Tamaki Nozomu Presents Dance In The Vampire Bund 9

DANCE IN THE VAMPIRE BUND

9

NOZOMU TAMAKI

J'ai lâché le paquet.

Qu'on m'enferme.

qu'on me lynche.

Comprenne qui pourra :

Je suis un mensonge

qui dit toujours la vérité

I have sent the parcel.

Imprison me for it,

lynch me for it, if you will.

All that matters is that

those who know understand:

I am a liar,

who always speaks the truth.

Jean Cocteau. Le Paquet rouge

Dance In The Vampire Bund 9

Contents

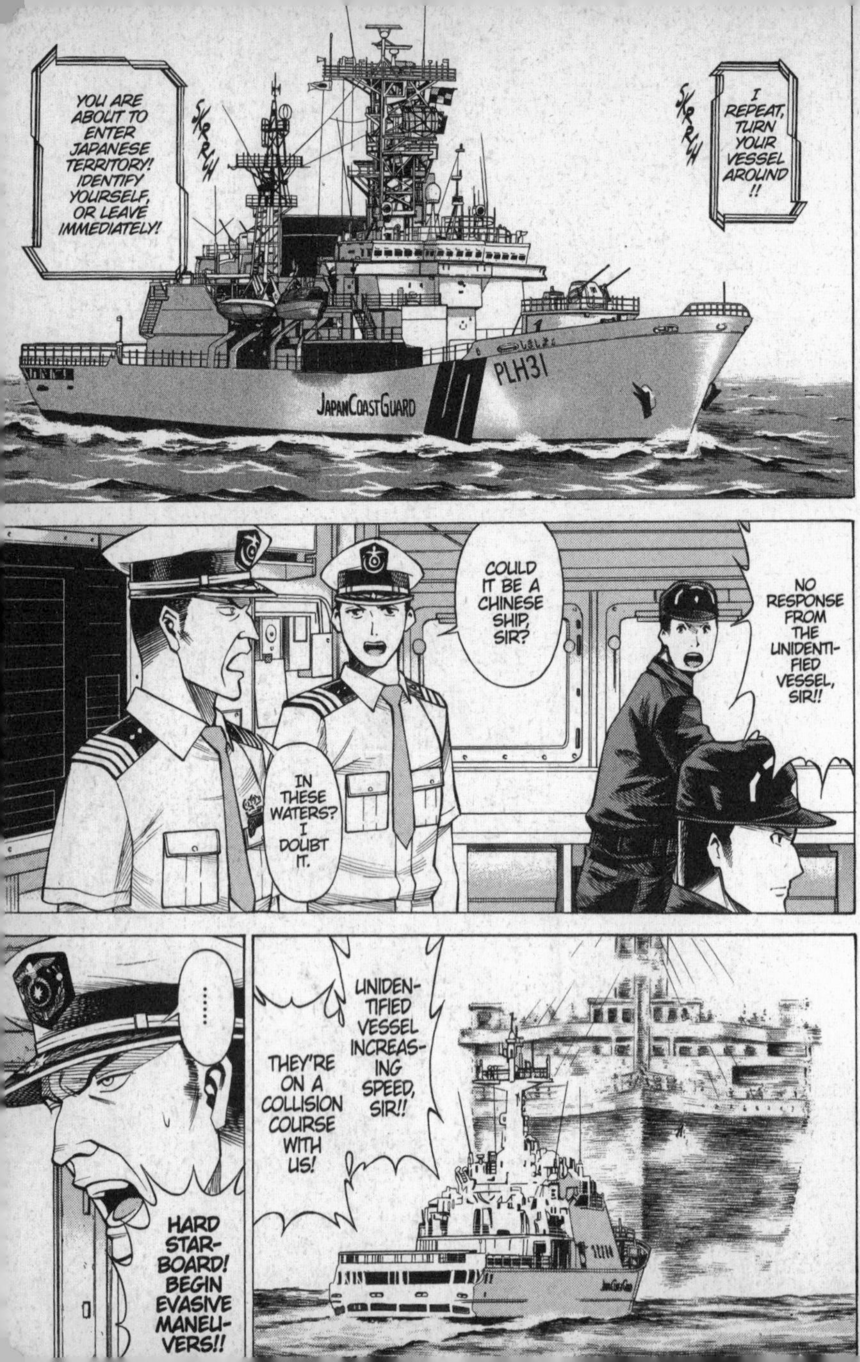
YOU ARE ABOUT TO ENTER JAPANESE TERRITORY! IDENTIFY YOURSELF, OR LEAVE IMMEDIATELY!
SKRCH
I REPEAT, TURN YOUR VESSEL AROUND!!
SKRCH
PLH31
JAPAN COAST GUARD
NO RESPONSE FROM THE UNIDENTIFIED VESSEL, SIR!!
COULD IT BE A CHINESE SHIP, SIR?
IN THESE WATERS? I DOUBT IT.
UNIDENTIFIED VESSEL INCREASING SPEED, SIR!!
THEY'RE ON A COLLISION COURSE WITH US!
......
HARD STARBOARD! BEGIN EVASIVE MANEUVERS!!

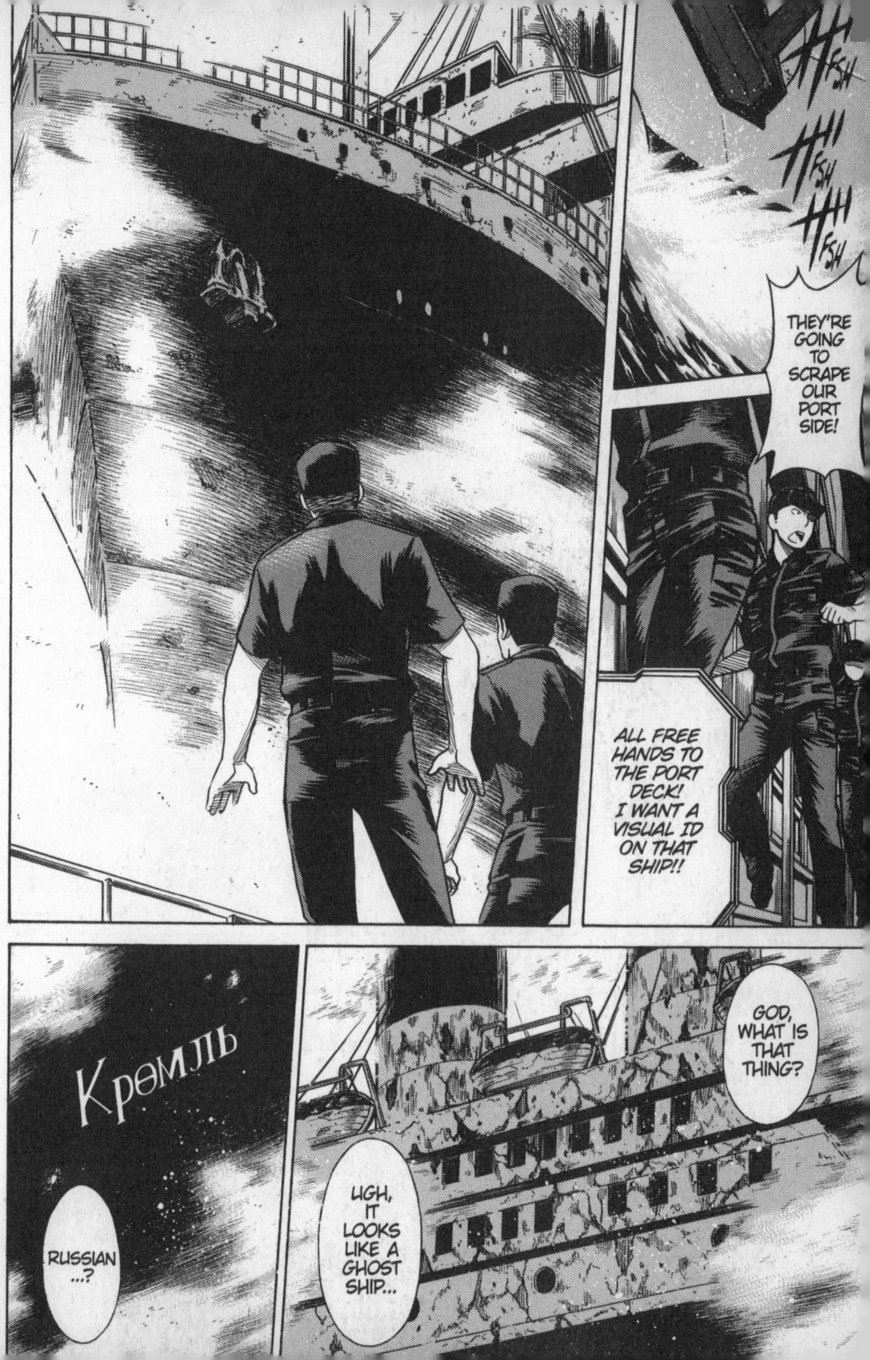
FSH
FSH
FSH
THEY'RE GOING TO SCRAPE OUR PORT SIDE!
ALL FREE HANDS TO THE PORT DECK! I WANT A VISUAL ID ON THAT SHIP!!
GOD, WHAT IS THAT THING?
UGH, IT LOOKS LIKE A GHOST SHIP...
Крөмль
RUSSIAN ...?

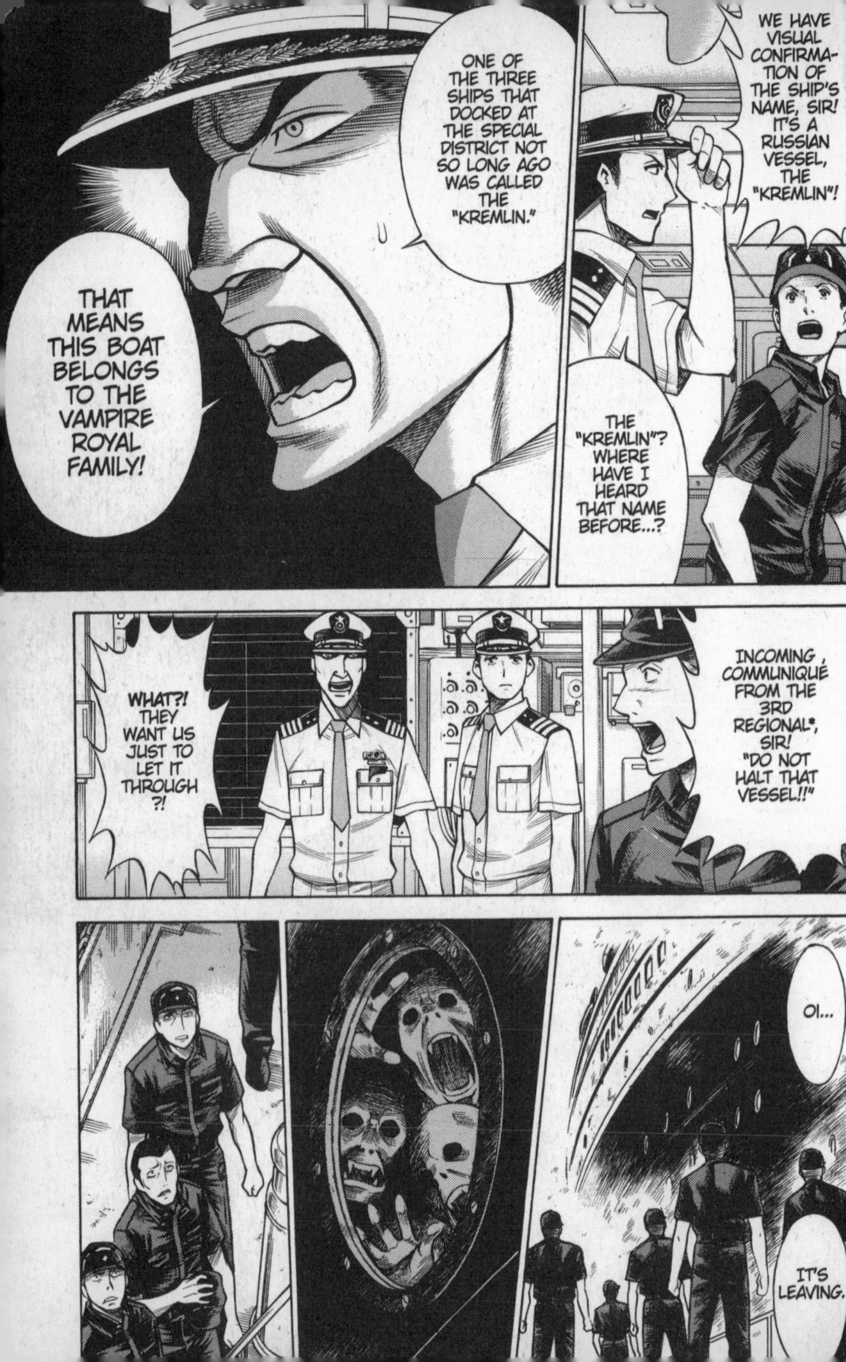
WE HAVE VISUAL CONFIRMATION OF THE SHIP'S NAME, SIR! IT'S A RUSSIAN VESSEL, THE "KREMLIN"!
THE "KREMLIN"? WHERE HAVE I HEARD THAT NAME BEFORE...?
ONE OF THE THREE SHIPS THAT DOCKED AT THE SPECIAL DISTRICT NOT SO LONG AGO WAS CALLED THE "KREMLIN."
THAT MEANS THIS BOAT BELONGS TO THE VAMPIRE ROYAL FAMILY!
INCOMING COMMUNIQUÉ FROM THE 3RD REGIONAL*, SIR! "DO NOT HALT THAT VESSEL!!"
WHAT?! THEY WANT US JUST TO LET IT THROUGH ?!
OI...
IT'S LEAVING.

*3rd Regional = Japanese 3rd Regional Coast Guard Headquarters

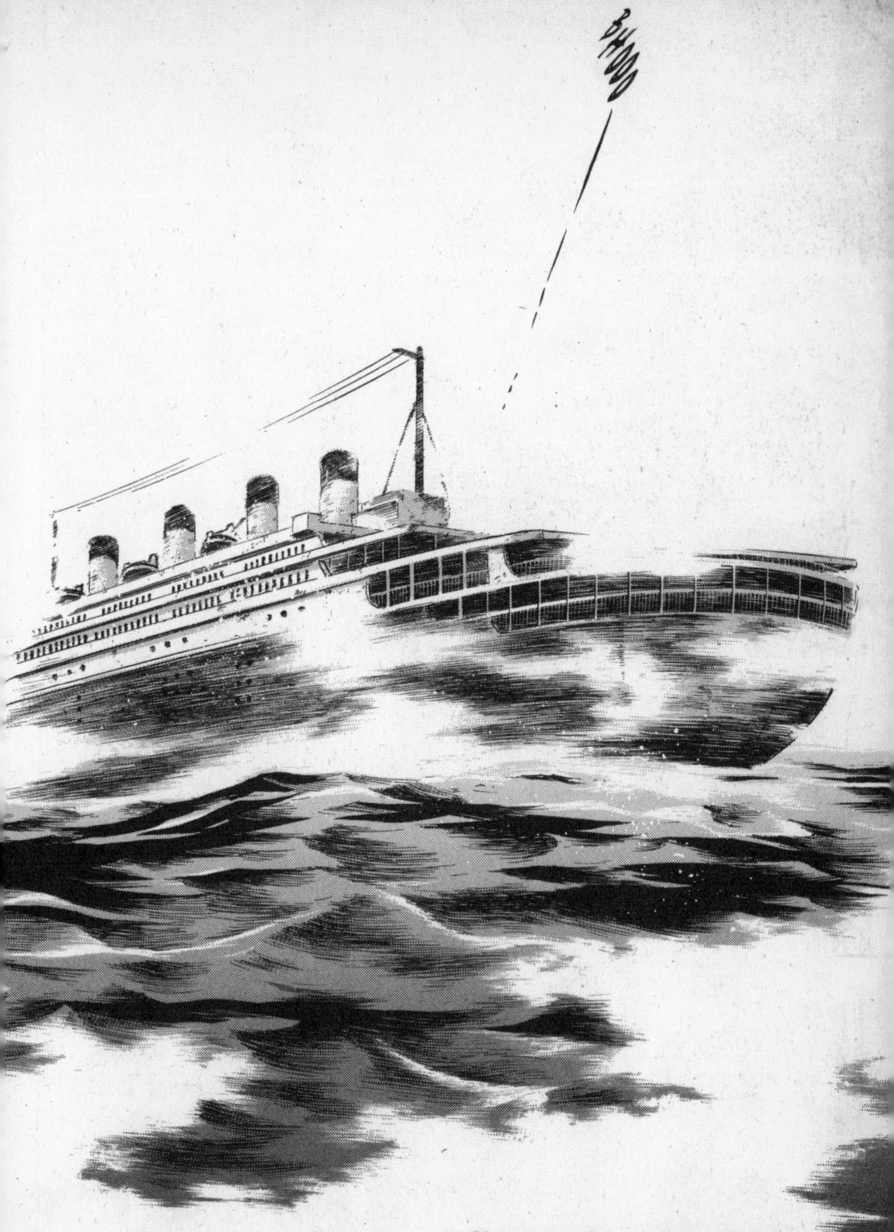
BHOOO

Chapter 50: Aftershocks

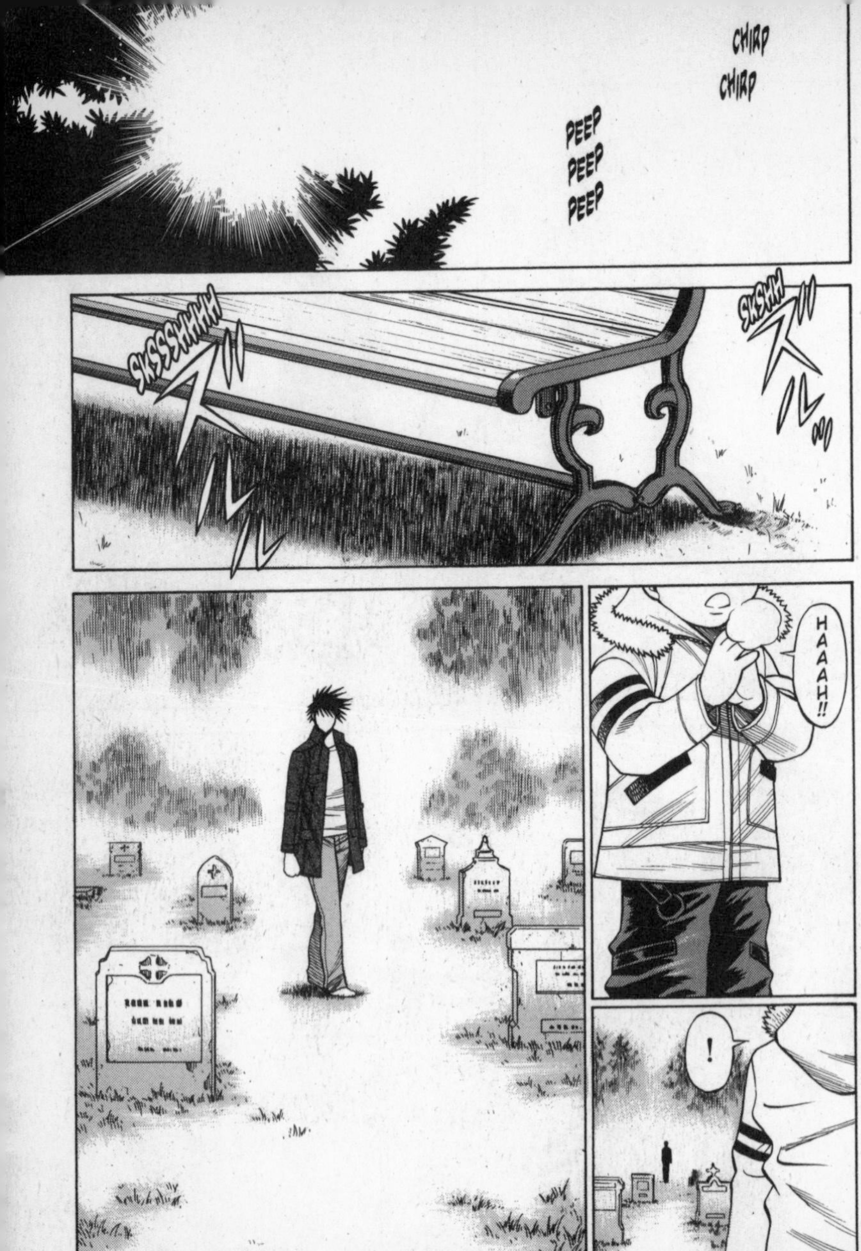
CHIRP
CHIRP
PEEP
PEEP
PEEP
SKSHH
SKSSSHHHH
HAAAAH!!
!

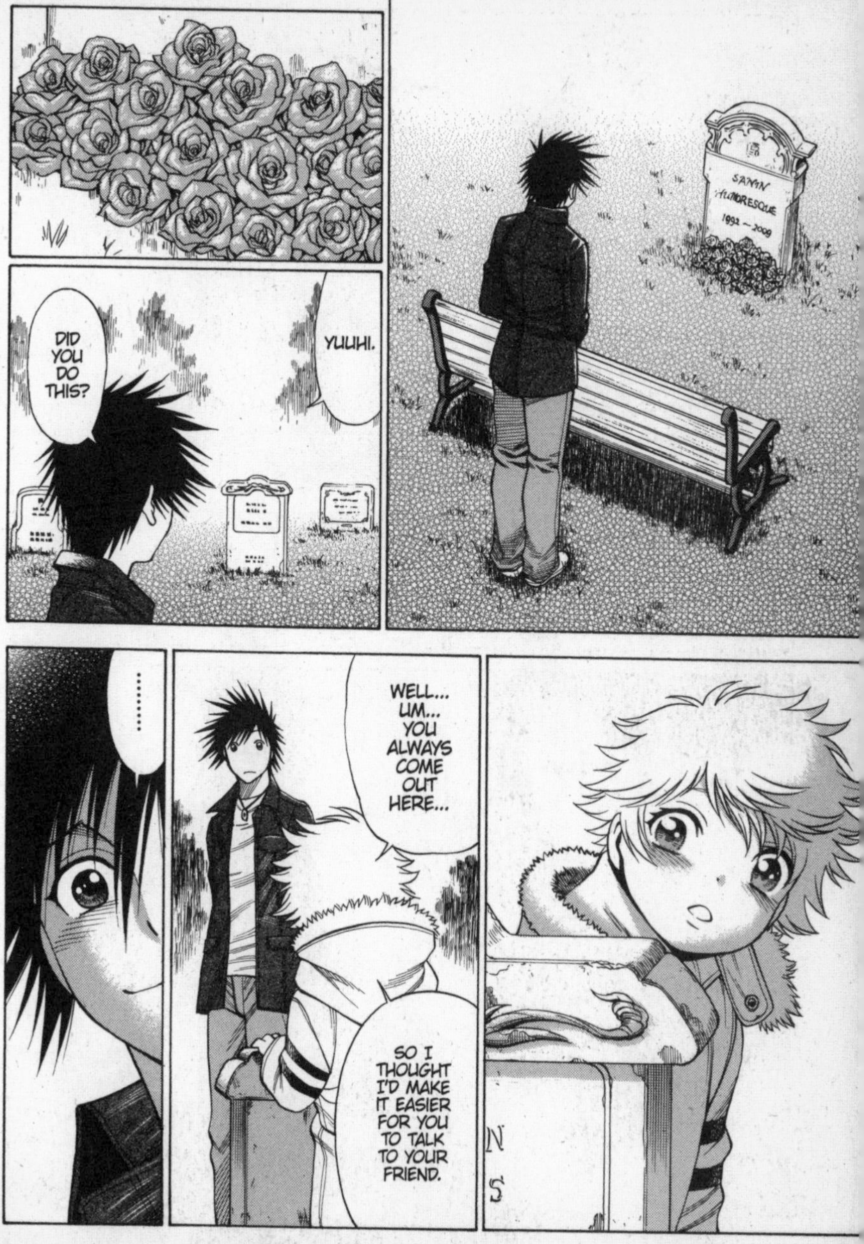
SANIN HUMORESQUE
1992 — 2009
YUUHI.
DID YOU DO THIS?
WELL... UM... YOU ALWAYS COME OUT HERE...
SO I THOUGHT I'D MAKE IT EASIER FOR YOU TO TALK TO YOUR FRIEND.
......

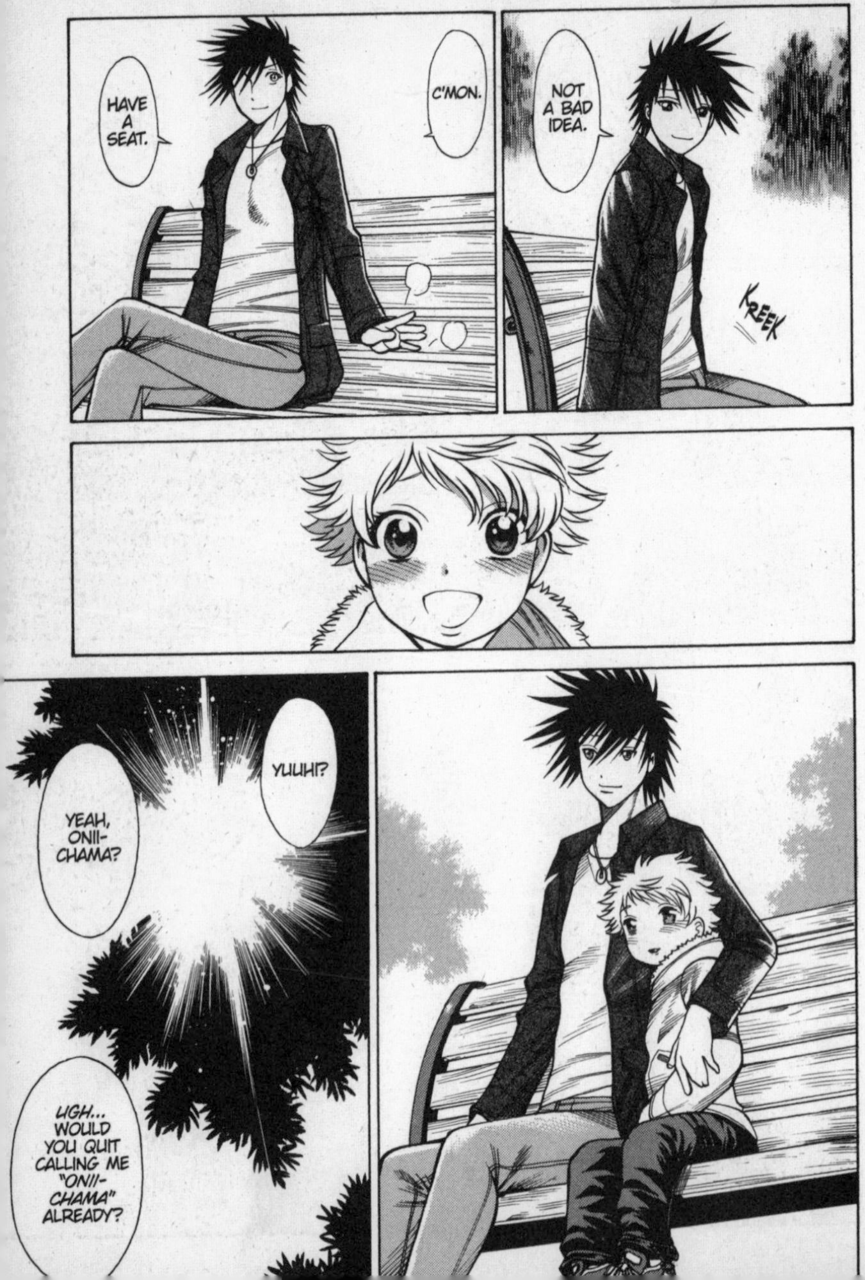
NOT A BAD IDEA.
KREEK
C'MON.
HAVE A SEAT.
YUUHI?
YEAH, ONII-CHAMA?
UGH... WOULD YOU QUIT CALLING ME "ONII-CHAMA" ALREADY?

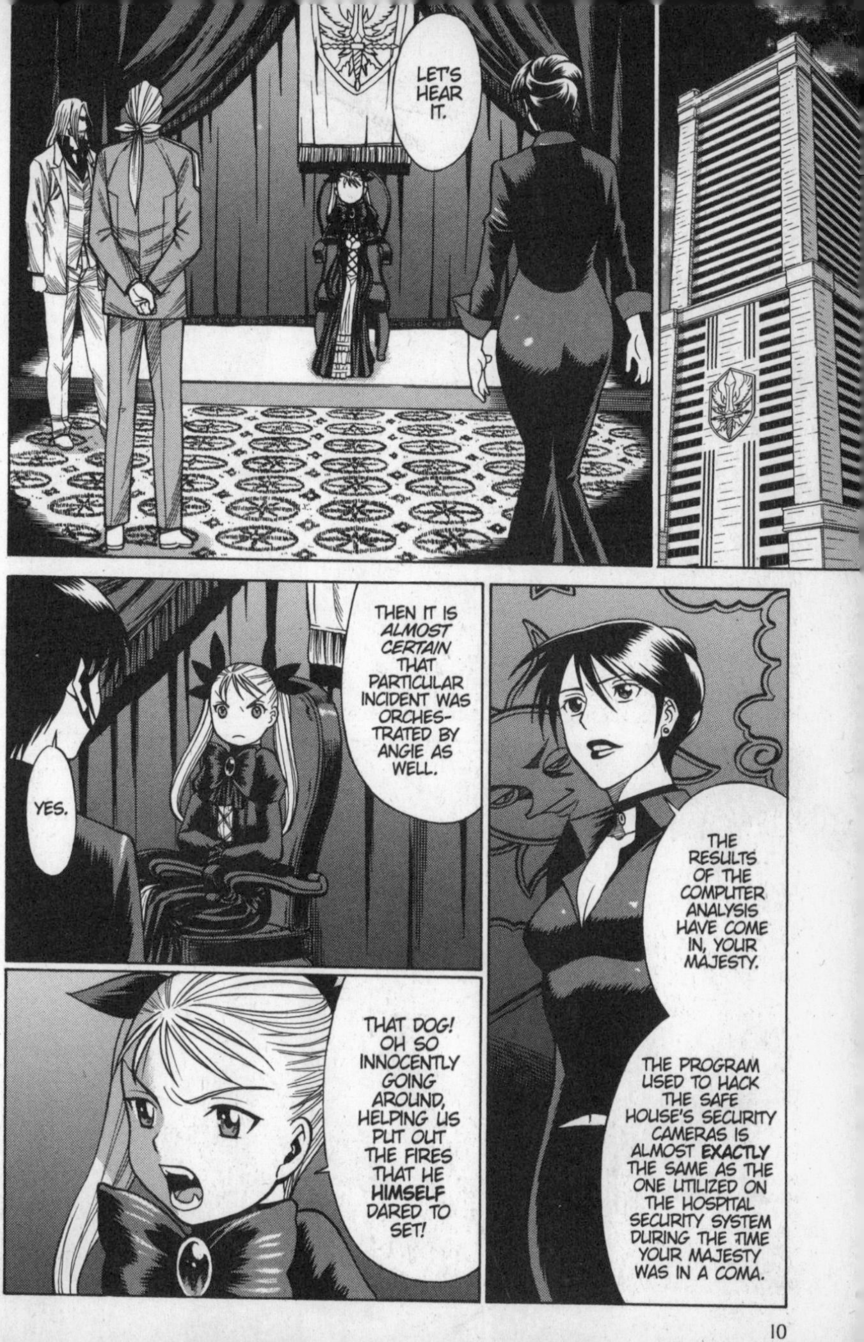

LET'S HEAR IT.
THE RESULTS OF THE COMPUTER ANALYSIS HAVE COME IN, YOUR MAJESTY.
THE PROGRAM USED TO HACK THE SAFE HOUSE'S SECURITY CAMERAS IS ALMOST EXACTLY THE SAME AS THE ONE UTILIZED ON THE HOSPITAL SECURITY SYSTEM DURING THE TIME YOUR MAJESTY WAS IN A COMA.
THEN IT IS ALMOST CERTAIN THAT PARTICULAR INCIDENT WAS ORCHESTRATED BY ANGIE AS WELL.
YES.
THAT DOG! OH SO INNOCENTLY GOING AROUND, HELPING US PUT OUT THE FIRES THAT HE HIMSELF DARED TO SET!

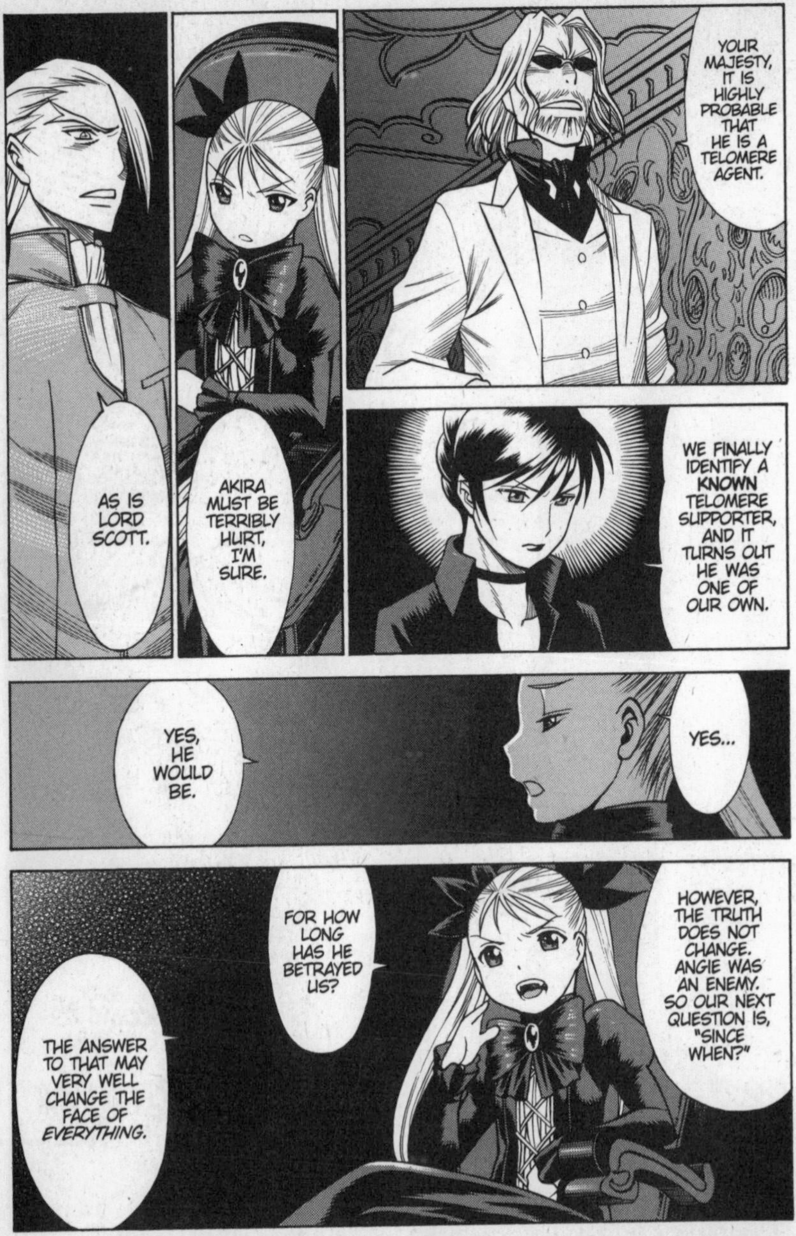
YOUR MAJESTY, IT IS HIGHLY PROBABLE THAT HE IS A TELOMERE AGENT.
WE FINALLY IDENTIFY A KNOWN TELOMERE SUPPORTER, AND IT TURNS OUT HE WAS ONE OF OUR OWN.
AKIRA MUST BE TERRIBLY HURT, I'M SURE.
AS IS LORD SCOTT.
YES...
YES, HE WOULD BE.
HOWEVER, THE TRUTH DOES NOT CHANGE. ANGIE WAS AN ENEMY. SO OUR NEXT QUESTION IS, "SINCE WHEN?"
FOR HOW LONG HAS HE BETRAYED US?
THE ANSWER TO THAT MAY VERY WELL CHANGE THE FACE OF *EVERYTHING*.

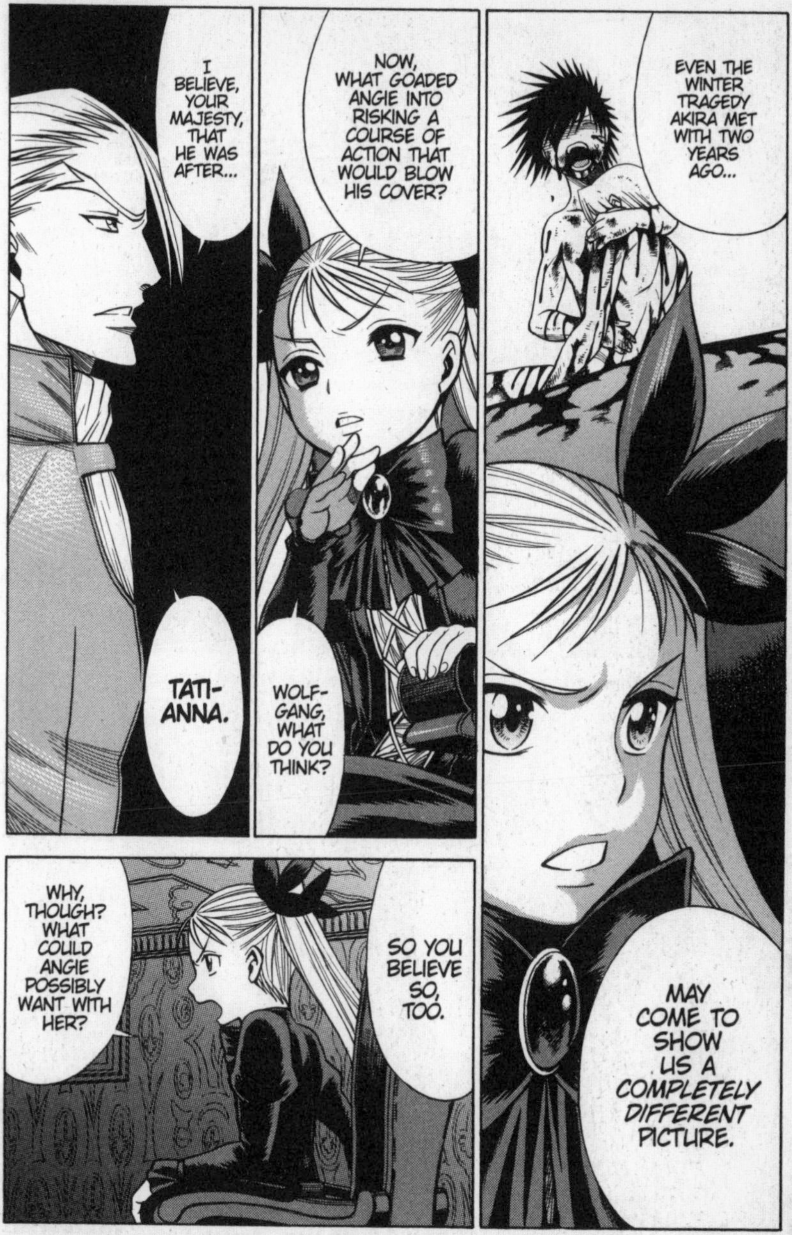
EVEN THE WINTER TRAGEDY AKIRA MET WITH TWO YEARS AGO...
MAY COME TO SHOW US A COMPLETELY DIFFERENT PICTURE.
NOW, WHAT GOADED ANGIE INTO RISKING A COURSE OF ACTION THAT WOULD BLOW HIS COVER?
WOLF-GANG, WHAT DO YOU THINK?
I BELIEVE, YOUR MAJESTY, THAT HE WAS AFTER...
TATI-ANNA.
SO YOU BELIEVE SO, TOO.
WHY, THOUGH? WHAT COULD ANGIE POSSIBLY WANT WITH HER?

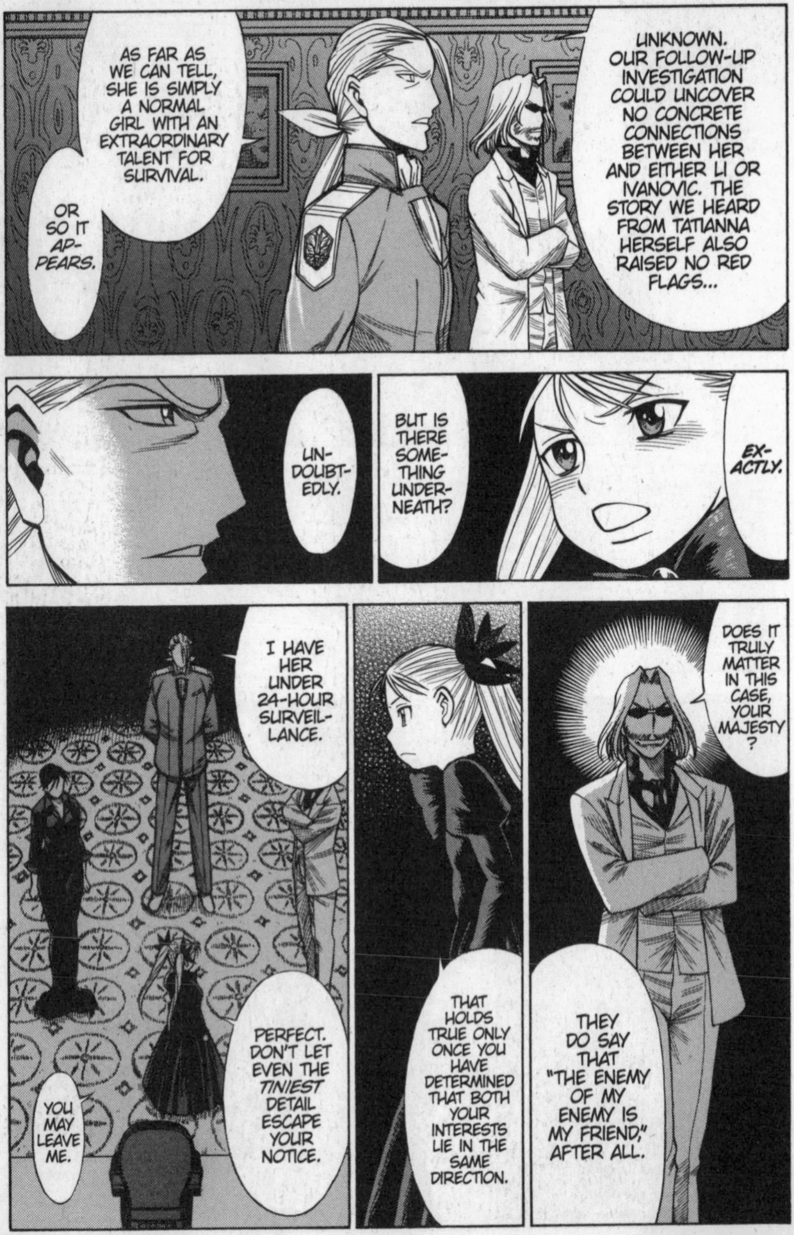
UNKNOWN. OUR FOLLOW-UP INVESTIGATION COULD UNCOVER NO CONCRETE CONNECTIONS BETWEEN HER AND EITHER LI OR IVANOVIC. THE STORY WE HEARD FROM TATIANNA HERSELF ALSO RAISED NO RED FLAGS...
AS FAR AS WE CAN TELL, SHE IS SIMPLY A NORMAL GIRL WITH AN EXTRAORDINARY TALENT FOR SURVIVAL.
OR SO IT AP-PEARS.
EX-ACTLY.
BUT IS THERE SOME-THING UNDER-NEATH?
UN-DOUBT-EDLY.
DOES IT TRULY MATTER IN THIS CASE, YOUR MAJESTY ?
THEY DO SAY THAT "THE ENEMY OF MY ENEMY IS MY FRIEND," AFTER ALL.
THAT HOLDS TRUE ONLY ONCE YOU HAVE DETERMINED THAT BOTH YOUR INTERESTS LIE IN THE SAME DIRECTION.
I HAVE HER UNDER 24-HOUR SURVEIL-LANCE.
PERFECT. DON'T LET EVEN THE *TINIEST* DETAIL ESCAPE YOUR NOTICE.
YOU MAY LEAVE ME.

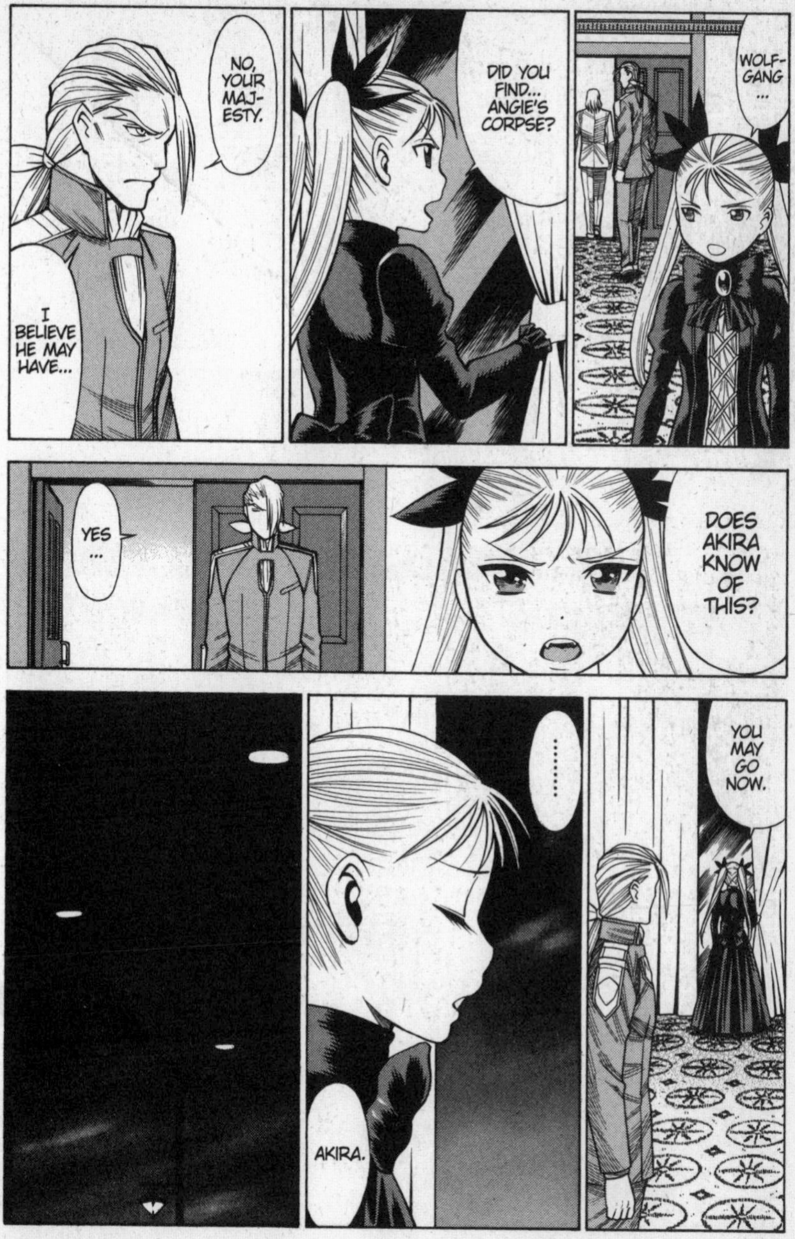
WOLF-GANG ...
DID YOU FIND... ANGIE'S CORPSE?
NO, YOUR MAJ-ESTY.
I BELIEVE HE MAY HAVE...
DOES AKIRA KNOW OF THIS?
YES ...
YOU MAY GO NOW.
......
AKIRA.

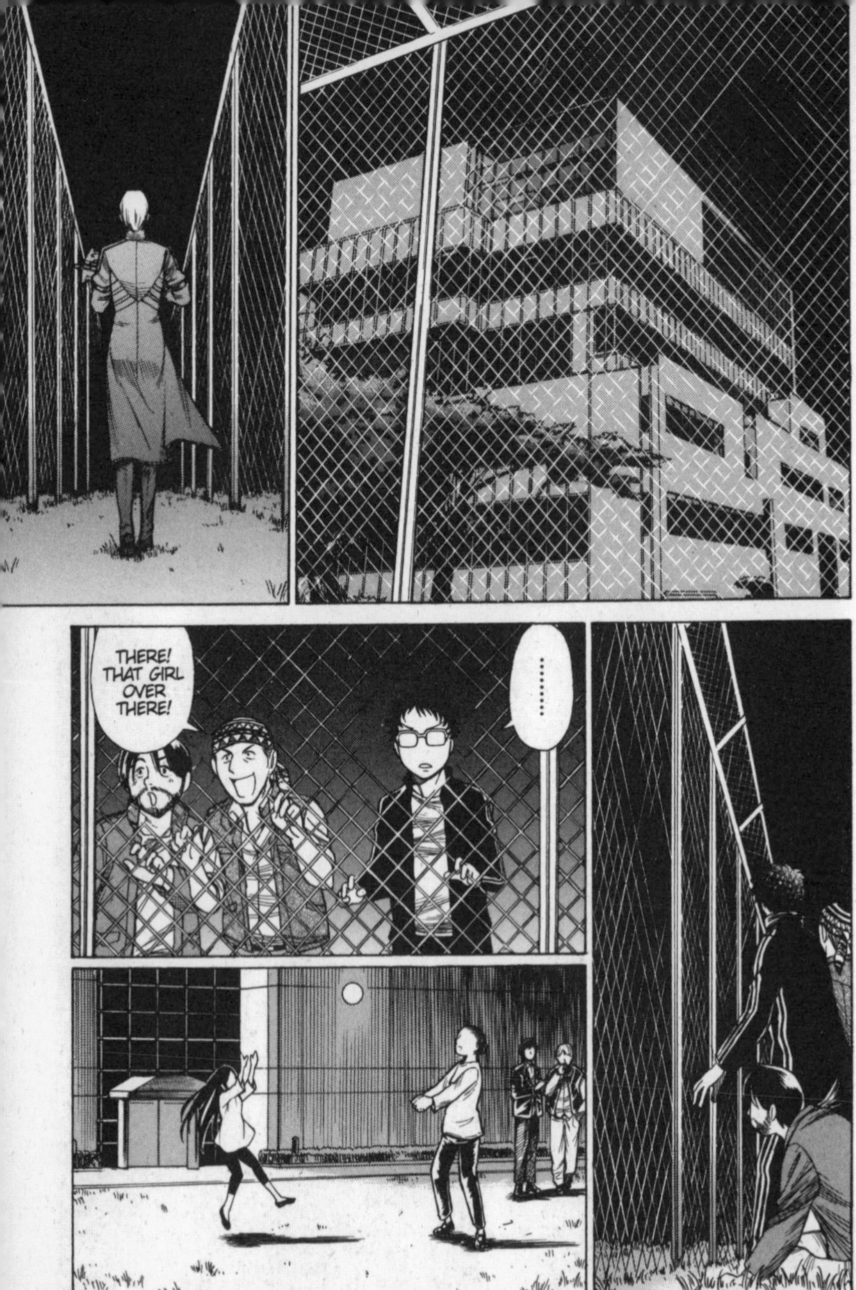

....
THERE! THAT GIRL OVER THERE!

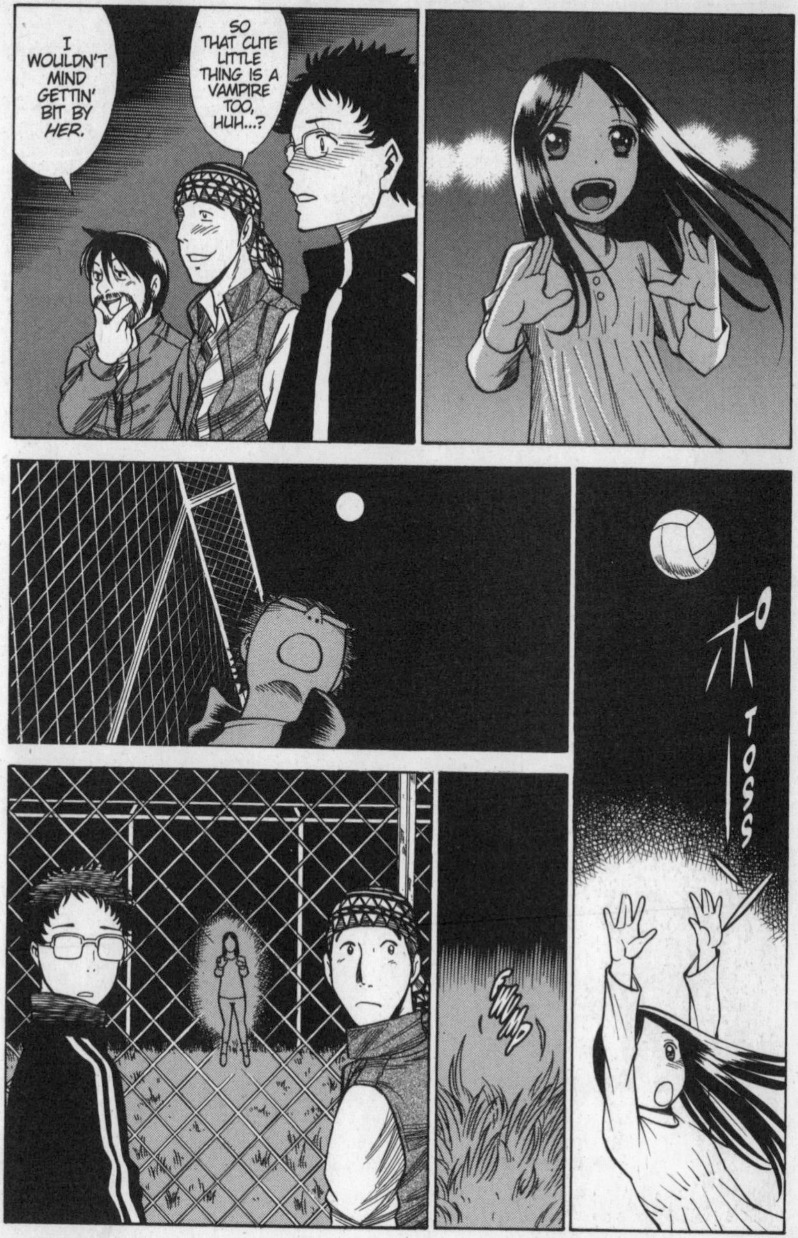
SO THAT CUTE LITTLE THING IS A VAMPIRE TOO, HUH...?
I WOULDN'T MIND GETTIN' BIT BY *HER*.
TOSS
FWUMP

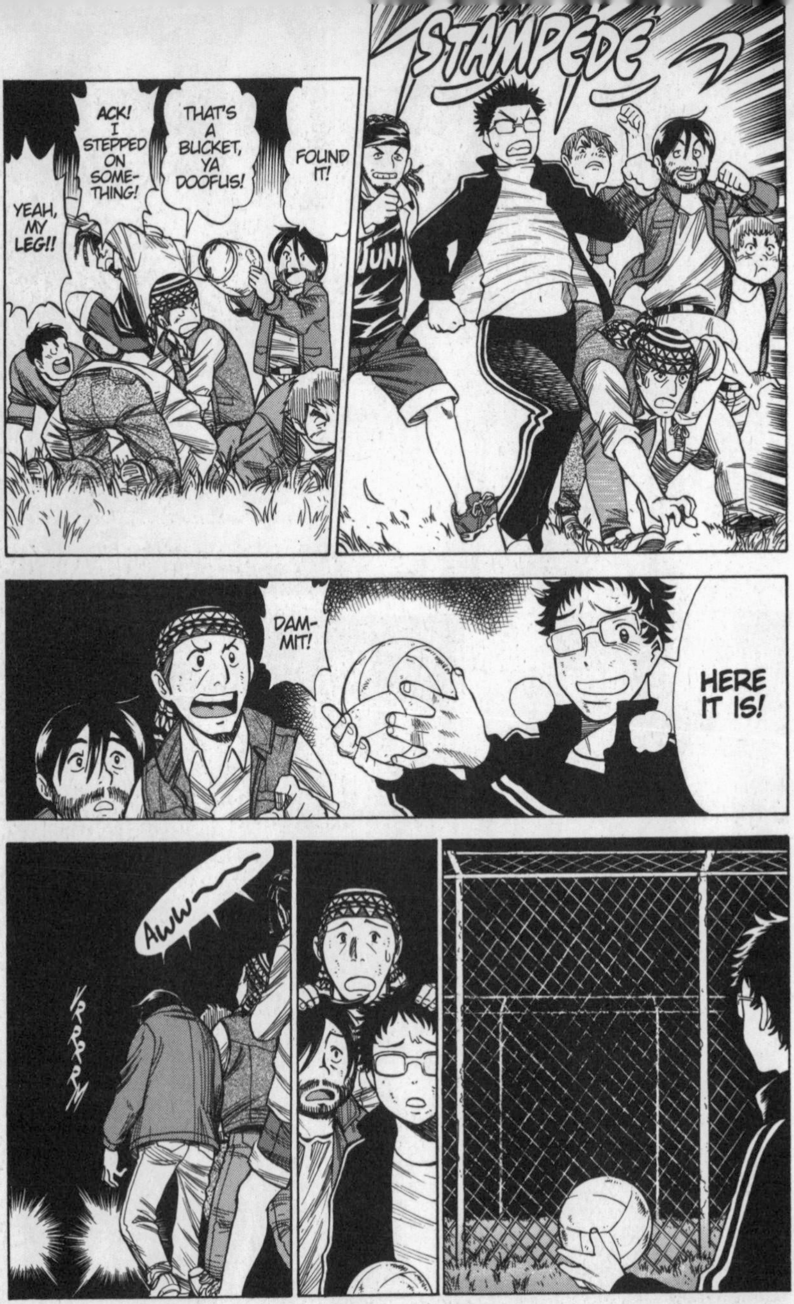
STAMPEDE
FOUND IT!
THAT'S A BUCKET, YA DOOFUS!
ACK! I STEPPED ON SOME-THING!
YEAH, MY LEG!!
HERE IT IS!
DAM-MIT!
AWW~~
VRRRRM

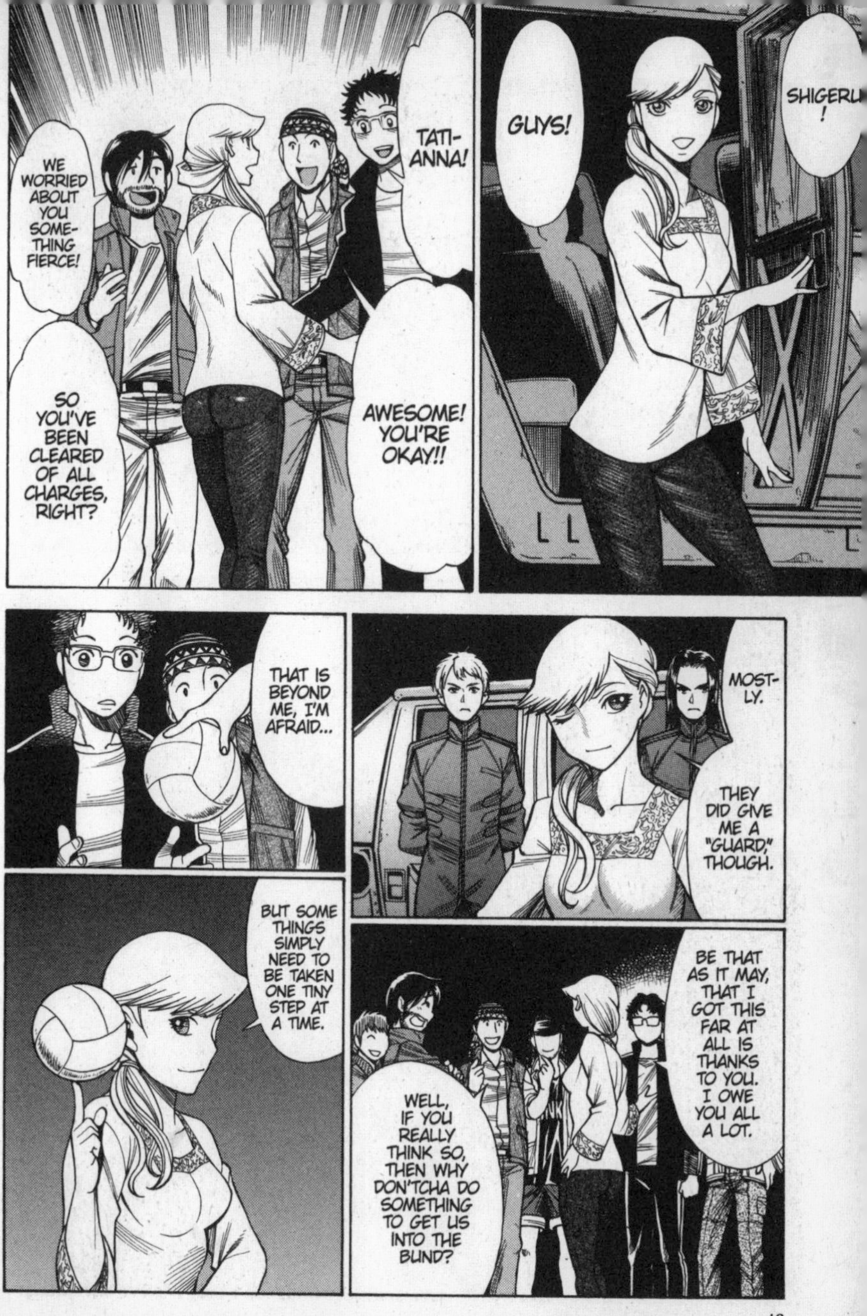
SHIGERU!
GUYS!
TATI-ANNA!
AWESOME! YOU'RE OKAY!!
WE WORRIED ABOUT YOU SOME-THING FIERCE!
SO YOU'VE BEEN CLEARED OF ALL CHARGES, RIGHT?
MOST-LY.
THEY DID GIVE ME A "GUARD," THOUGH.
BE THAT AS IT MAY, THAT I GOT THIS FAR AT ALL IS THANKS TO YOU. I OWE YOU ALL A LOT.
WELL, IF YOU REALLY THINK SO, THEN WHY DON'TCHA DO SOMETHING TO GET US INTO THE BUND?
THAT IS BEYOND ME, I'M AFRAID...
BUT SOME THINGS SIMPLY NEED TO BE TAKEN ONE TINY STEP AT A TIME.

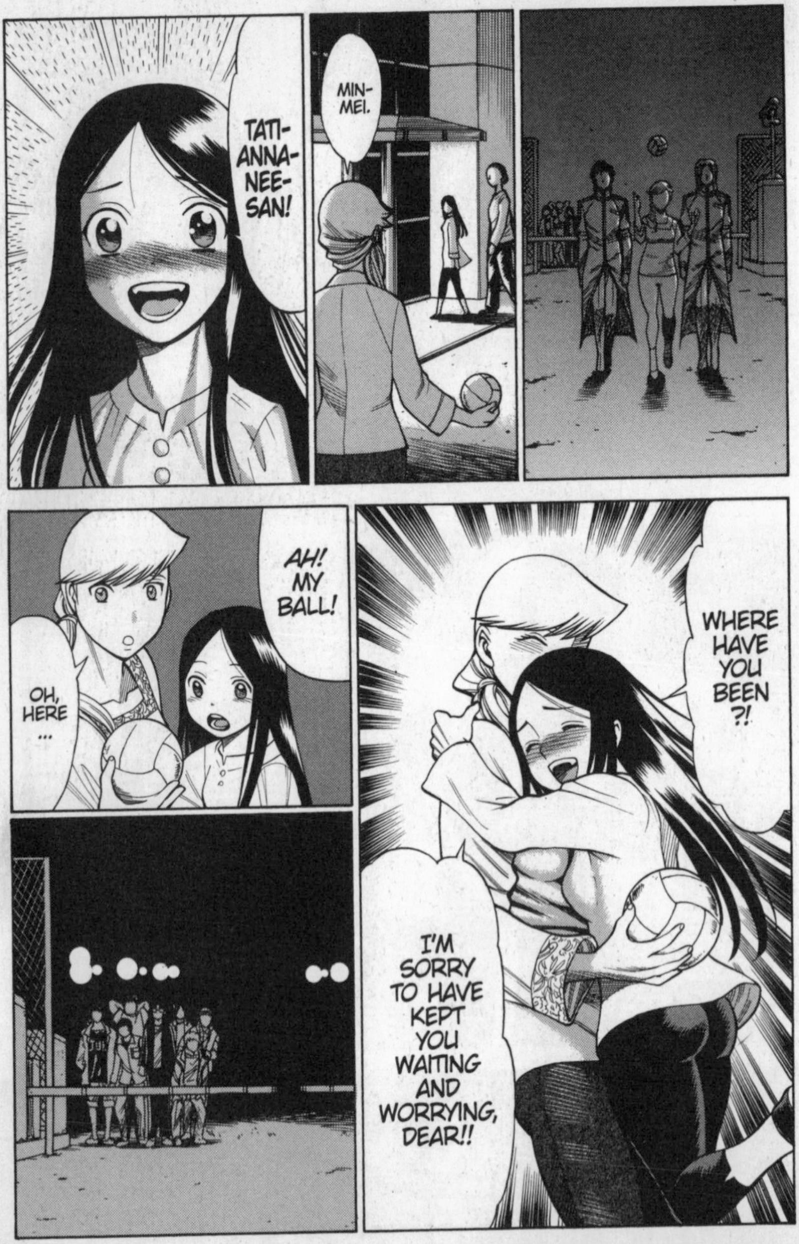
MIN-MEI.
TATI-ANNA-NEE-SAN!
WHERE HAVE YOU BEEN?!
I'M SORRY TO HAVE KEPT YOU WAITING AND WORRYING, DEAR!!
AH! MY BALL!
OH, HERE ...

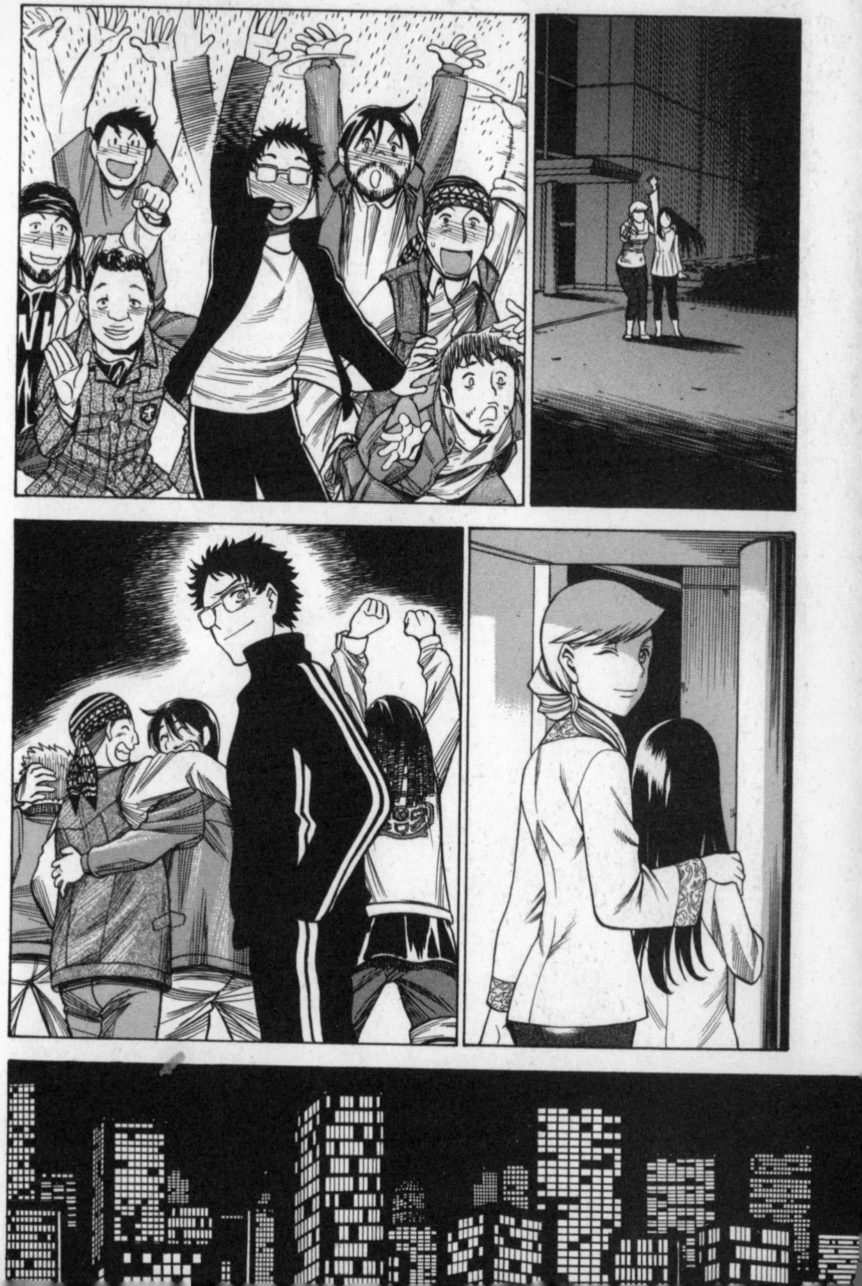

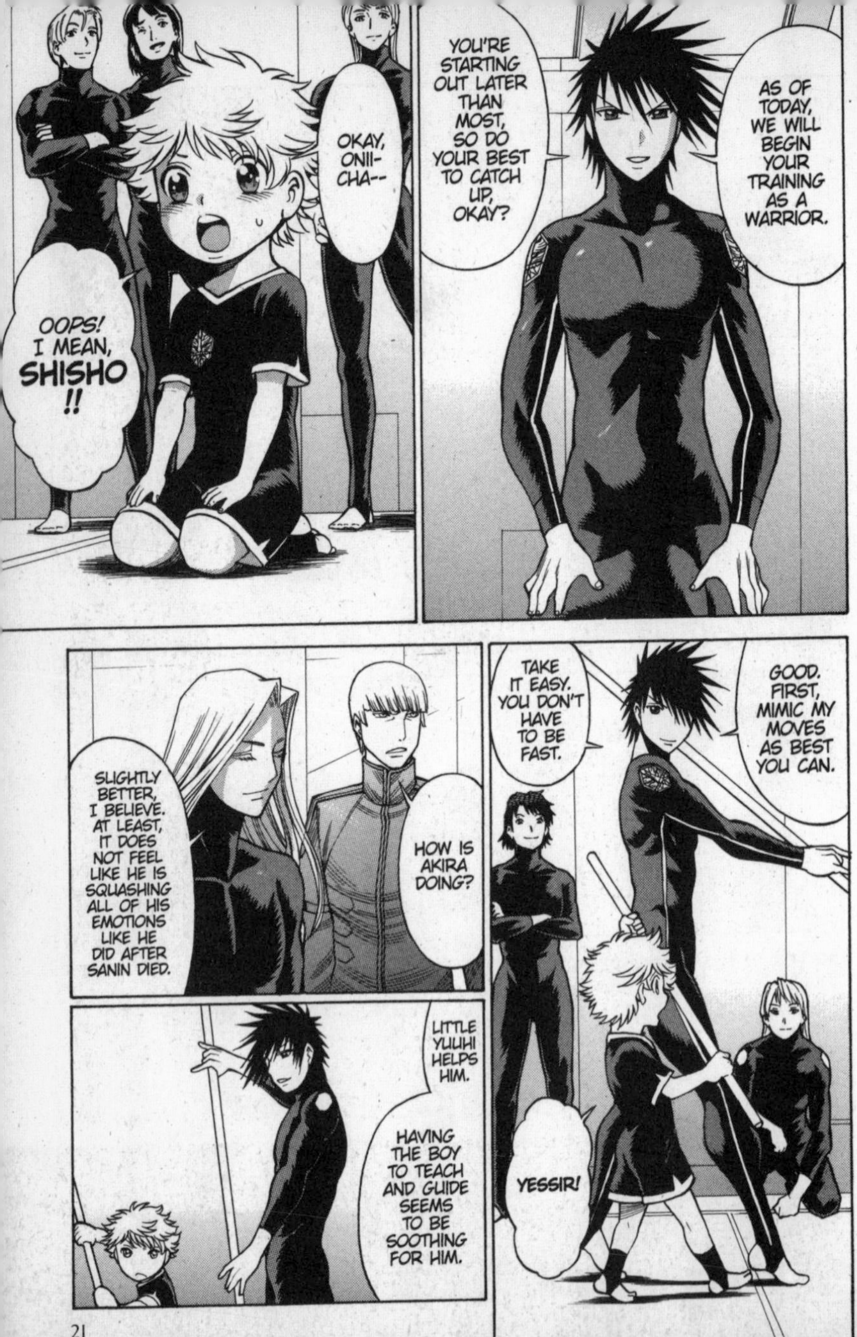
AS OF TODAY, WE WILL BEGIN YOUR TRAINING AS A WARRIOR.
YOU'RE STARTING OUT LATER THAN MOST, SO DO YOUR BEST TO CATCH UP, OKAY?
OKAY, ONII-CHA--
OOPS! I MEAN, SHISHO!!
GOOD. FIRST, MIMIC MY MOVES AS BEST YOU CAN.
TAKE IT EASY. YOU DON'T HAVE TO BE FAST.
YESSIR!
HOW IS AKIRA DOING?
SLIGHTLY BETTER, I BELIEVE. AT LEAST, IT DOES NOT FEEL LIKE HE IS SQUASHING ALL OF HIS EMOTIONS LIKE HE DID AFTER SANIN DIED.
LITTLE YUUHI HELPS HIM.
HAVING THE BOY TO TEACH AND GUIDE SEEMS TO BE SOOTHING FOR HIM.

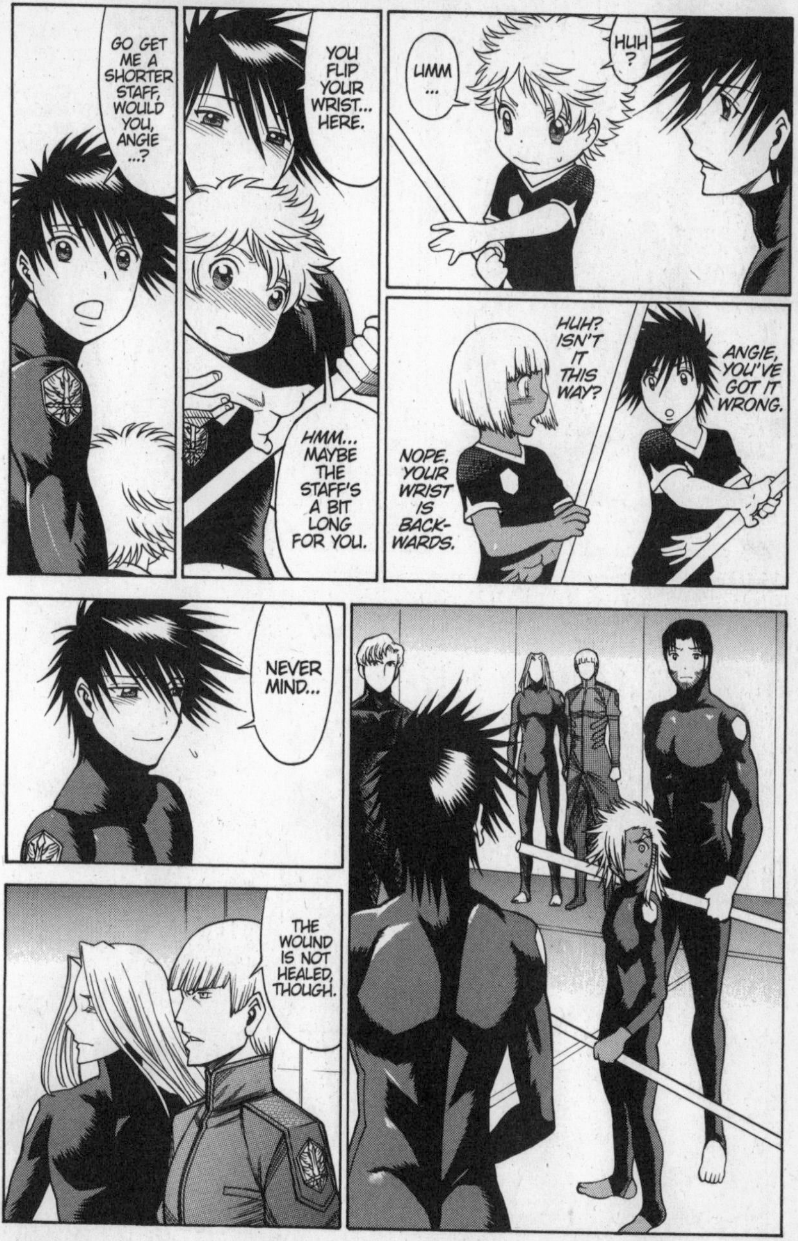
HUH?
UMM...
ANGIE, YOU'VE GOT IT WRONG.
HUH? ISN'T IT THIS WAY?
NOPE. YOUR WRIST IS BACK-WARDS.
YOU FLIP YOUR WRIST... HERE.
HMM... MAYBE THE STAFF'S A BIT LONG FOR YOU.
GO GET ME A SHORTER STAFF, WOULD YOU, ANGIE ...?
NEVER MIND...
THE WOUND IS NOT HEALED, THOUGH.

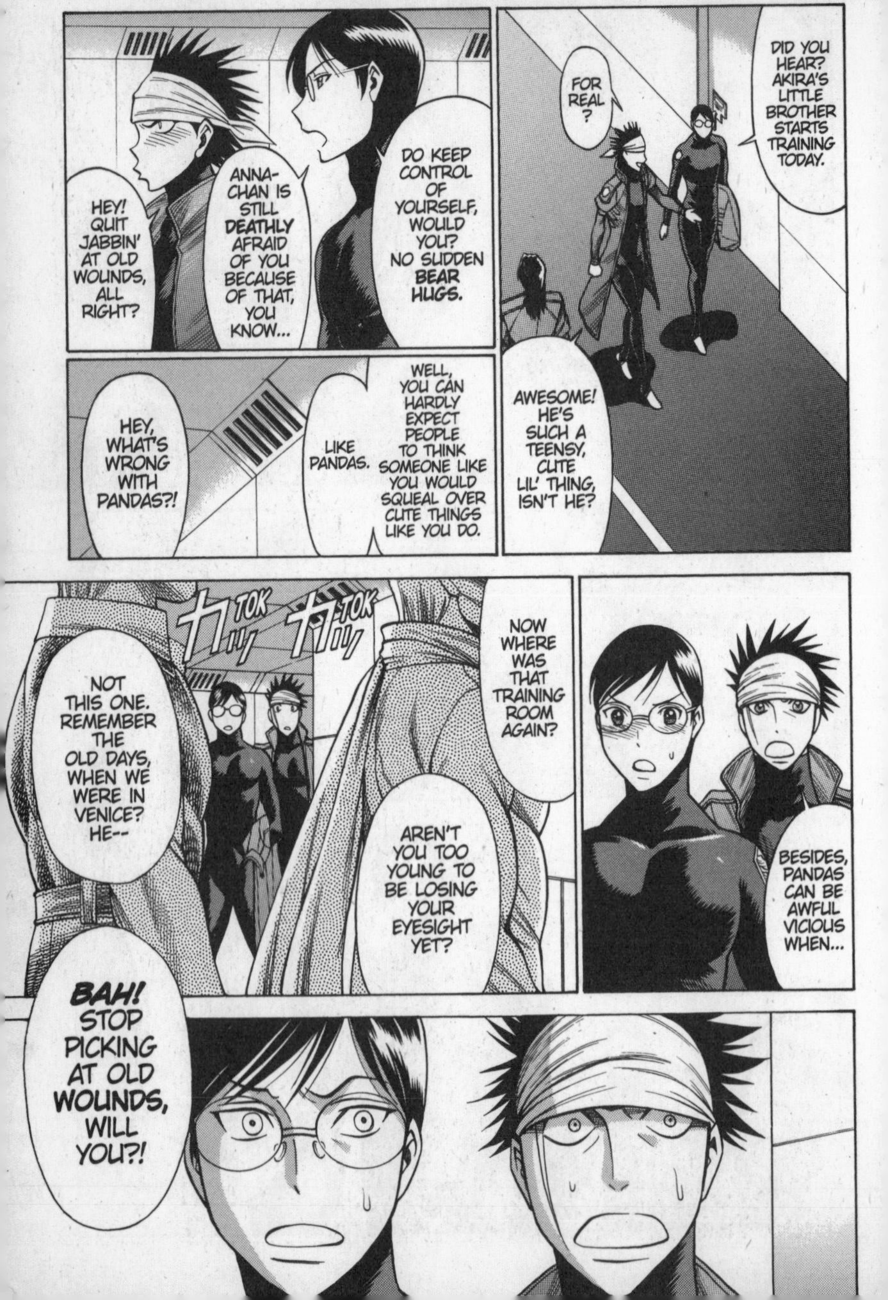
DID YOU HEAR? AKIRA'S LITTLE BROTHER STARTS TRAINING TODAY.
FOR REAL?
AWESOME! HE'S SUCH A TEENSY, CUTE LIL' THING, ISN'T HE?
DO KEEP CONTROL OF YOURSELF, WOULD YOU? NO SUDDEN BEAR HUGS.
ANNA-CHAN IS STILL DEATHLY AFRAID OF YOU BECAUSE OF THAT, YOU KNOW...
HEY! QUIT JABBIN' AT OLD WOUNDS, ALL RIGHT?
WELL, YOU CAN HARDLY EXPECT PEOPLE TO THINK SOMEONE LIKE YOU WOULD SQUEAL OVER CUTE THINGS LIKE YOU DO.
LIKE PANDAS.
HEY, WHAT'S WRONG WITH PANDAS?!
NOW WHERE WAS THAT TRAINING ROOM AGAIN?
BESIDES, PANDAS CAN BE AWFUL VICIOUS WHEN...
TOK
TOK
AREN'T YOU TOO YOUNG TO BE LOSING YOUR EYESIGHT YET?
NOT THIS ONE. REMEMBER THE OLD DAYS, WHEN WE WERE IN VENICE? HE--
BAH! STOP PICKING AT OLD WOUNDS, WILL YOU?!

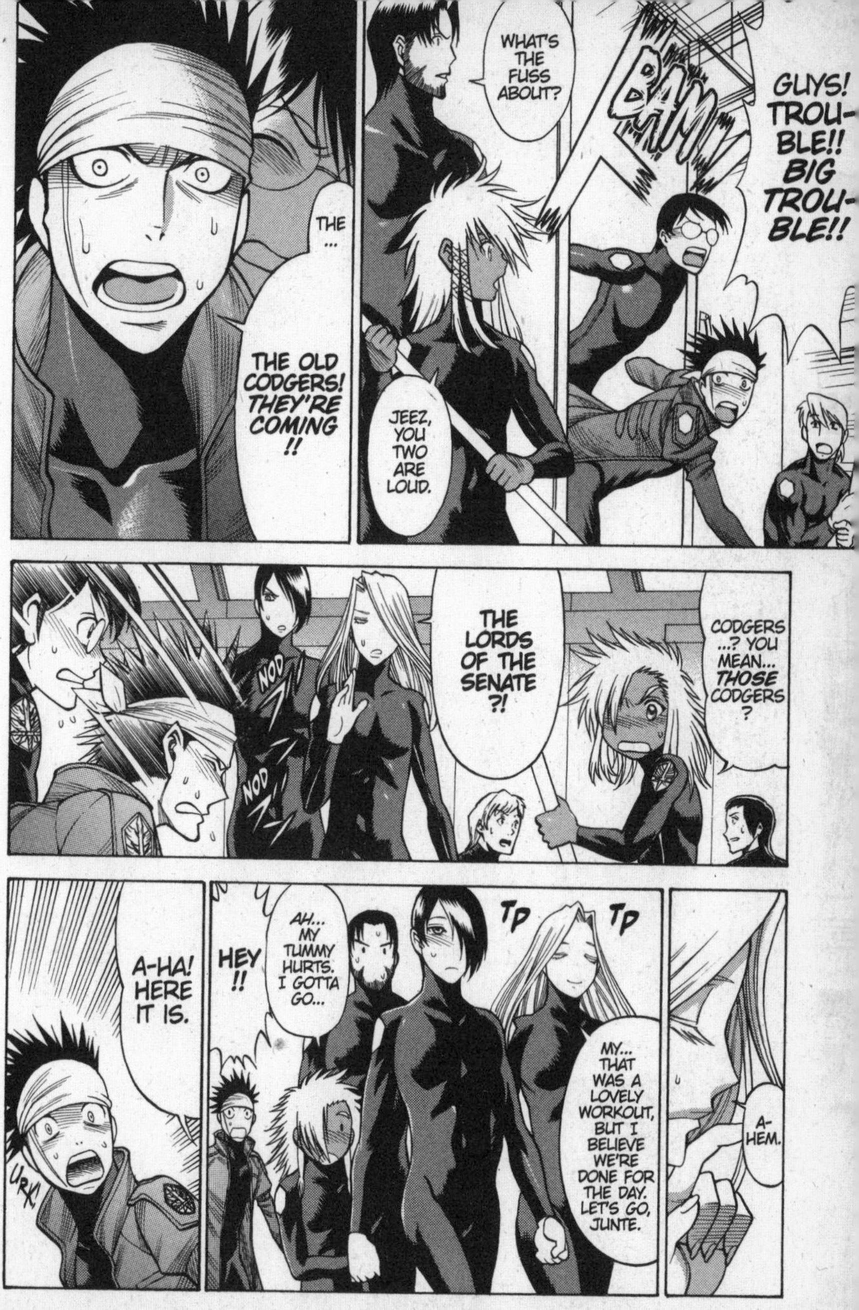
GUYS! TROUBLE!! BIG TROUBLE!!
BAM
WHAT'S THE FUSS ABOUT?
JEEZ, YOU TWO ARE LOUD.
THE ...
THE OLD CODGERS! THEY'RE COMING!!
CODGERS ...? YOU MEAN... THOSE CODGERS?
THE LORDS OF THE SENATE?!
NOD
NOD
A-HEM.
MY... THAT WAS A LOVELY WORKOUT, BUT I BELIEVE WE'RE DONE FOR THE DAY. LET'S GO, JUNTE.
TP
TP
AH... MY TUMMY HURTS. I GOTTA GO...
HEY!!
A-HA! HERE IT IS.
URK!

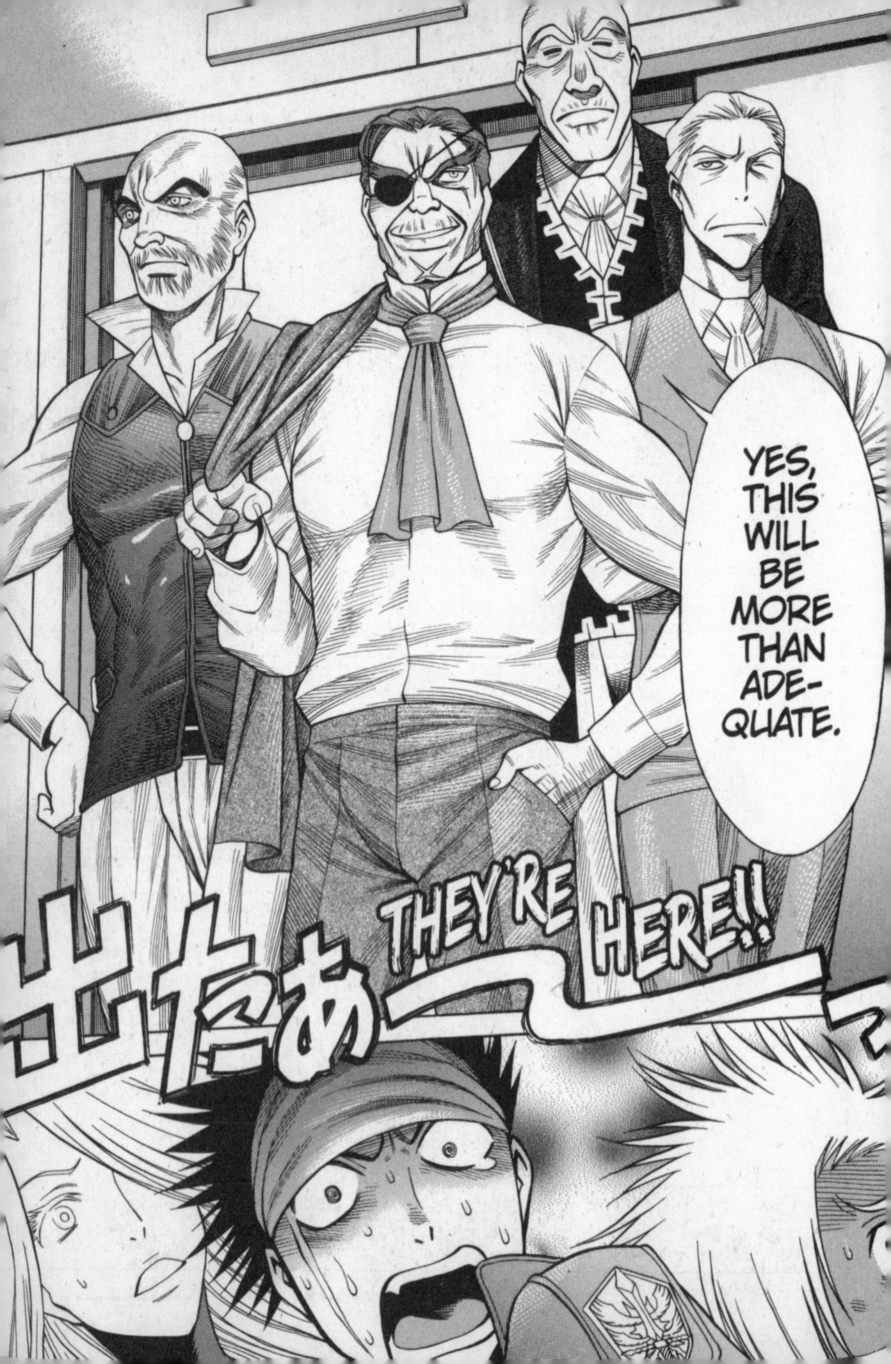
YES, THIS WILL BE MORE THAN ADE-QUATE.
出たあ――っ
THEY'RE HERE!!

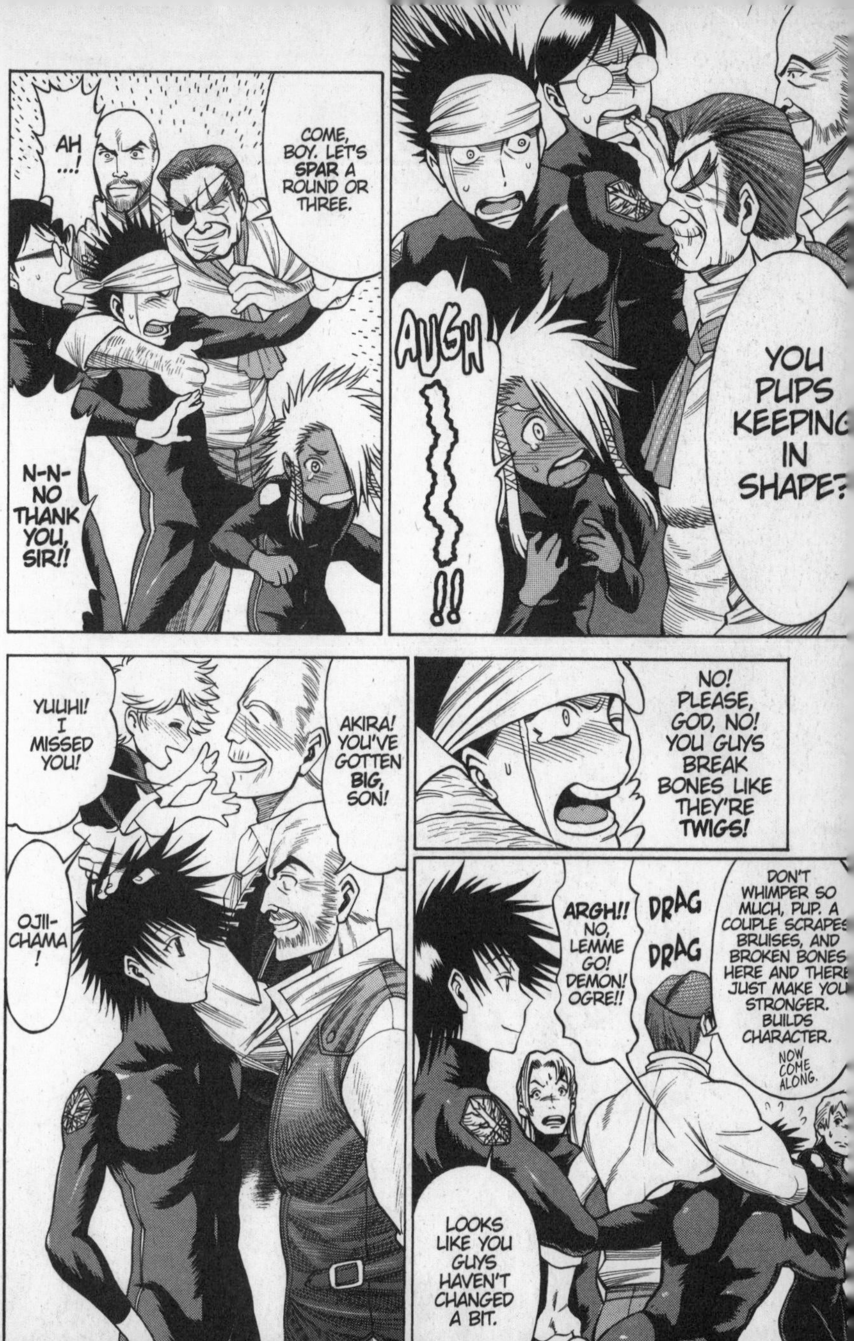
YOU PUPS KEEPING IN SHAPE?
AUGH!!
COME, BOY. LET'S SPAR A ROUND OR THREE.
AH ...!
N-N-NO THANK YOU, SIR!!
NO! PLEASE, GOD, NO! YOU GUYS BREAK BONES LIKE THEY'RE TWIGS!
DON'T WHIMPER SO MUCH, PUP. A COUPLE SCRAPES, BRUISES, AND BROKEN BONES HERE AND THERE JUST MAKE YOU STRONGER. BUILDS CHARACTER.
NOW COME ALONG.
DRAG
DRAG
ARGH!! NO, LEMME GO! DEMON! OGRE!!
LOOKS LIKE YOU GUYS HAVEN'T CHANGED A BIT.
AKIRA! YOU'VE GOTTEN BIG, SON!
YUUHI! I MISSED YOU!
OJII-CHAMA!

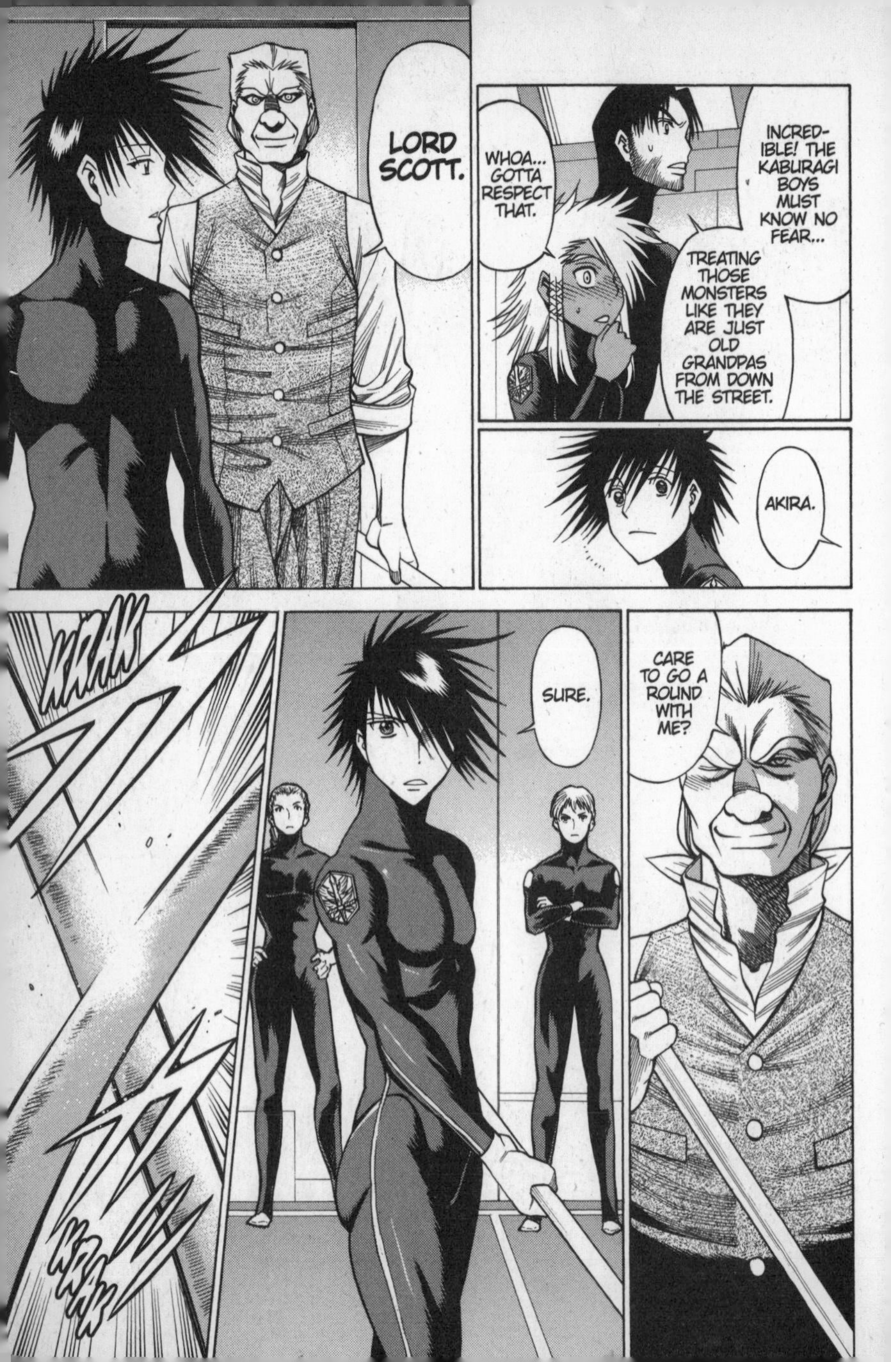
INCRED-IBLE! THE KABURAGI BOYS MUST KNOW NO FEAR...
TREATING THOSE MONSTERS LIKE THEY ARE JUST OLD GRANDPAS FROM DOWN THE STREET.
WHOA... GOTTA RESPECT THAT.
AKIRA.
LORD SCOTT.
CARE TO GO A ROUND WITH ME?
SURE.

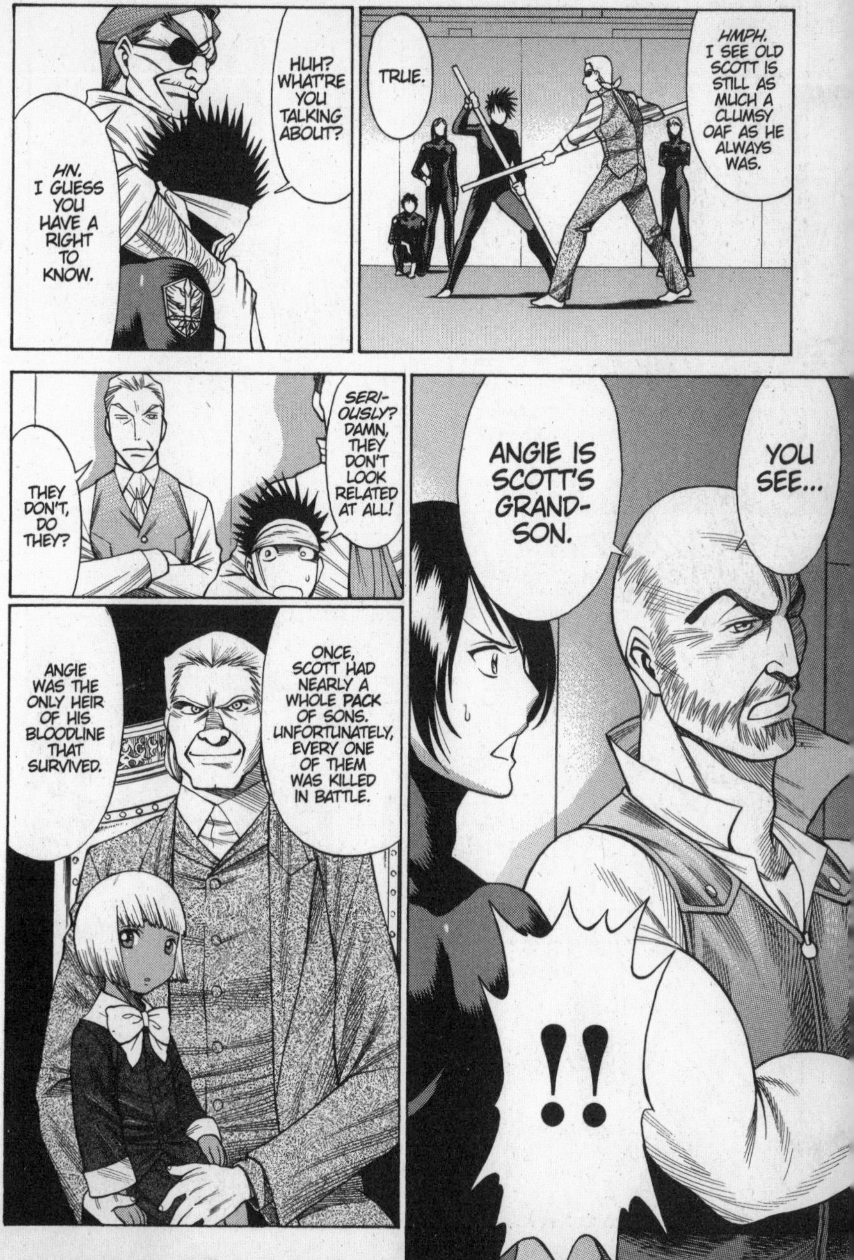
HMPH. I SEE OLD SCOTT IS STILL AS MUCH A CLUMSY OAF AS HE ALWAYS WAS.
TRUE.
HUH? WHAT'RE YOU TALKING ABOUT?
HN. I GUESS YOU HAVE A RIGHT TO KNOW.
YOU SEE...
ANGIE IS SCOTT'S GRAND-SON.
!!
SERI-OUSLY? DAMN, THEY DON'T LOOK RELATED AT ALL!
THEY DON'T, DO THEY?
ONCE, SCOTT HAD NEARLY A WHOLE PACK OF SONS. UNFORTUNATELY, EVERY ONE OF THEM WAS KILLED IN BATTLE.
ANGIE WAS THE ONLY HEIR OF HIS BLOODLINE THAT SURVIVED.

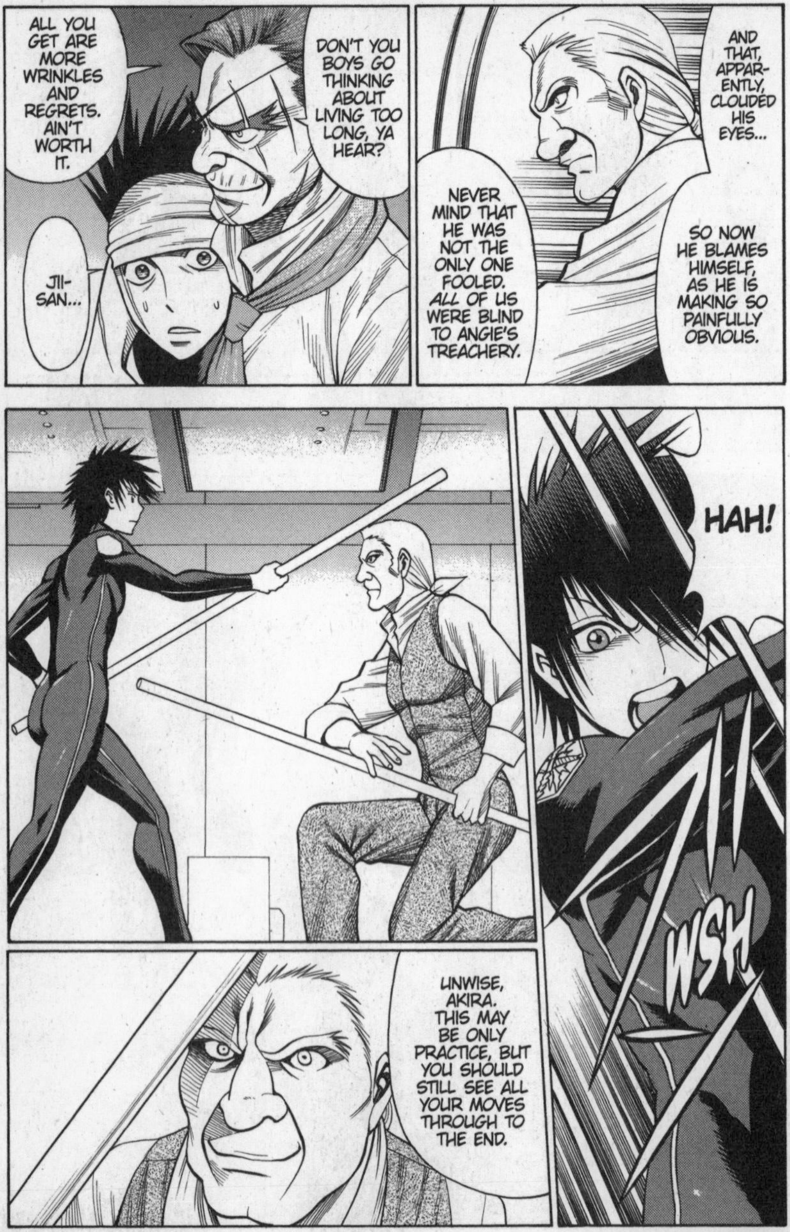

AND THAT, APPARENTLY, CLOUDED HIS EYES...
SO NOW HE BLAMES HIMSELF, AS HE IS MAKING SO PAINFULLY OBVIOUS.
NEVER MIND THAT HE WAS NOT THE ONLY ONE FOOLED. *ALL* OF US WERE BLIND TO ANGIE'S TREACHERY.
DON'T YOU BOYS GO THINKING ABOUT LIVING TOO LONG, YA HEAR?
ALL YOU GET ARE MORE WRINKLES AND REGRETS. AIN'T WORTH IT.
JII-SAN...
HAH!
WSH
UNWISE, AKIRA. THIS MAY BE ONLY PRACTICE, BUT YOU SHOULD STILL SEE ALL YOUR MOVES THROUGH TO THE END.

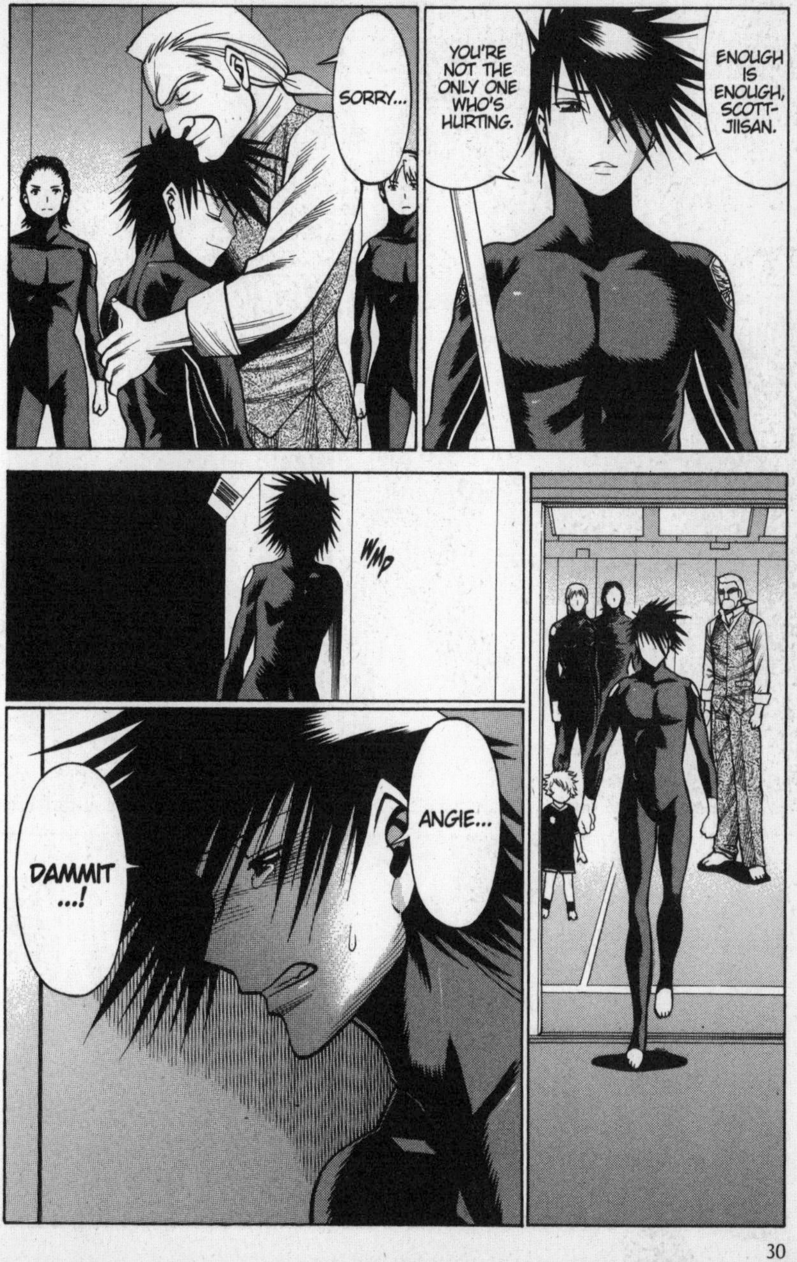
ENOUGH IS ENOUGH, SCOTT-JIISAN.
YOU'RE NOT THE ONLY ONE WHO'S HURTING.
SORRY...
WMP
ANGIE...
DAMMIT ...!

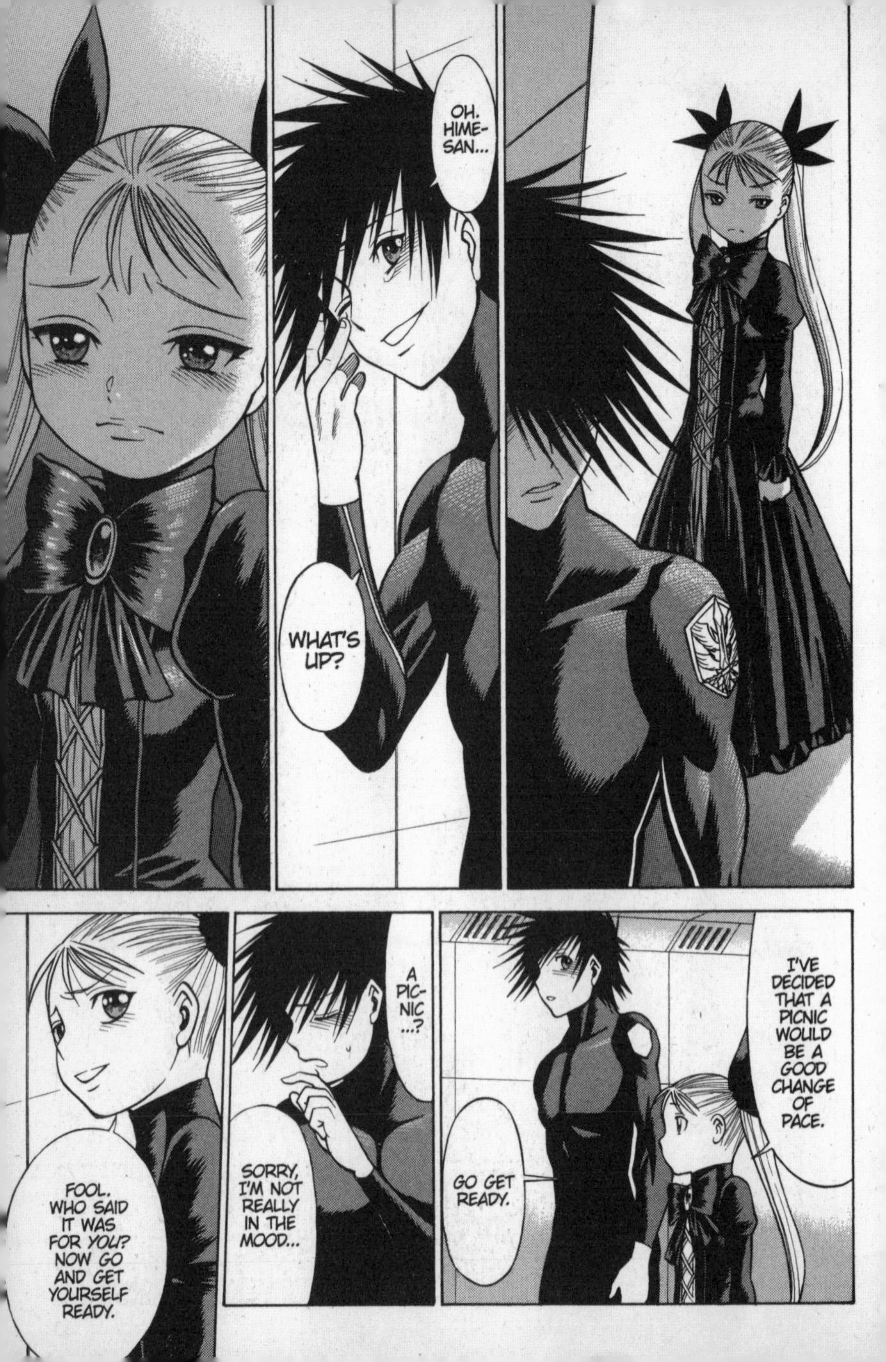
OH. HIME-SAN...
WHAT'S UP?
I'VE DECIDED THAT A PICNIC WOULD BE A GOOD CHANGE OF PACE.
GO GET READY.
A PICNIC...?
SORRY, I'M NOT REALLY IN THE MOOD...
FOOL. WHO SAID IT WAS FOR YOU? NOW GO AND GET YOURSELF READY.

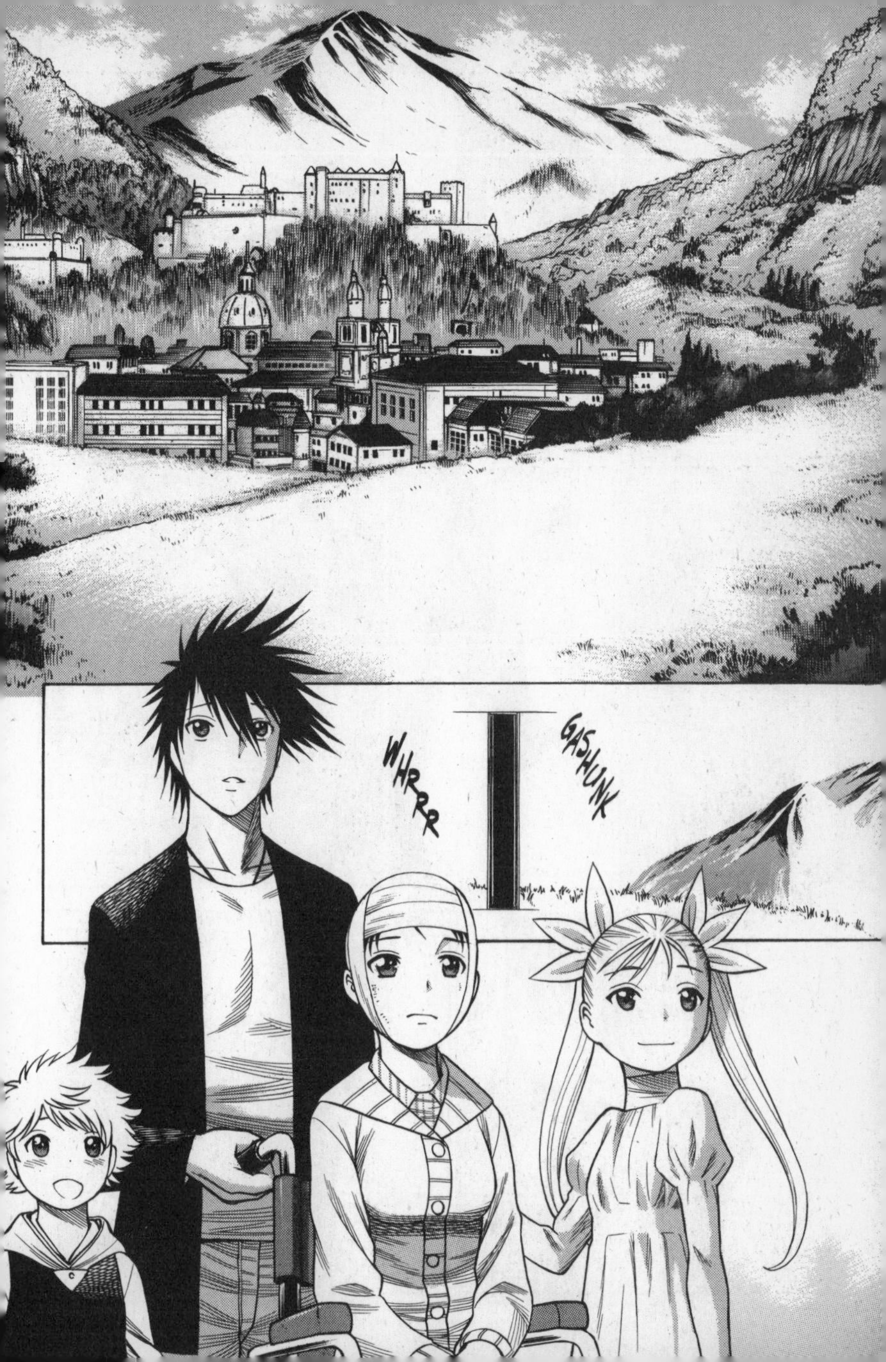
GASHUNK
WHRRR

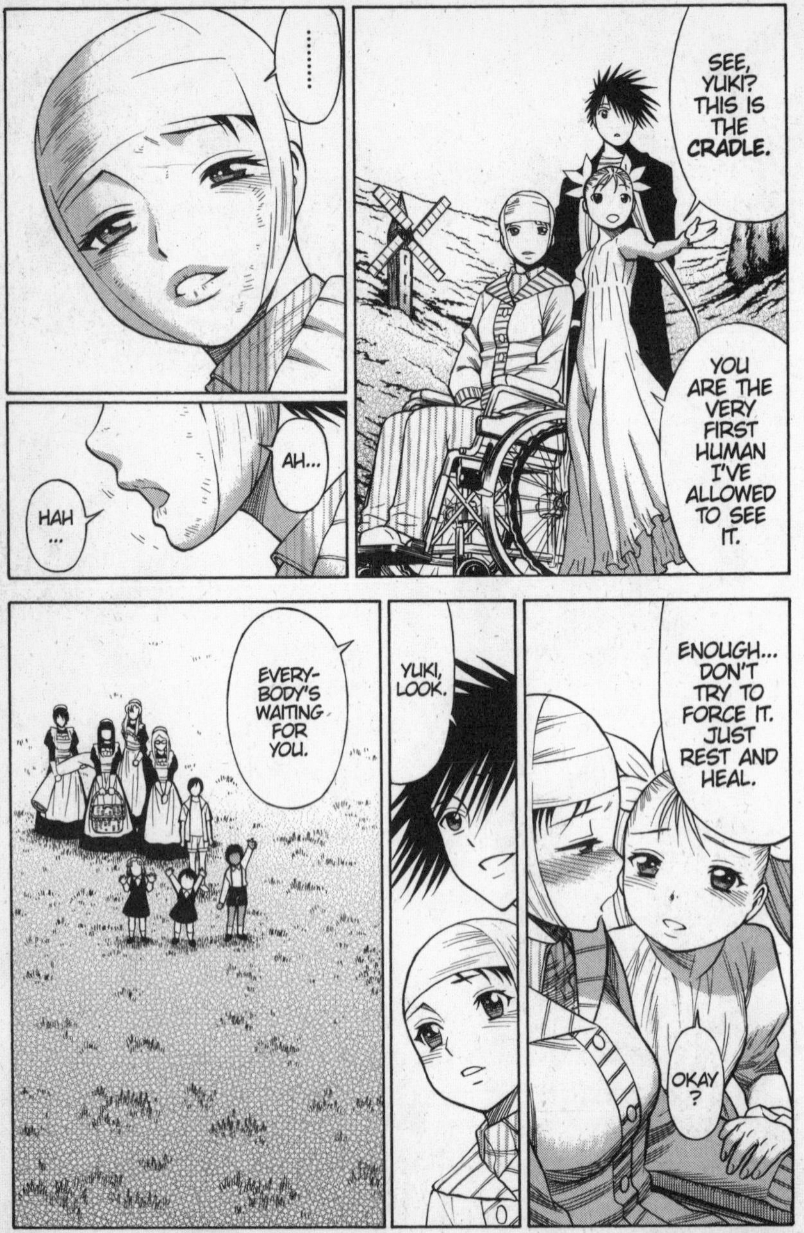
SEE, YUKI? THIS IS THE CRADLE.
YOU ARE THE VERY FIRST HUMAN I'VE ALLOWED TO SEE IT.
......
AH...
HAH...
ENOUGH... DON'T TRY TO FORCE IT. JUST REST AND HEAL.
OKAY?
YUKI, LOOK.
EVERYBODY'S WAITING FOR YOU.

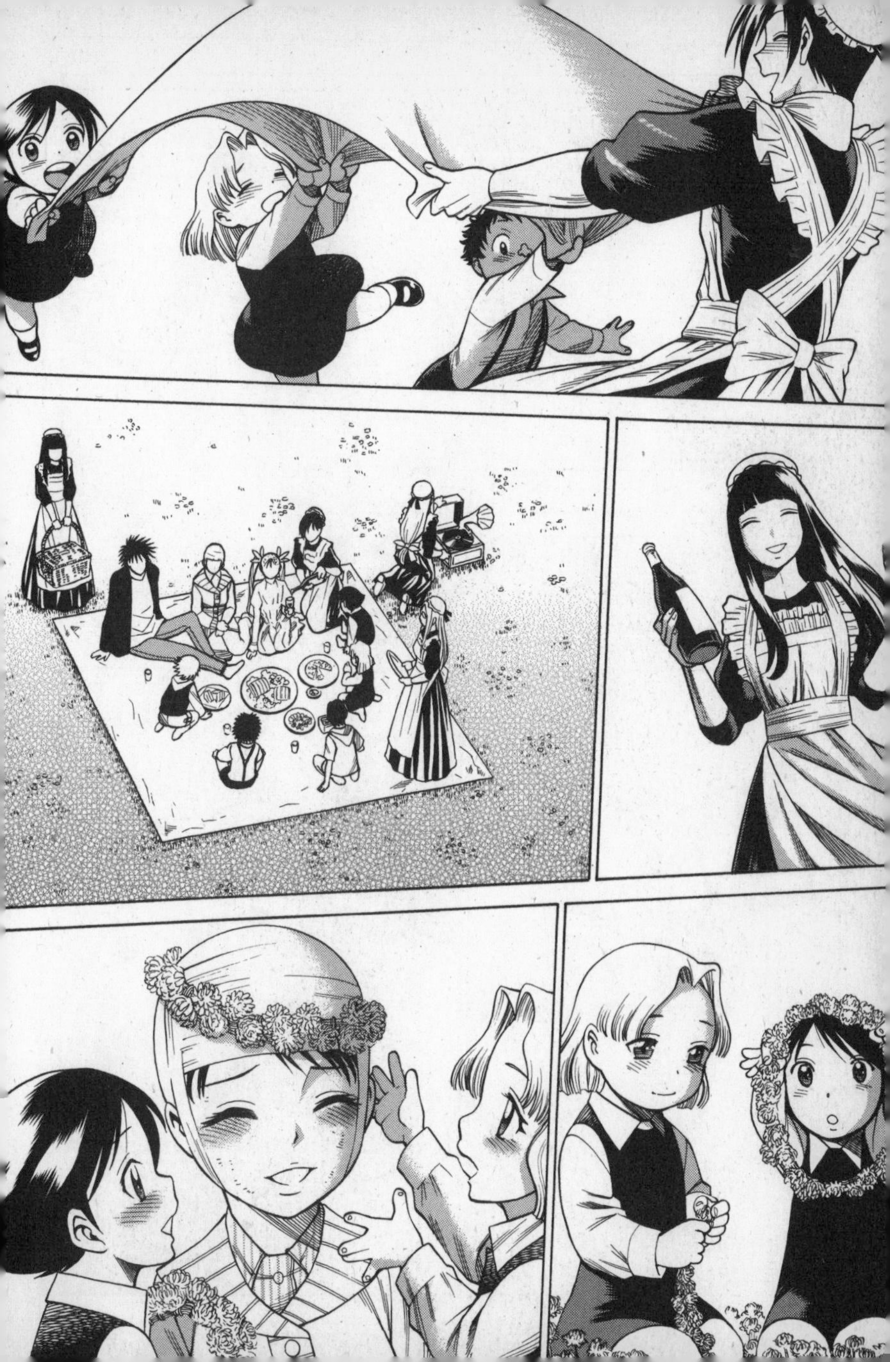

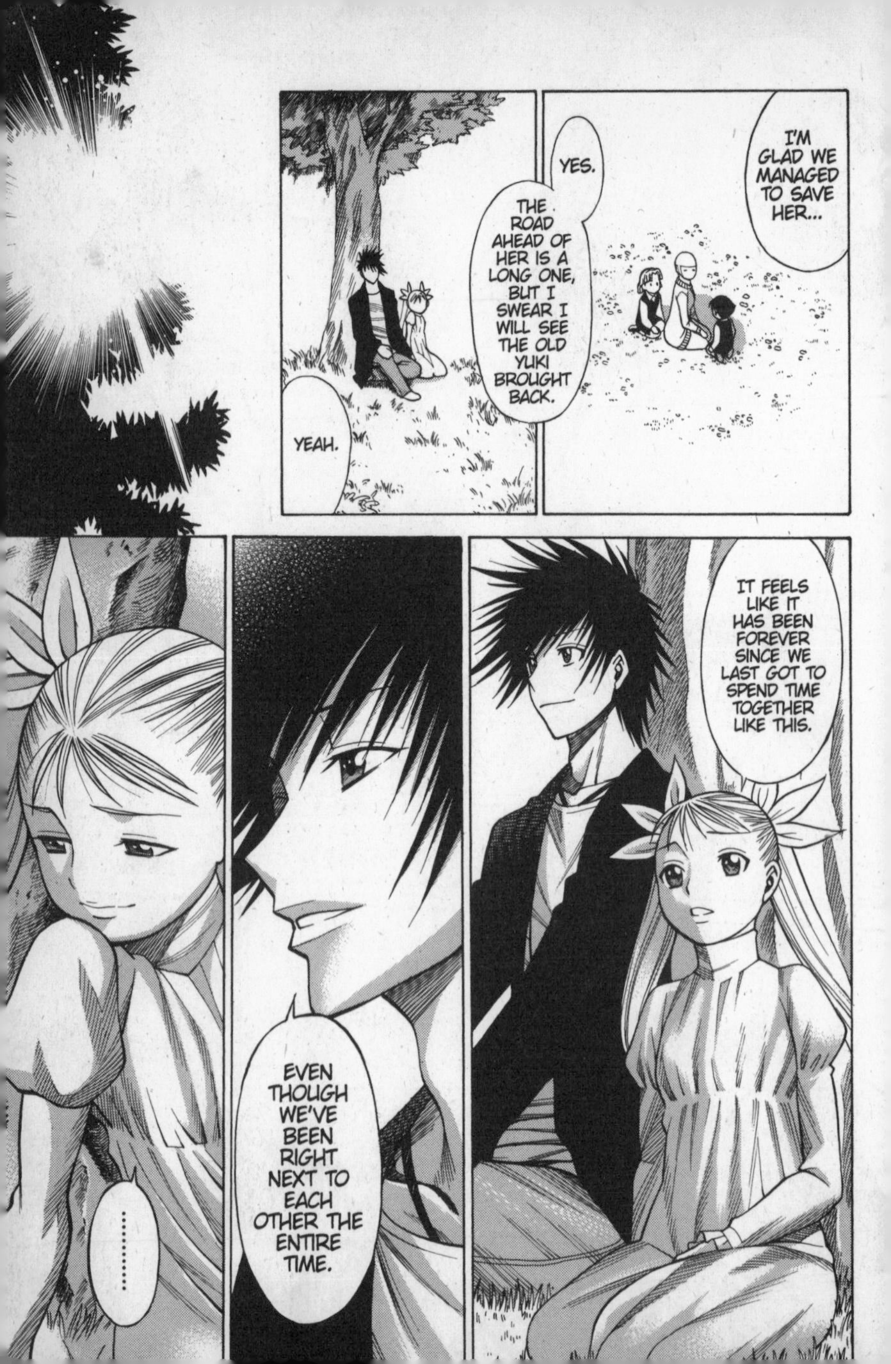
I'M GLAD WE MANAGED TO SAVE HER...
YES.
THE ROAD AHEAD OF HER IS A LONG ONE, BUT I SWEAR I WILL SEE THE OLD YUKI BROUGHT BACK.
YEAH.
IT FEELS LIKE IT HAS BEEN FOREVER SINCE WE LAST GOT TO SPEND TIME TOGETHER LIKE THIS.
EVEN THOUGH WE'VE BEEN RIGHT NEXT TO EACH OTHER THE ENTIRE TIME.
......

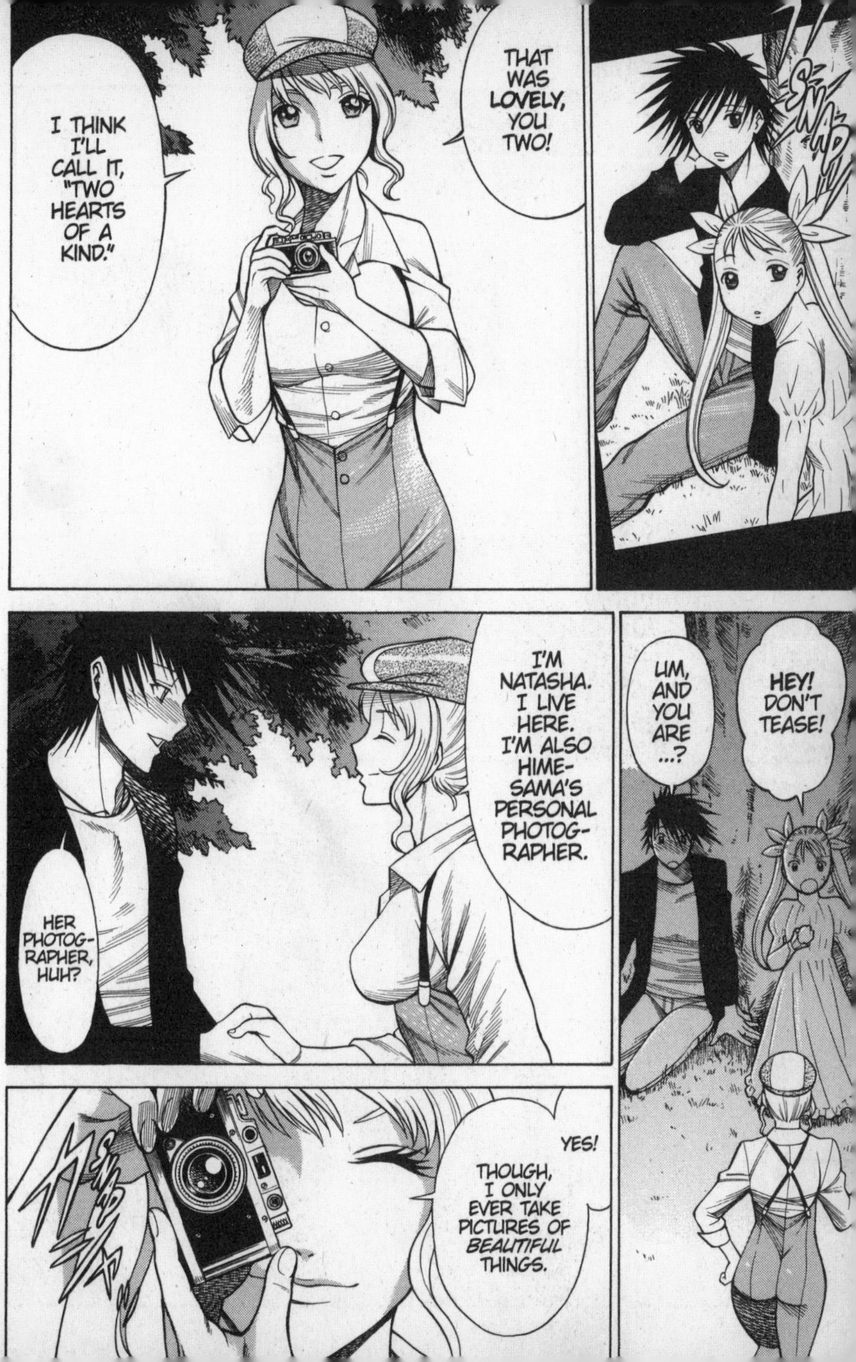
SNAP!
THAT WAS LOVELY, YOU TWO!
I THINK I'LL CALL IT, "TWO HEARTS OF A KIND."
HEY! DON'T TEASE!
UM, AND YOU ARE ...?
I'M NATASHA. I LIVE HERE. I'M ALSO HIME-SAMA'S PERSONAL PHOTOG-RAPHER.
HER PHOTOG-RAPHER, HUH?
YES!
THOUGH, I ONLY EVER TAKE PICTURES OF *BEAUTIFUL* THINGS.

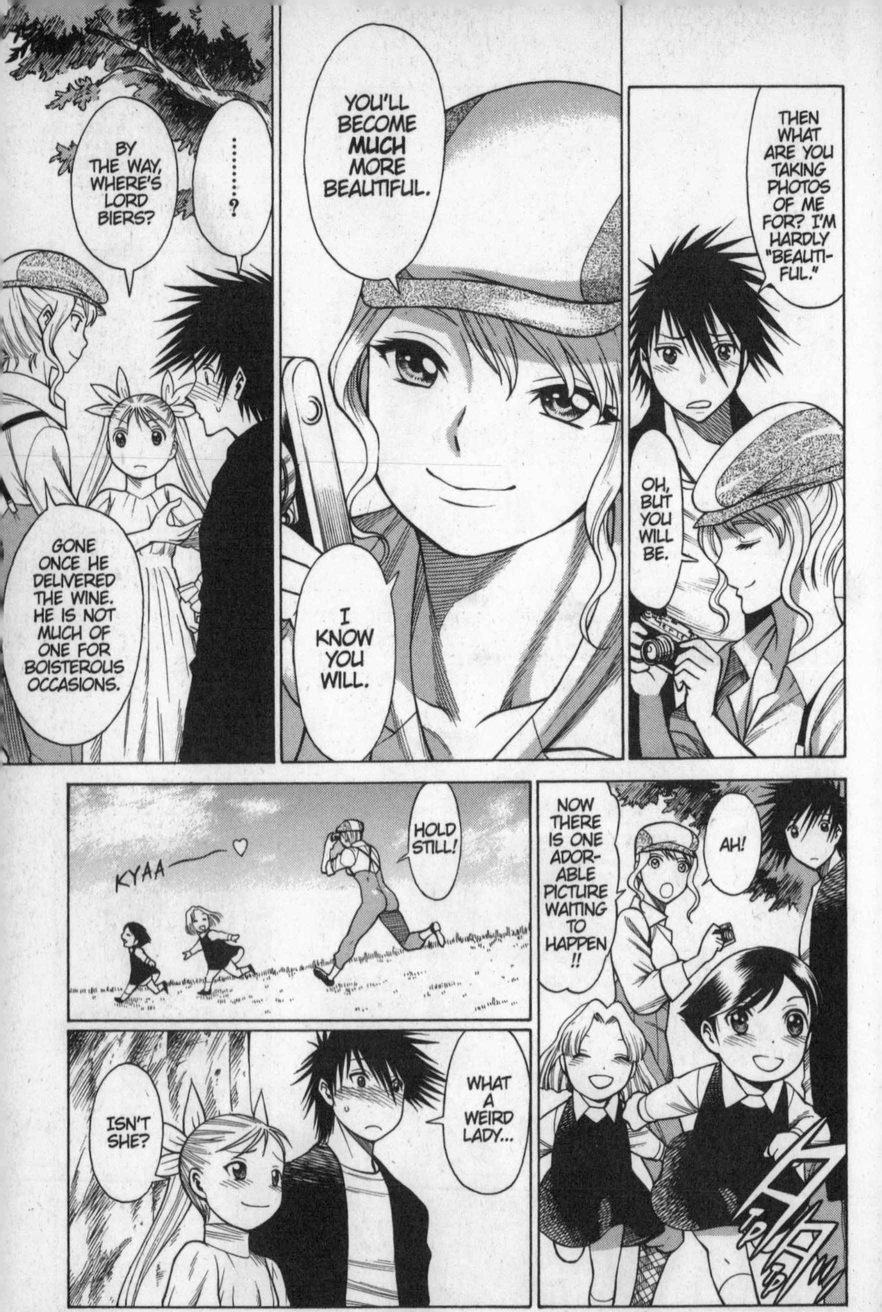
THEN WHAT ARE YOU TAKING PHOTOS OF ME FOR? I'M HARDLY "BEAUTIFUL."
OH, BUT YOU WILL BE.
YOU'LL BECOME MUCH MORE BEAUTIFUL.
I KNOW YOU WILL.
......?
BY THE WAY, WHERE'S LORD BIERS?
GONE ONCE HE DELIVERED THE WINE. HE IS NOT MUCH OF ONE FOR BOISTEROUS OCCASIONS.
AH!
NOW THERE IS ONE ADORABLE PICTURE WAITING TO HAPPEN !!
HOLD STILL!
KYAA
WHAT A WEIRD LADY...
ISN'T SHE?

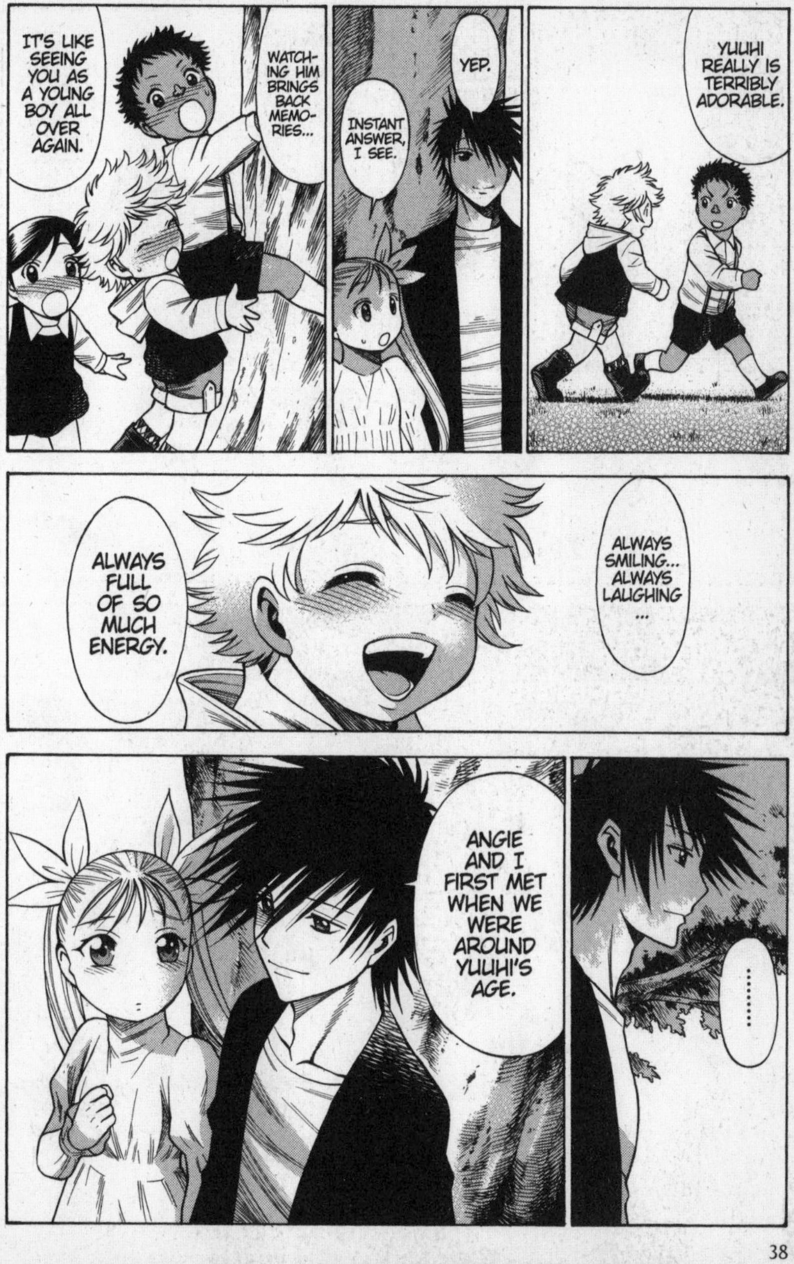
YUUHI REALLY IS TERRIBLY ADORABLE.
YEP.
INSTANT ANSWER, I SEE.
WATCHING HIM BRINGS BACK MEMORIES...
IT'S LIKE SEEING YOU AS A YOUNG BOY ALL OVER AGAIN.
ALWAYS SMILING... ALWAYS LAUGHING...
ALWAYS FULL OF SO MUCH ENERGY.
....
ANGIE AND I FIRST MET WHEN WE WERE AROUND YUUHI'S AGE.

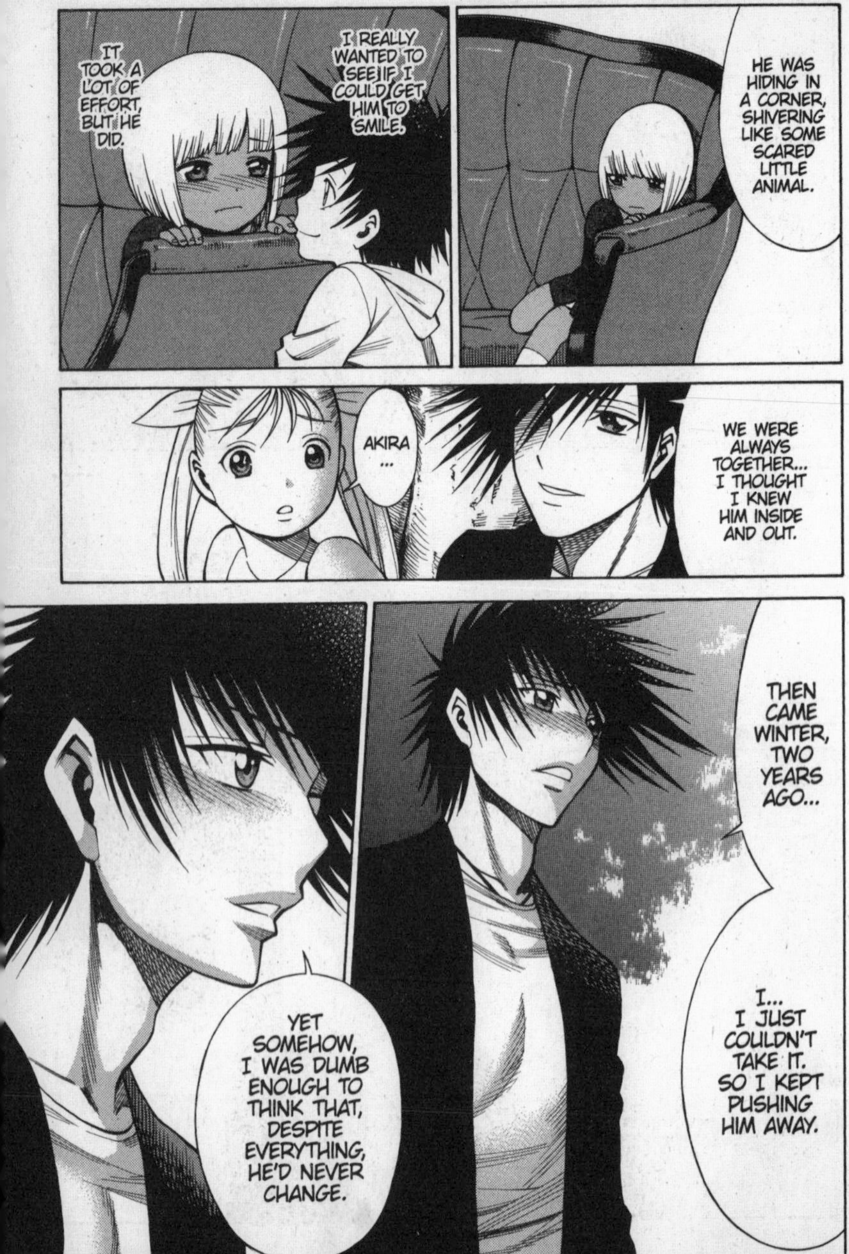
HE WAS HIDING IN A CORNER, SHIVERING LIKE SOME SCARED LITTLE ANIMAL.
I REALLY WANTED TO SEE IF I COULD GET HIM TO SMILE.
IT TOOK A LOT OF EFFORT, BUT HE DID.
WE WERE ALWAYS TOGETHER... I THOUGHT I KNEW HIM INSIDE AND OUT.
AKIRA ...
THEN CAME WINTER, TWO YEARS AGO...
I... I JUST COULDN'T TAKE IT. SO I KEPT PUSHING HIM AWAY.
YET SOMEHOW, I WAS DUMB ENOUGH TO THINK THAT, DESPITE EVERYTHING, HE'D NEVER CHANGE.

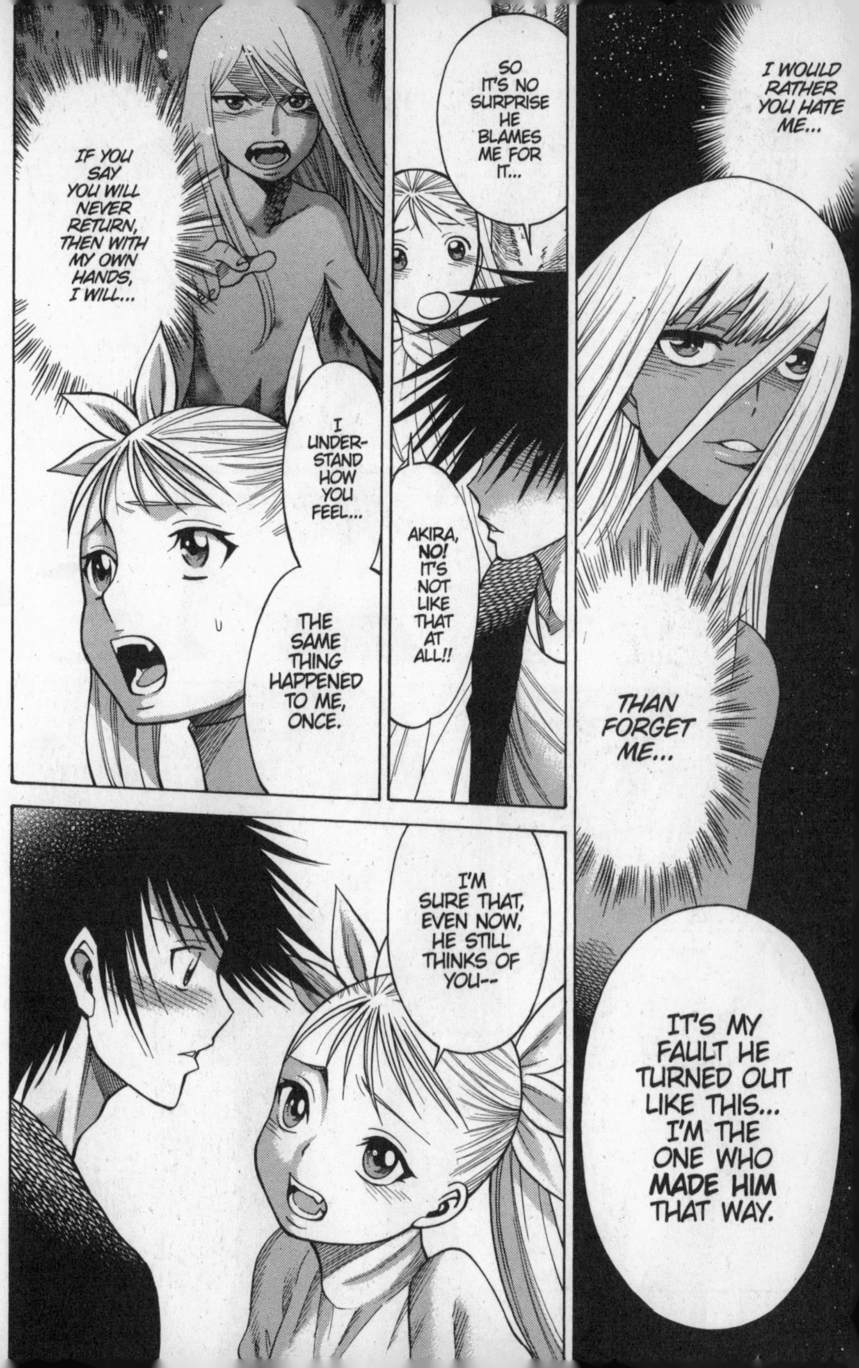
I WOULD RATHER YOU HATE ME...
THAN FORGET ME...
IT'S MY FAULT HE TURNED OUT LIKE THIS... I'M THE ONE WHO MADE HIM THAT WAY.
SO IT'S NO SURPRISE HE BLAMES ME FOR IT...
AKIRA, NO! IT'S NOT LIKE THAT AT ALL!!
IF YOU SAY YOU WILL NEVER RETURN, THEN WITH MY OWN HANDS, I WILL...
I UNDER-STAND HOW YOU FEEL...
THE SAME THING HAPPENED TO ME, ONCE.
I'M SURE THAT, EVEN NOW, HE STILL THINKS OF YOU--

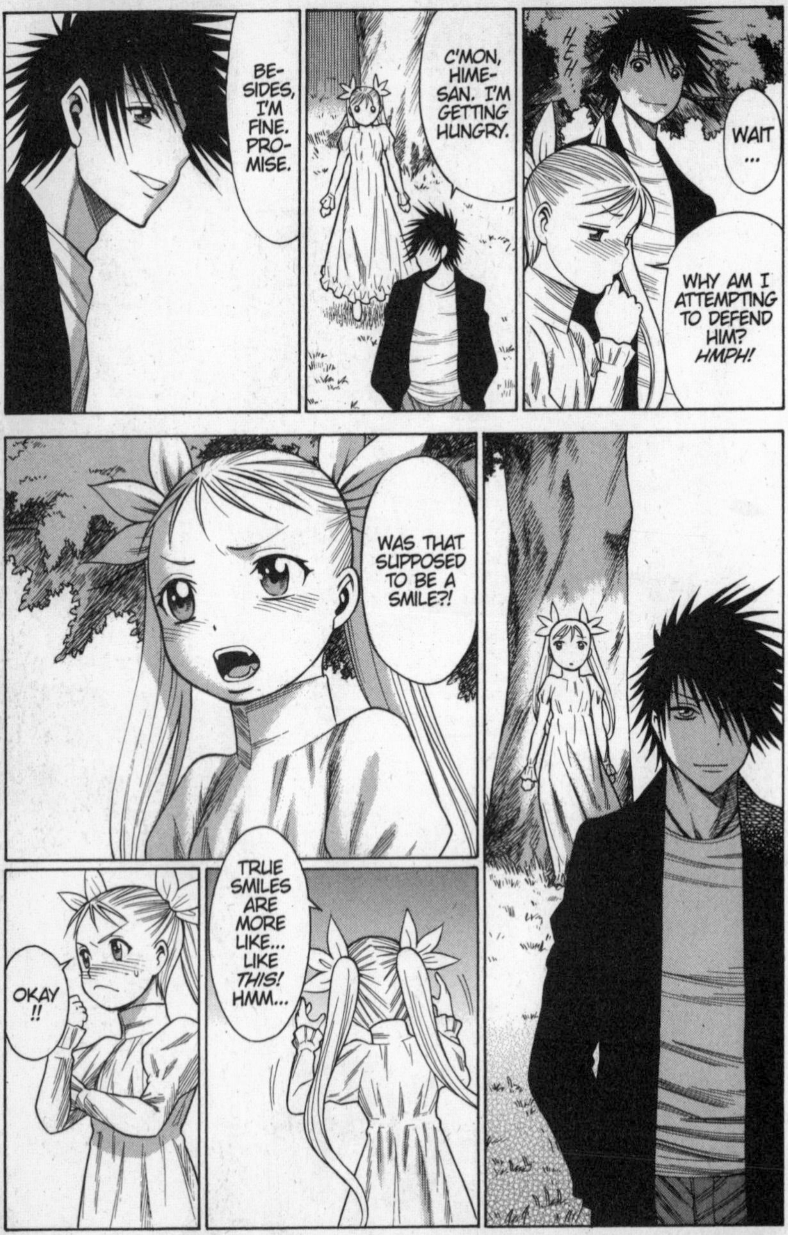
WAIT ...
HEH!
WHY AM I ATTEMPTING TO DEFEND HIM? *HMPH!*
C'MON, HIME-SAN. I'M GETTING HUNGRY.
BE-SIDES, I'M FINE. PRO-MISE.
WAS THAT SUPPOSED TO BE A SMILE?!
TRUE SMILES ARE MORE LIKE... LIKE *THIS!* HMM...
OKAY !!

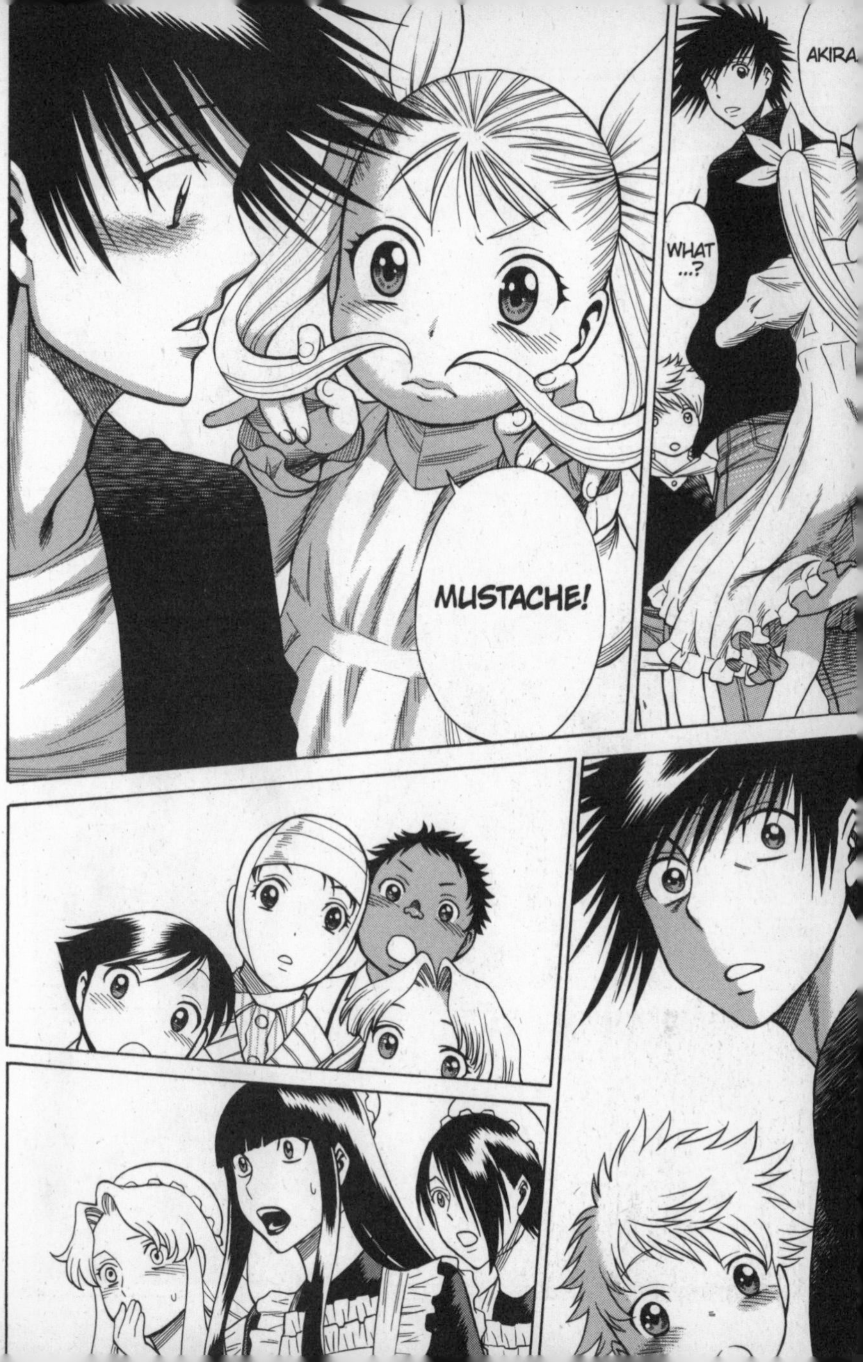
AKIRA.
WHAT ...?
MUSTACHE!

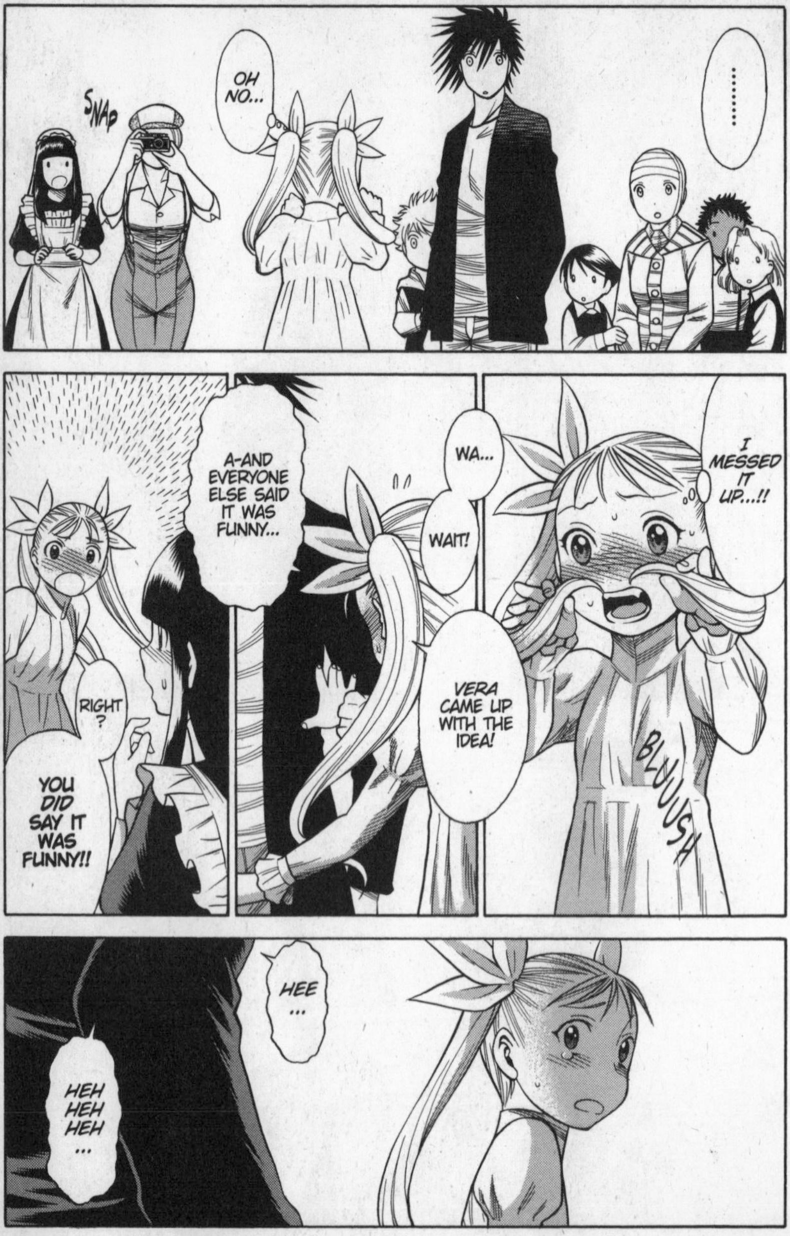
......
OH NO...
SNAP
I MESSED IT UP...!!
VERA CAME UP WITH THE IDEA!
BLUUUSH
WA...
WAIT!
A-AND EVERYONE ELSE SAID IT WAS FUNNY...
RIGHT?
YOU DID SAY IT WAS FUNNY!!
HEE...
HEH HEH HEH...

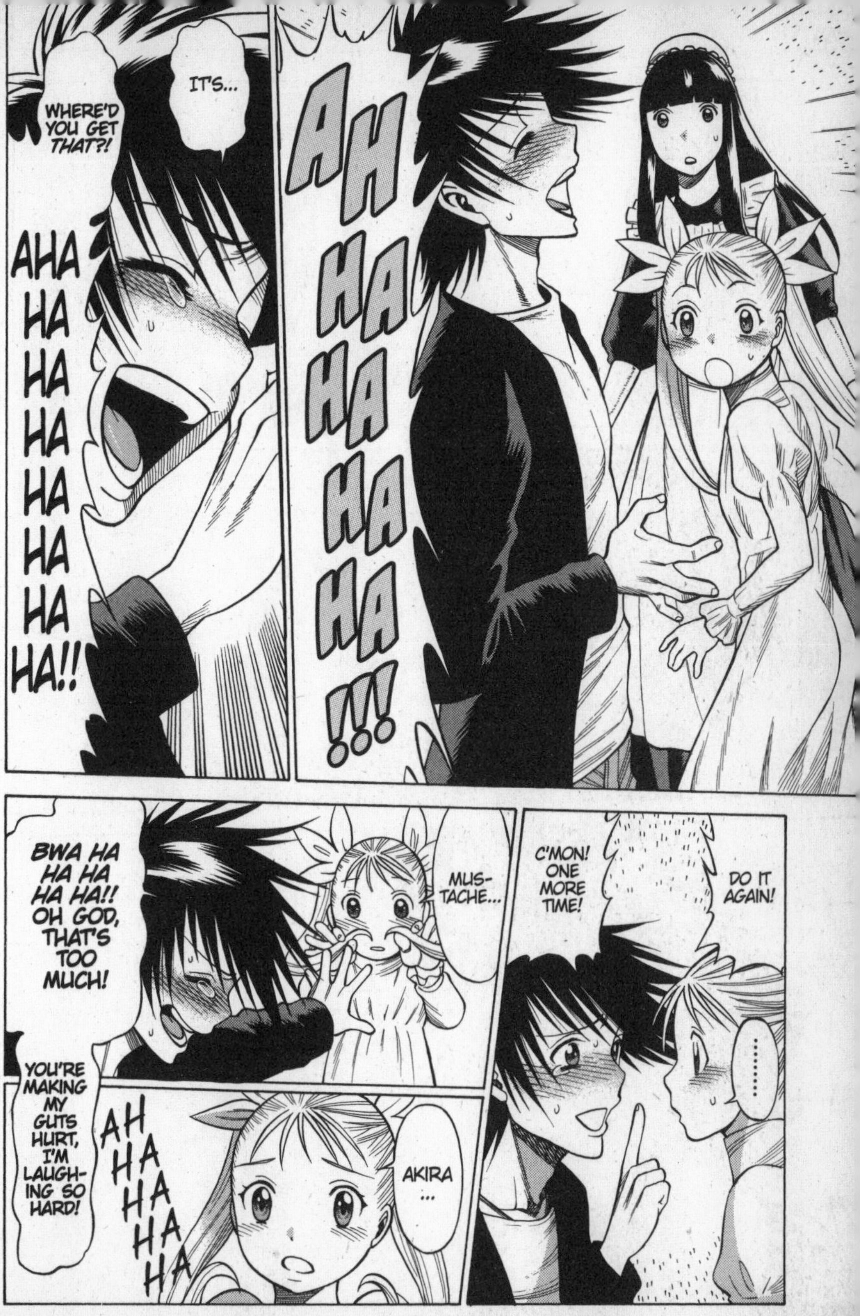
AHHAHAHAHAHAHA!!!
IT'S...
WHERE'D YOU GET THAT?!
AHAHAHAHAHAHAHAHAHAHAHAHA!!
DO IT AGAIN!
C'MON! ONE MORE TIME!
......
MUS-TACHE...
BWA HA HA HA HA HA!! OH GOD, THAT'S TOO MUCH!
AKIRA ...
AHAHAHAHAHA
YOU'RE MAKING MY GUTS HURT, I'M LAUGHING SO HARD!

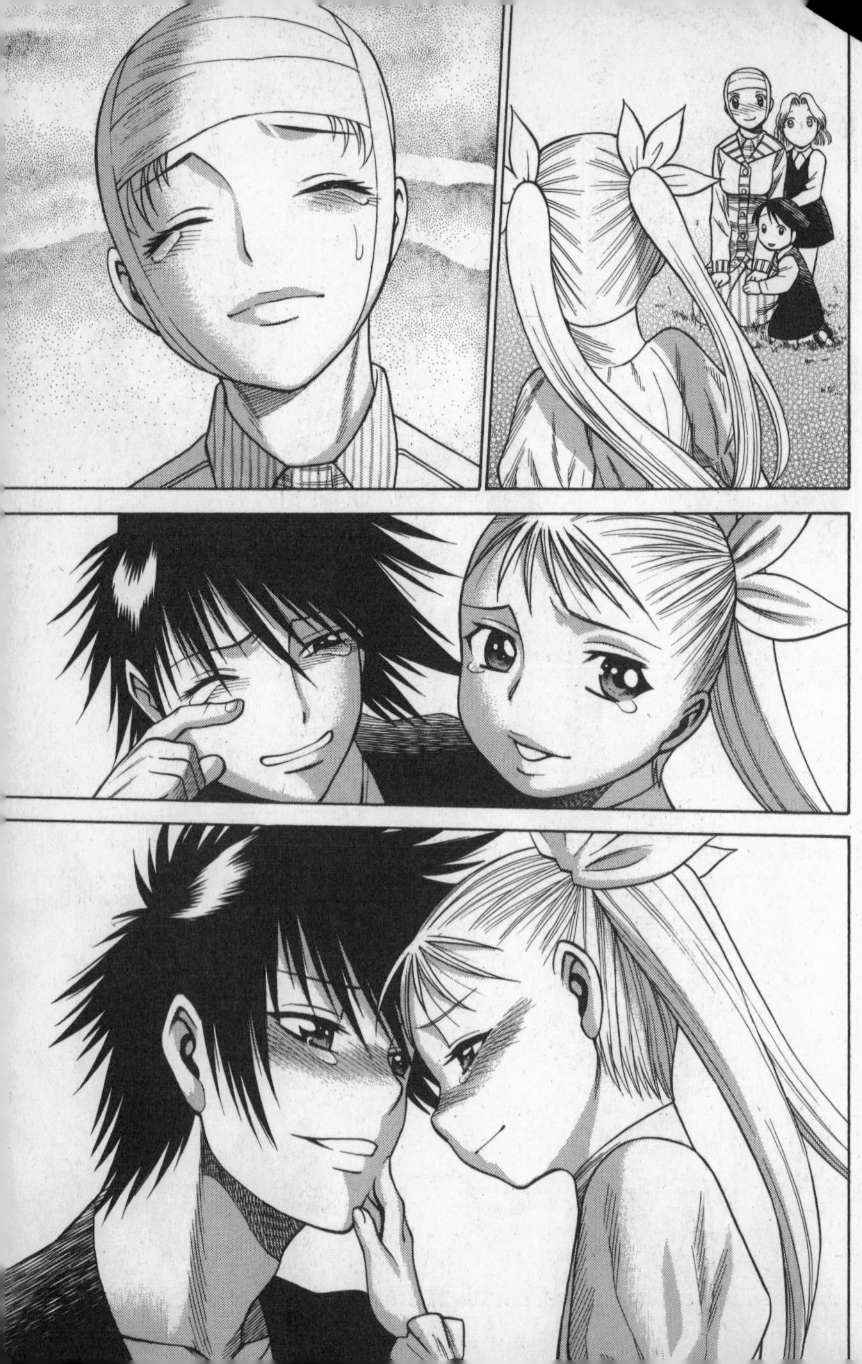

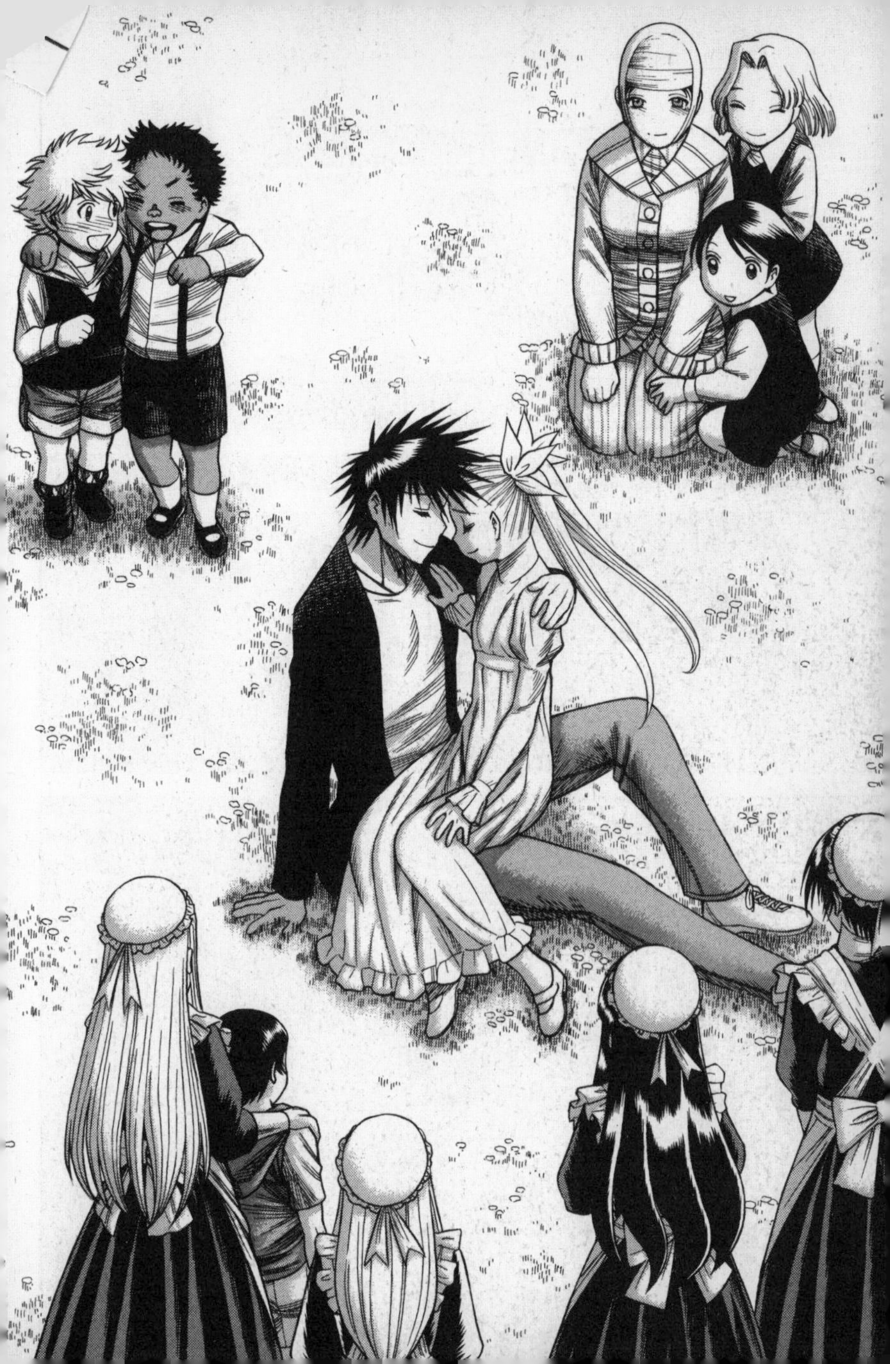

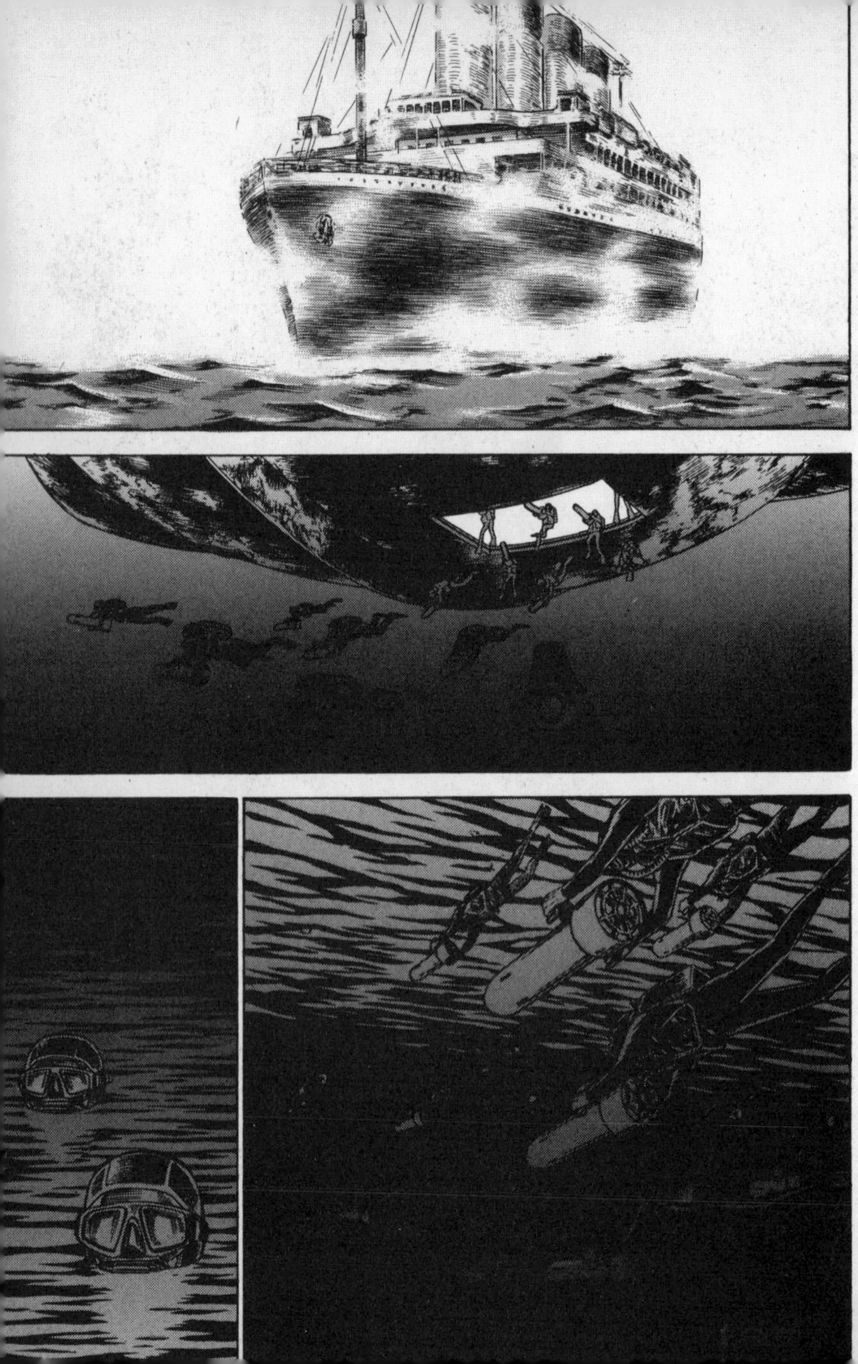

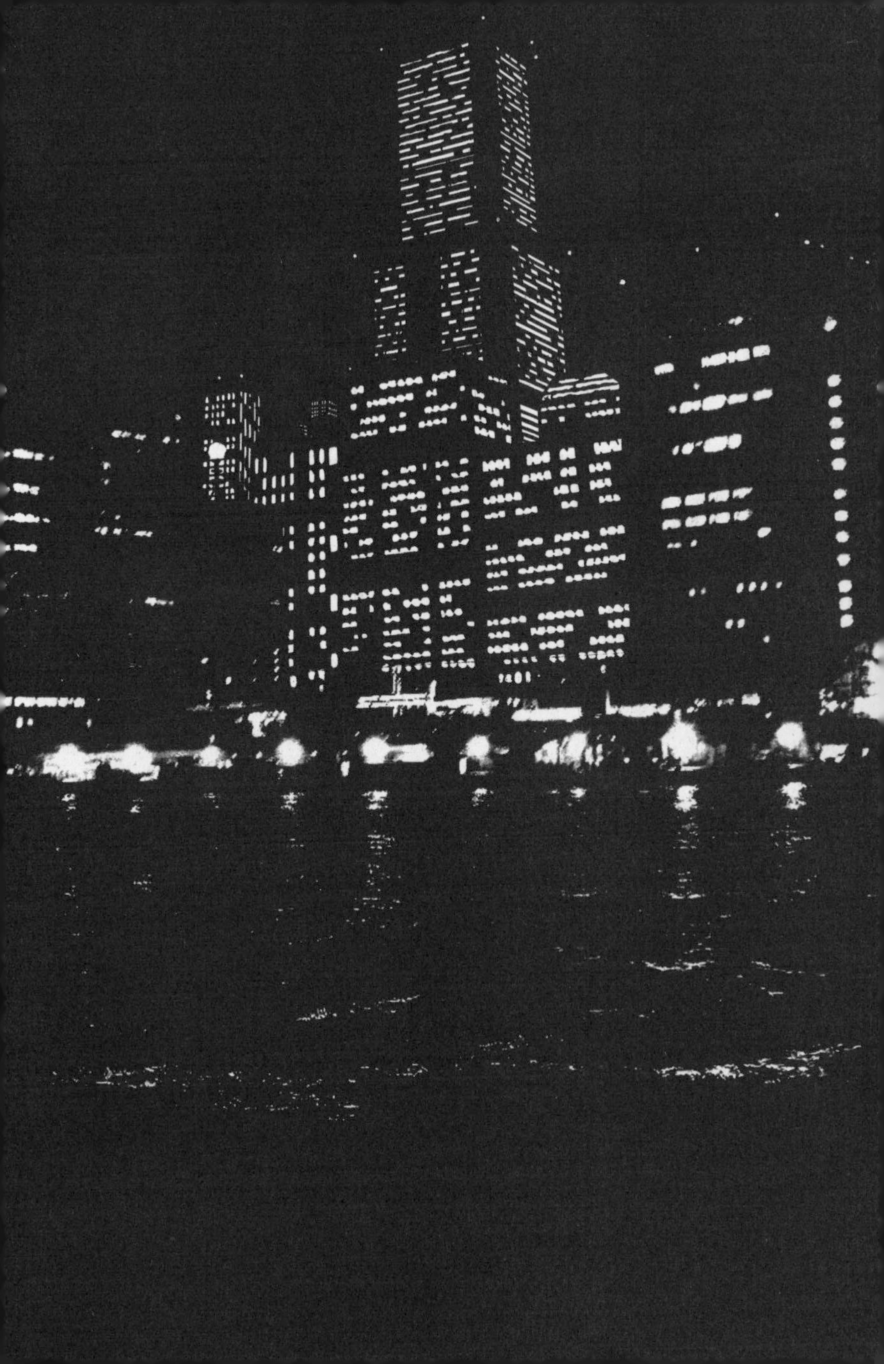

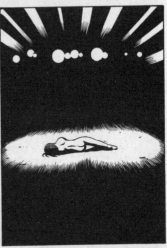

I
DON'T
...

IS
SHE
DEAD
?

TMP

TMP

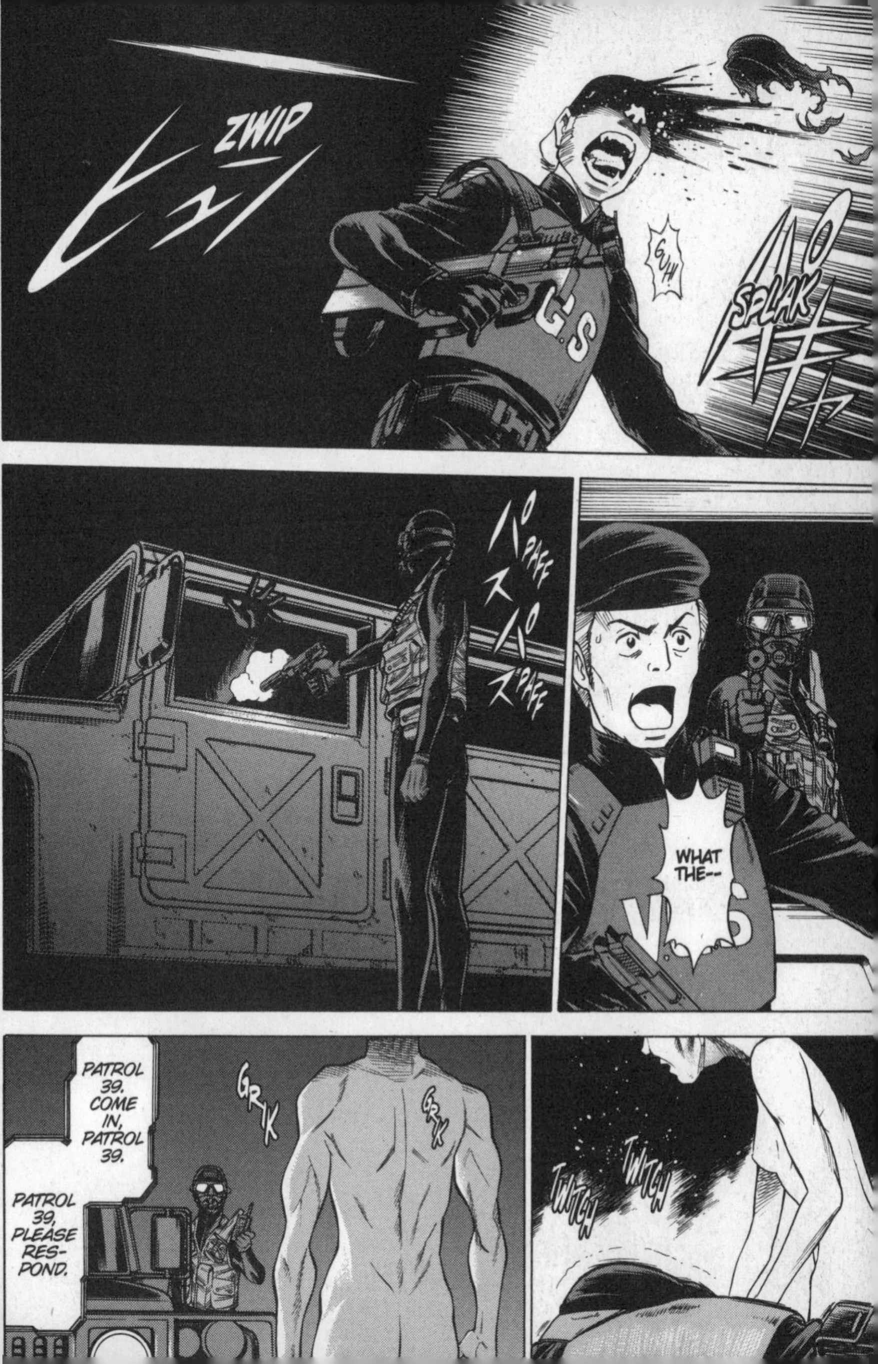
GUH!
SPLAK
ZWIP
WHAT THE--
PAFF
PAFF
TWITCH
TWITCH
PATROL 39. COME IN, PATROL 39.
PATROL 39, PLEASE RESPOND.
GRIK
GRIK

Chapter 51: The First to Come

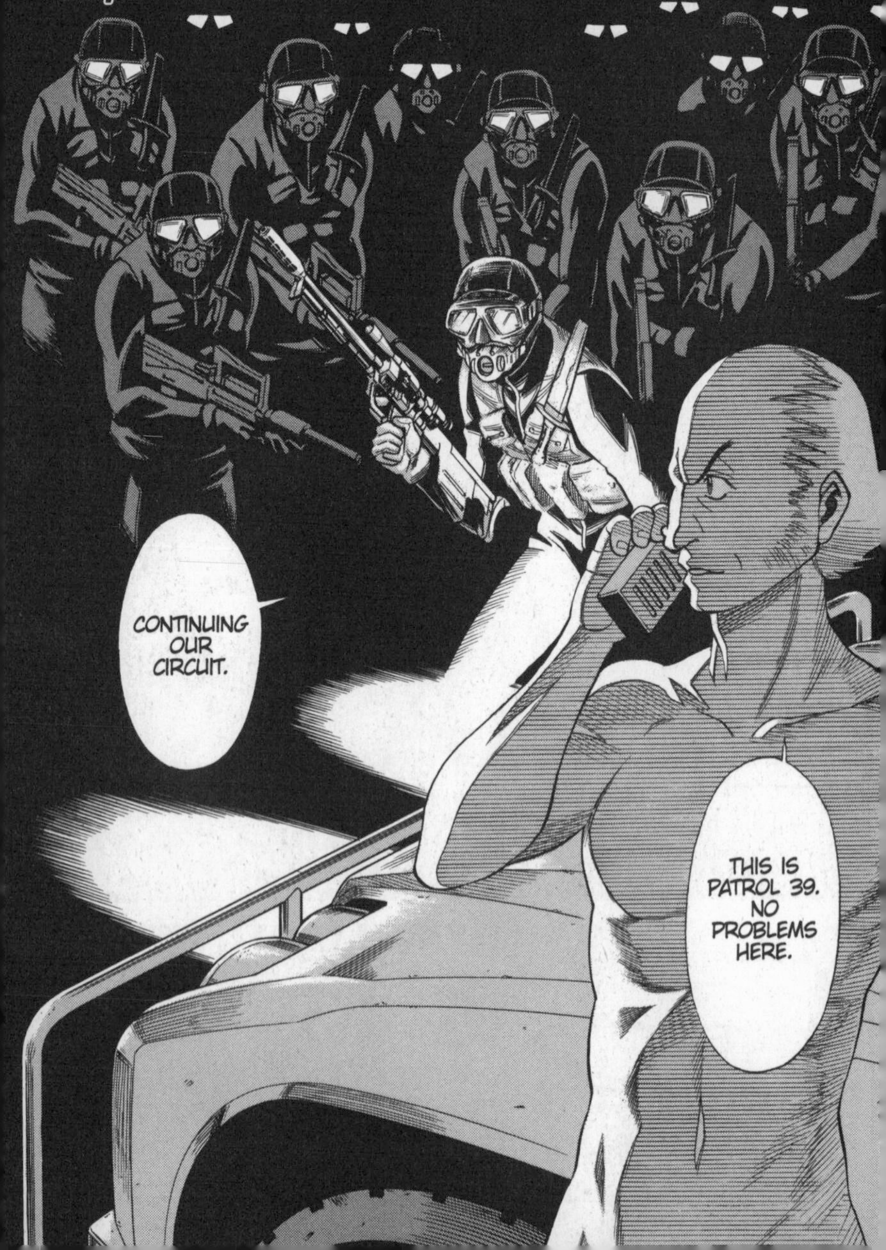
THIS IS PATROL 39. NO PROBLEMS HERE.
CONTINUING OUR CIRCUIT.

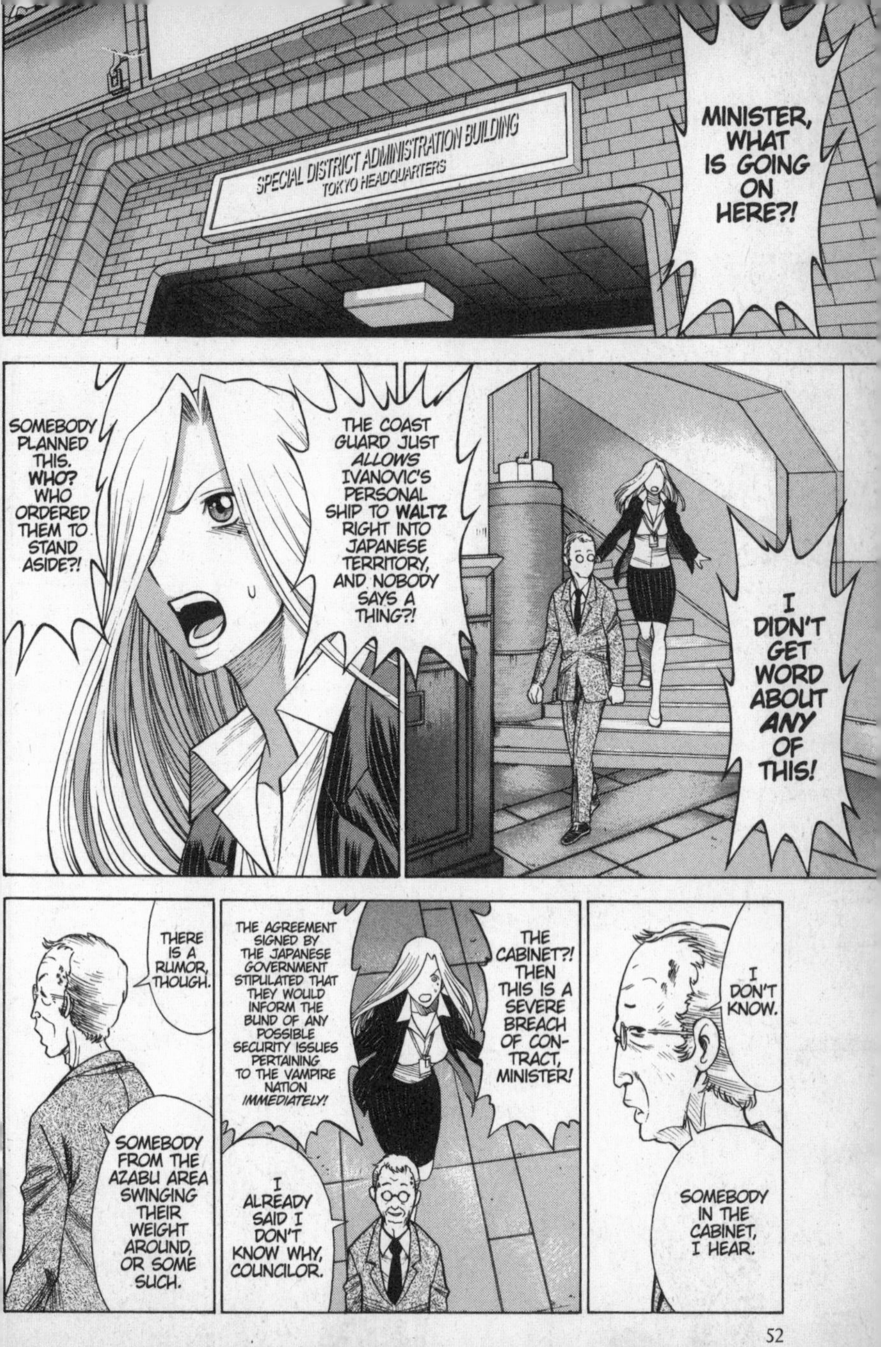
SPECIAL DISTRICT ADMINISTRATION BUILDING
TOKYO HEADQUARTERS
MINISTER, WHAT IS GOING ON HERE?!
I DIDN'T GET WORD ABOUT *ANY* OF THIS!
THE COAST GUARD JUST *ALLOWS* IVANOVIC'S PERSONAL SHIP TO **WALTZ** RIGHT INTO JAPANESE TERRITORY, AND NOBODY SAYS A THING?!
SOMEBODY PLANNED THIS. **WHO?** WHO ORDERED THEM TO STAND ASIDE?!
I DON'T KNOW.
SOMEBODY IN THE CABINET, I HEAR.
THE CABINET?! THEN THIS IS A SEVERE BREACH OF CON-TRACT, MINISTER!
THE AGREEMENT SIGNED BY THE JAPANESE GOVERNMENT STIPULATED THAT THEY WOULD INFORM THE BUND OF ANY POSSIBLE SECURITY ISSUES PERTAINING TO THE VAMPIRE NATION *IMMEDIATELY!*
I ALREADY SAID I DON'T KNOW WHY, COUNCILOR.
THERE IS A RUMOR, THOUGH.
SOMEBODY FROM THE AZABU AREA SWINGING THEIR WEIGHT AROUND, OR SOME SUCH.

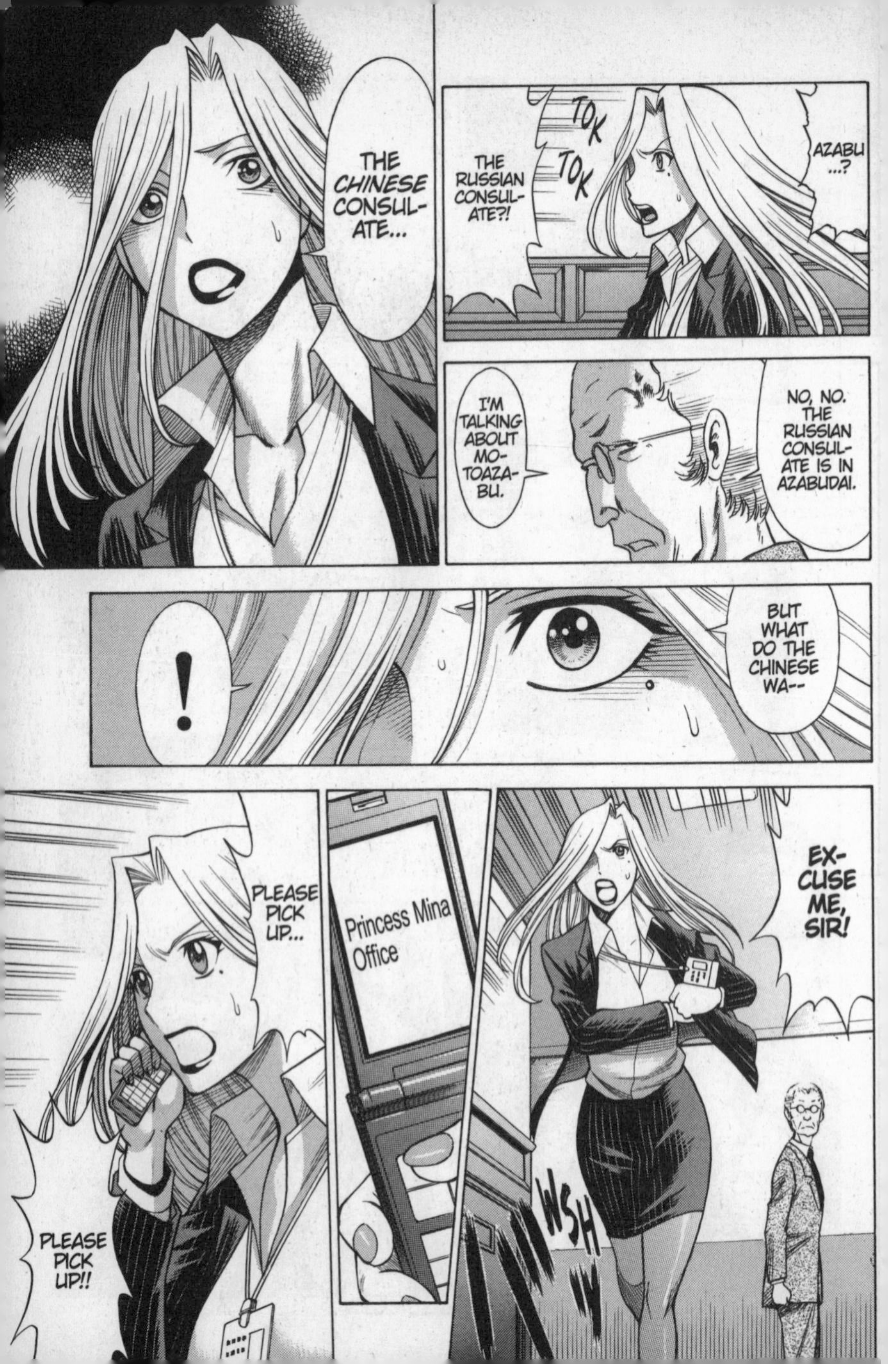
AZABU ...?
TOK TOK
THE RUSSIAN CONSUL-ATE?!
NO, NO. THE RUSSIAN CONSUL-ATE IS IN AZABUDAI.
I'M TALKING ABOUT MO-TOAZA-BU.
THE CHINESE CONSUL-ATE...
BUT WHAT DO THE CHINESE WA--
!
EX-CUSE ME, SIR!
WSH
Princess Mina Office
PLEASE PICK UP...
PLEASE PICK UP!!

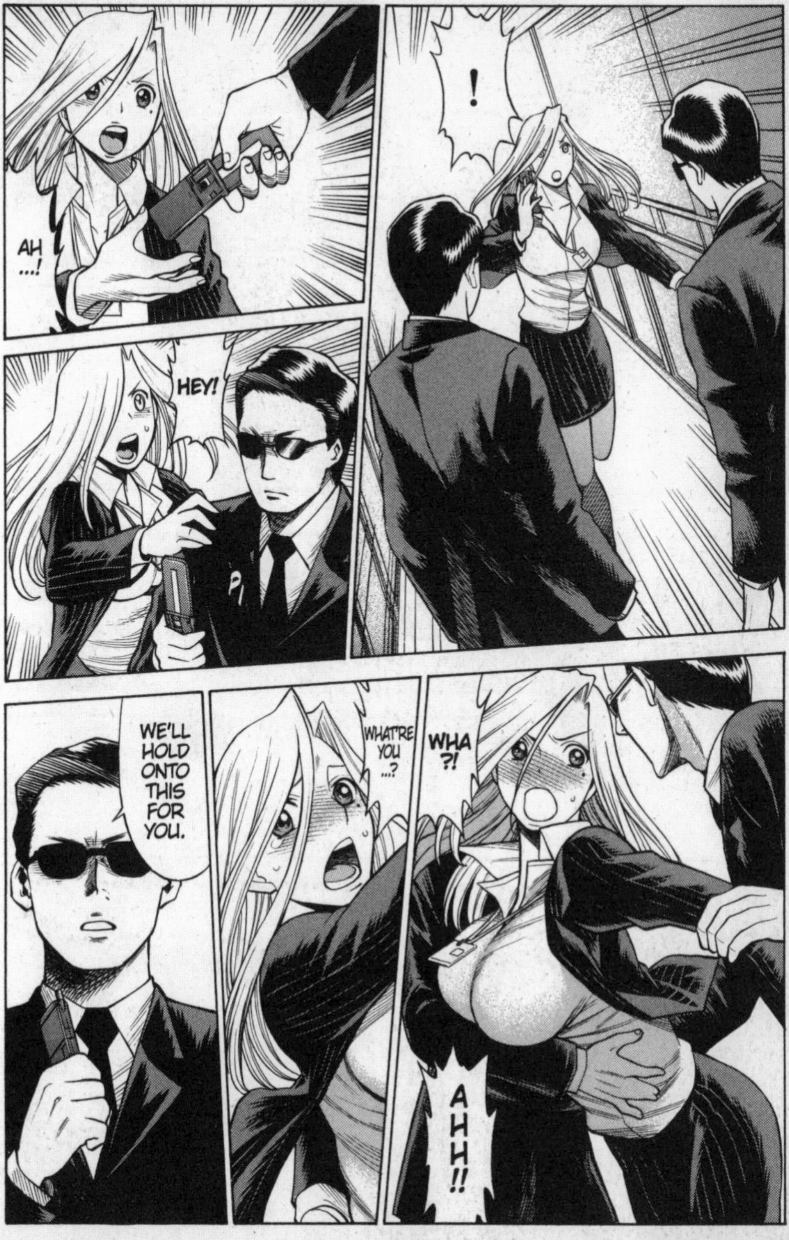
!
AH ...!
HEY!
WHA ?!
AHH!!
WHAT'RE YOU ...?
WE'LL HOLD ONTO THIS FOR YOU.

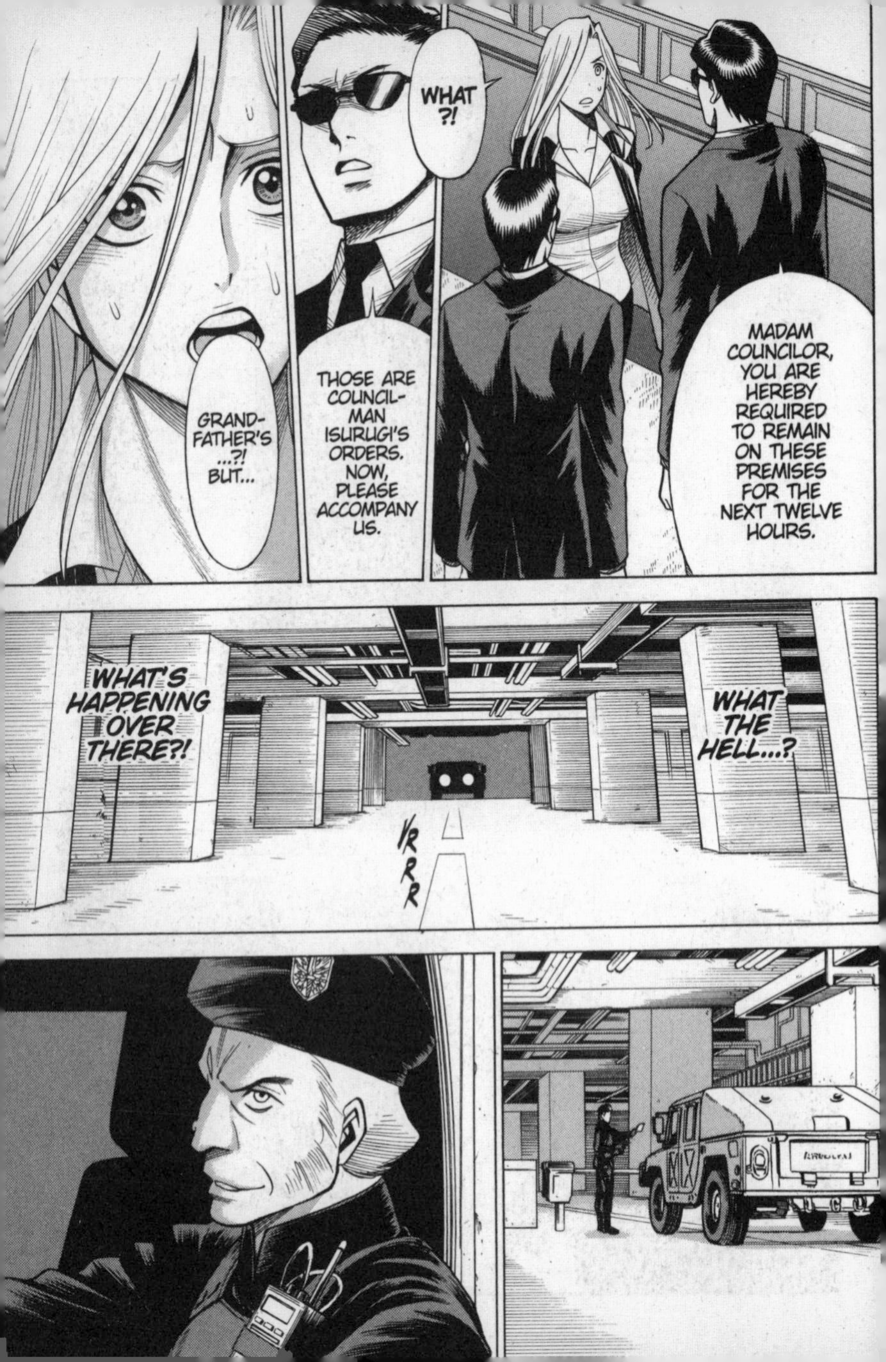
MADAM COUNCILOR, YOU ARE HEREBY REQUIRED TO REMAIN ON THESE PREMISES FOR THE NEXT TWELVE HOURS.
WHAT ?!
THOSE ARE COUNCILMAN ISURUGI'S ORDERS. NOW, PLEASE ACCOMPANY US.
GRANDFATHER'S ...?! BUT...
WHAT THE HELL...?
WHAT'S HAPPENING OVER THERE?!
VRRR

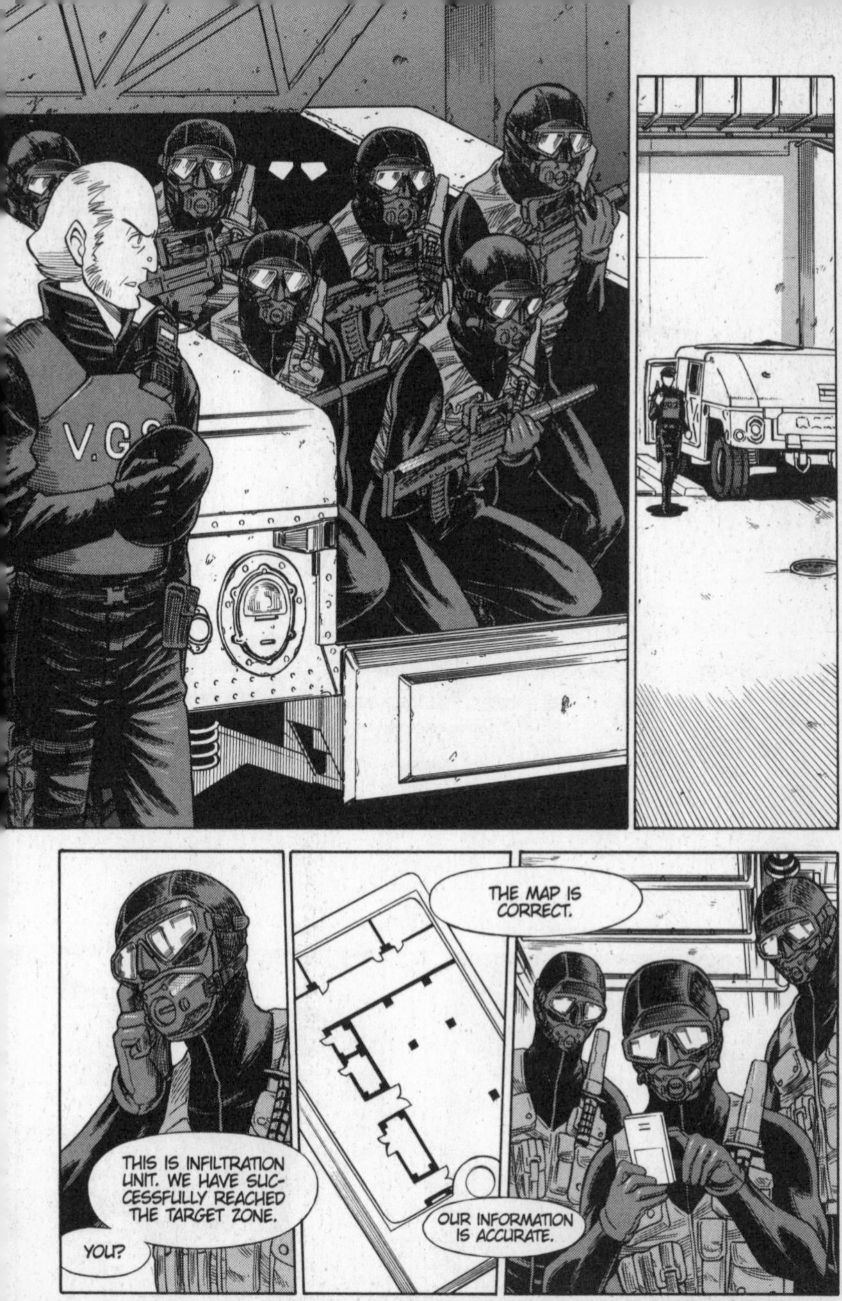
V.G.S
THE MAP IS CORRECT.
OUR INFORMATION IS ACCURATE.
THIS IS INFILTRATION UNIT. WE HAVE SUCCESSFULLY REACHED THE TARGET ZONE.
YOU?

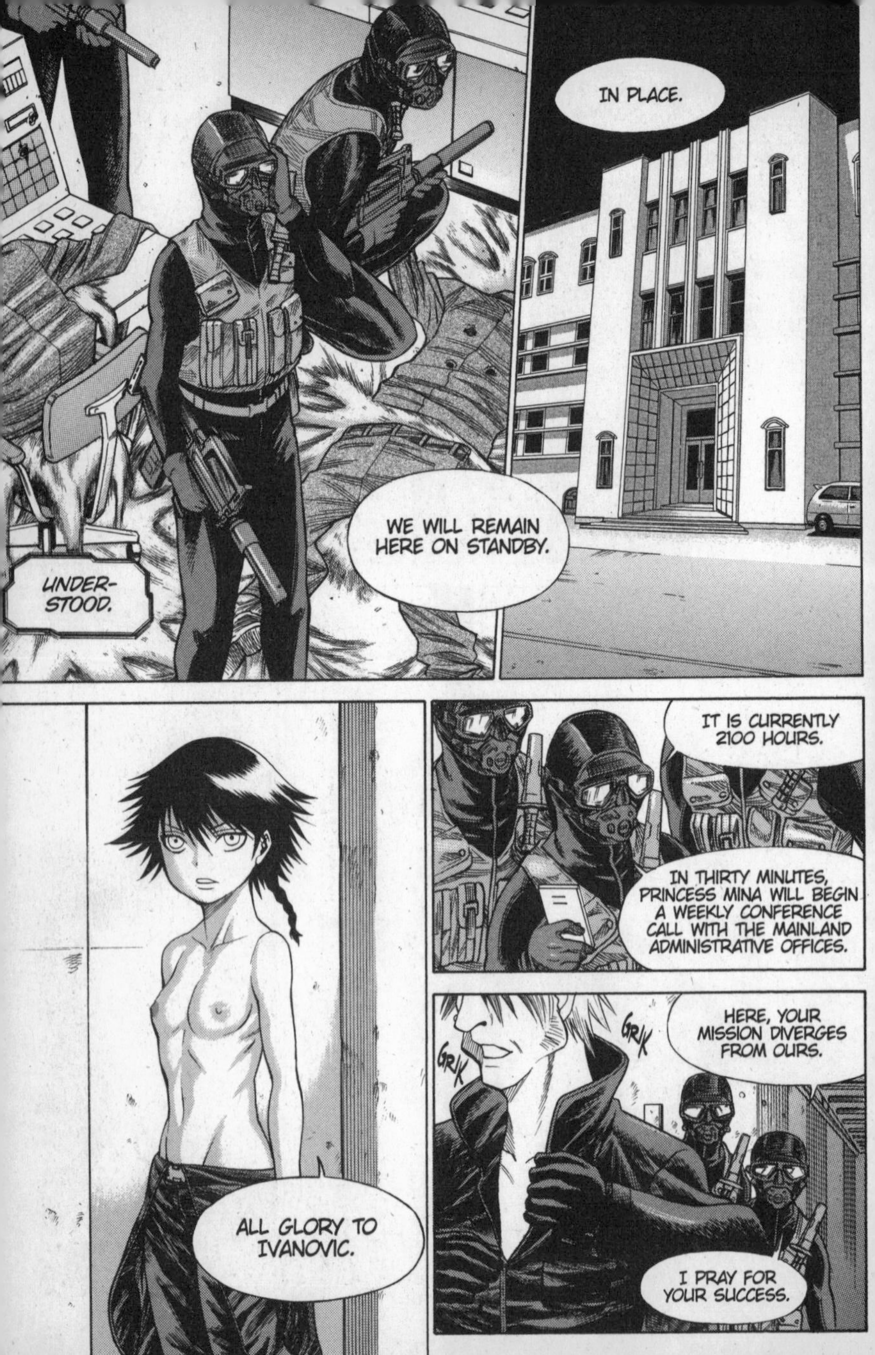
IN PLACE.
WE WILL REMAIN HERE ON STANDBY.
UNDER-STOOD.
IT IS CURRENTLY 2100 HOURS.
IN THIRTY MINUTES, PRINCESS MINA WILL BEGIN A WEEKLY CONFERENCE CALL WITH THE MAINLAND ADMINISTRATIVE OFFICES.
HERE, YOUR MISSION DIVERGES FROM OURS.
GRIK GRIK
I PRAY FOR YOUR SUCCESS.
ALL GLORY TO IVANOVIC.

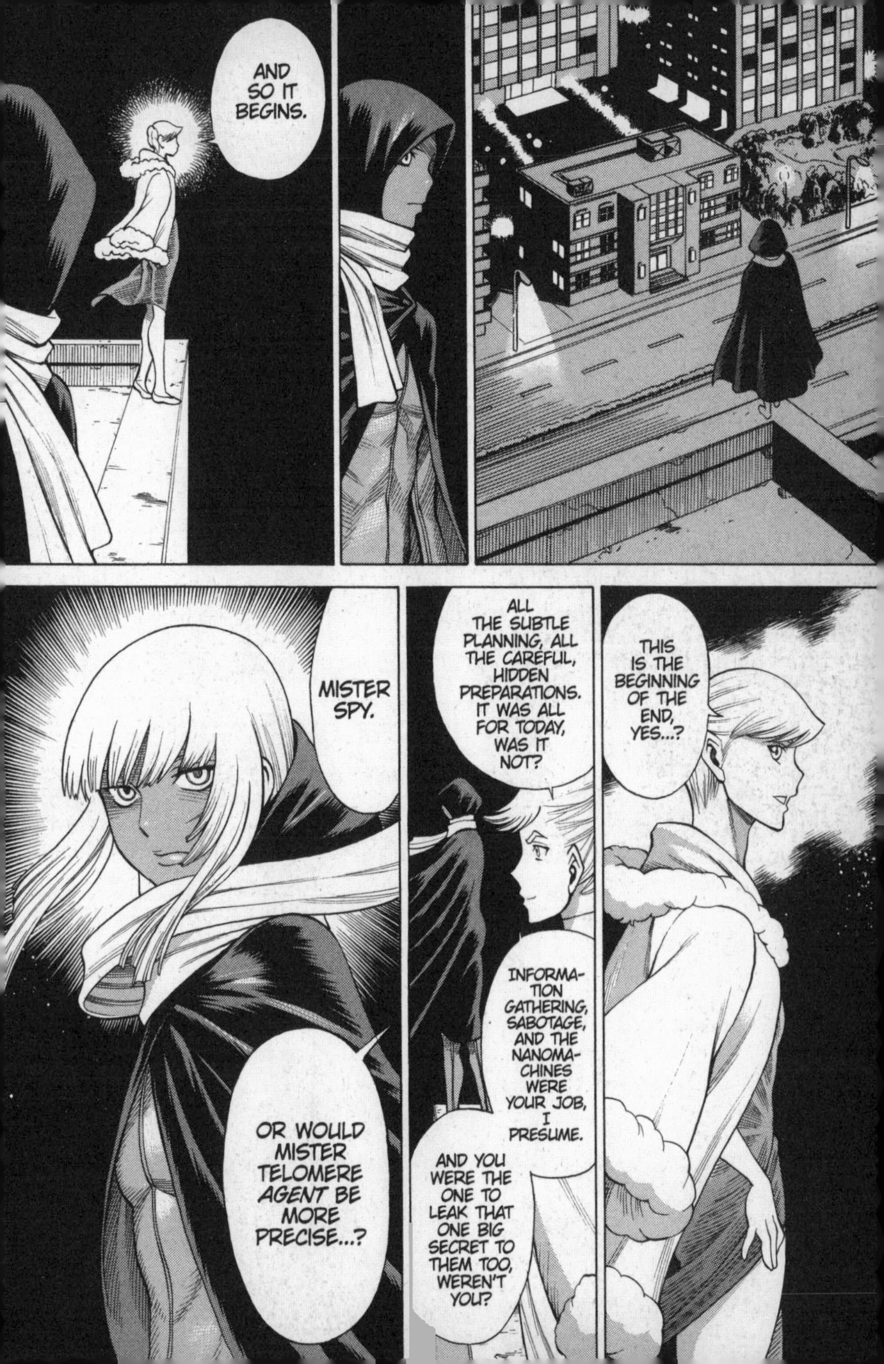
AND SO IT BEGINS.
THIS IS THE BEGINNING OF THE END, YES...?
ALL THE SUBTLE PLANNING, ALL THE CAREFUL, HIDDEN PREPARATIONS. IT WAS ALL FOR TODAY, WAS IT NOT?
INFORMATION-GATHERING, SABOTAGE, AND THE NANOMACHINES WERE YOUR JOB, I PRESUME.
AND YOU WERE THE ONE TO LEAK THAT ONE BIG SECRET TO THEM TOO, WEREN'T YOU?
MISTER SPY.
OR WOULD MISTER TELOMERE AGENT BE MORE PRECISE...?

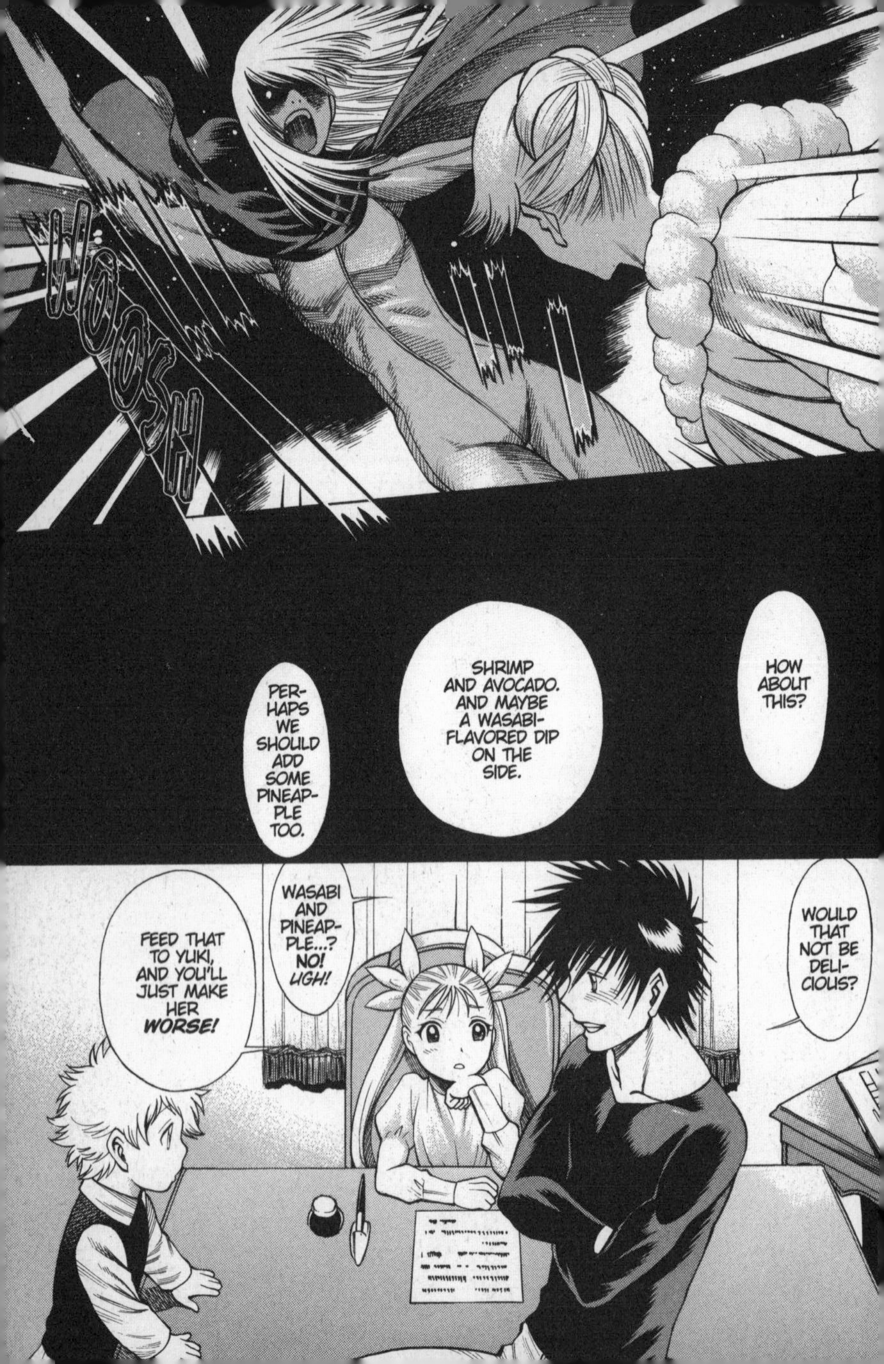
WOOSH
HOW ABOUT THIS?
SHRIMP AND AVOCADO. AND MAYBE A WASABI-FLAVORED DIP ON THE SIDE.
PER-HAPS WE SHOULD ADD SOME PINEAP-PLE TOO.
WOULD THAT NOT BE DELI-CIOUS?
WASABI AND PINEAP-PLE...? NO! UGH!
FEED THAT TO YUKI, AND YOU'LL JUST MAKE HER WORSE!

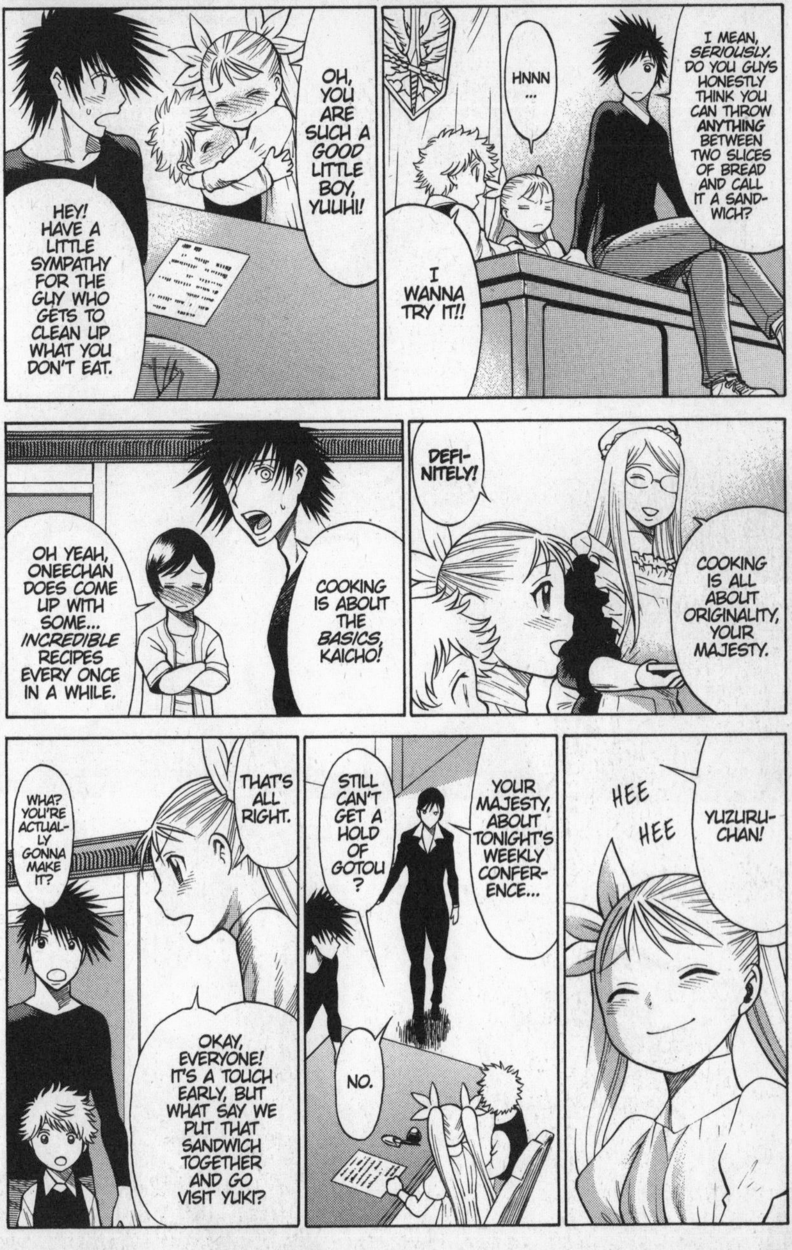
I MEAN, *SERIOUSLY.* DO YOU GUYS HONESTLY THINK YOU CAN THROW ANYTHING BETWEEN TWO SLICES OF BREAD AND CALL IT A SANDWICH?
HNNN...
I WANNA TRY IT!!
OH, YOU ARE SUCH A *GOOD* LITTLE BOY, YUUHI!
HEY! HAVE A LITTLE SYMPATHY FOR THE GUY WHO GETS TO CLEAN UP WHAT YOU DON'T EAT.
COOKING IS ALL ABOUT ORIGINALITY, YOUR MAJESTY.
DEFI-NITELY!
COOKING IS ABOUT THE *BASICS,* KAICHO!
OH YEAH, ONEECHAN DOES COME UP WITH SOME... *INCREDIBLE* RECIPES EVERY ONCE IN A WHILE.
YUZURU-CHAN!
HEE HEE
YOUR MAJESTY, ABOUT TONIGHT'S WEEKLY CONFERENCE...
STILL CAN'T GET A HOLD OF GOTOU?
NO.
THAT'S ALL RIGHT.
OKAY, EVERYONE! IT'S A TOUCH EARLY, BUT WHAT SAY WE PUT THAT SANDWICH TOGETHER AND GO VISIT YUKI?
WHA? YOU'RE ACTUALLY GONNA MAKE IT?

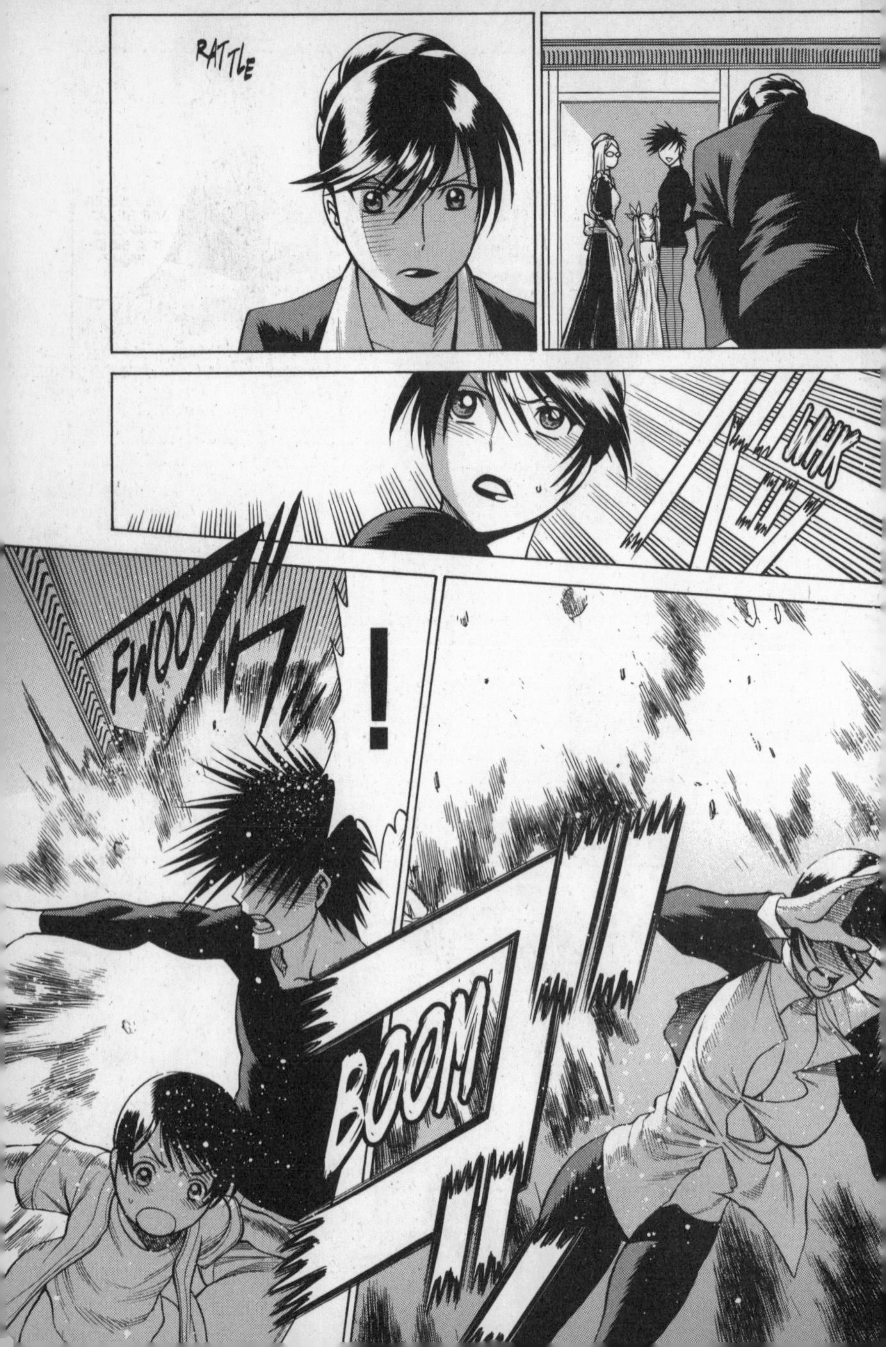
RATTLE
WHK
FWOOM
!
BOOM

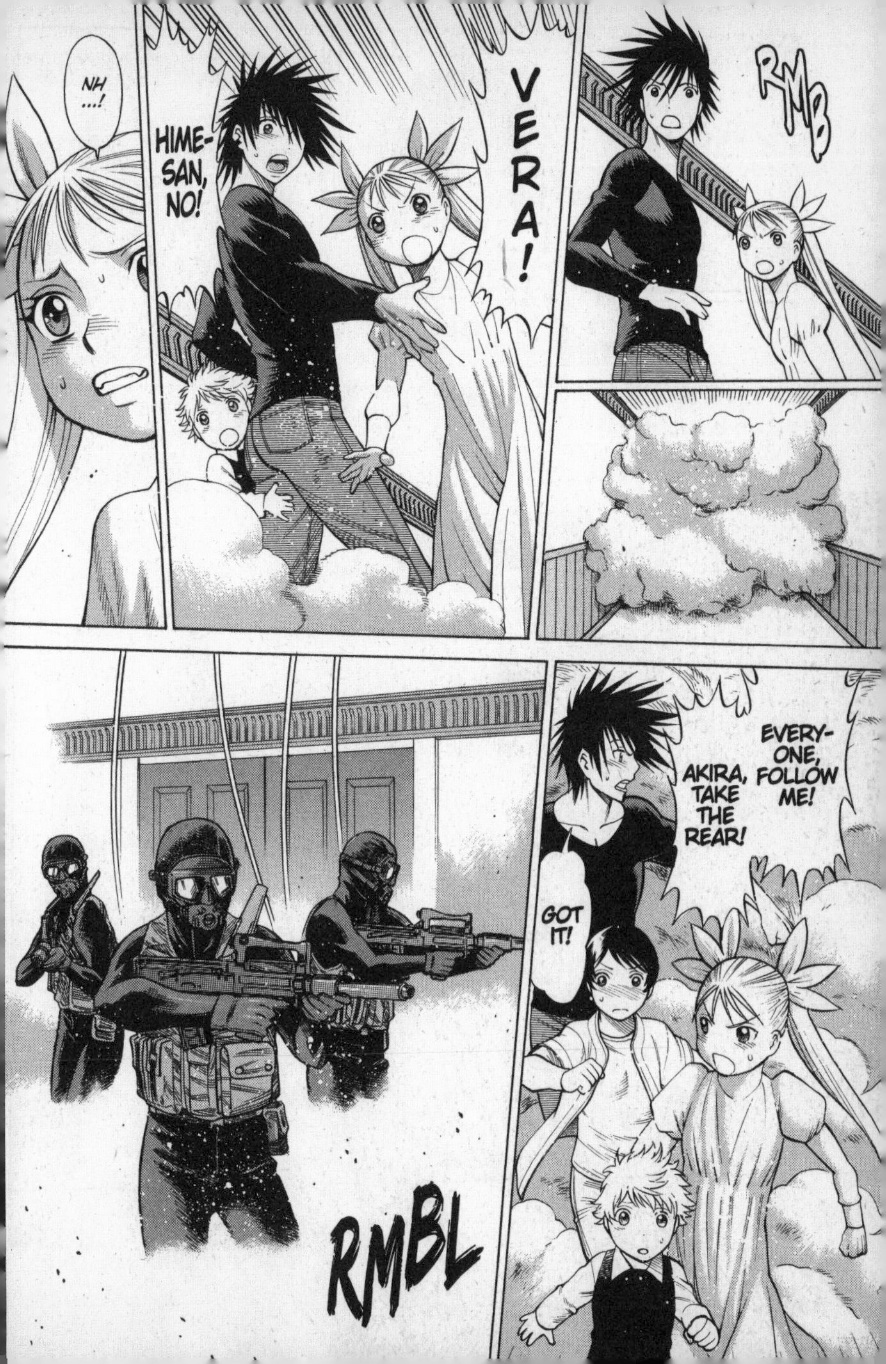
RMB
VERA!
HIME-SAN, NO!
NH ...!
EVERY-ONE, FOLLOW ME!
AKIRA, TAKE THE REAR!
GOT IT!
RMBL

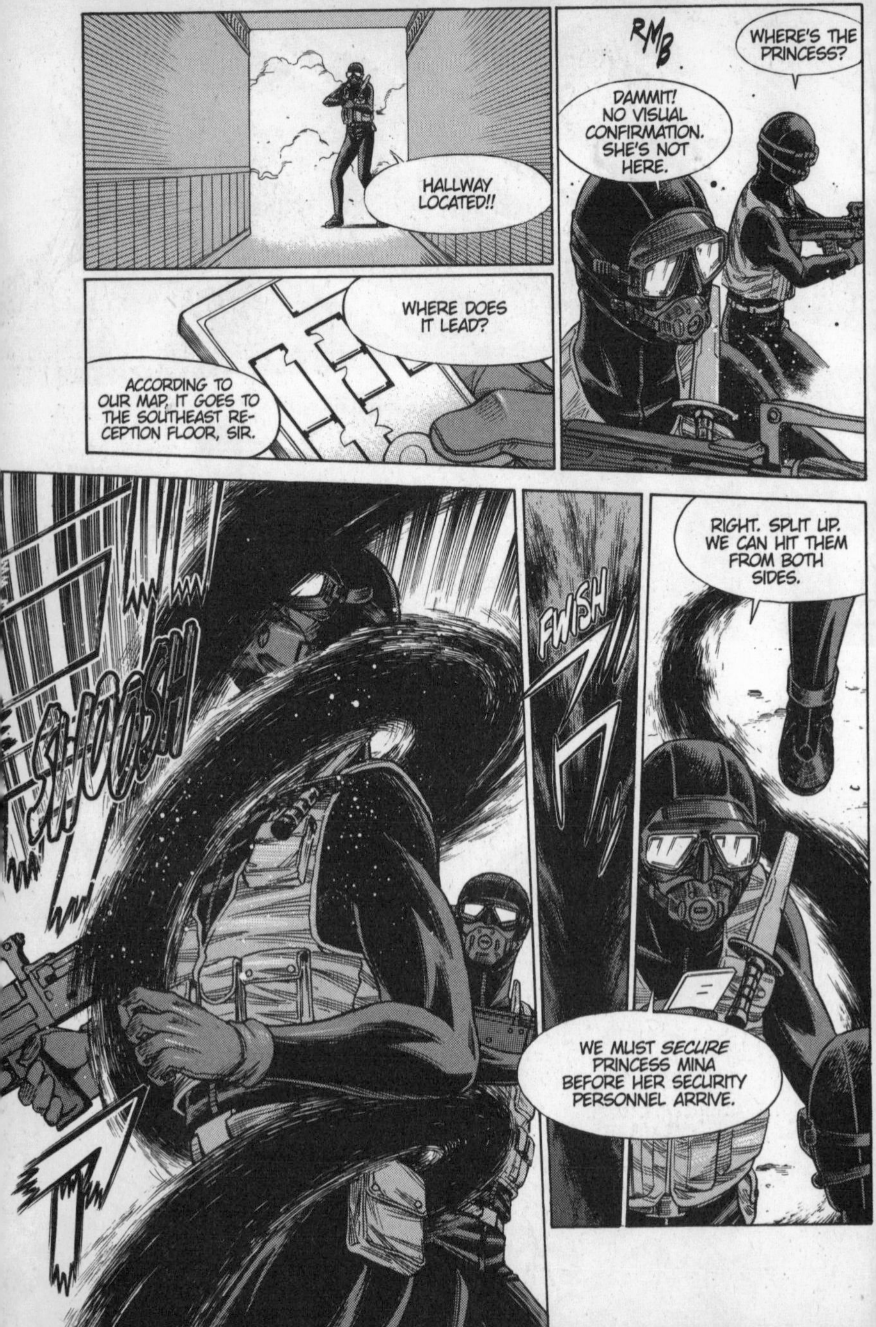
WHERE'S THE PRINCESS?
RMB
DAMMIT! NO VISUAL CONFIRMATION. SHE'S NOT HERE.
HALLWAY LOCATED!!
WHERE DOES IT LEAD?
ACCORDING TO OUR MAP, IT GOES TO THE SOUTHEAST RE-CEPTION FLOOR, SIR.
RIGHT. SPLIT UP. WE CAN HIT THEM FROM BOTH SIDES.
WE MUST *SECURE* PRINCESS MINA BEFORE HER SECURITY PERSONNEL ARRIVE.
FWISH
SWOOSH

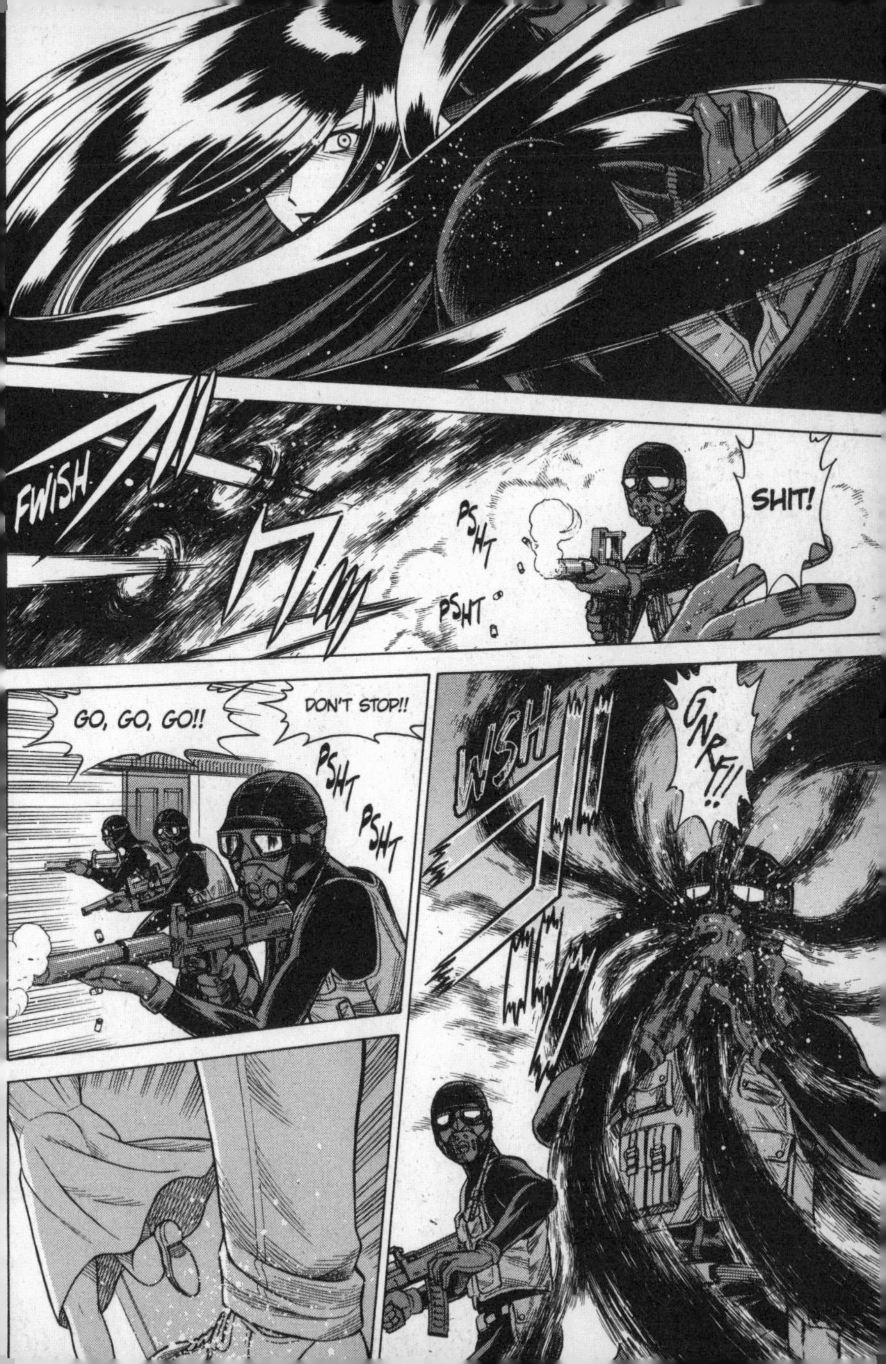
SHIT!
PSHT
PSHT
FWISH
GNRF!!
WSH
DON'T STOP!!
GO, GO, GO!!
PSHT
PSHT

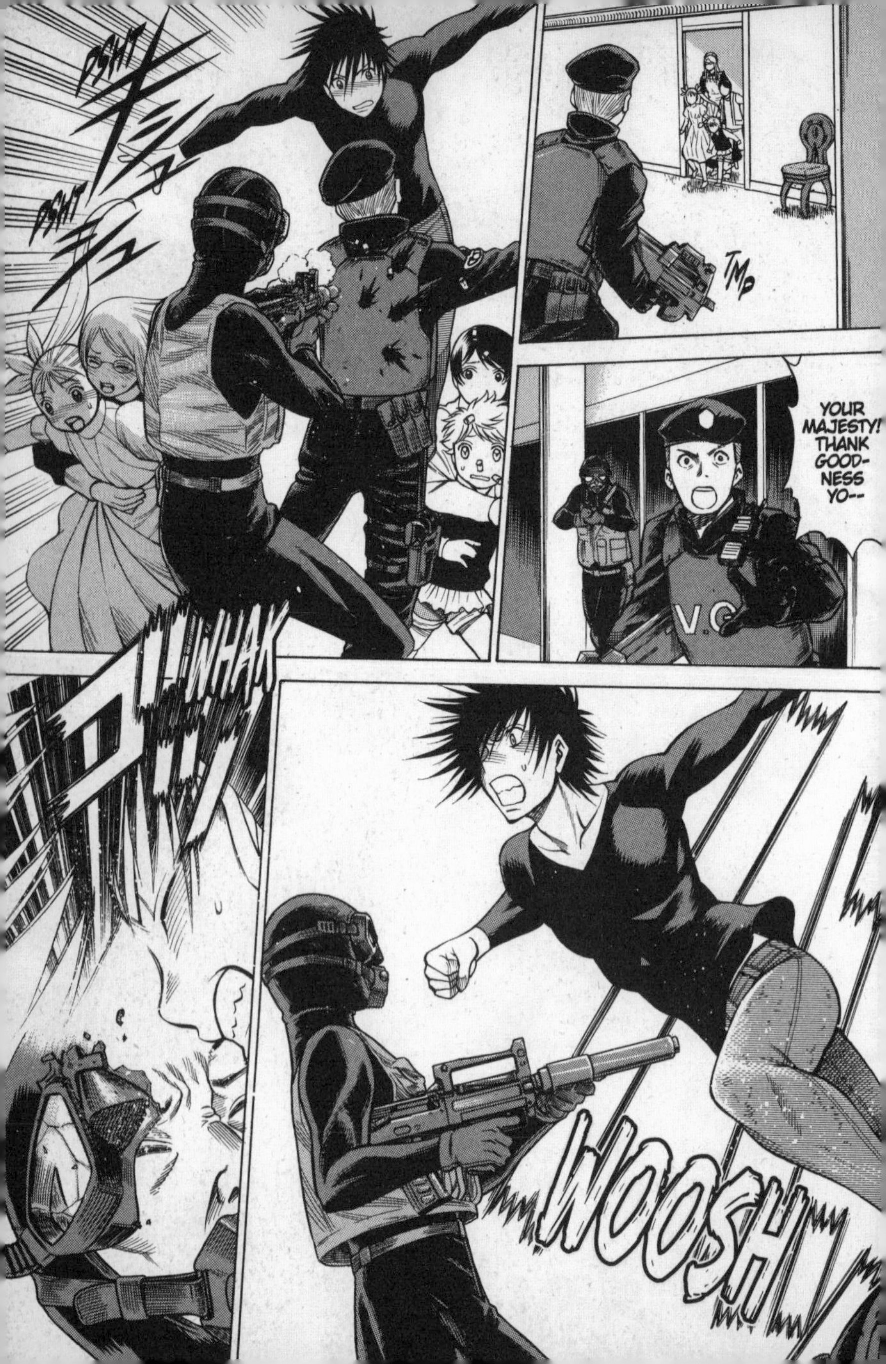
TMP
YOUR MAJESTY! THANK GOODNESS YO--
PSHT
PSHT
WOOSH
WHAK

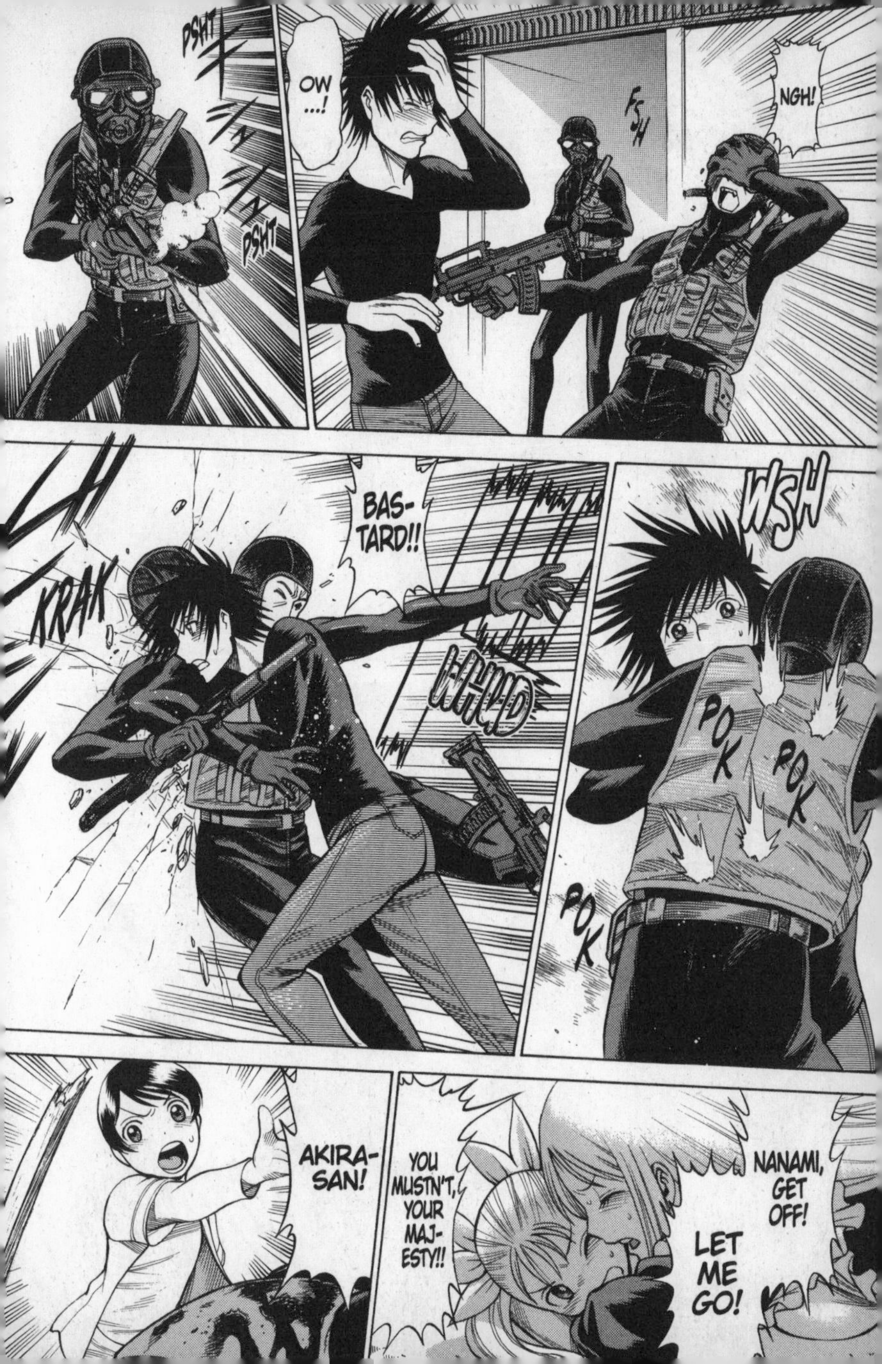
NGH!
FSH
OW ...!
PSHT
PSHT
WSH
POK
POK
POK
BAS-TARD!!
WHUD
KRAK
NANAMI, GET OFF!
LET ME GO!
YOU MUSTN'T, YOUR MAJ-ESTY!!
AKIRA-SAN!

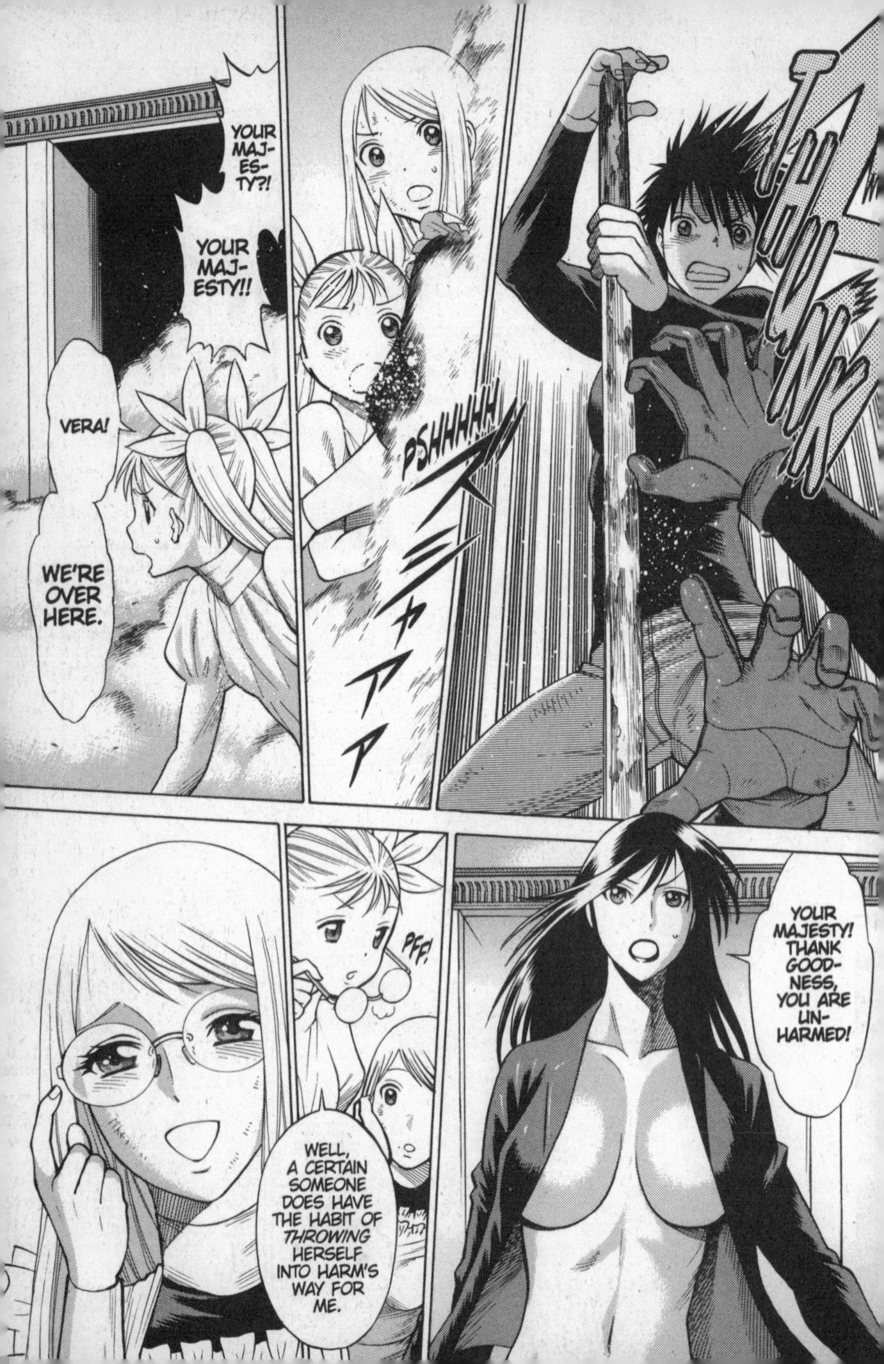
THUNK
PSHHHHH
YOUR MAJ-ES-TY?!
YOUR MAJ-ESTY!!
VERA!
WE'RE OVER HERE.
YOUR MAJESTY! THANK GOOD-NESS, YOU ARE UN-HARMED!
PFF!
WELL, A CERTAIN SOMEONE DOES HAVE THE HABIT OF THROWING HERSELF INTO HARM'S WAY FOR ME.

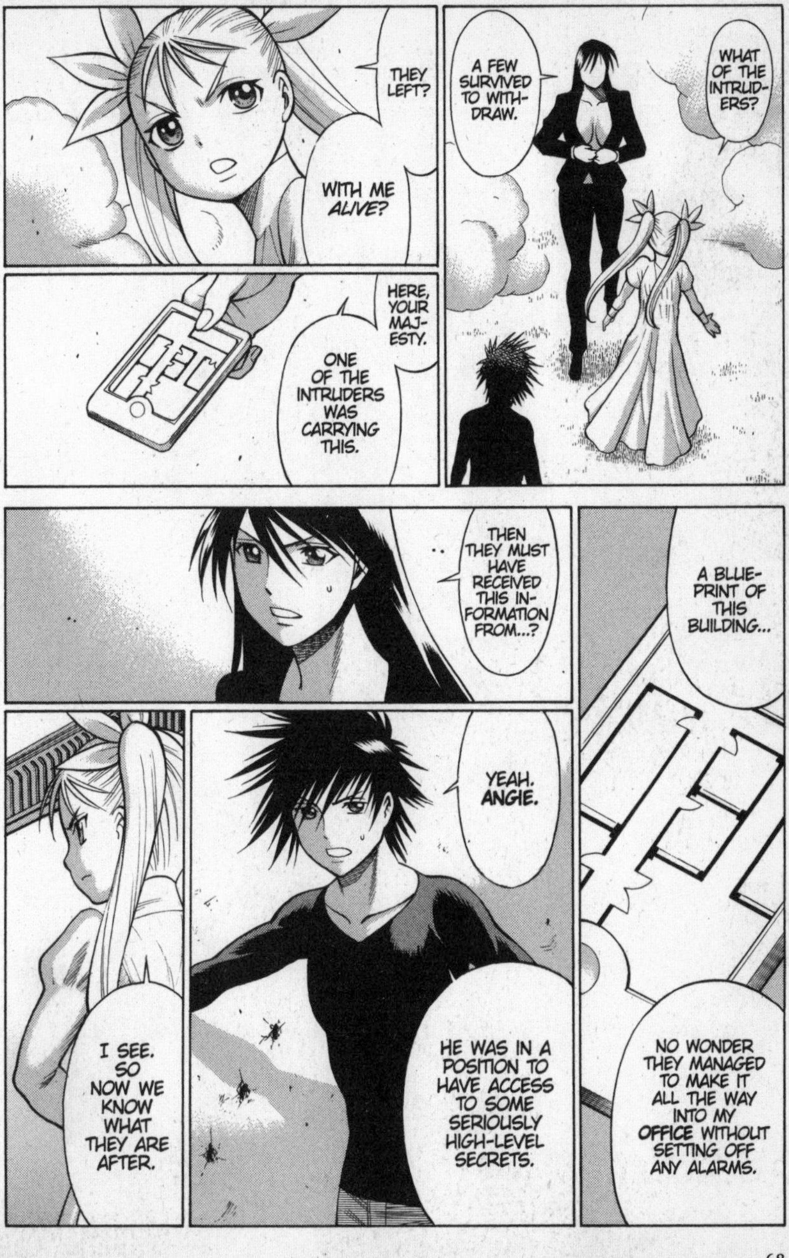
WHAT OF THE INTRUDERS?
A FEW SURVIVED TO WITHDRAW.
THEY LEFT?
WITH ME *ALIVE?*
HERE, YOUR MAJESTY.
ONE OF THE INTRUDERS WAS CARRYING THIS.
A BLUEPRINT OF THIS BUILDING...
NO WONDER THEY MANAGED TO MAKE IT ALL THE WAY INTO MY OFFICE WITHOUT SETTING OFF ANY ALARMS.
THEN THEY MUST HAVE RECEIVED THIS INFORMATION FROM...?
YEAH. ANGIE.
HE WAS IN A POSITION TO HAVE ACCESS TO SOME SERIOUSLY HIGH-LEVEL SECRETS.
I SEE. SO NOW WE KNOW WHAT THEY ARE AFTER.

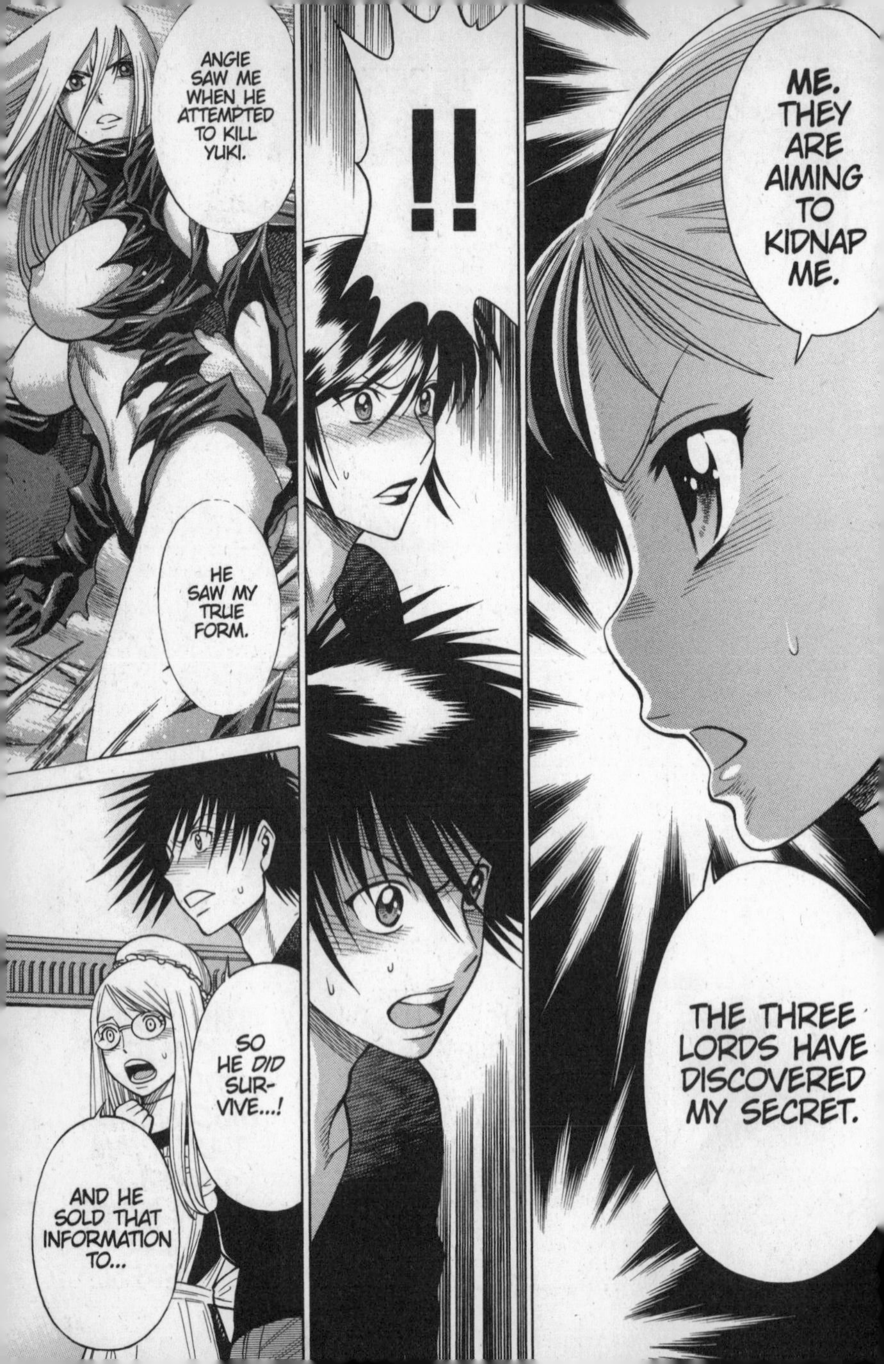

ME. THEY ARE AIMING TO KIDNAP ME.
THE THREE LORDS HAVE DISCOVERED MY SECRET.
!!
ANGIE SAW ME WHEN HE ATTEMPTED TO KILL YUKI.
HE SAW MY TRUE FORM.
SO HE *DID* SUR-VIVE...!
AND HE SOLD THAT INFORMATION TO...

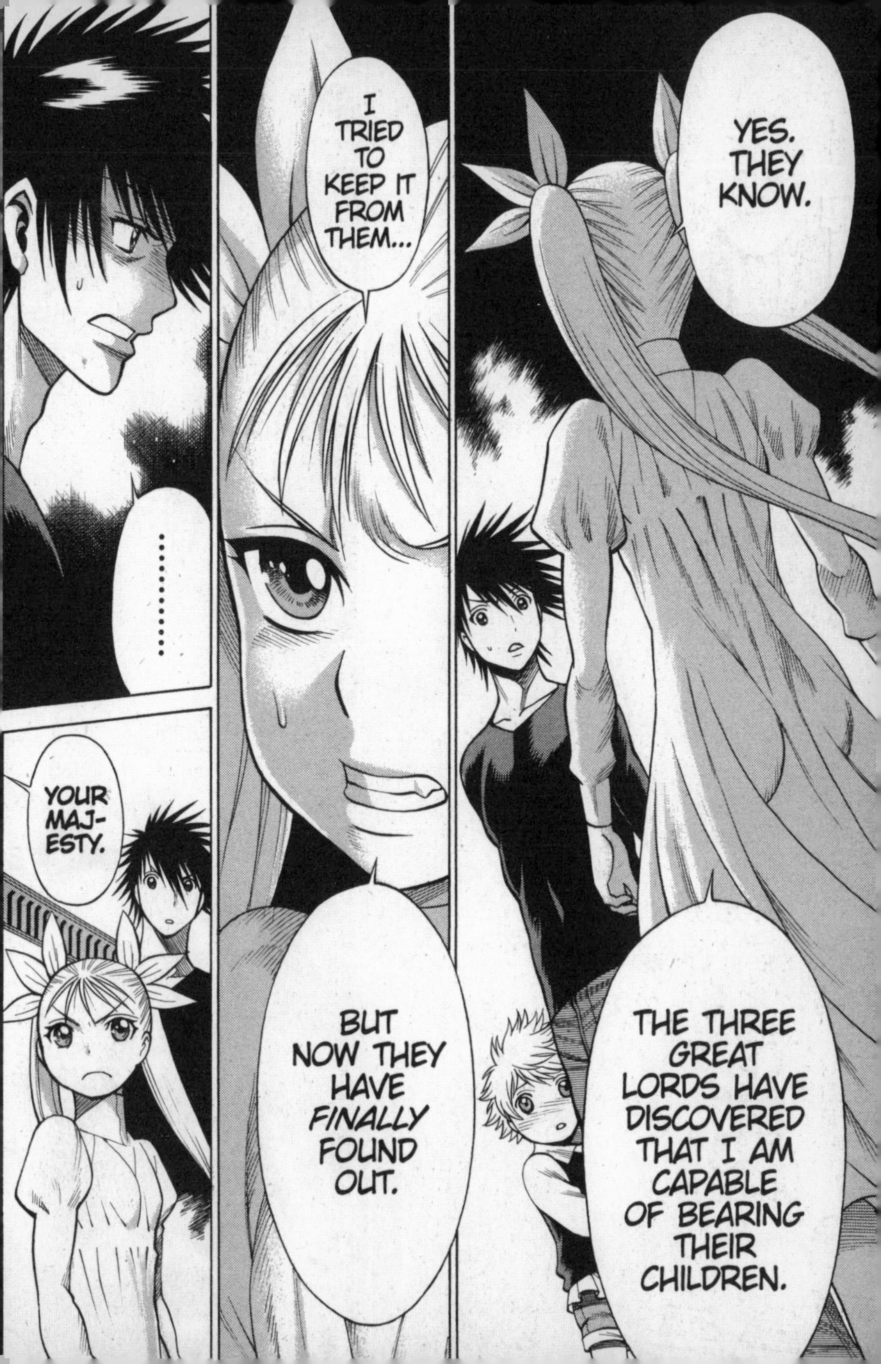

YES. THEY KNOW.
THE THREE GREAT LORDS HAVE DISCOVERED THAT I AM CAPABLE OF BEARING THEIR CHILDREN.
I TRIED TO KEEP IT FROM THEM...
BUT NOW THEY HAVE *FINALLY* FOUND OUT.
....
YOUR MAJ-ESTY.

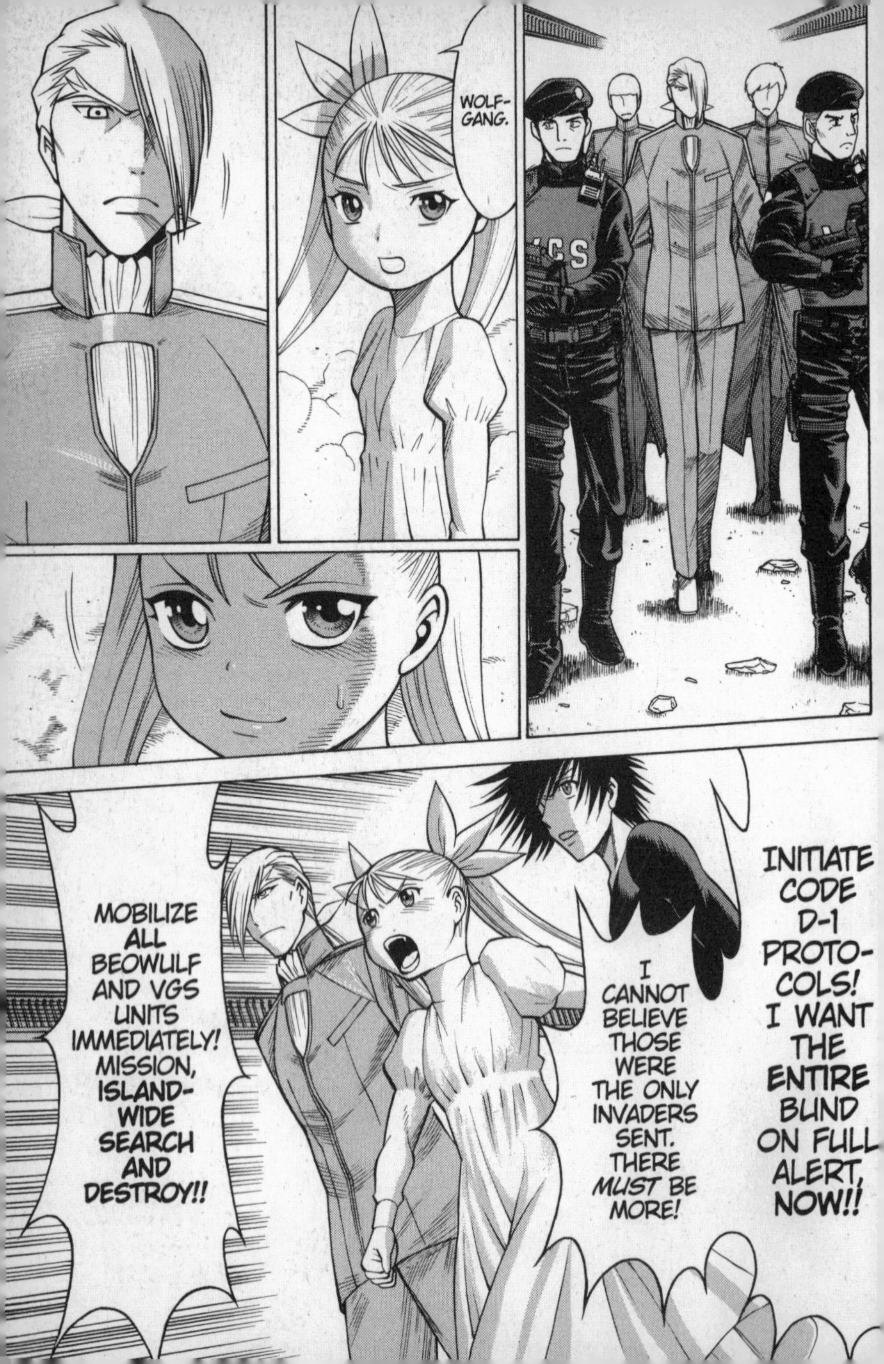
WOLF-GANG.
INITIATE CODE D-1 PROTOCOLS! I WANT THE ENTIRE BLIND ON FULL ALERT, NOW!!
I CANNOT BELIEVE THOSE WERE THE ONLY INVADERS SENT. THERE *MUST* BE MORE!
MOBILIZE ALL BEOWULF AND VGS UNITS IMMEDIATELY! MISSION, ISLAND-WIDE SEARCH AND DESTROY!!

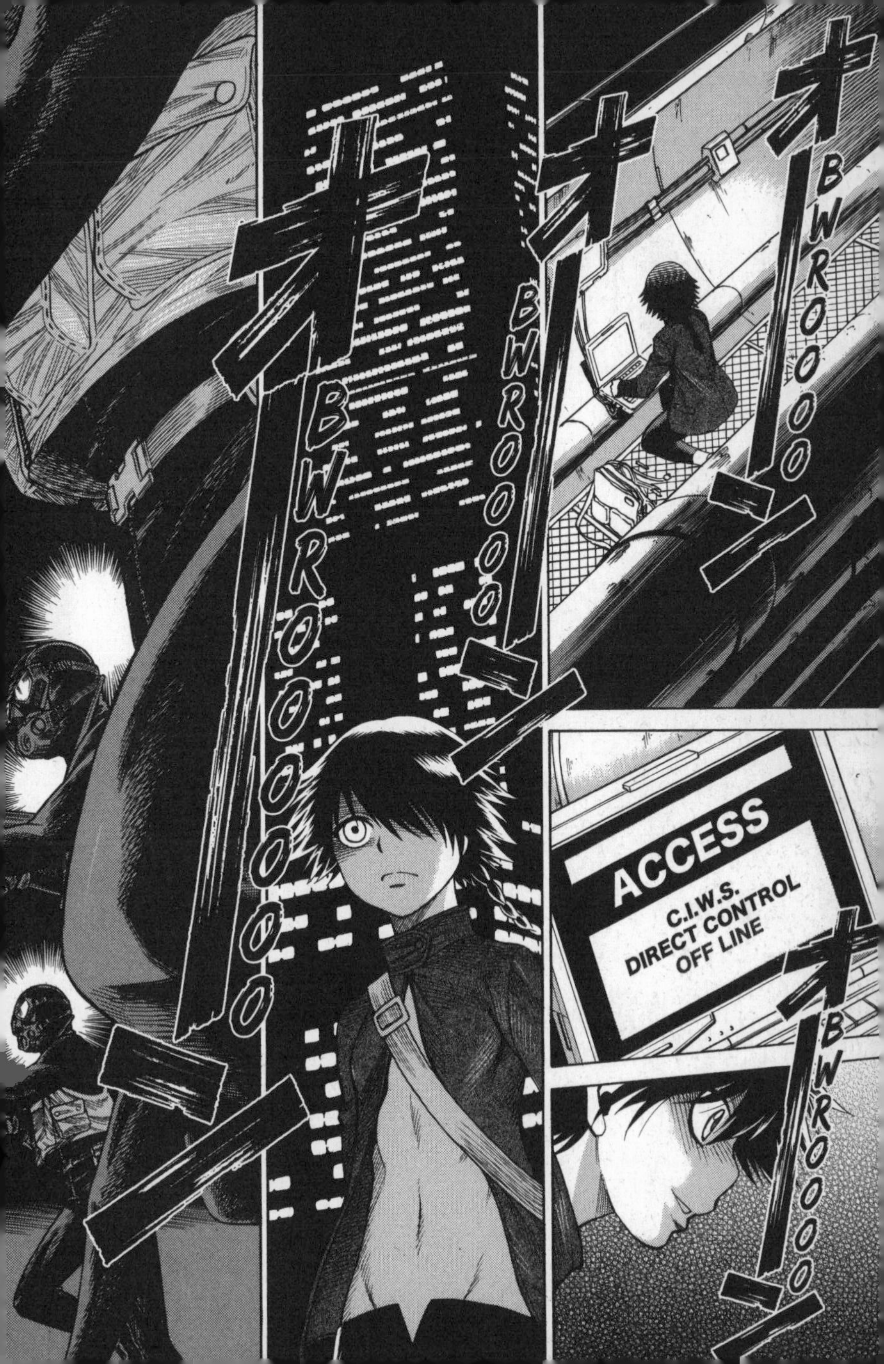
オー
BWROOOOO
オー
BWROOOOO
ACCESS
C.I.W.S.
DIRECT CONTROL
OFF LINE
オ
BWROOOOO
オー
BWROOOOOOOO

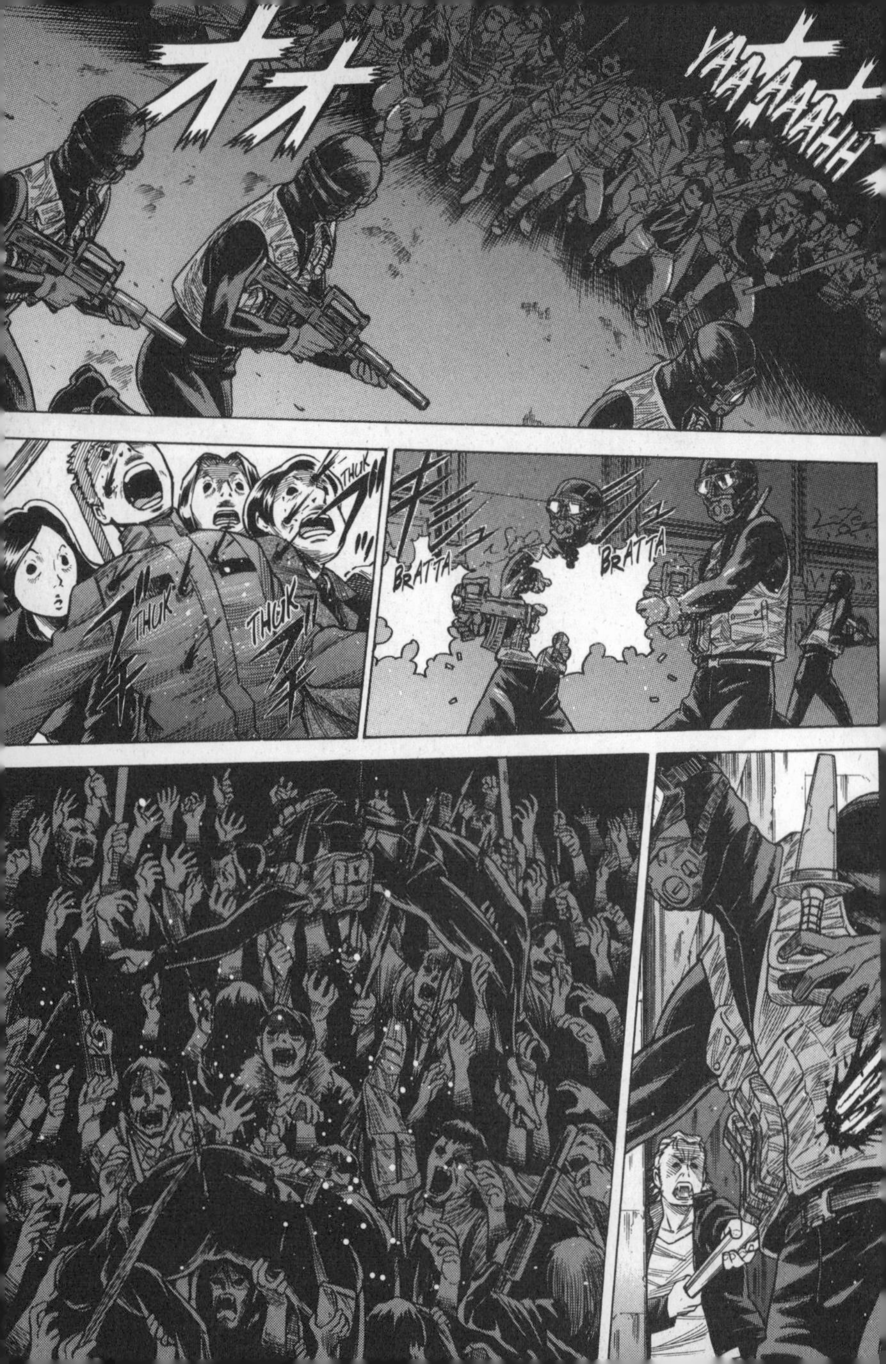
YAAAAAHH
オオ
BRATTA
BRATTA
THUK
THUK
THUK

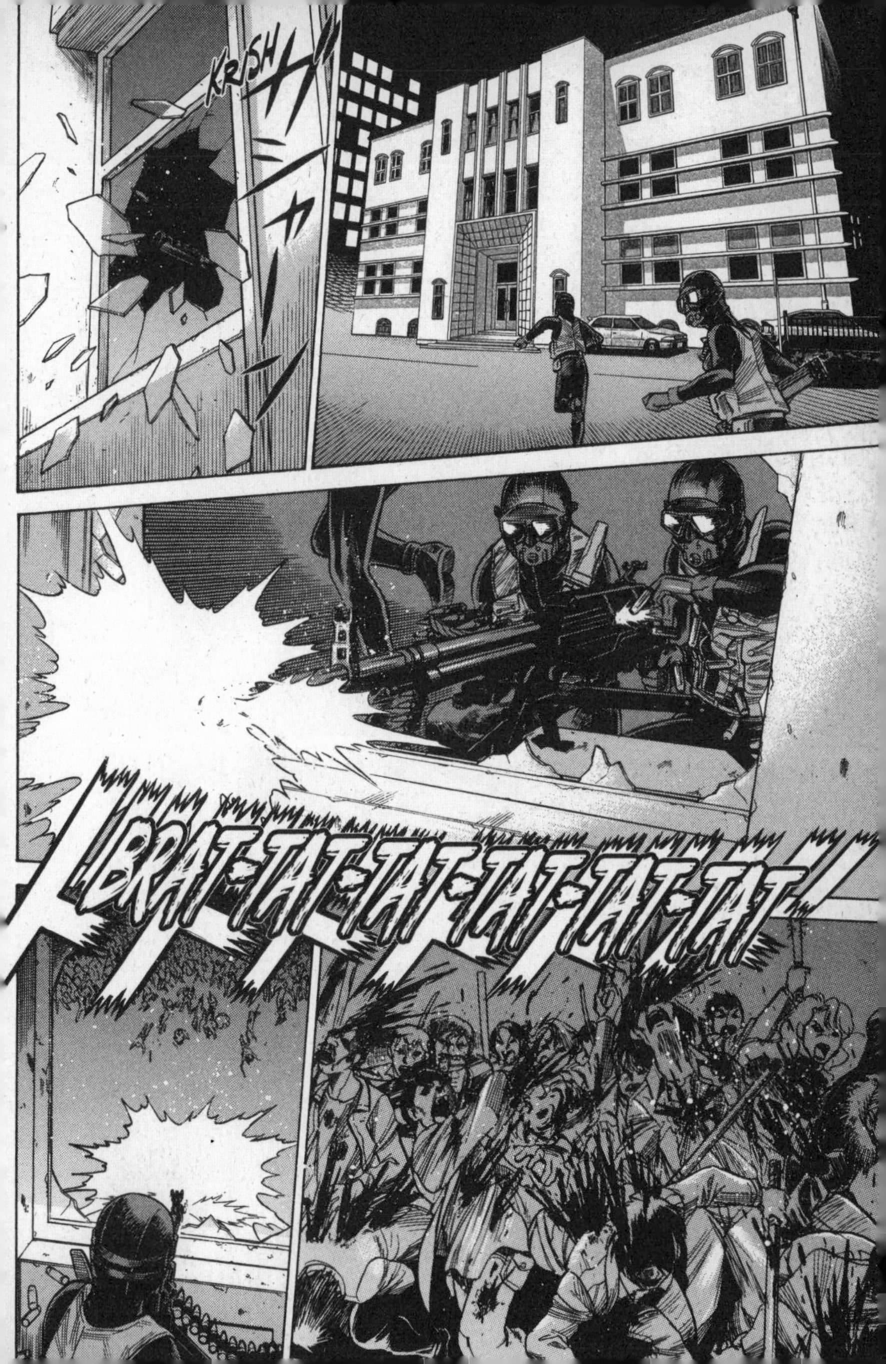
KRISH
BRAT-TAT-TAT-TAT-TAT-TAT!

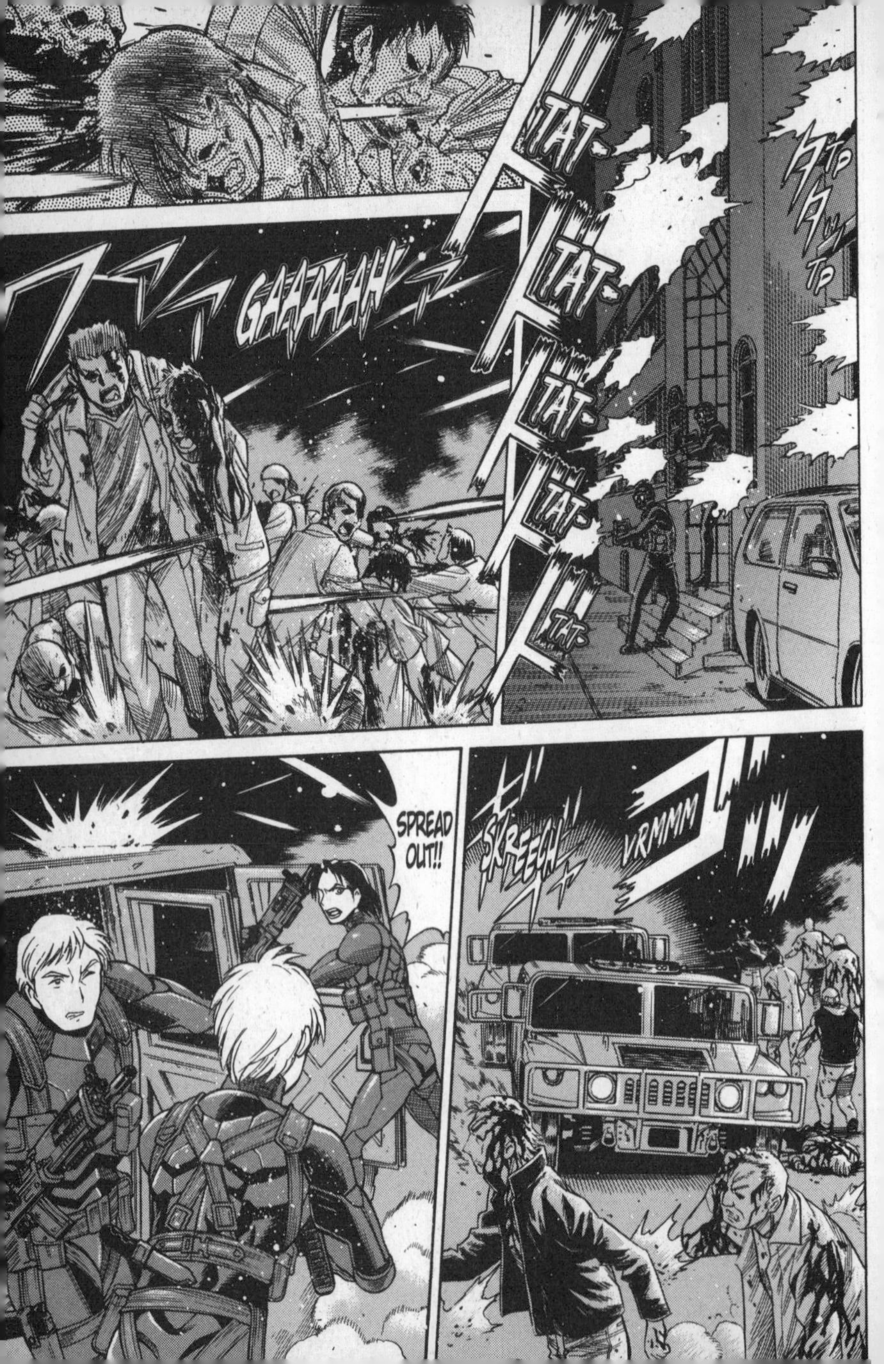
TP
TP
TAT-TAT-TAT-TAT-TAT-
GAAAAAH
SKREECH
VRMMM
SPREAD OUT!!

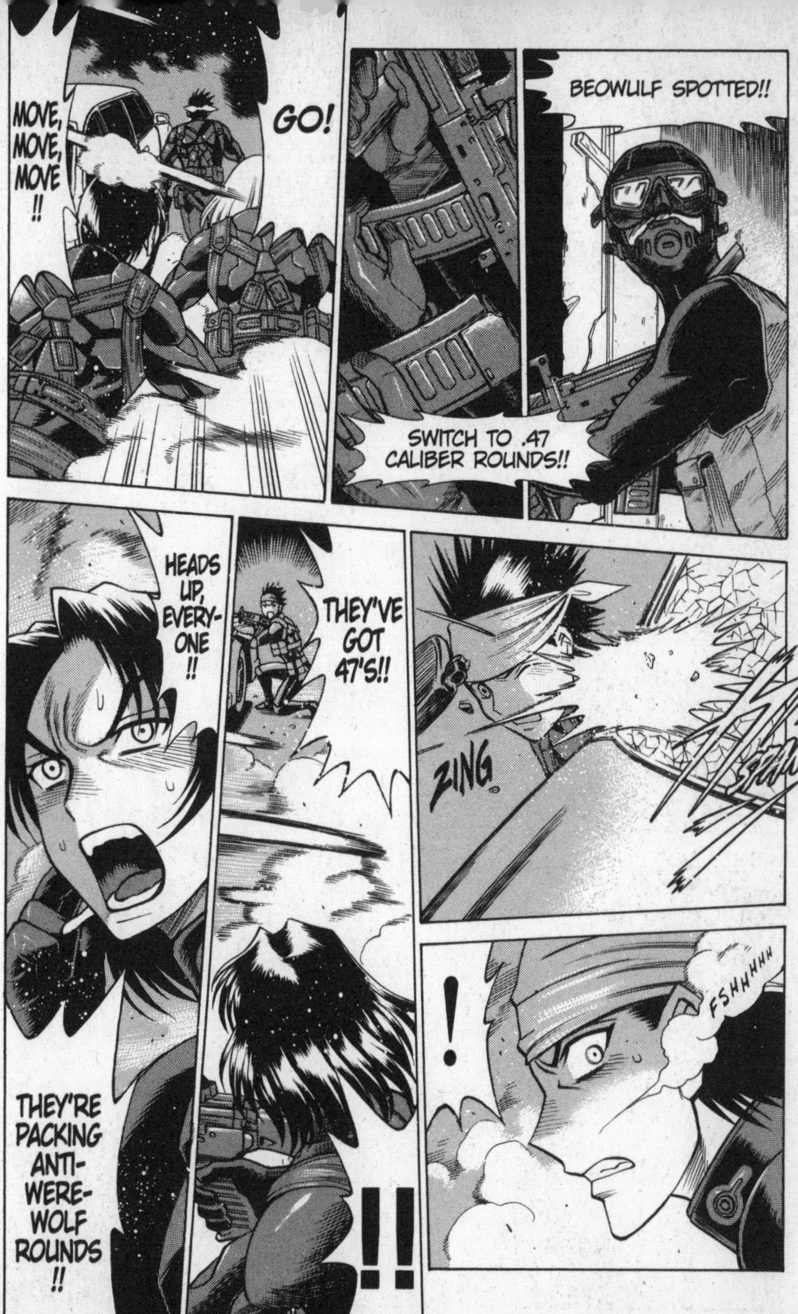
BEOWULF SPOTTED!!
SWITCH TO .47 CALIBER ROUNDS!!
GO!
MOVE, MOVE, MOVE!!
ZING
FSHHHHH
!
THEY'VE GOT 47'S!!
!!
HEADS UP, EVERY-ONE!!
THEY'RE PACKING ANTI-WERE-WOLF ROUNDS!!

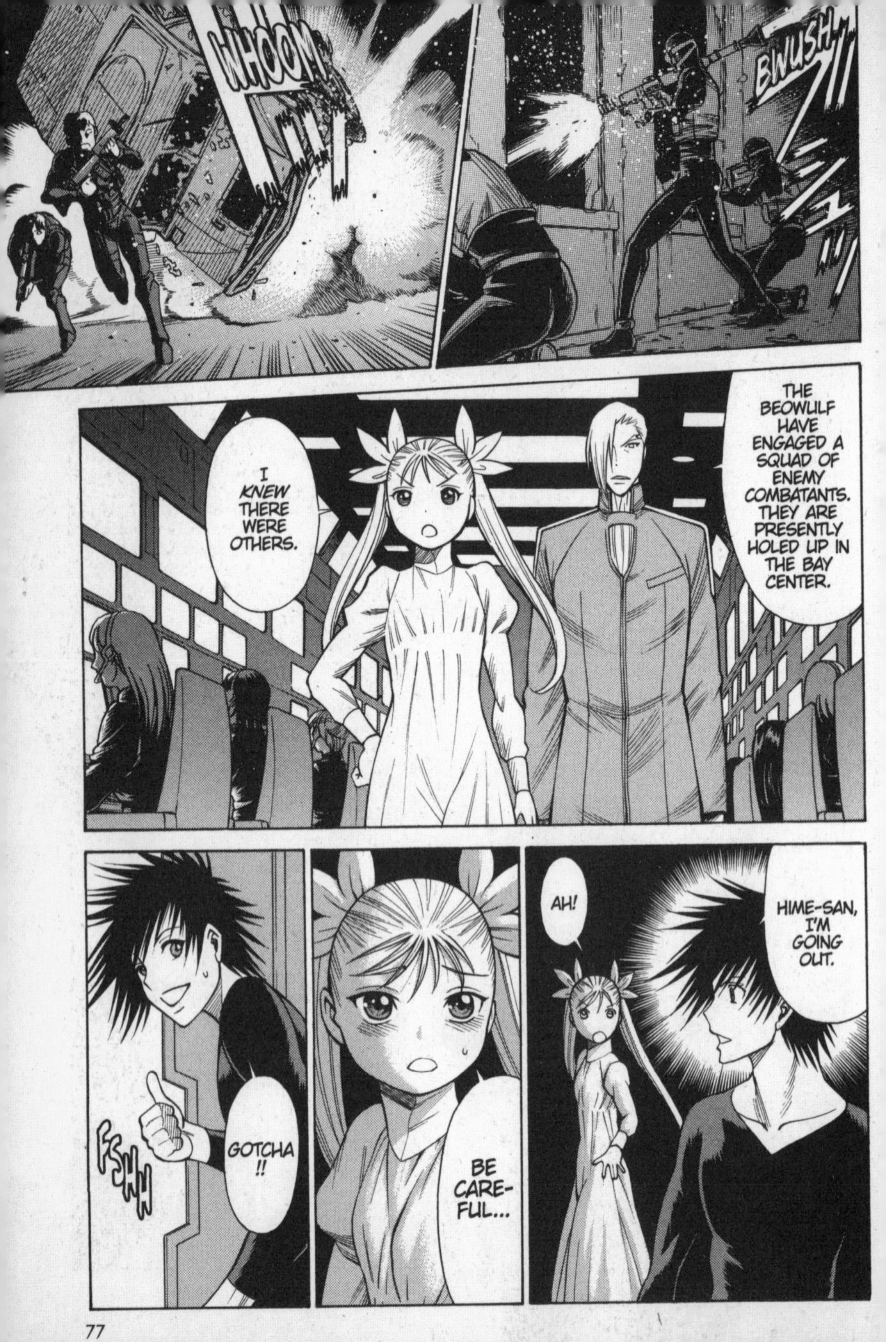
BWUSH
WHOOM
THE BEOWULF HAVE ENGAGED A SQUAD OF ENEMY COMBATANTS. THEY ARE PRESENTLY HOLED UP IN THE BAY CENTER.
I KNEW THERE WERE OTHERS.
HIME-SAN, I'M GOING OUT.
AH!
BE CAREFUL...
GOTCHA!!
FSHH

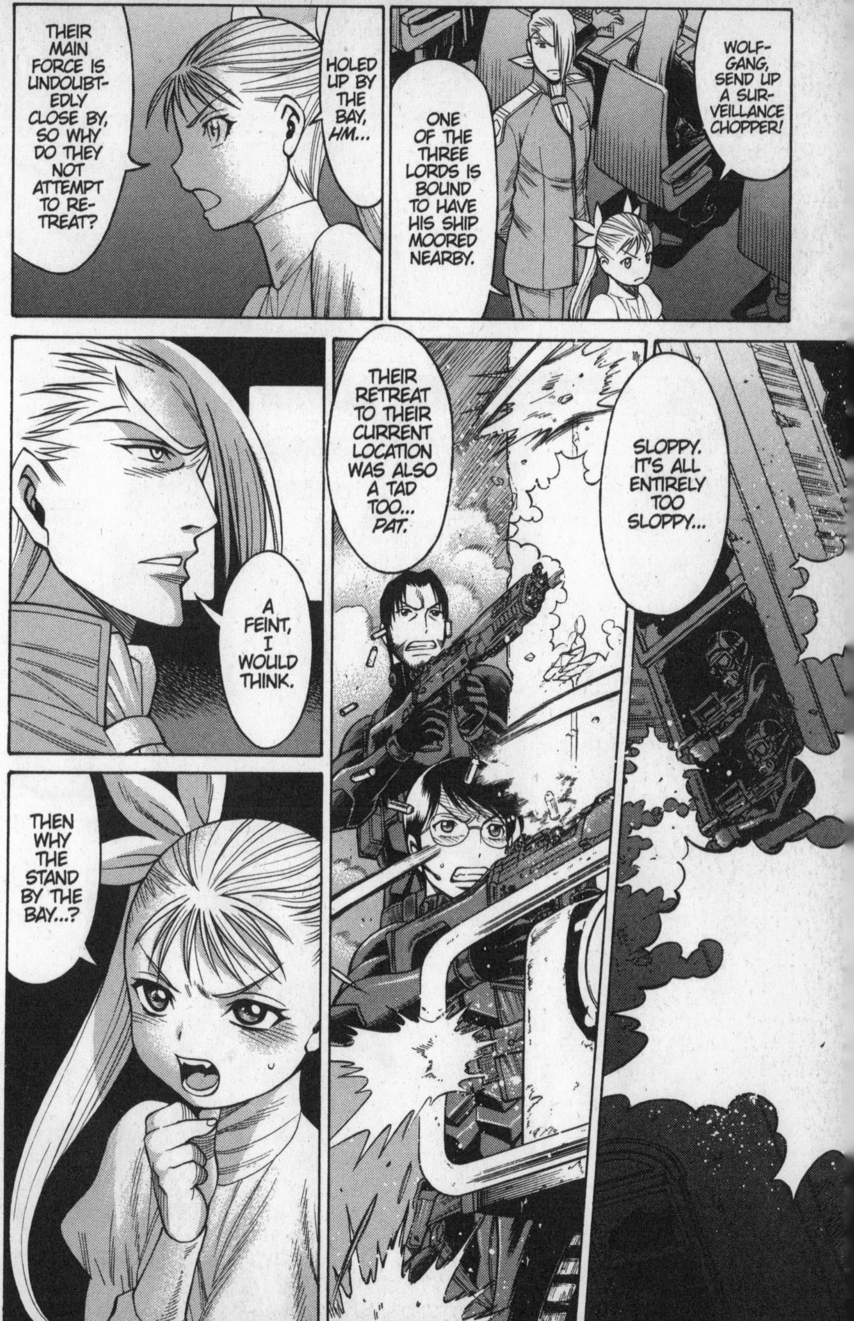
WOLF-GANG, SEND UP A SUR-VEILLANCE CHOPPER!
ONE OF THE THREE LORDS IS BOUND TO HAVE HIS SHIP MOORED NEARBY.
HOLED UP BY THE BAY, *HM*...
THEIR MAIN FORCE IS UNDOUBT-EDLY CLOSE BY, SO WHY DO THEY NOT ATTEMPT TO RE-TREAT?
SLOPPY. IT'S ALL ENTIRELY TOO SLOPPY...
THEIR RETREAT TO THEIR CURRENT LOCATION WAS ALSO A TAD TOO... *PAT*.
A FEINT, I WOULD THINK.
THEN WHY THE STAND BY THE BAY...?

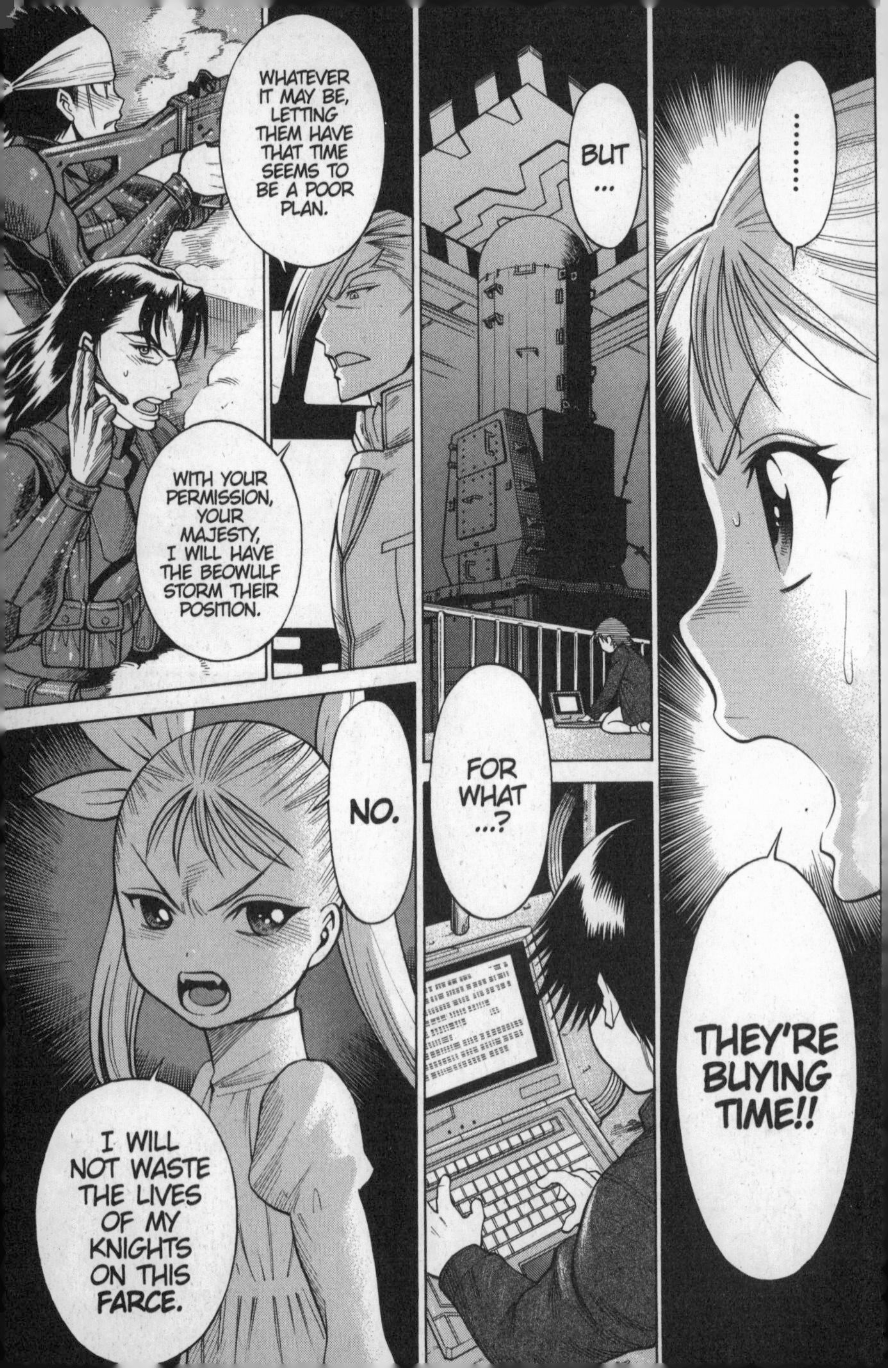
......
THEY'RE BUYING TIME!!
BUT ...
FOR WHAT ...?
WHATEVER IT MAY BE, LETTING THEM HAVE THAT TIME SEEMS TO BE A POOR PLAN.
WITH YOUR PERMISSION, YOUR MAJESTY, I WILL HAVE THE BEOWULF STORM THEIR POSITION.
NO.
I WILL NOT WASTE THE LIVES OF MY KNIGHTS ON THIS FARCE.

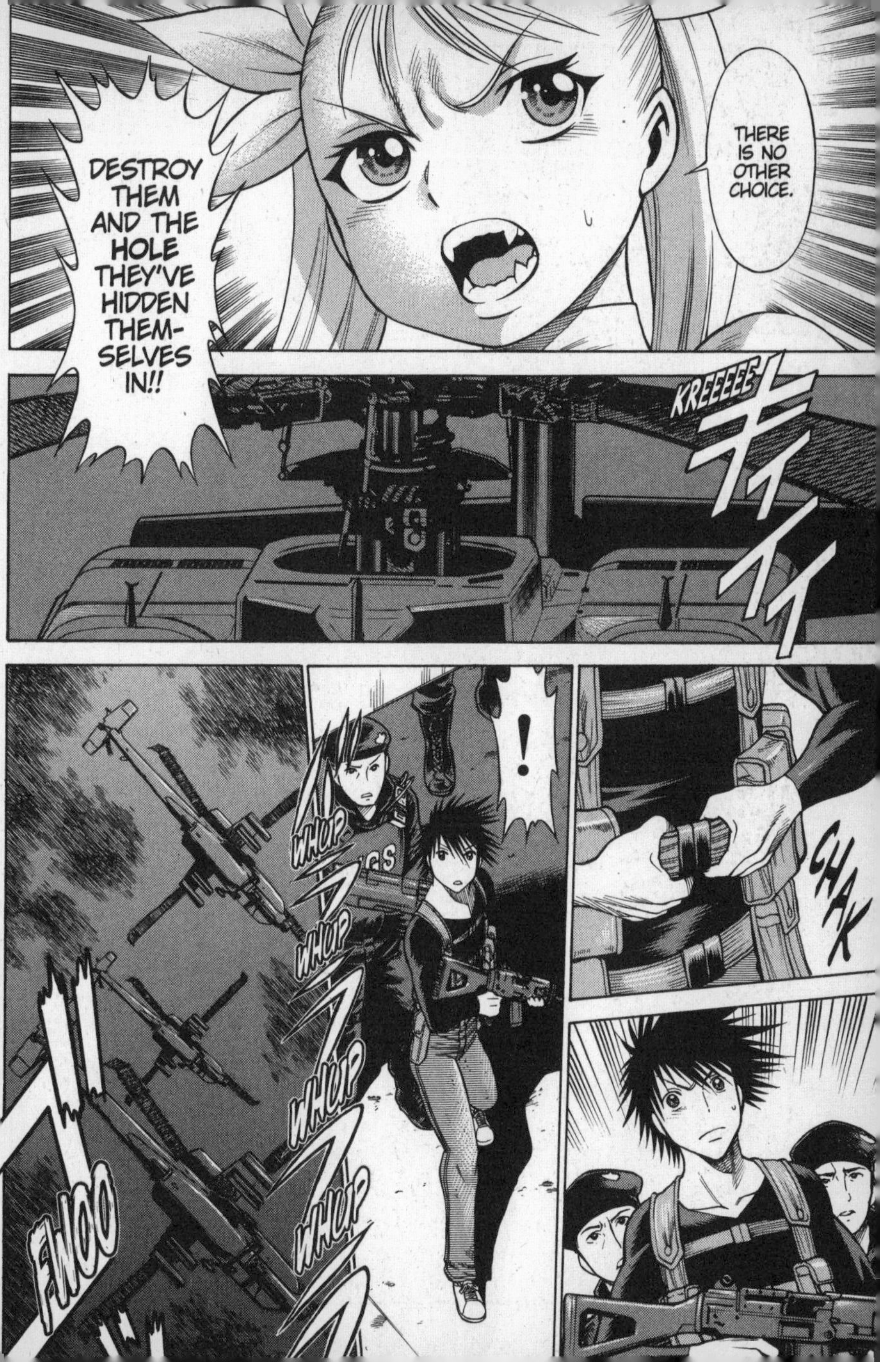

THERE IS NO OTHER CHOICE.
DESTROY THEM AND THE HOLE THEY'VE HIDDEN THEM-SELVES IN!!
KREEEEE
キィィィ
CHAK
!
WHUP
WHUP
WHUP
WHUP
WHUP
FWOO

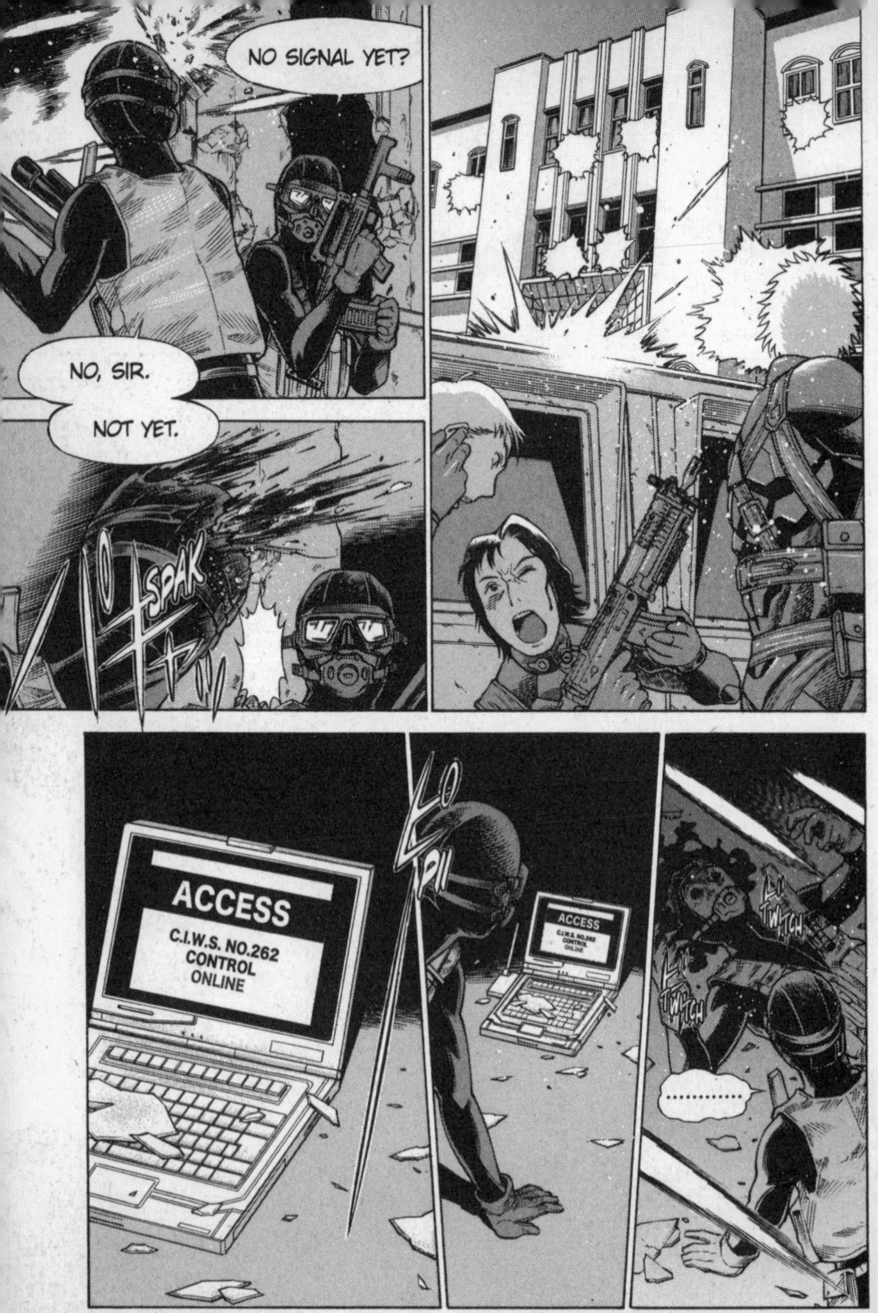
NO SIGNAL YET?
NO, SIR.
NOT YET.
SPAK
TWITCH
TWITCH
....
ACCESS
C.I.W.S. NO.262
CONTROL
ONLINE
ACCESS
C.I.W.S. NO.262
CONTROL
ONLINE

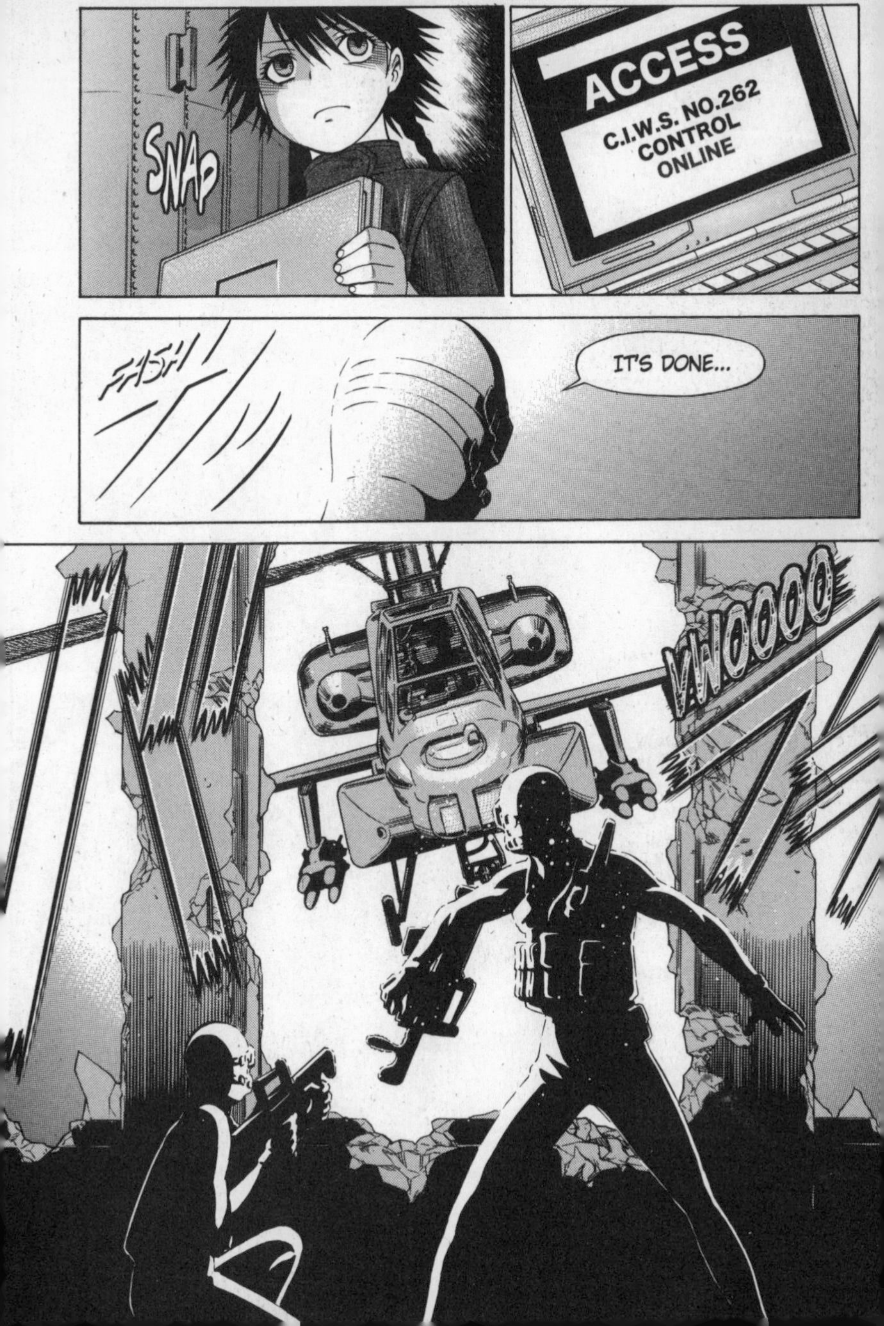
ACCESS
C.I.W.S. NO.262 CONTROL ONLINE
SNAP
IT'S DONE...
FASH
VWOOOO

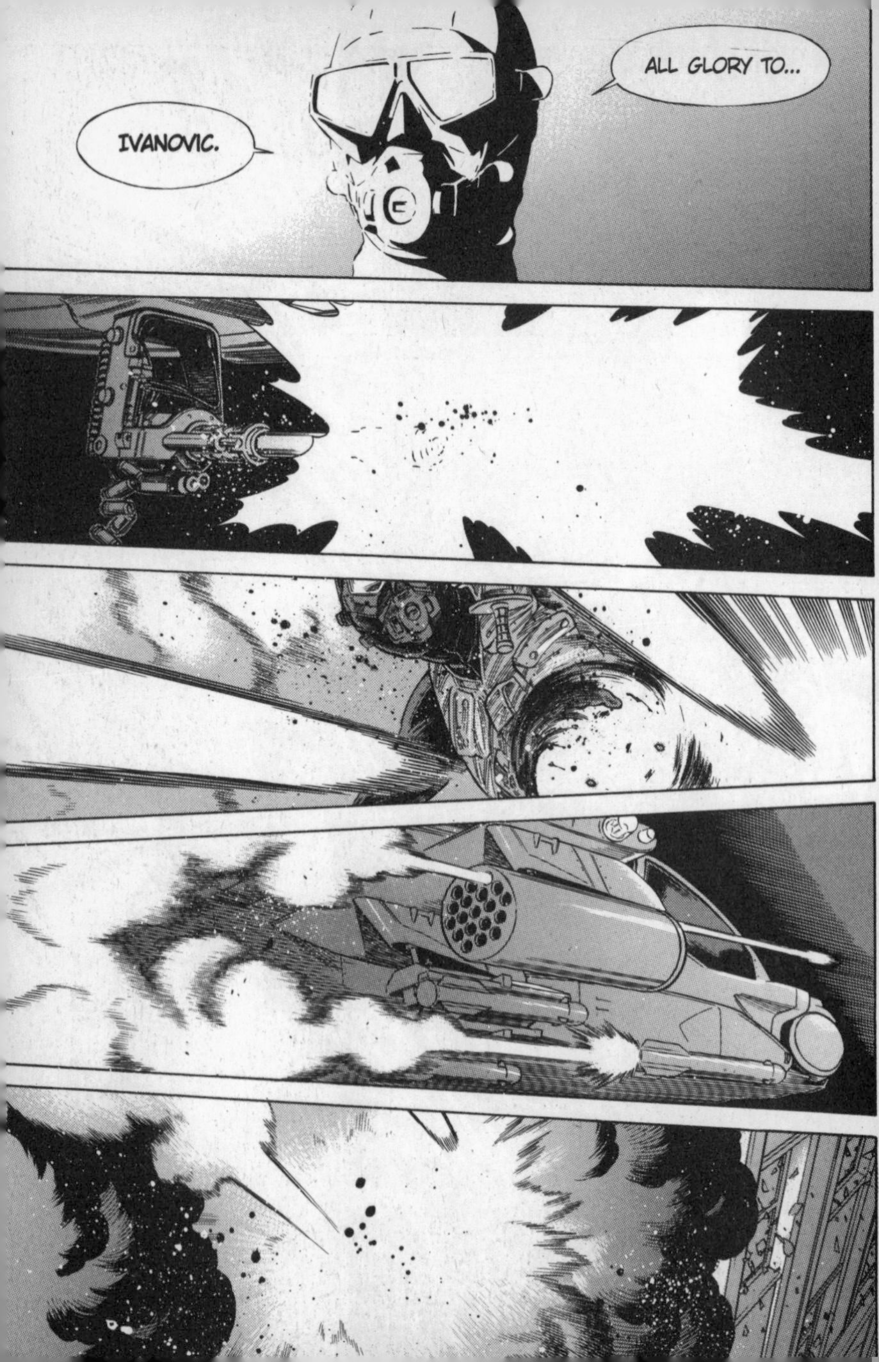
ALL GLORY TO...
IVANOVIC.

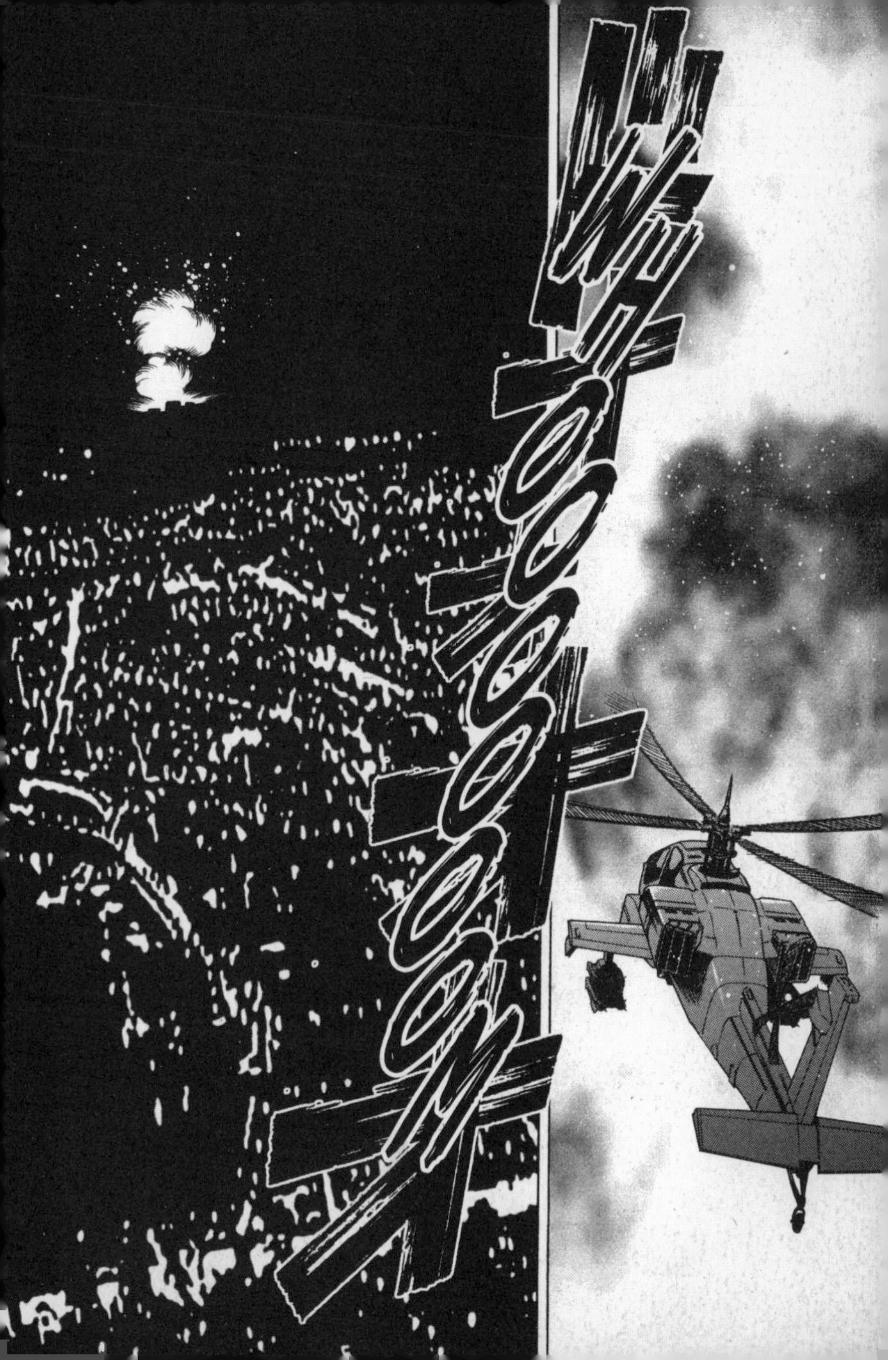
WHOOOOOOM

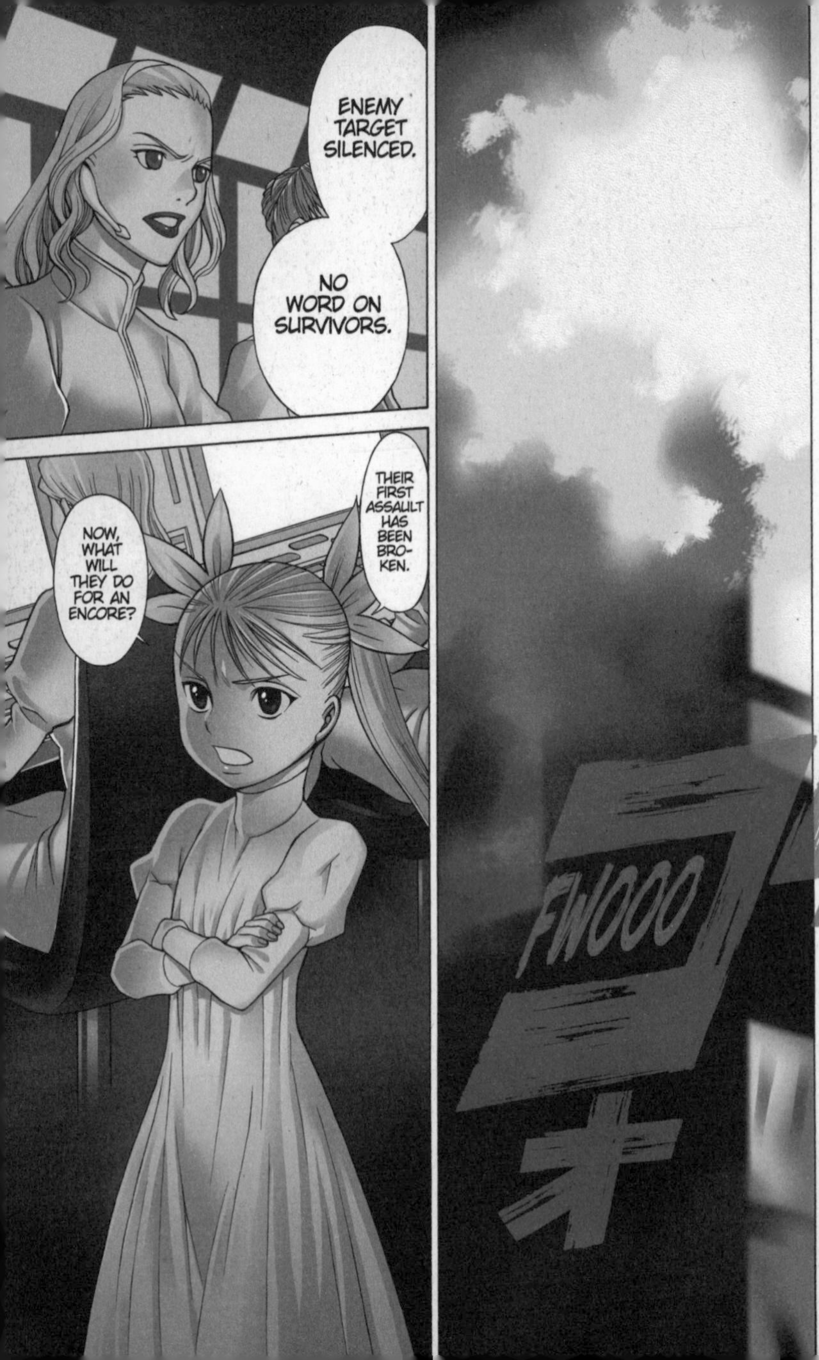
FWOOO
ENEMY TARGET SILENCED.
NO WORD ON SURVIVORS.
THEIR FIRST ASSAULT HAS BEEN BRO-KEN.
NOW, WHAT WILL THEY DO FOR AN ENCORE?

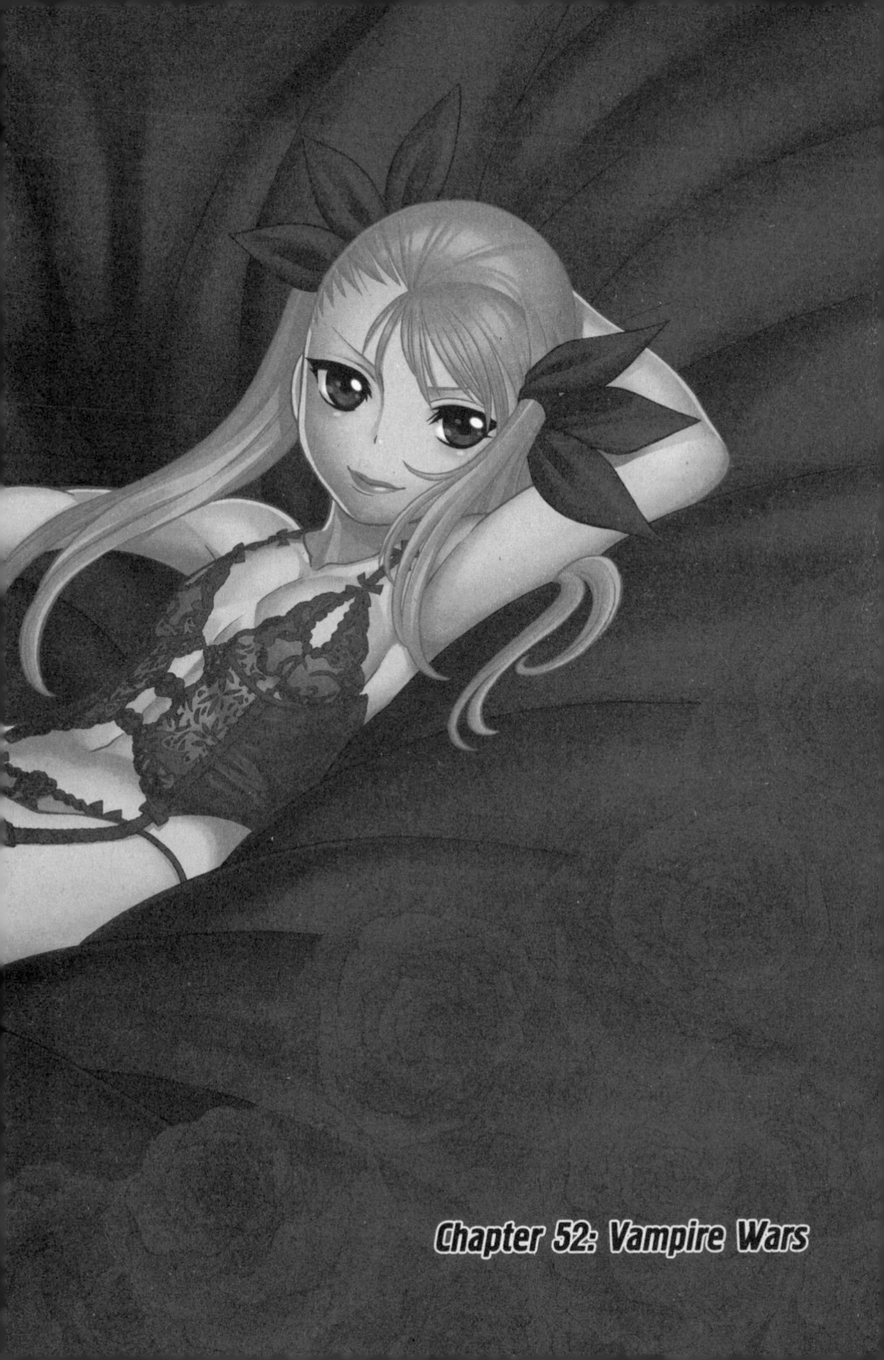

Chapter 52: Vampire Wars

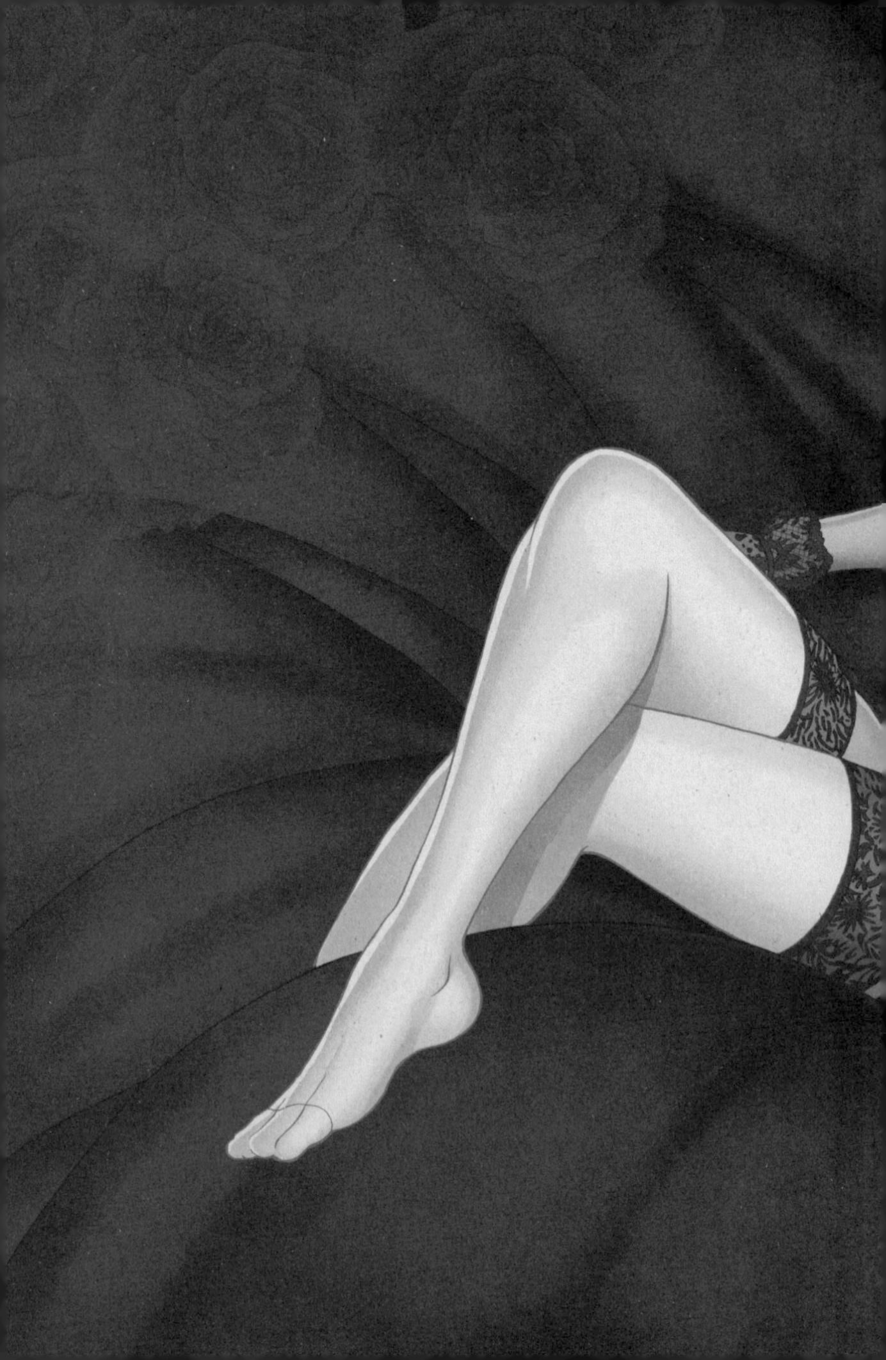

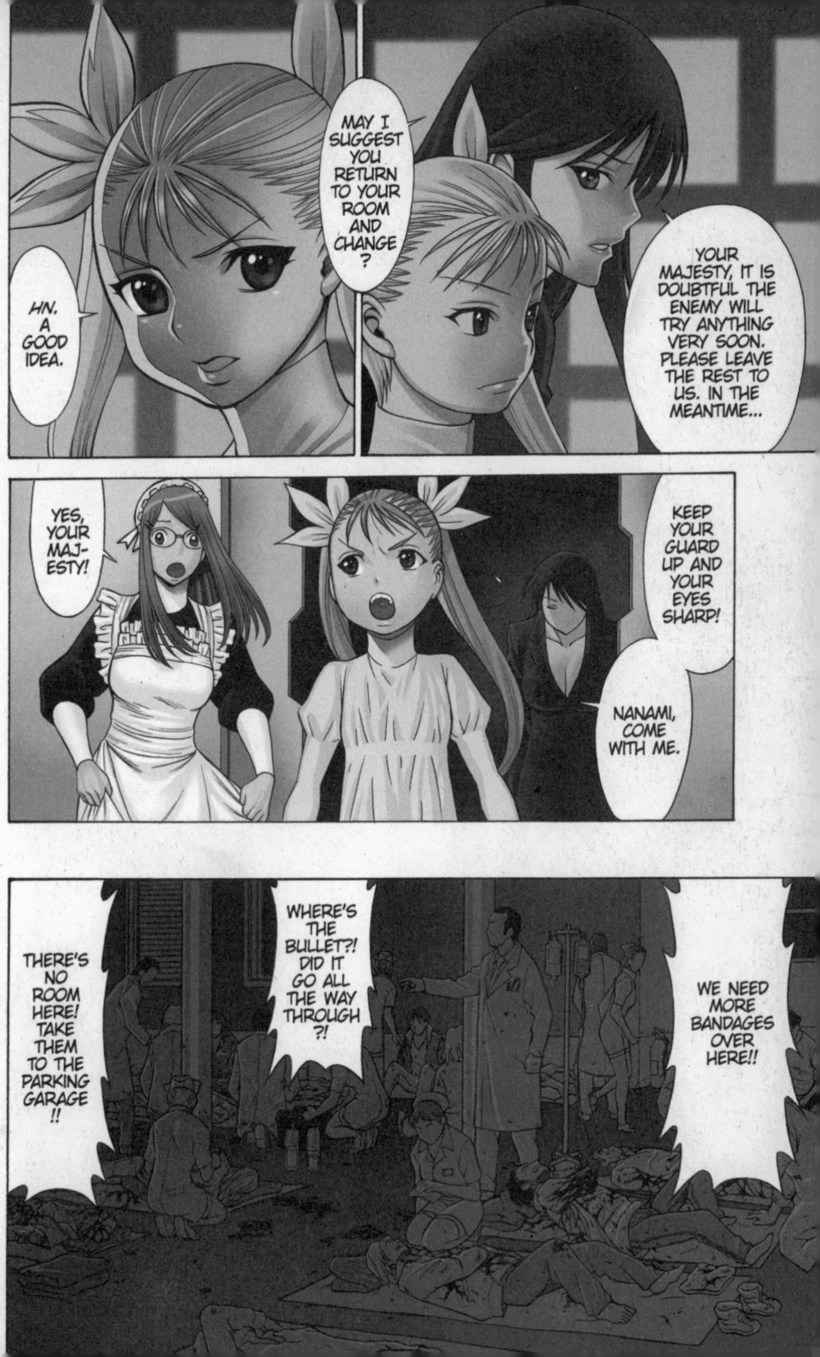
YOUR MAJESTY, IT IS DOUBTFUL THE ENEMY WILL TRY ANYTHING VERY SOON. PLEASE LEAVE THE REST TO US. IN THE MEANTIME...
MAY I SUGGEST YOU RETURN TO YOUR ROOM AND CHANGE?
HN. A GOOD IDEA.
KEEP YOUR GUARD UP AND YOUR EYES SHARP!
NANAMI, COME WITH ME.
YES, YOUR MAJ-ESTY!
WE NEED MORE BANDAGES OVER HERE!!
WHERE'S THE BULLET?! DID IT GO ALL THE WAY THROUGH?!
THERE'S NO ROOM HERE! TAKE THEM TO THE PARKING GARAGE!!

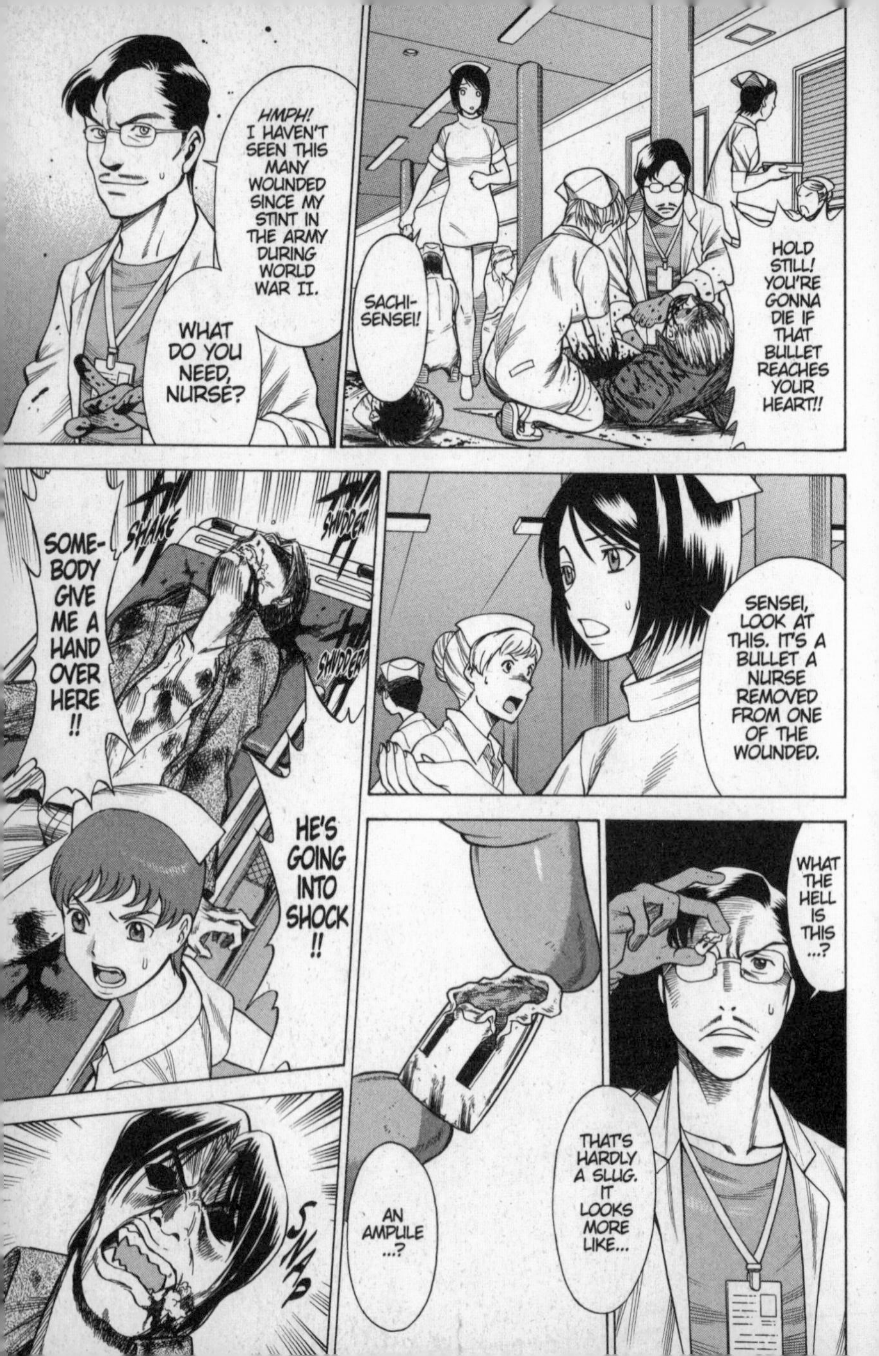
HOLD STILL! YOU'RE GONNA DIE IF THAT BULLET REACHES YOUR HEART!!
SACHI-SENSEI!
HMPH! I HAVEN'T SEEN THIS MANY WOUNDED SINCE MY STINT IN THE ARMY DURING WORLD WAR II.
WHAT DO YOU NEED, NURSE?
SENSEI, LOOK AT THIS. IT'S A BULLET A NURSE REMOVED FROM ONE OF THE WOUNDED.
WHAT THE HELL IS THIS ...?
THAT'S HARDLY A SLUG. IT LOOKS MORE LIKE...
AN AMPULE ...?
SHUDDER
SHUDDER
SHAKE
SOME-BODY GIVE ME A HAND OVER HERE!!
HE'S GOING INTO SHOCK!!
SNAP

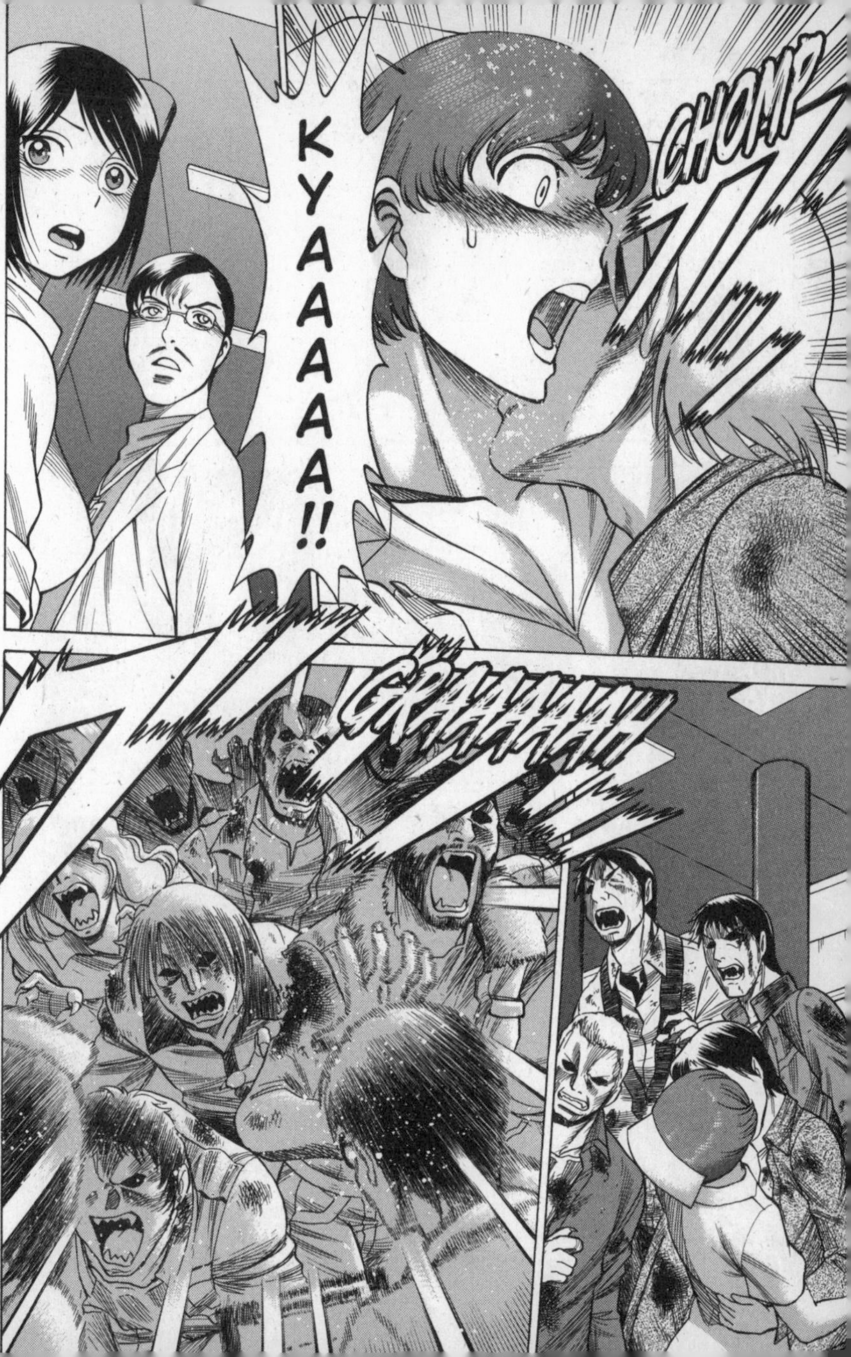
CHOMP
KYAAAAAA!!
GRAAAAAH

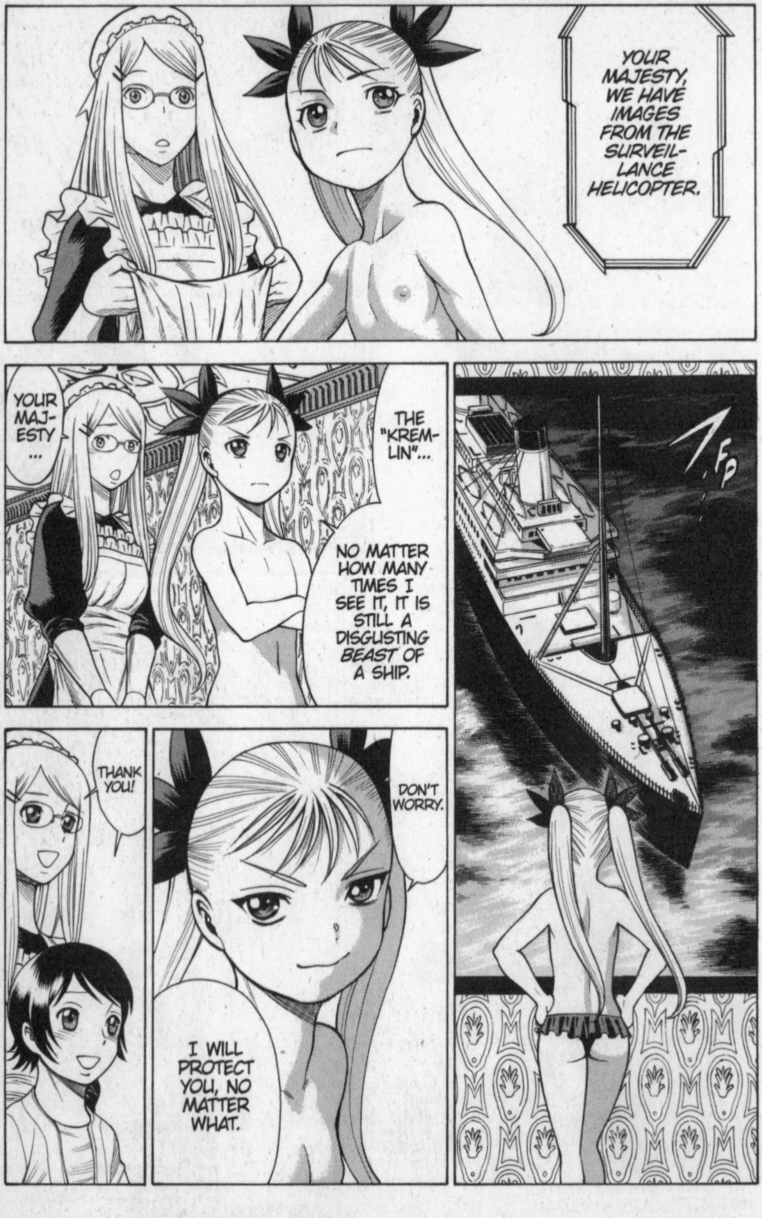
YOUR MAJESTY, WE HAVE IMAGES FROM THE SURVEIL-LANCE HELICOPTER.
FP
THE "KREM-LIN"...
NO MATTER HOW MANY TIMES I SEE IT, IT IS STILL A DISGUSTING *BEAST* OF A SHIP.
YOUR MAJ-ESTY ...
DON'T WORRY.
I WILL PROTECT YOU, NO MATTER WHAT.
THANK YOU!

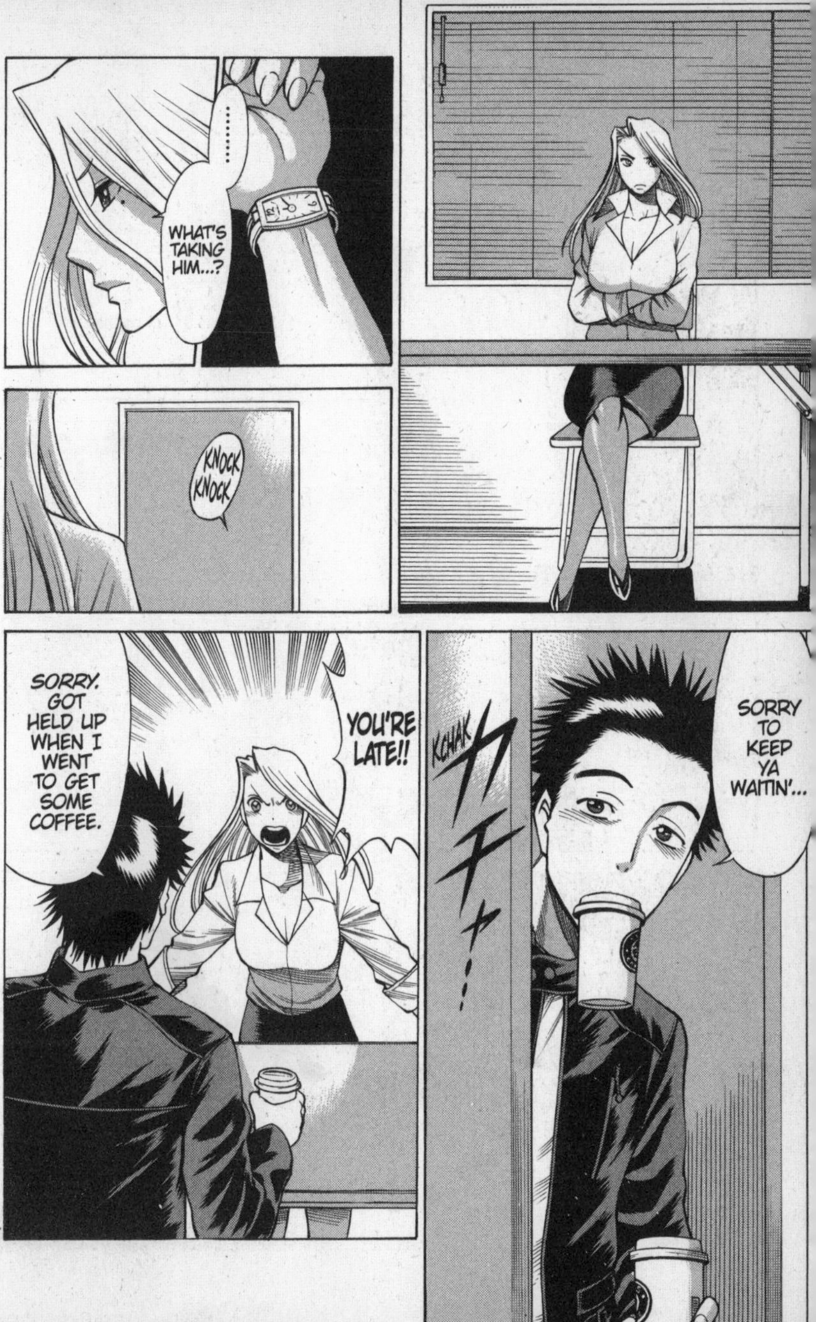
......
WHAT'S TAKING HIM...?
KNOCK KNOCK
KCHAK
SORRY TO KEEP YA WAITIN'...
YOU'RE LATE!!
SORRY. GOT HELD UP WHEN I WENT TO GET SOME COFFEE.

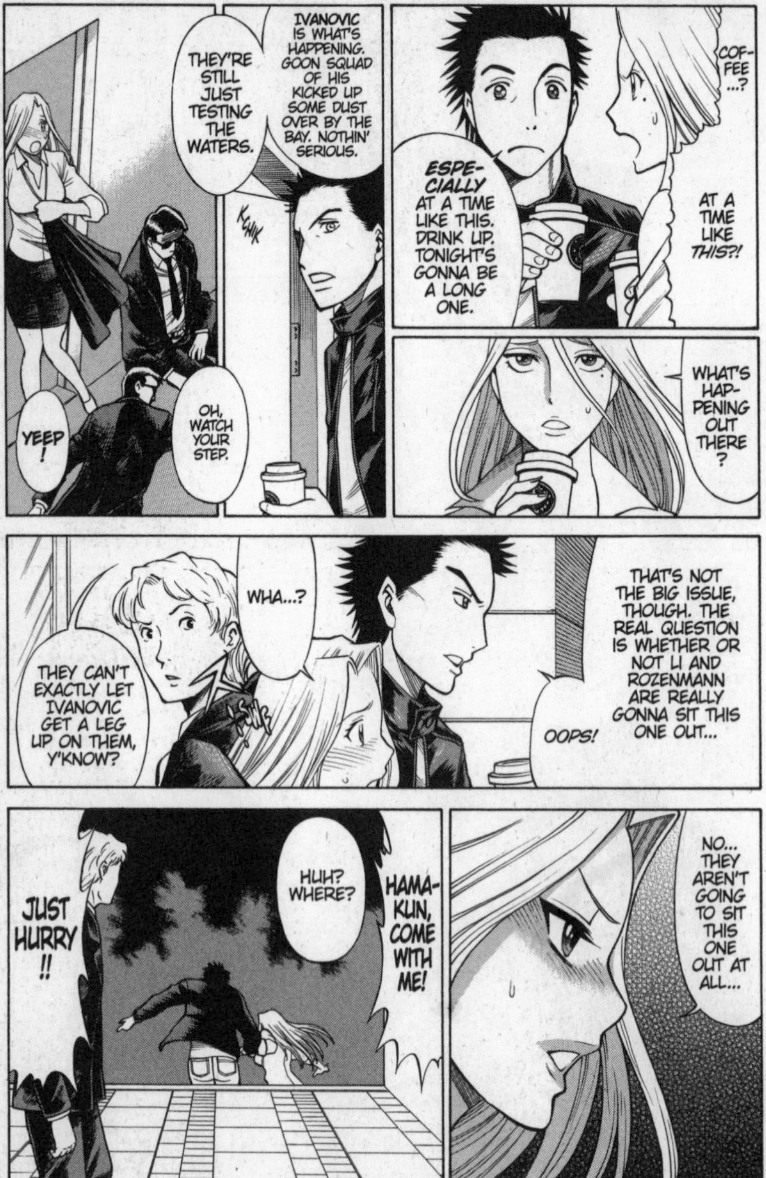
COF-FEE ...?
ESPE-CIALLY AT A TIME LIKE THIS. DRINK UP. TONIGHT'S GONNA BE A LONG ONE.
AT A TIME LIKE THIS?!
WHAT'S HAP-PENING OUT THERE ?
IVANOVIC IS WHAT'S HAPPENING. GOON SQUAD OF HIS KICKED UP SOME DUST OVER BY THE BAY. NOTHIN' SERIOUS.
THEY'RE STILL JUST TESTING THE WATERS.
KCHIK
OH, WATCH YOUR STEP.
YEEP !
THAT'S NOT THE BIG ISSUE, THOUGH. THE REAL QUESTION IS WHETHER OR NOT LI AND ROZENMANN ARE REALLY GONNA SIT THIS ONE OUT...
OOPS!
WHA...?
THEY CAN'T EXACTLY LET IVANOVIC GET A LEG UP ON THEM, Y'KNOW?
NO... THEY AREN'T GOING TO SIT THIS ONE OUT AT ALL...
HAMA-KUN, COME WITH ME!
HUH? WHERE?
JUST HURRY !!

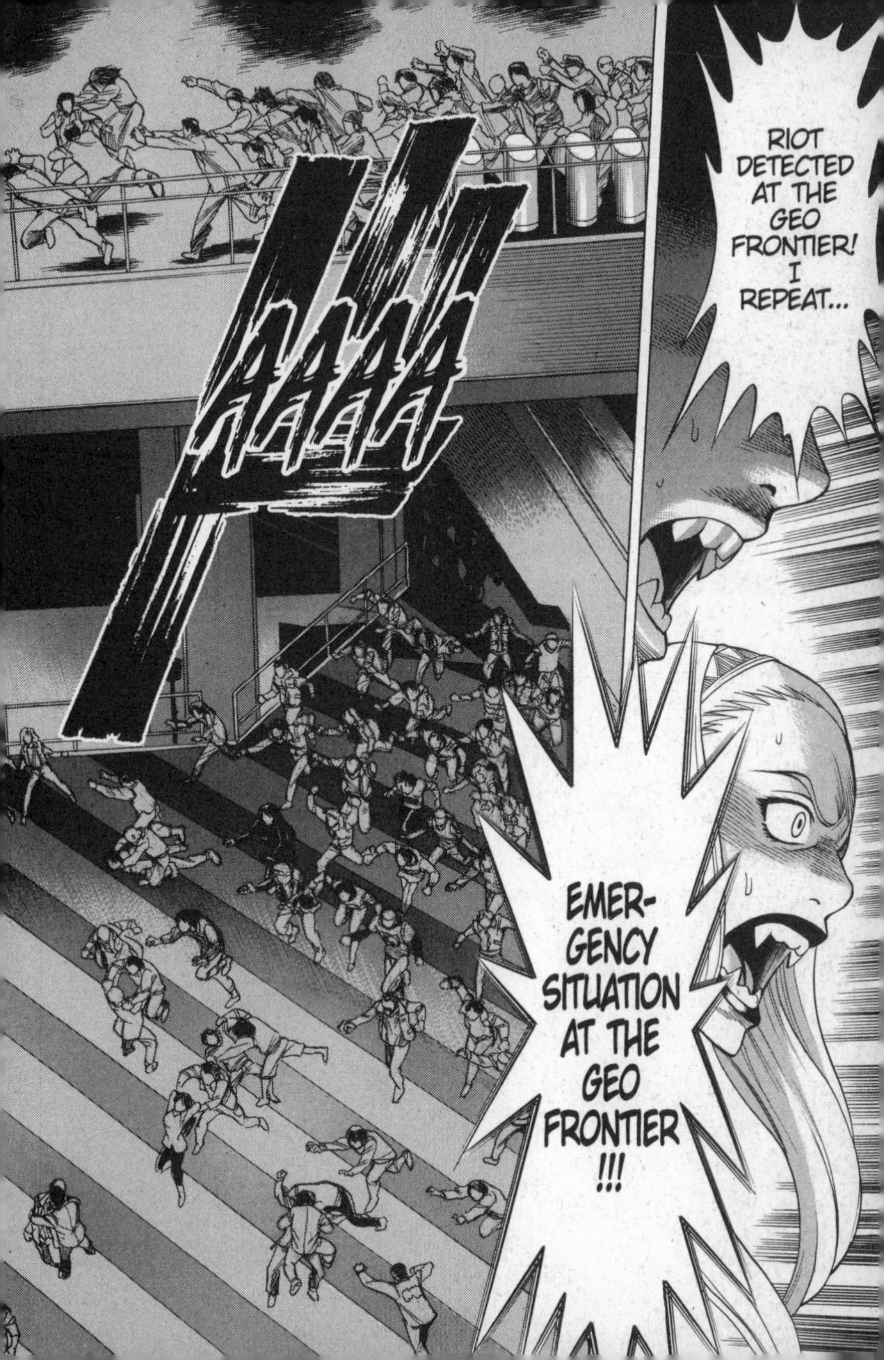

RIOT DETECTED AT THE GEO FRONTIER! I REPEAT...
EMERGENCY SITUATION AT THE GEO FRONTIER!!!

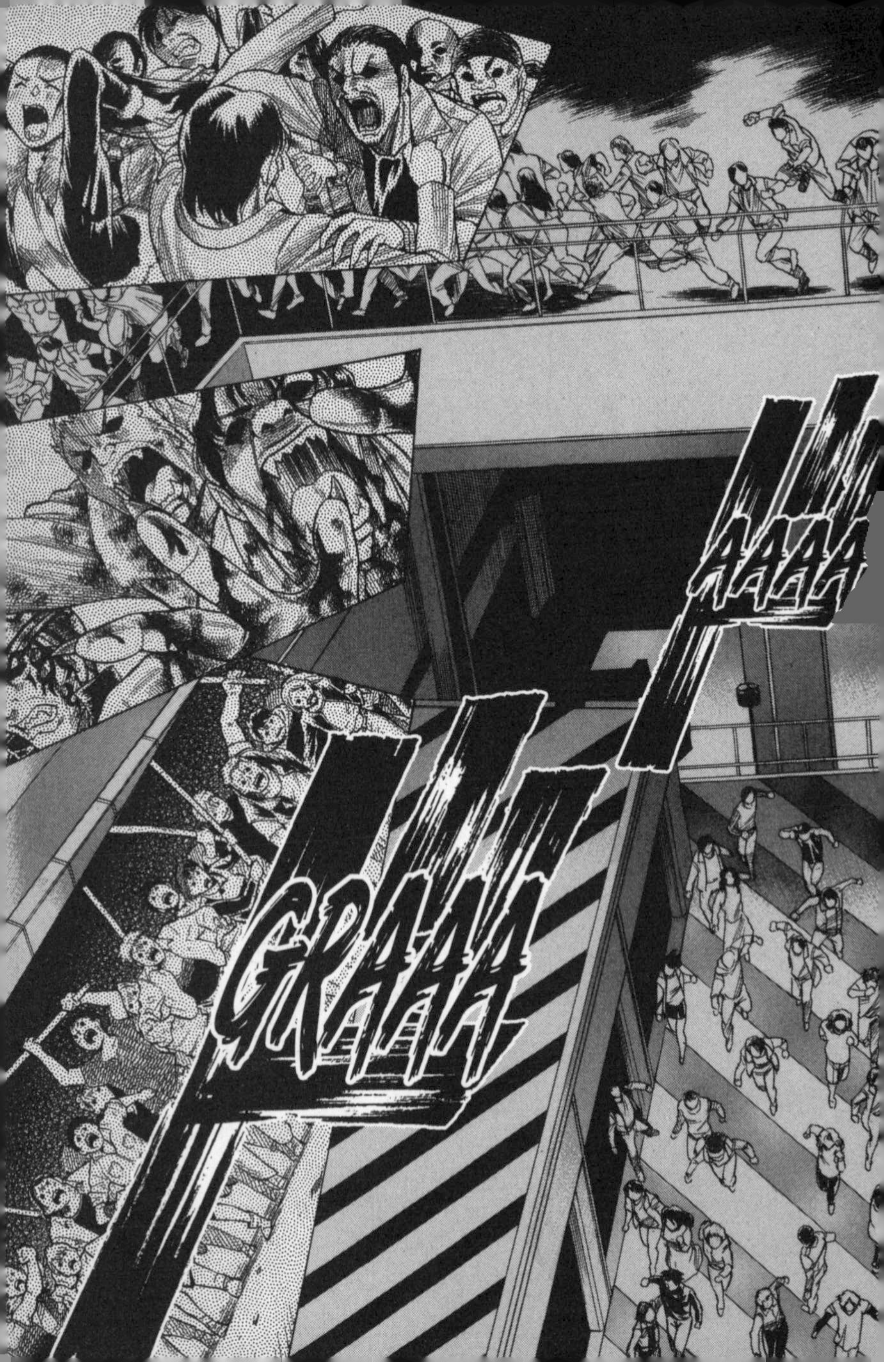
AAAA
GRAAAA

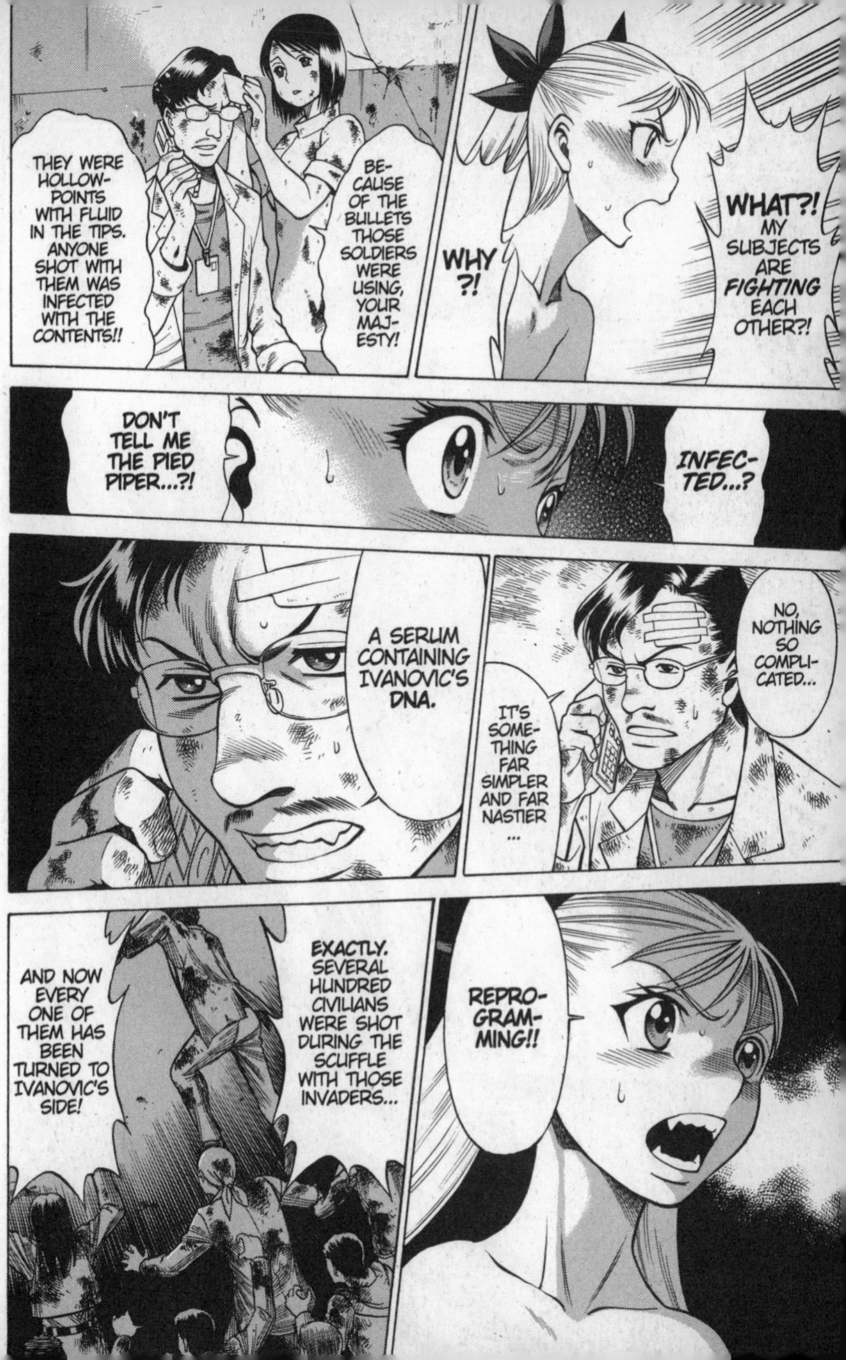
WHAT?! MY SUBJECTS ARE FIGHTING EACH OTHER?!
WHY ?!
BECAUSE OF THE BULLETS THOSE SOLDIERS WERE USING, YOUR MAJESTY!
THEY WERE HOLLOW-POINTS WITH FLUID IN THE TIPS. ANYONE SHOT WITH THEM WAS INFECTED WITH THE CONTENTS!!
INFECTED...?
DON'T TELL ME THE PIED PIPER...?!
NO, NOTHING SO COMPLICATED...
IT'S SOMETHING FAR SIMPLER AND FAR NASTIER ...
A SERUM CONTAINING IVANOVIC'S DNA.
REPROGRAMMING!!
EXACTLY. SEVERAL HUNDRED CIVILIANS WERE SHOT DURING THE SCUFFLE WITH THOSE INVADERS...
AND NOW EVERY ONE OF THEM HAS BEEN TURNED TO IVANOVIC'S SIDE!

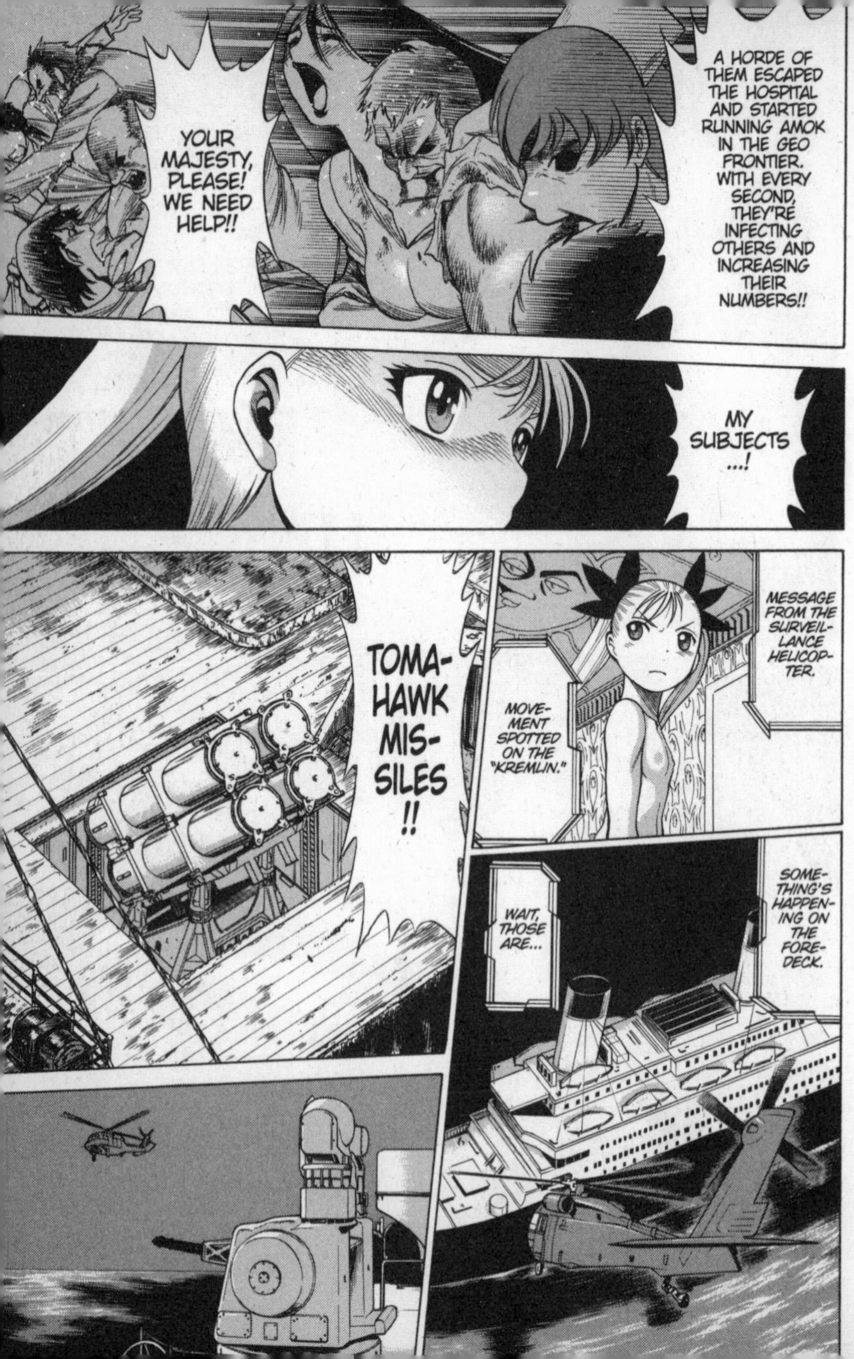
A HORDE OF THEM ESCAPED THE HOSPITAL AND STARTED RUNNING AMOK IN THE GEO FRONTIER. WITH EVERY SECOND, THEY'RE INFECTING OTHERS AND INCREASING THEIR NUMBERS!!
YOUR MAJESTY, PLEASE! WE NEED HELP!!
MY SUBJECTS ...!
MESSAGE FROM THE SURVEIL-LANCE HELICOP-TER.
MOVE-MENT SPOTTED ON THE "KREMLIN."
SOME-THING'S HAPPEN-ING ON THE FORE-DECK.
WAIT, THOSE ARE...
TOMA-HAWK MIS-SILES !!

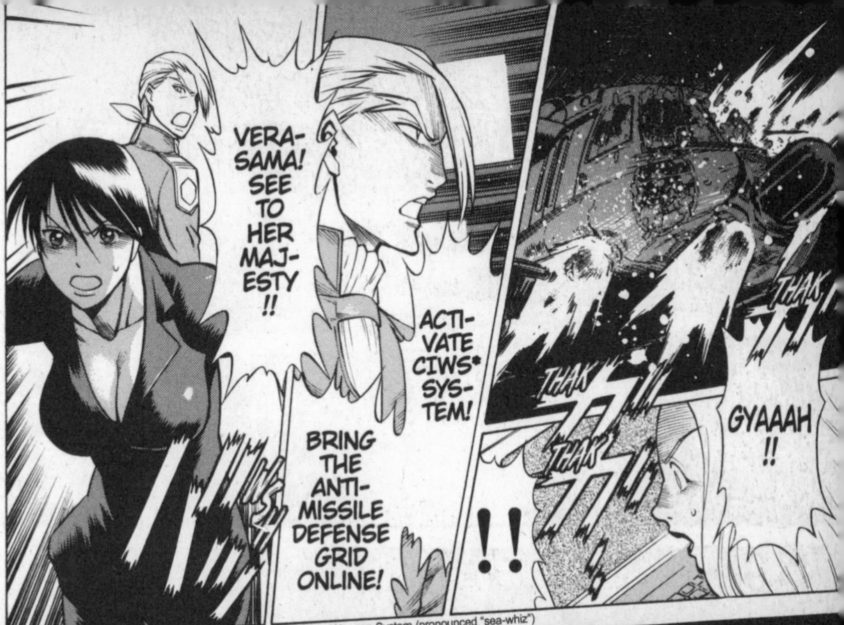
THAK
GYAAAH !!
THAK
THAK
!!
VERA-SAMA! SEE TO HER MAJESTY !!
ACTIVATE CIWS* SYSTEM!
BRING THE ANTI-MISSILE DEFENSE GRID ONLINE!

*CIWS = Close-In Weapon System (pronounced "sea-whiz")

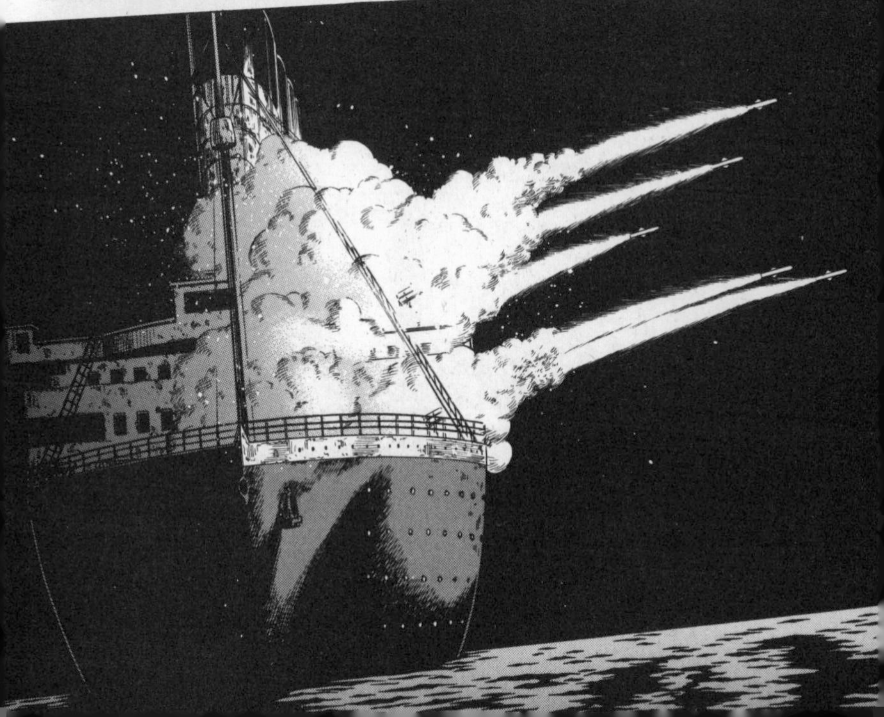

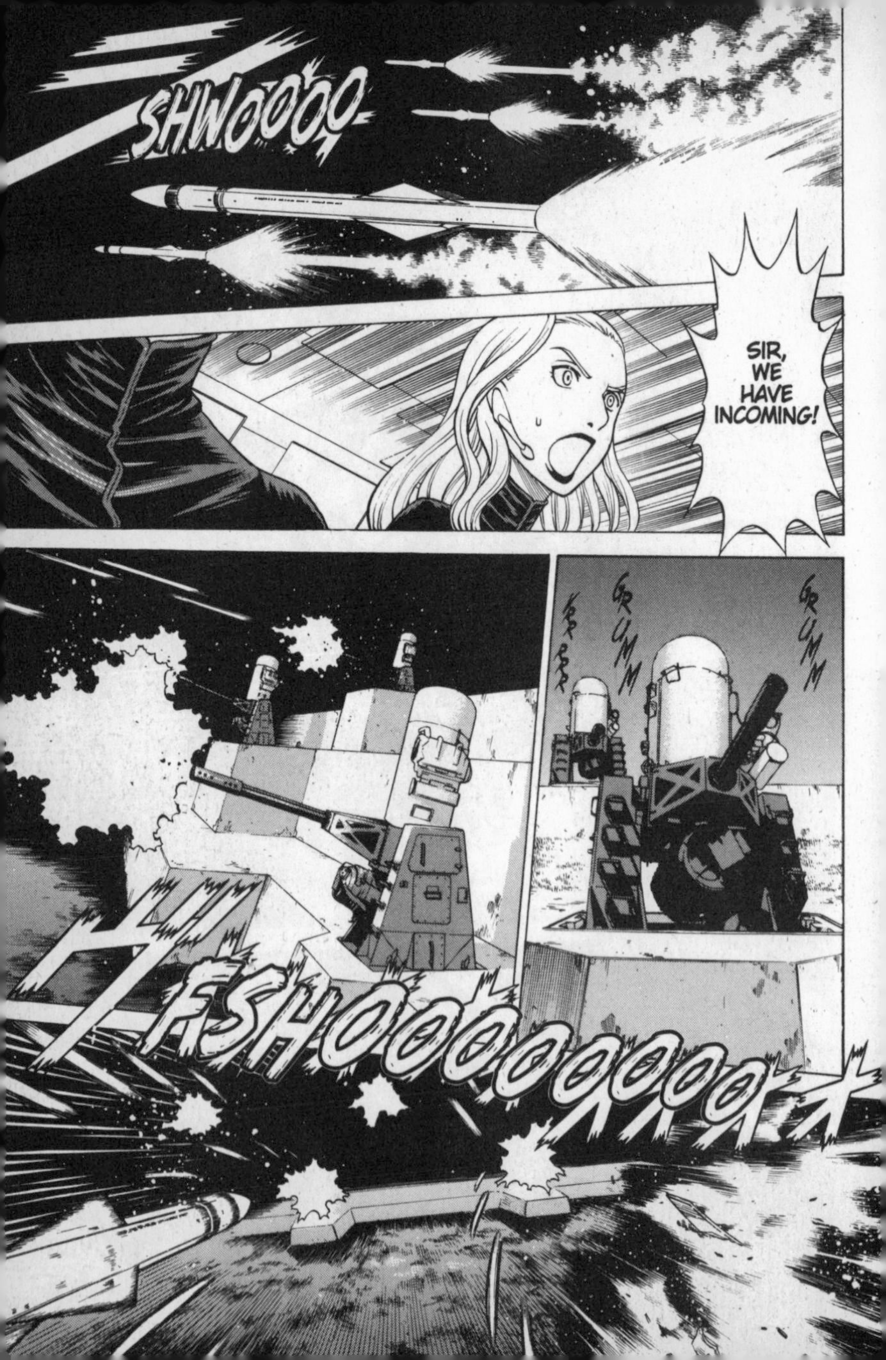
SHWOOOO
SIR, WE HAVE INCOMING!
GRUMM
KRRRRR
GRUMM
FSHOOOOOOOOO

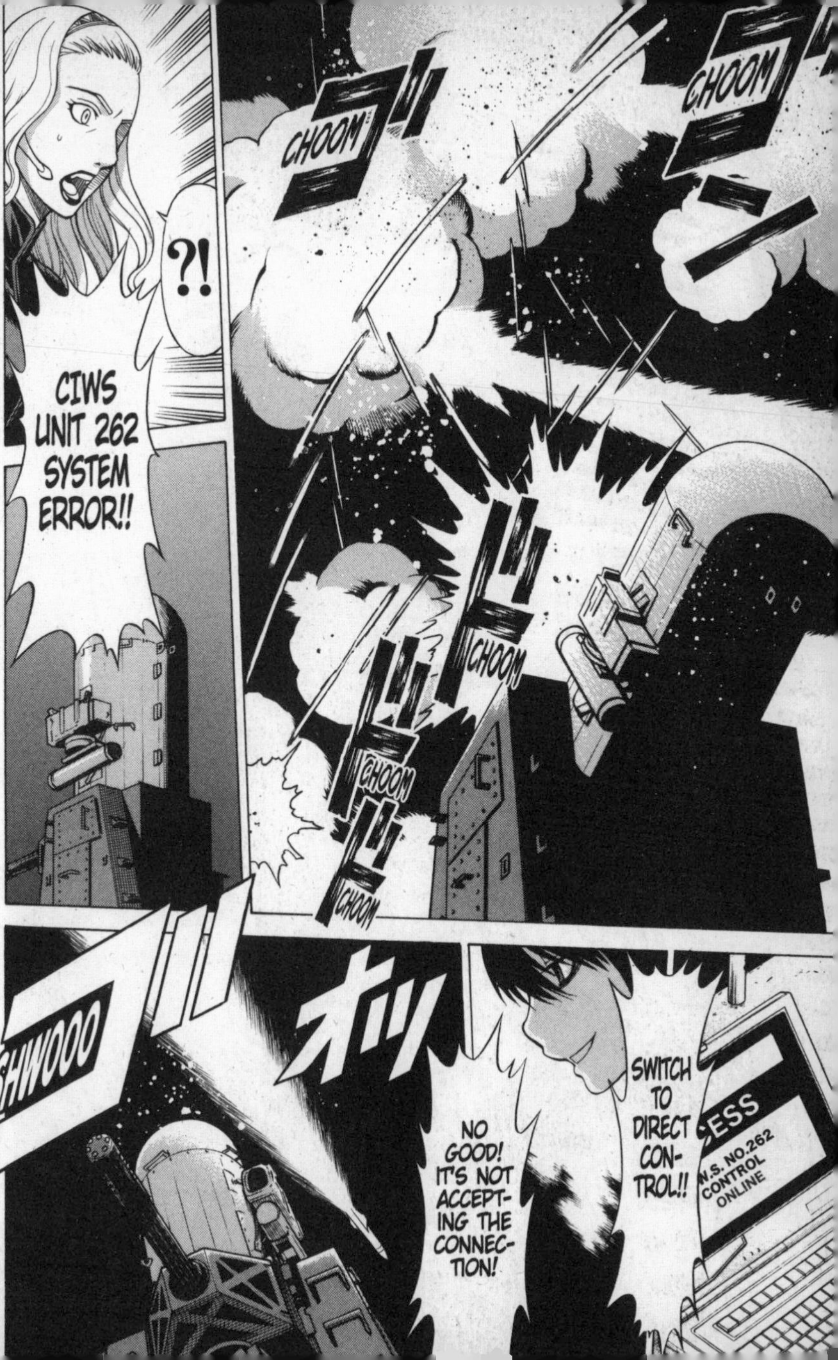
CHOOM
CHOOM
CHOOM
CHOOM
CHOOM
?!
CIWS UNIT 262 SYSTEM ERROR!!
SWITCH TO DIRECT CON-TROL!!
ESS
W.S. NO.262 CONTROL ONLINE
NO GOOD! IT'S NOT ACCEPT-ING THE CONNEC-TION!
オッ
SHWOOO

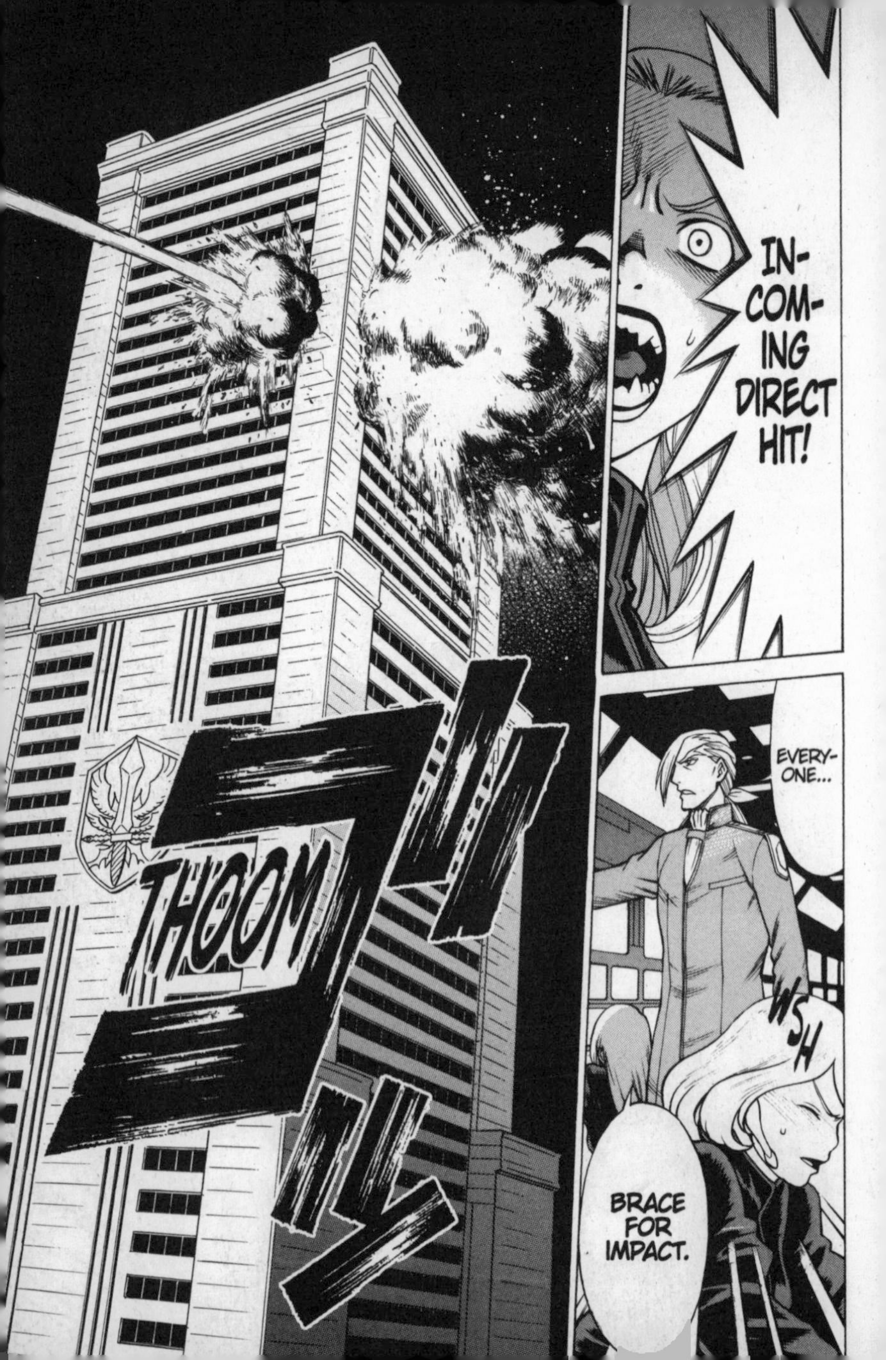
IN-COMING DIRECT HIT!
EVERY-ONE...
WSH
BRACE FOR IMPACT.
THOOM

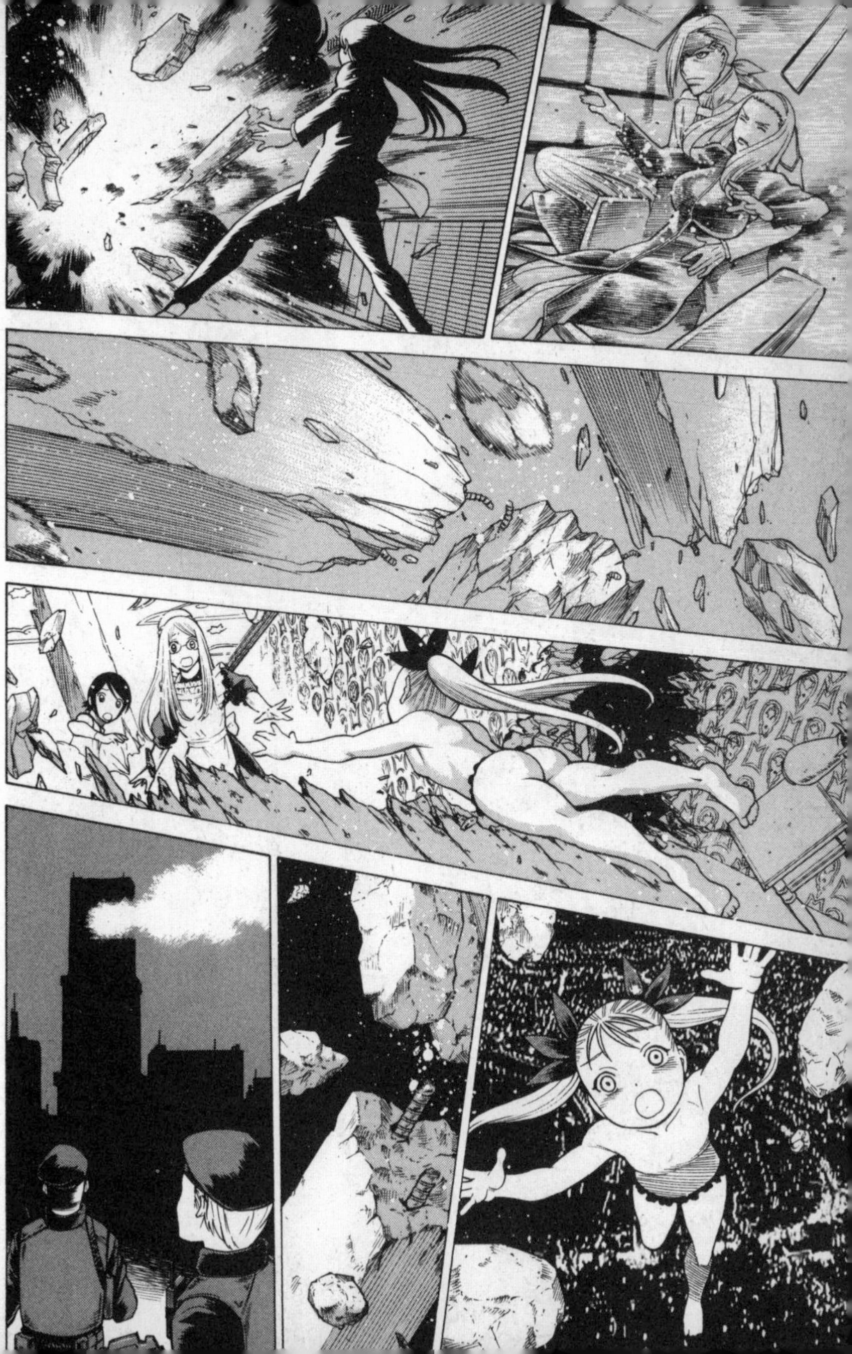

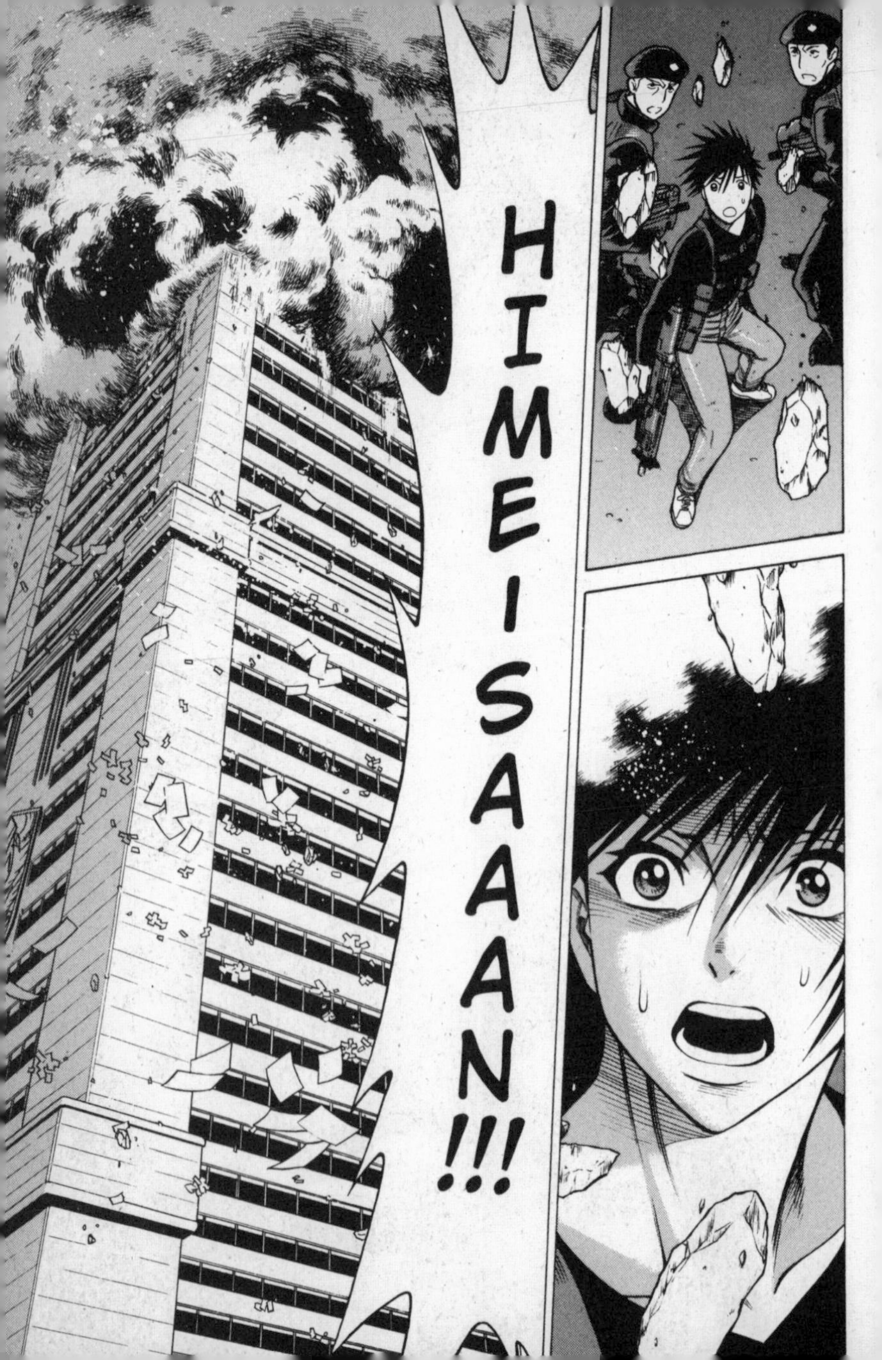
HIMEI SAAAN!!!

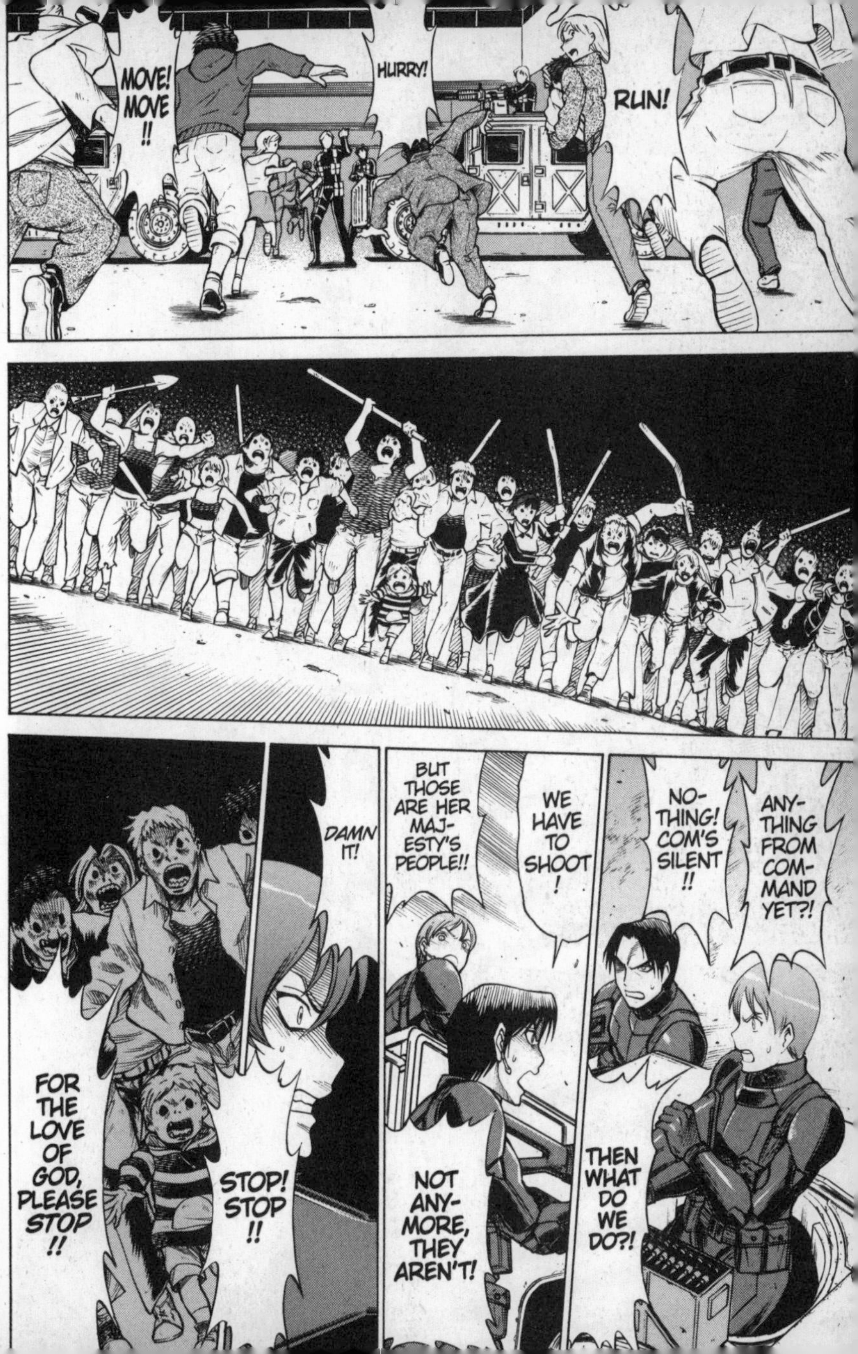
RUN!
HURRY!
MOVE! MOVE!!
ANYTHING FROM COMMAND YET?!
NOTHING! COM'S SILENT!!
THEN WHAT DO WE DO?!
WE HAVE TO SHOOT!
BUT THOSE ARE HER MAJESTY'S PEOPLE!!
NOT ANYMORE, THEY AREN'T!
DAMN IT!
STOP! STOP!!
FOR THE LOVE OF GOD, PLEASE STOP!!

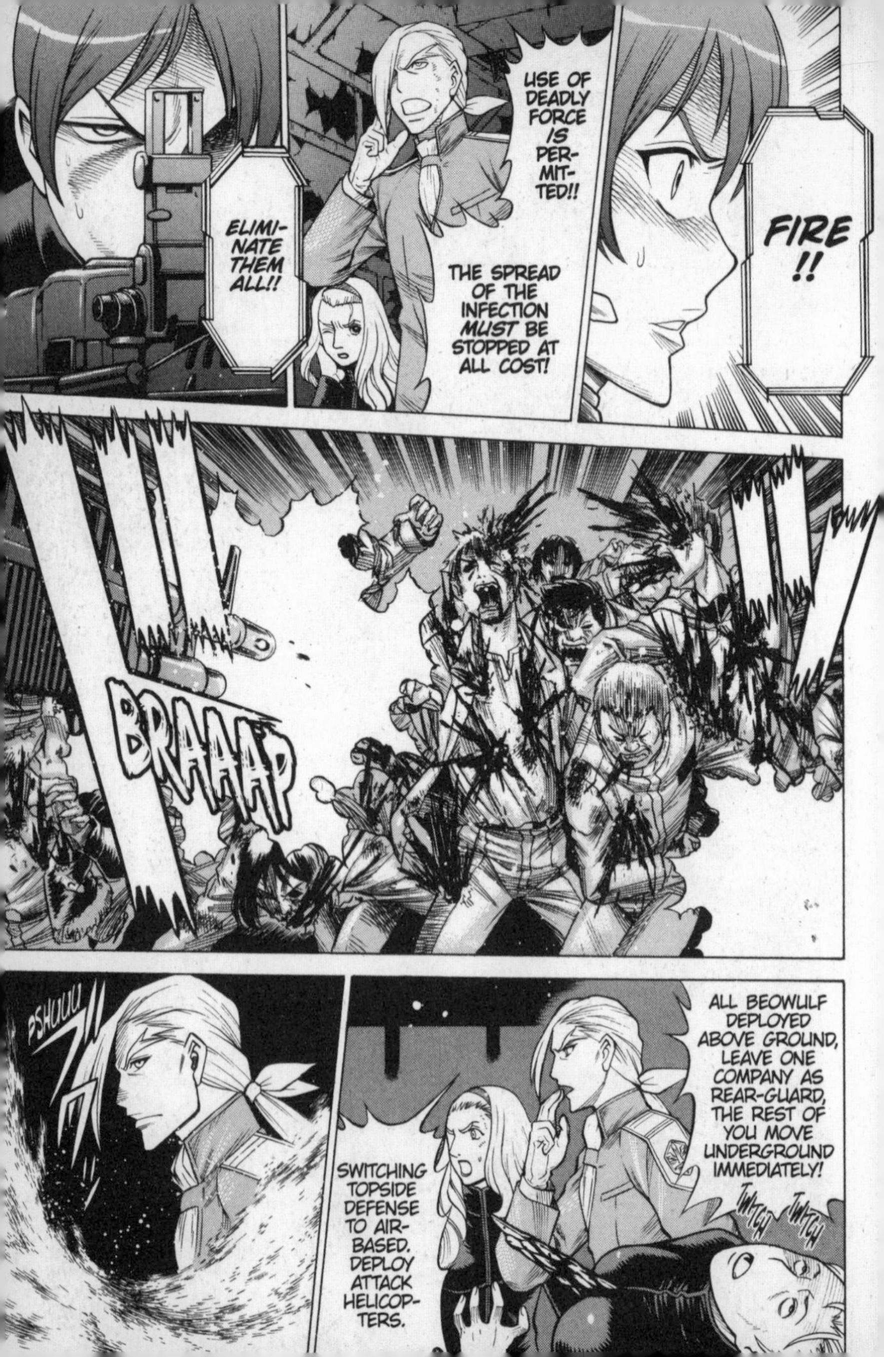
FIRE!!
USE OF DEADLY FORCE IS PERMITTED!!
THE SPREAD OF THE INFECTION MUST BE STOPPED AT ALL COST!
ELIMINATE THEM ALL!!
BRAAAP
ALL BEOWULF DEPLOYED ABOVE GROUND, LEAVE ONE COMPANY AS REAR-GUARD, THE REST OF YOU MOVE UNDERGROUND IMMEDIATELY!
SWITCHING TOPSIDE DEFENSE TO AIR-BASED. DEPLOY ATTACK HELICOPTERS.
TWITCH TWITCH
PSHUUU

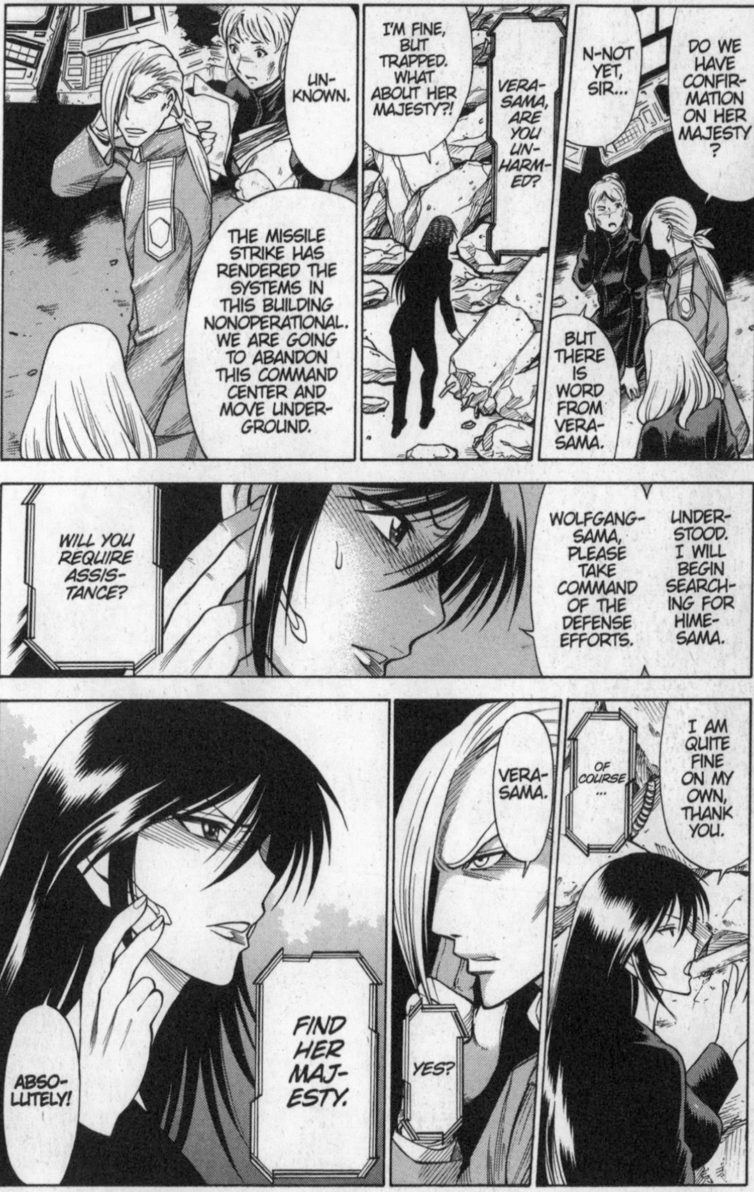
DO WE HAVE CONFIRMATION ON HER MAJESTY?
N-NOT YET, SIR...
BUT THERE IS WORD FROM VERA-SAMA.
VERA-SAMA, ARE YOU UNHARMED?
I'M FINE, BUT TRAPPED. WHAT ABOUT HER MAJESTY?!
UNKNOWN.
THE MISSILE STRIKE HAS RENDERED THE SYSTEMS IN THIS BUILDING NONOPERATIONAL. WE ARE GOING TO ABANDON THIS COMMAND CENTER AND MOVE UNDERGROUND.
UNDERSTOOD. I WILL BEGIN SEARCHING FOR HIME-SAMA.
WOLFGANG-SAMA, PLEASE TAKE COMMAND OF THE DEFENSE EFFORTS.
WILL YOU REQUIRE ASSISTANCE?
I AM QUITE FINE ON MY OWN, THANK YOU.
OF COURSE...
VERA-SAMA.
YES?
FIND HER MAJESTY.
ABSOLUTELY!

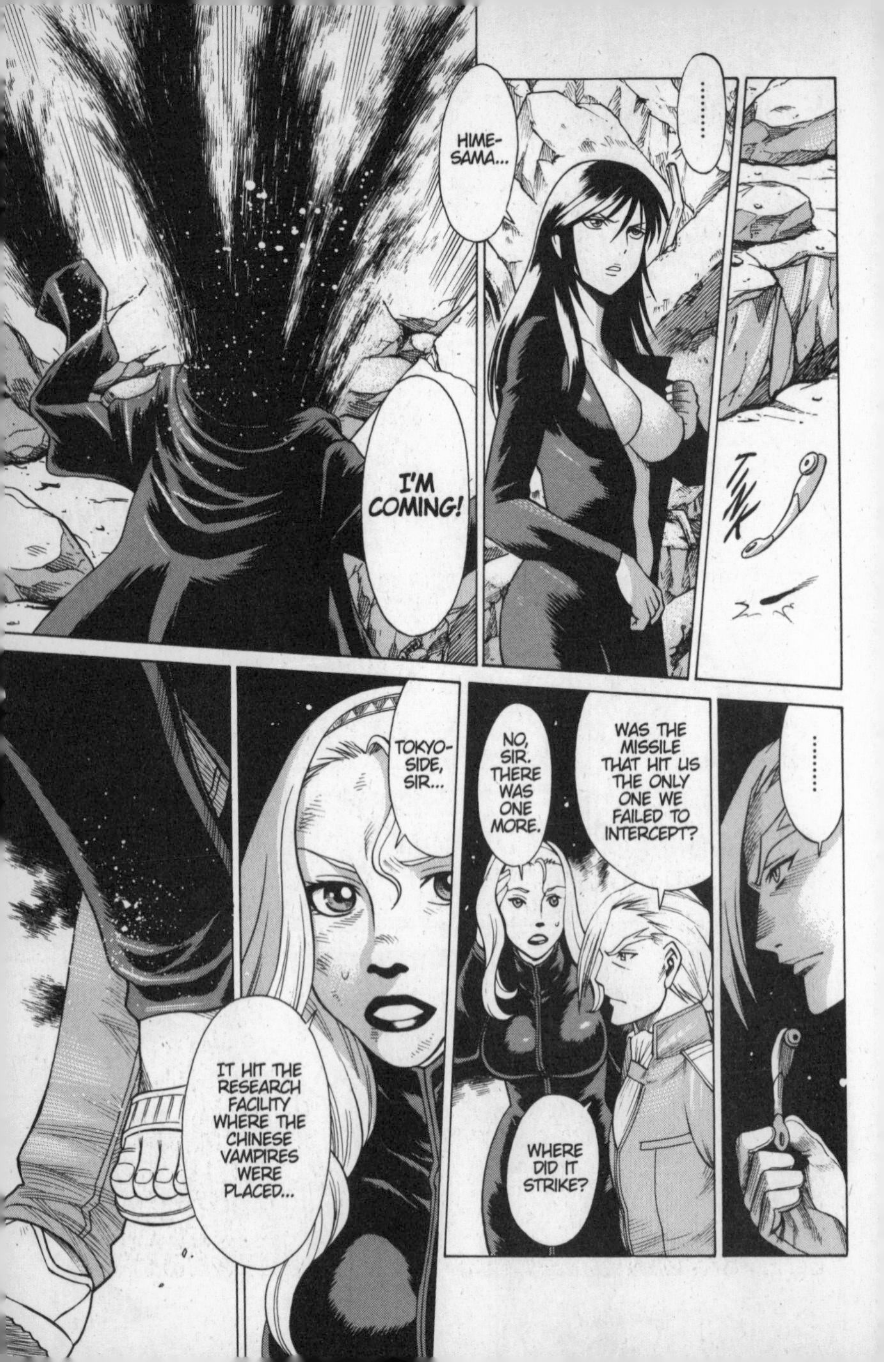

TINK
......
HIME-SAMA...
I'M COMING!
......
WAS THE MISSILE THAT HIT US THE ONLY ONE WE FAILED TO INTERCEPT?
NO, SIR. THERE WAS ONE MORE.
WHERE DID IT STRIKE?
TOKYO-SIDE, SIR...
IT HIT THE RESEARCH FACILITY WHERE THE CHINESE VAMPIRES WERE PLACED...

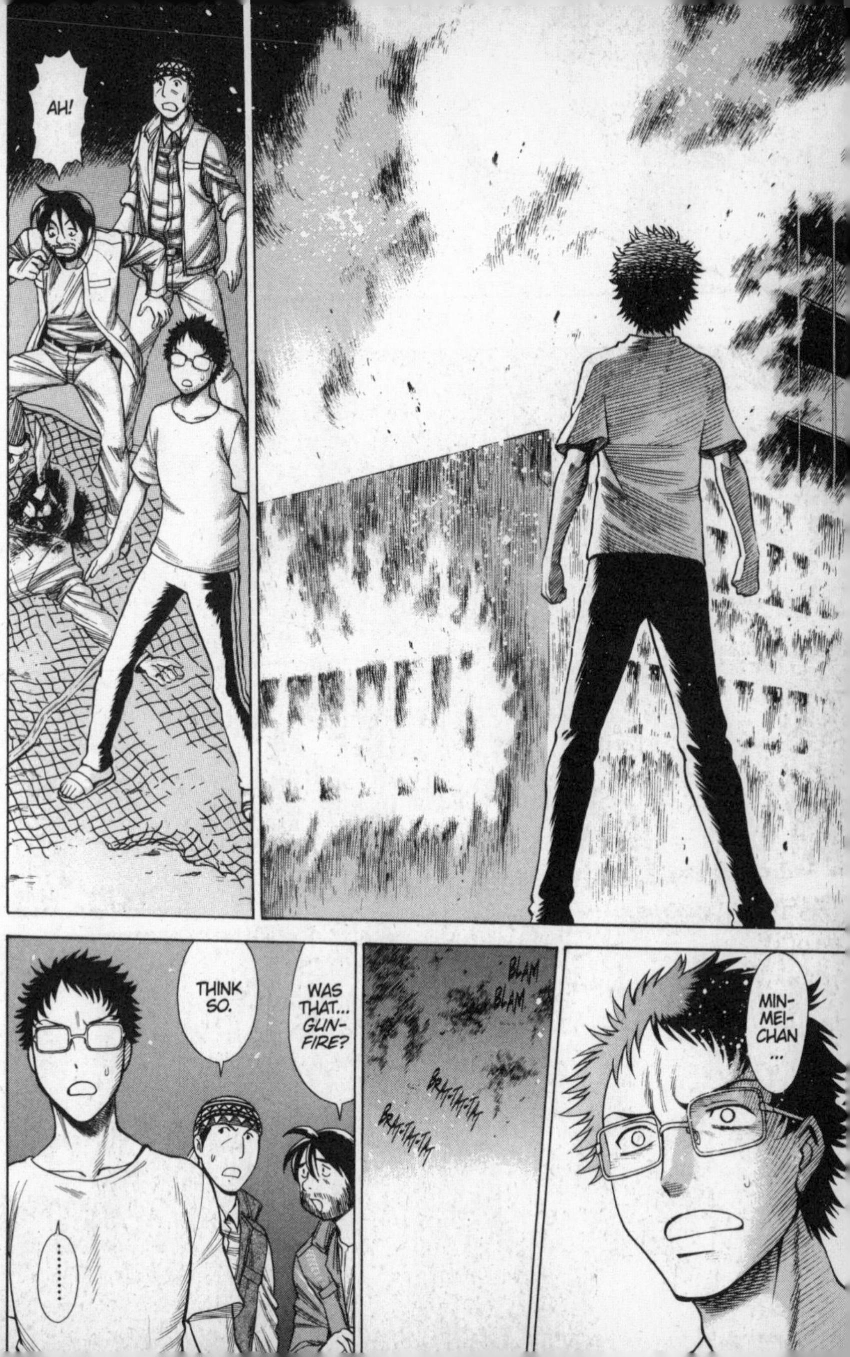
AH!
MIN-MEI-CHAN ...
BLAM
BLAM
BRA-TA-TA-TAT
BRA-TA-TA-TAT
WAS THAT... GUN-FIRE?
THINK SO.
......

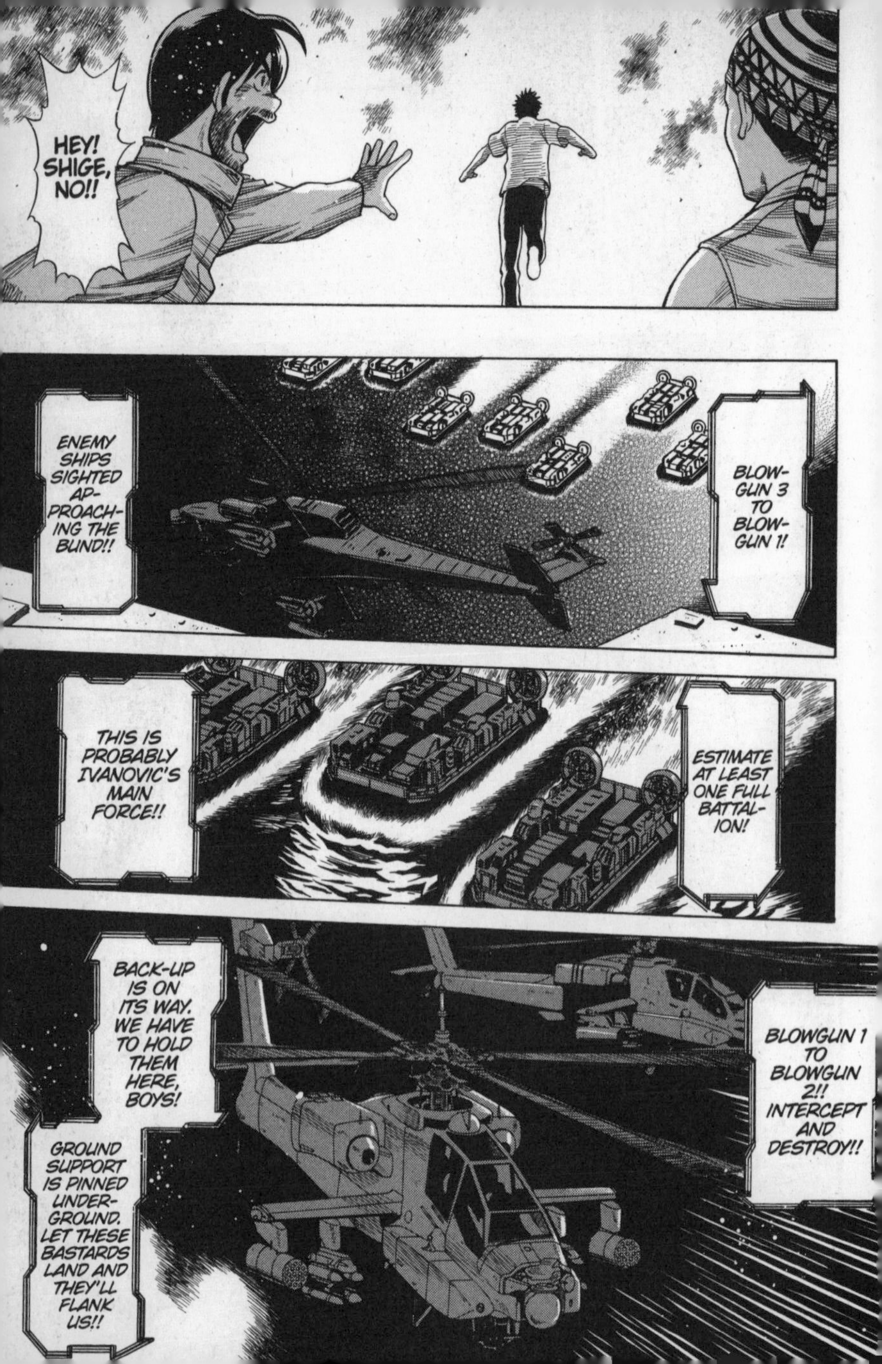
HEY! SHIGE, NO!!
BLOW-GUN 3 TO BLOW-GUN 1!
ENEMY SHIPS SIGHTED AP-PROACHING THE BUND!!
ESTIMATE AT LEAST ONE FULL BATTAL-ION!
THIS IS PROBABLY IVANOVIC'S MAIN FORCE!!
BLOWGUN 1 TO BLOWGUN 2!! INTERCEPT AND DESTROY!!
BACK-UP IS ON ITS WAY. WE HAVE TO HOLD THEM HERE, BOYS!
GROUND SUPPORT IS PINNED UNDER-GROUND. LET THESE BASTARDS LAND AND THEY'LL FLANK US!!

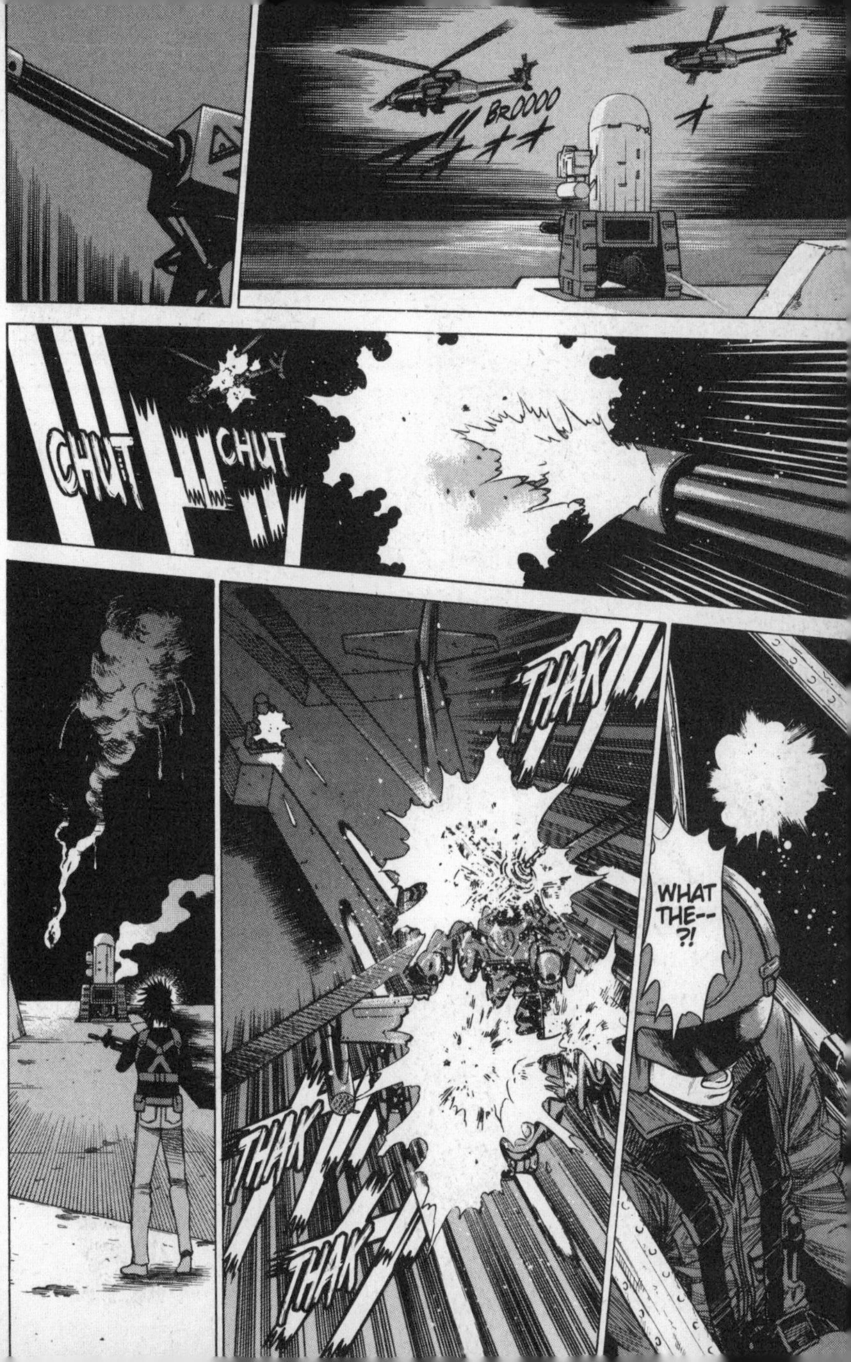
BROOOO
CHUT
CHUT
WHAT THE-- ?!
THAK
THAK
THAK

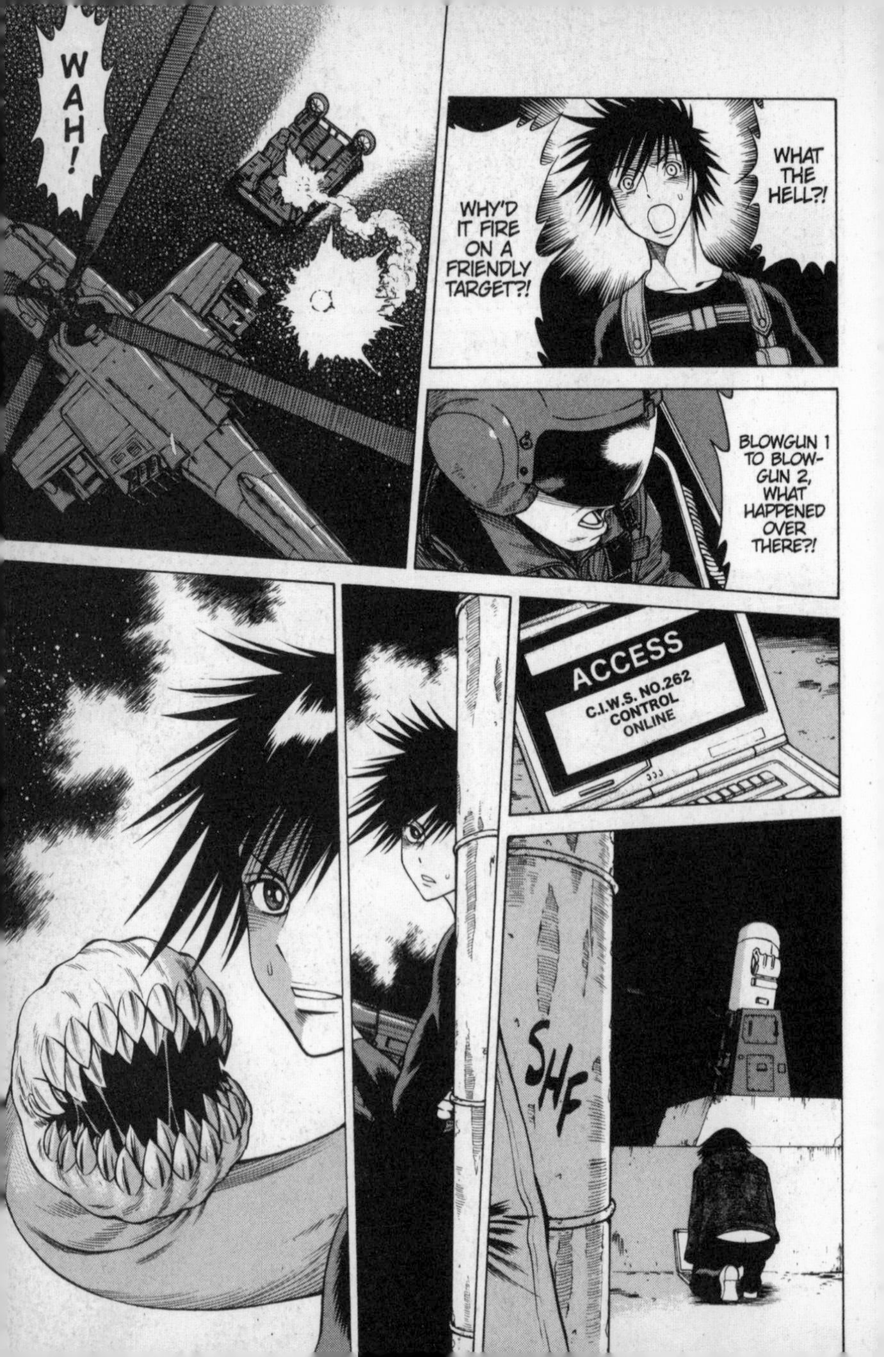
WHAT THE HELL?!
WHY'D IT FIRE ON A FRIENDLY TARGET?!
BLOWGUN 1 TO BLOWGUN 2, WHAT HAPPENED OVER THERE?!
WAH!
ACCESS
C.I.W.S. NO.262 CONTROL ONLINE
SHF

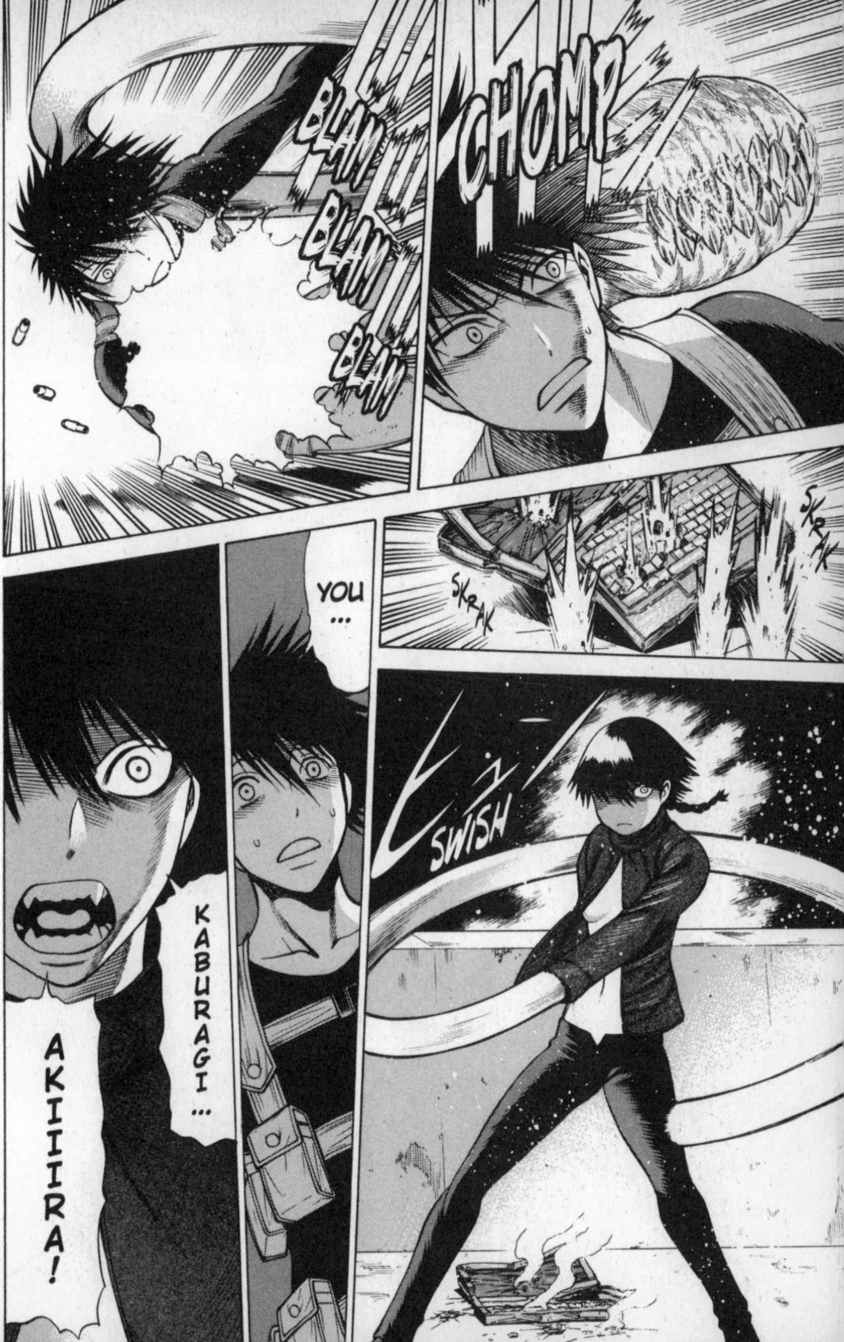
CHOMP
BLAM BLAM BLAM BLAM
SKRAK
SKRAK
SWISH
YOU ...
KABURAGI ...
AKIIIRA!

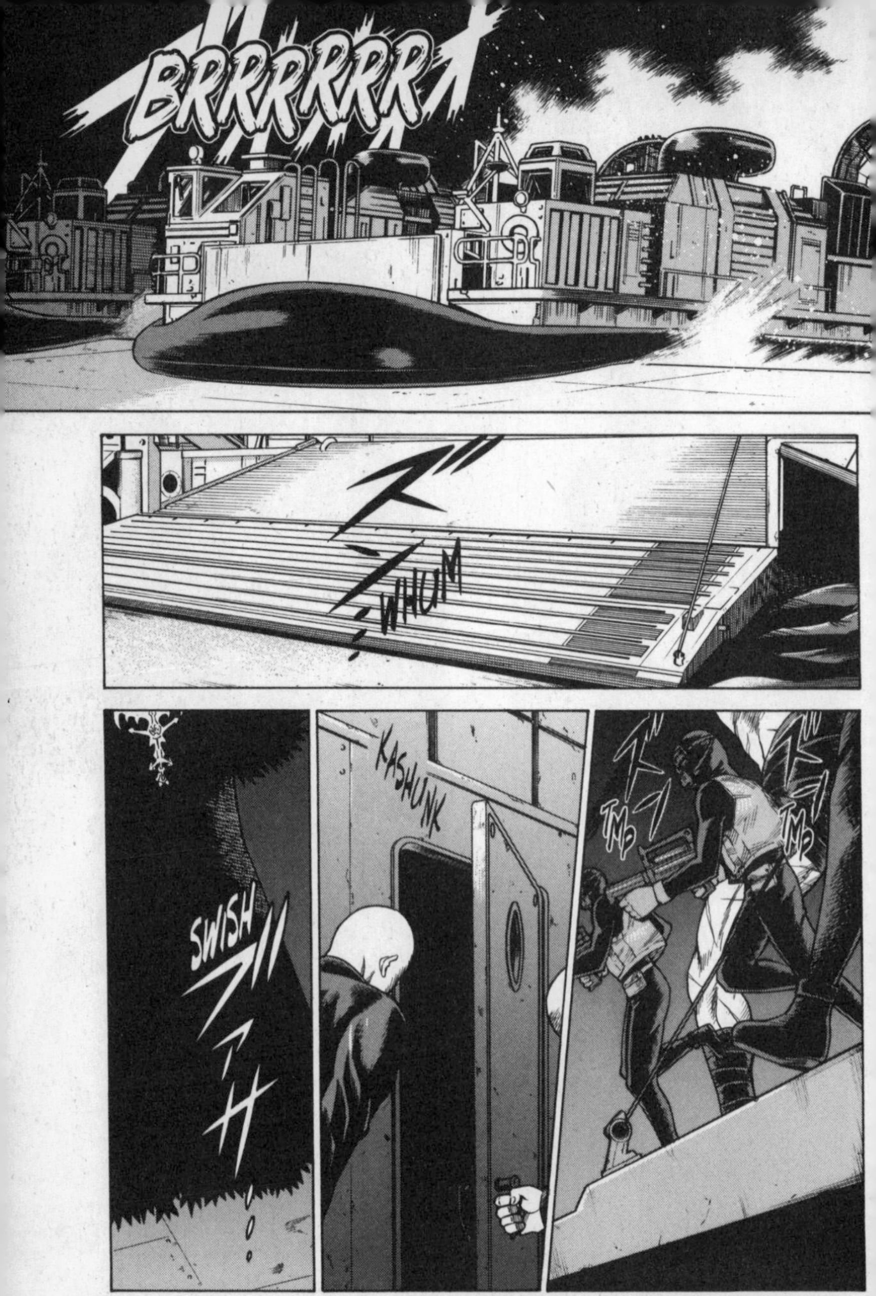
BRRRRRRR
WHUM
TMP
TMP
KASHUNK
SWISH

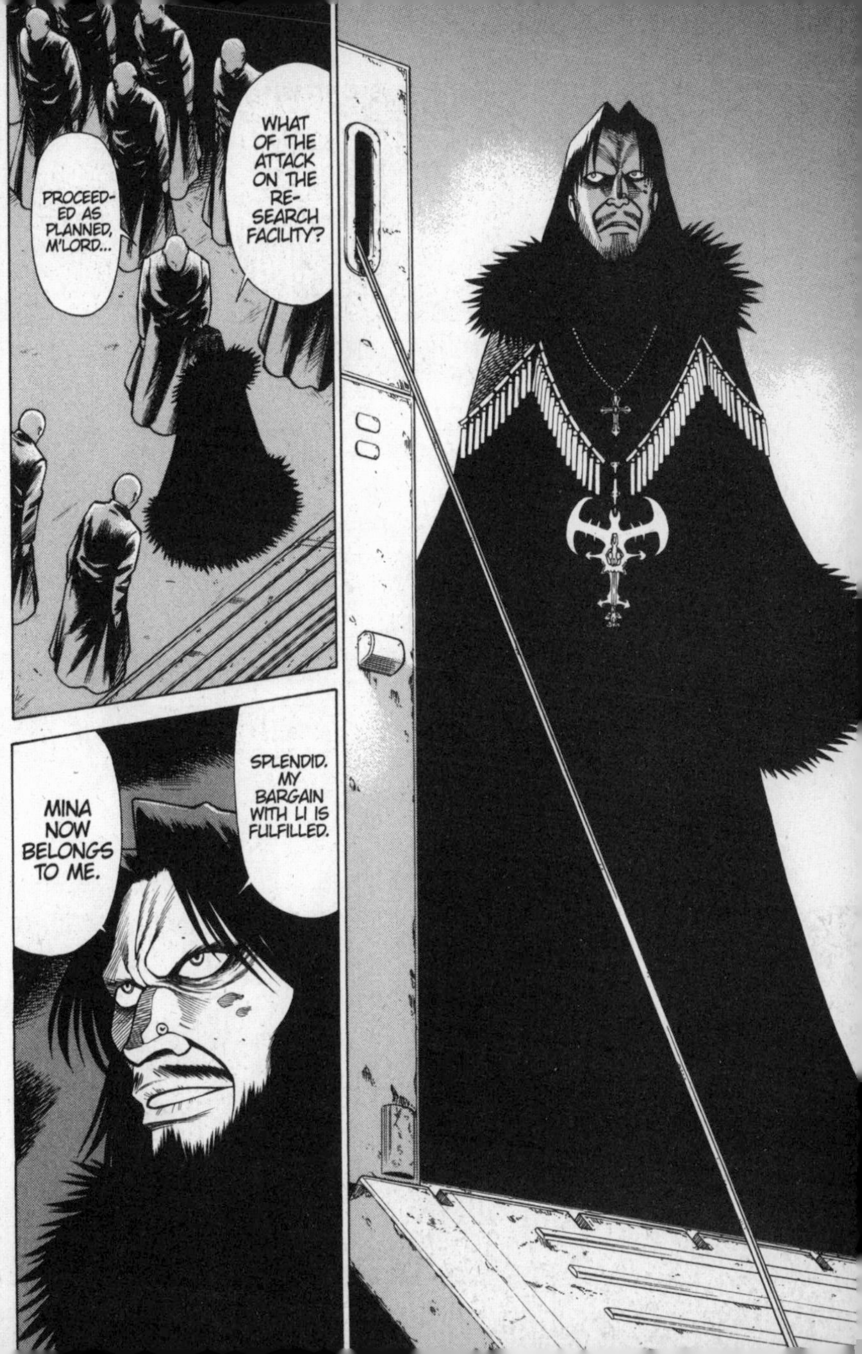
WHAT OF THE ATTACK ON THE RE-SEARCH FACILITY?
PROCEED-ED AS PLANNED, M'LORD...
SPLENDID. MY BARGAIN WITH LI IS FULFILLED.
MINA NOW BELONGS TO ME.

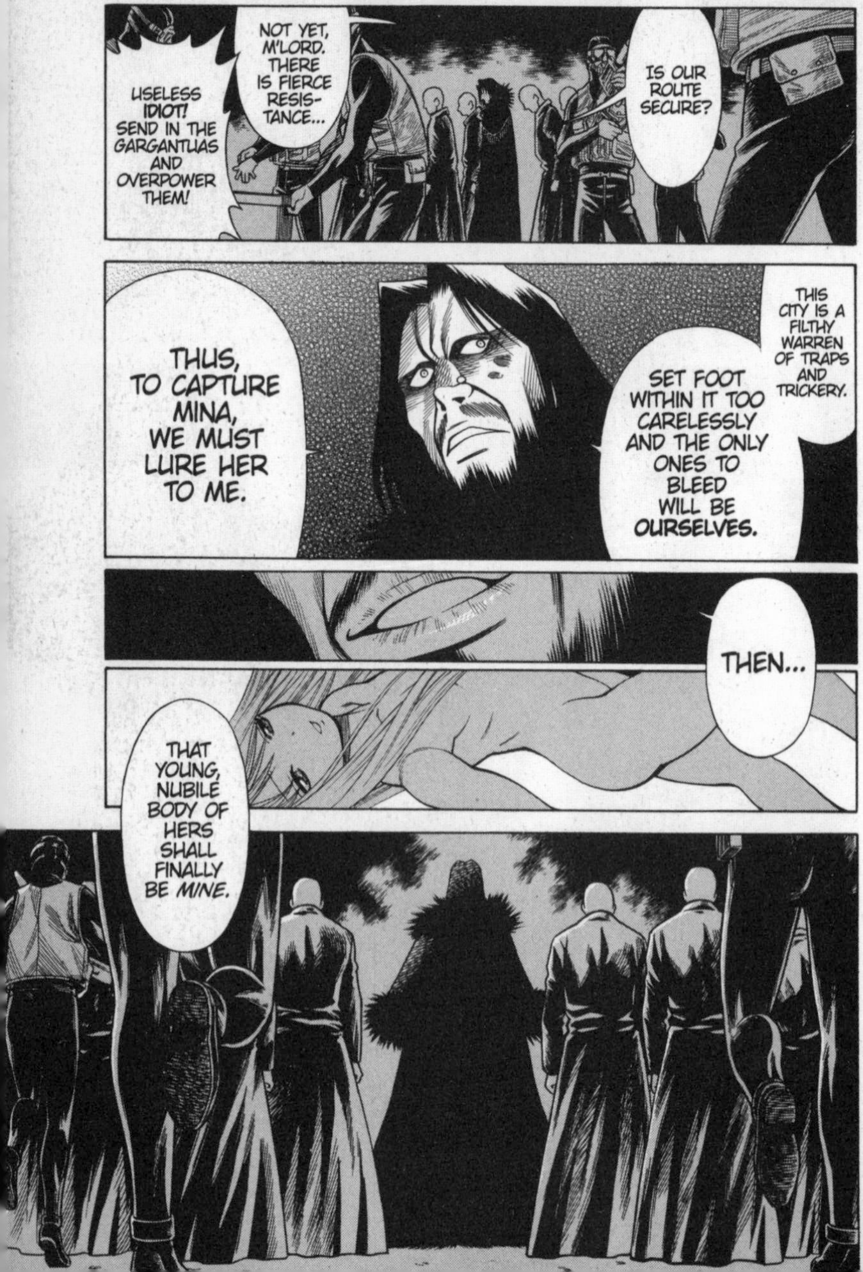
IS OUR ROUTE SECURE?
NOT YET, M'LORD. THERE IS FIERCE RESIS-TANCE...
USELESS IDIOT! SEND IN THE GARGANTUAS AND OVERPOWER THEM!
THIS CITY IS A FILTHY WARREN OF TRAPS AND TRICKERY.
SET FOOT WITHIN IT TOO CARELESSLY AND THE ONLY ONES TO BLEED WILL BE **OURSELVES.**
THUS, TO CAPTURE MINA, WE MUST LURE HER TO ME.
THEN...
THAT YOUNG, NUBILE BODY OF HERS SHALL FINALLY BE *MINE.*

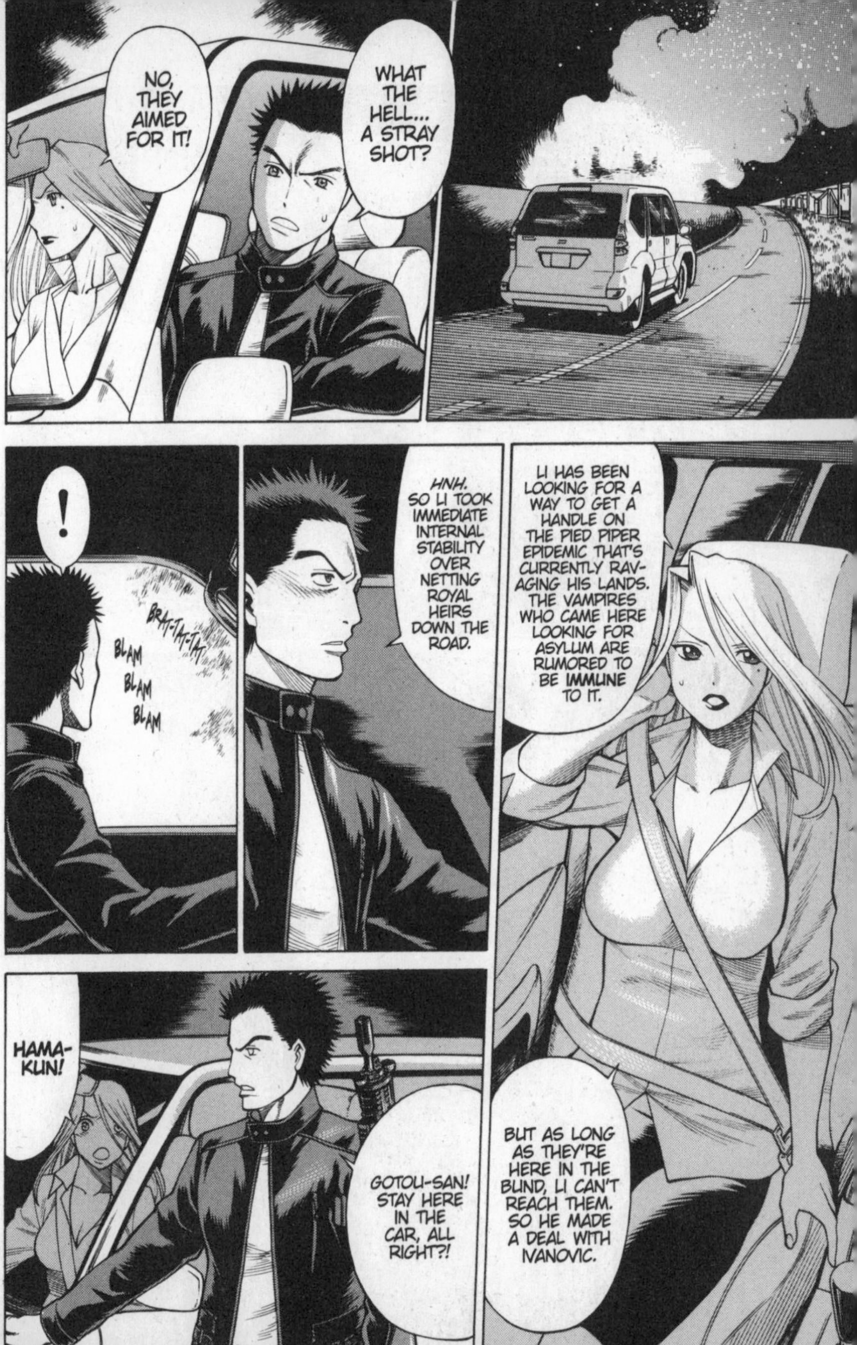
WHAT THE HELL... A STRAY SHOT?
NO, THEY AIMED FOR IT!
LI HAS BEEN LOOKING FOR A WAY TO GET A HANDLE ON THE PIED PIPER EPIDEMIC THAT'S CURRENTLY RAV-AGING HIS LANDS. THE VAMPIRES WHO CAME HERE LOOKING FOR ASYLUM ARE RUMORED TO BE IMMUNE TO IT.
BUT AS LONG AS THEY'RE HERE IN THE BUND, LI CAN'T REACH THEM. SO HE MADE A DEAL WITH IVANOVIC.
HNH. SO LI TOOK IMMEDIATE INTERNAL STABILITY OVER NETTING ROYAL HEIRS DOWN THE ROAD.
!
BRAT-TAT-TAT
BLAM
BLAM
BLAM
BLAM
GOTOU-SAN! STAY HERE IN THE CAR, ALL RIGHT?!
HAMA-KUN!

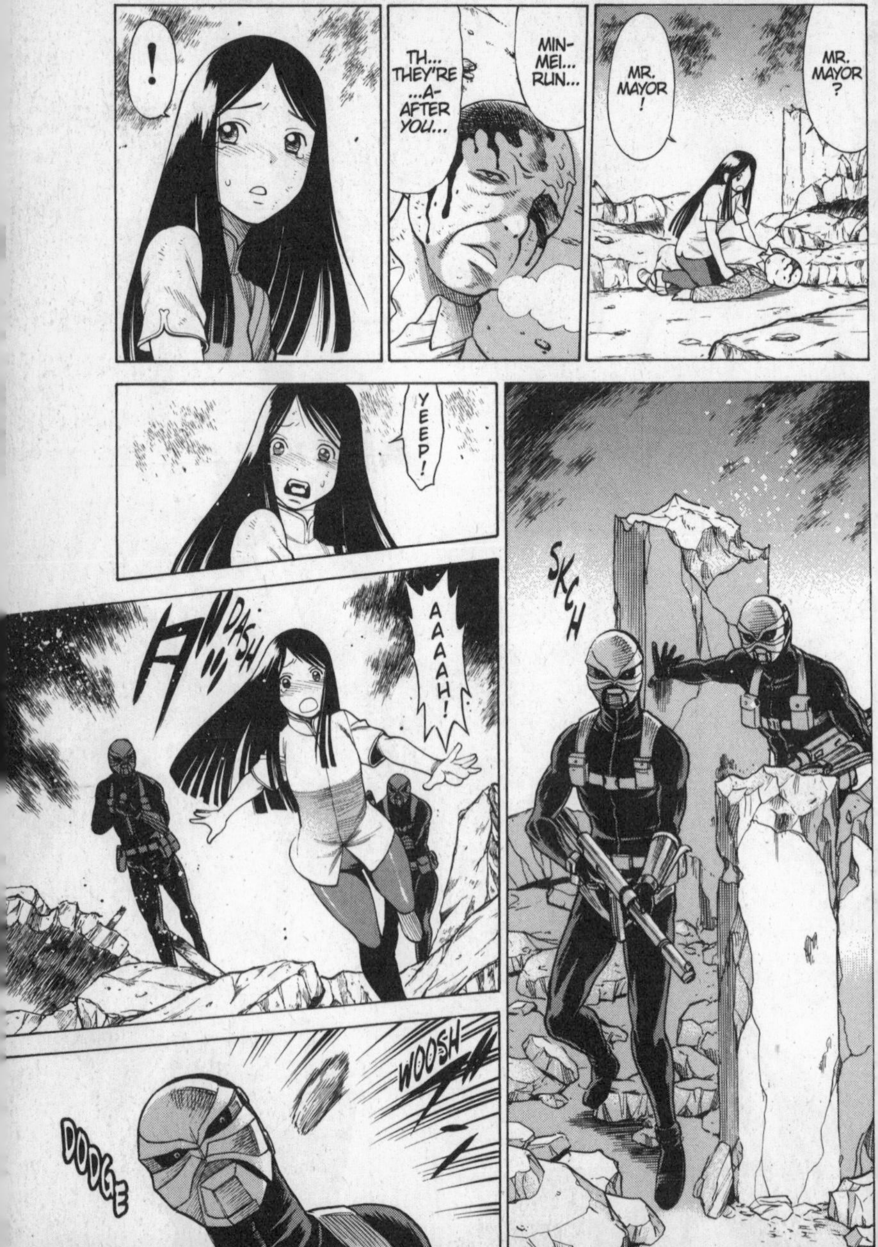
MR. MAYOR ?
MR. MAYOR !
MIN-MEI... RUN...
TH... THEY'RE ...A-AFTER YOU...
!
SKCH
YEEP!
AAAAH!
DASH
WOOSH
DODGE

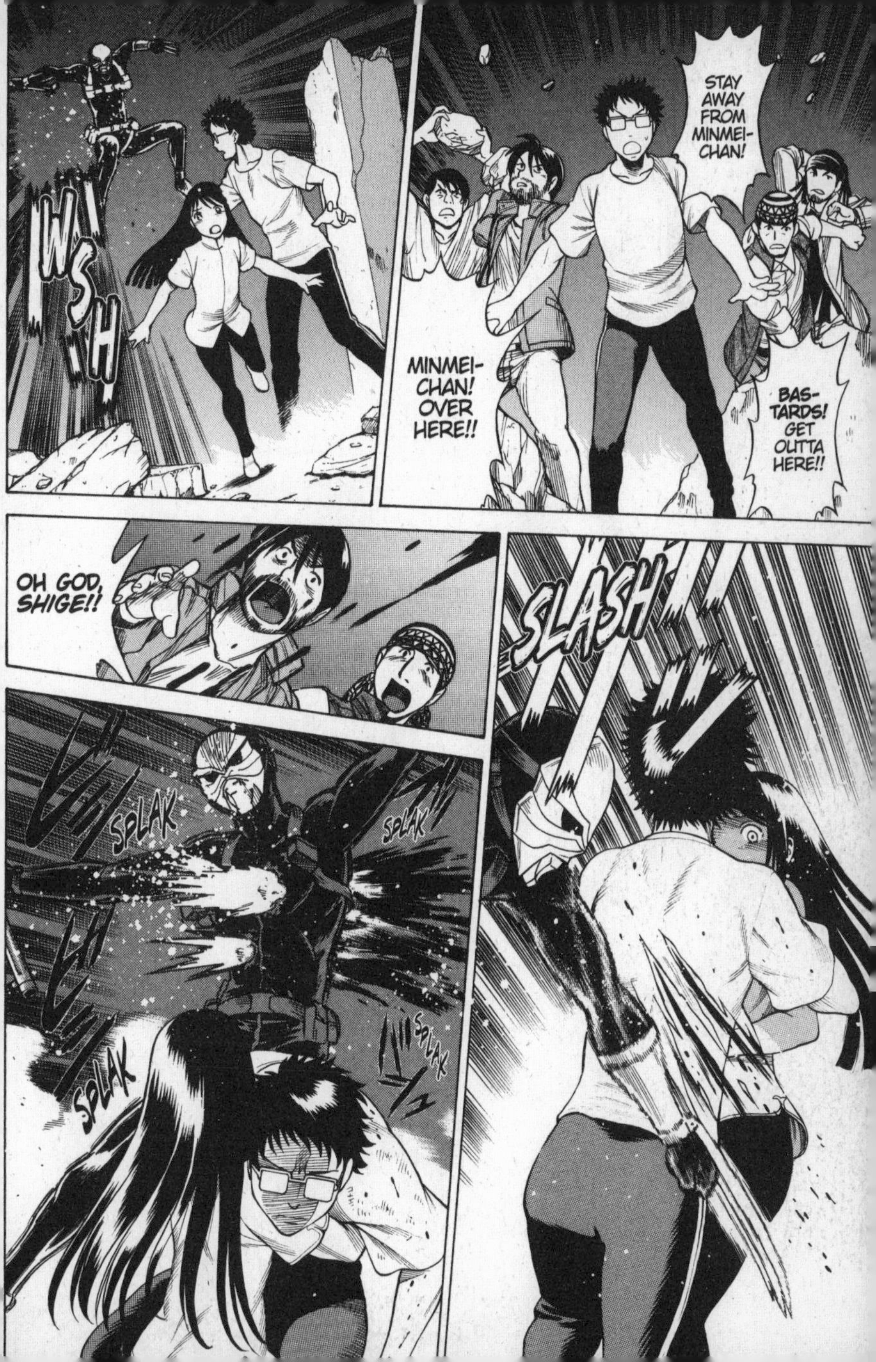
STAY AWAY FROM MINMEI-CHAN!
BAS-TARDS! GET OUTTA HERE!!
MINMEI-CHAN! OVER HERE!!
WSH
SLASH
OH GOD, SHIGE!!
SPLAK
SPLAK
SPLAK
SPLAK

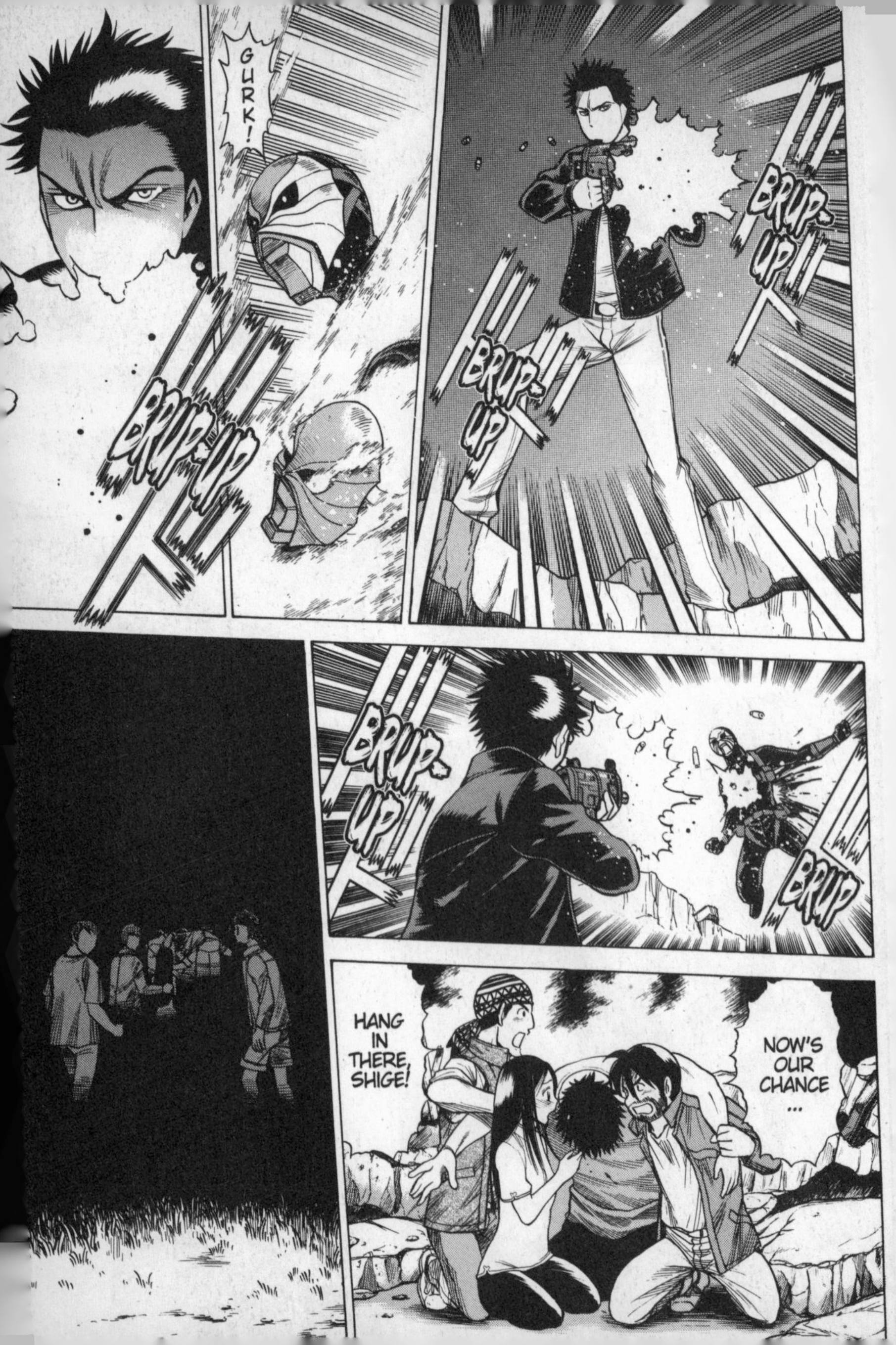
BRUP-UP
BRUP-UP
GURK!
BRUP-UP
BRUP-UP
BRUP
NOW'S OUR CHANCE ...
HANG IN THERE, SHIGE!

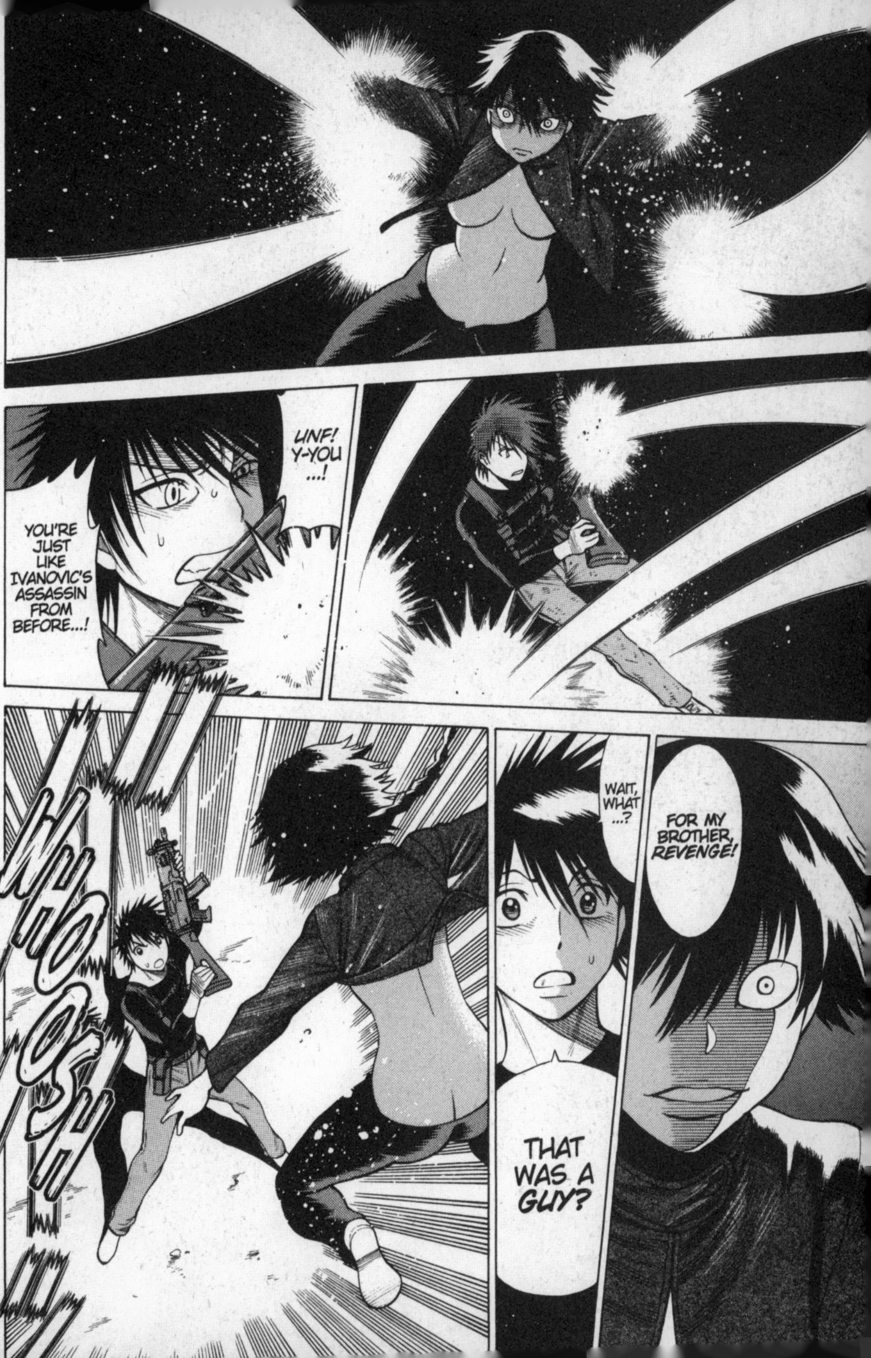
UNF! Y-YOU ...!
YOU'RE JUST LIKE IVANOVIC'S ASSASSIN FROM BEFORE...!
FOR MY BROTHER, REVENGE!
WAIT, WHAT ...?
THAT WAS A GUY?
WHOOOSH

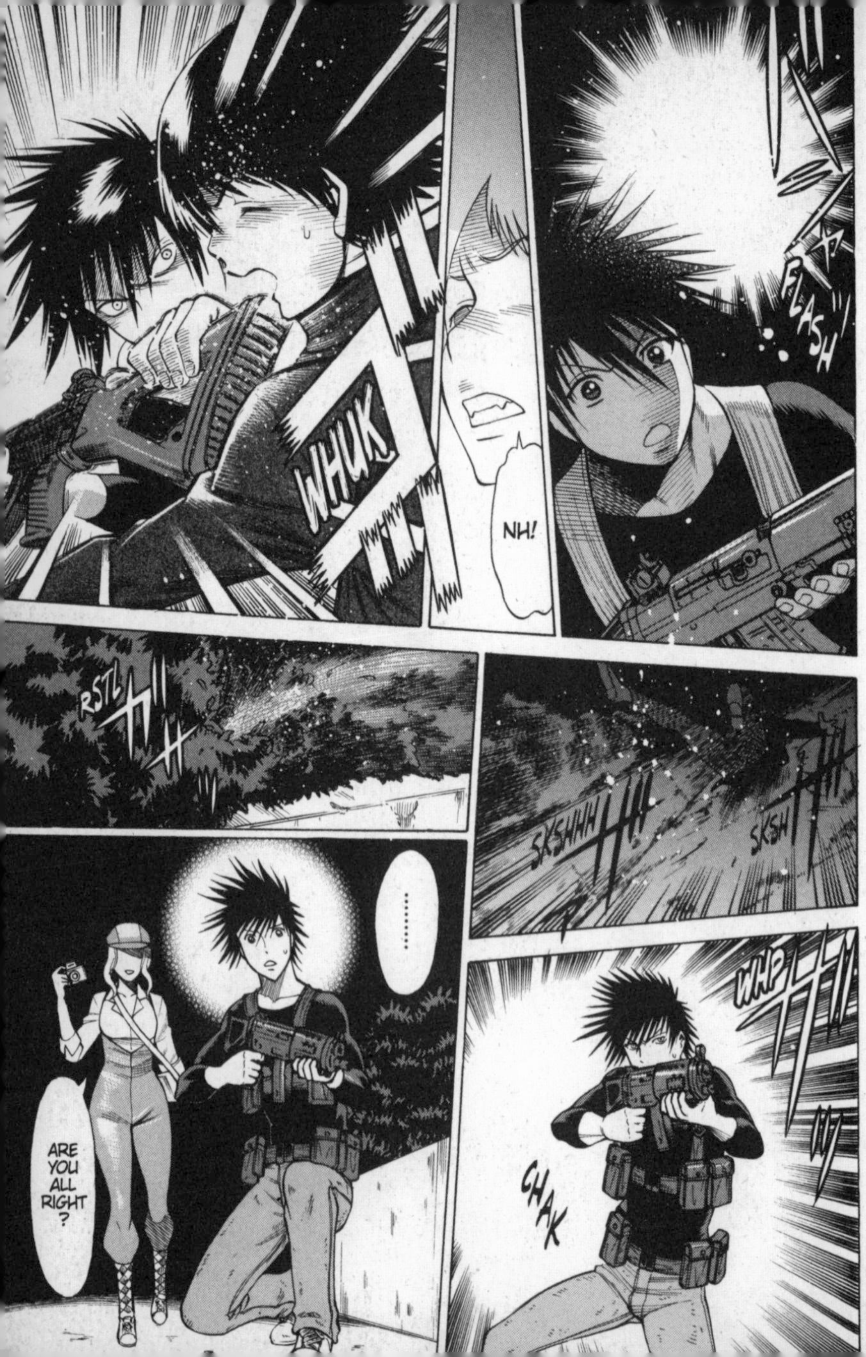
FLASH
NH!
WHUK
SKSH
SKSHHH
WHP
CHAK
RSTL
......
ARE YOU ALL RIGHT?

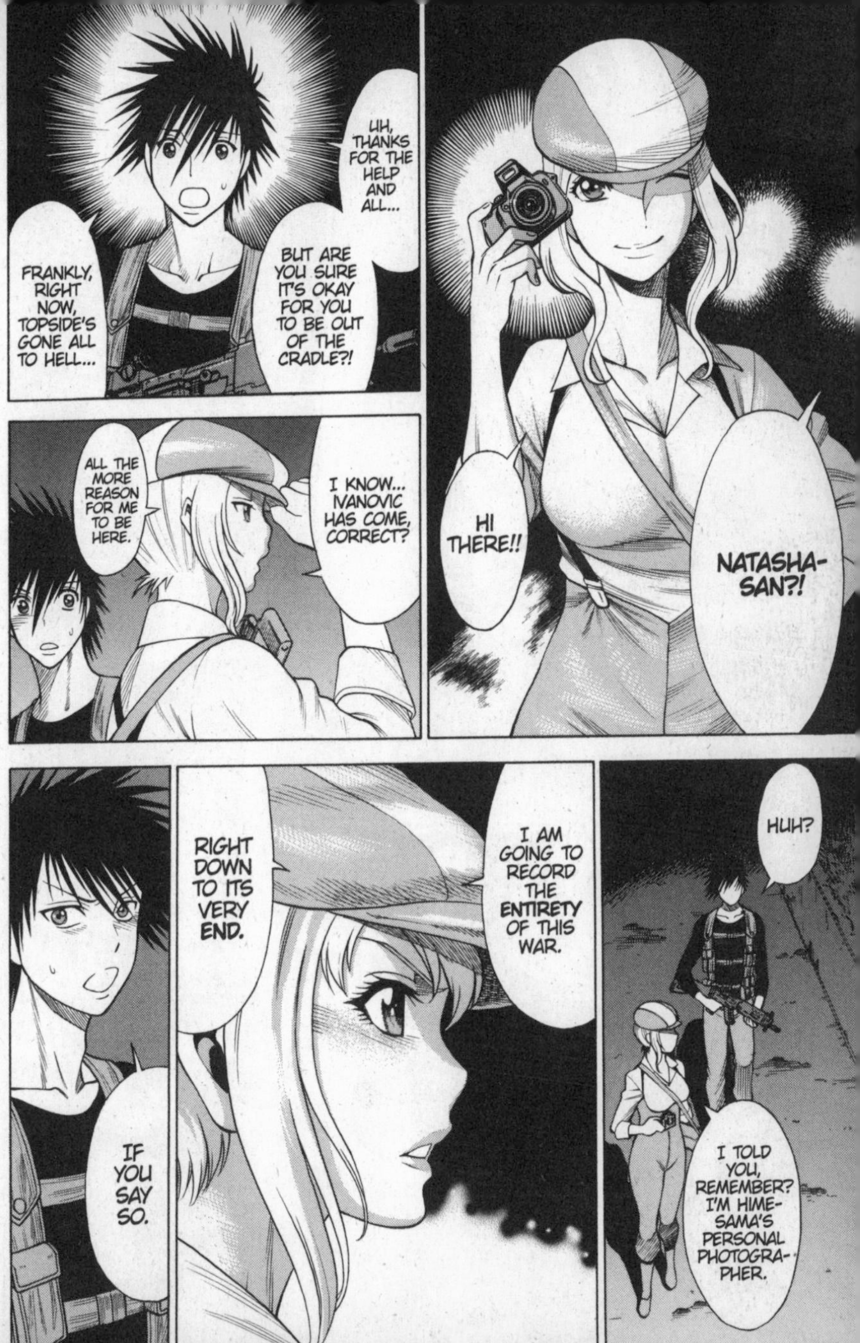
NATASHA-SAN?!
HI THERE!!
UH, THANKS FOR THE HELP AND ALL...
BUT ARE YOU SURE IT'S OKAY FOR YOU TO BE OUT OF THE CRADLE?!
FRANKLY, RIGHT NOW, TOPSIDE'S GONE ALL TO HELL...
I KNOW... IVANOVIC HAS COME, CORRECT?
ALL THE MORE REASON FOR ME TO BE HERE.
HUH?
I TOLD YOU, REMEMBER? I'M HIME-SAMA'S PERSONAL PHOTOGRA-PHER.
I AM GOING TO RECORD THE ENTIRETY OF THIS WAR.
RIGHT DOWN TO ITS VERY END.
IF YOU SAY SO.

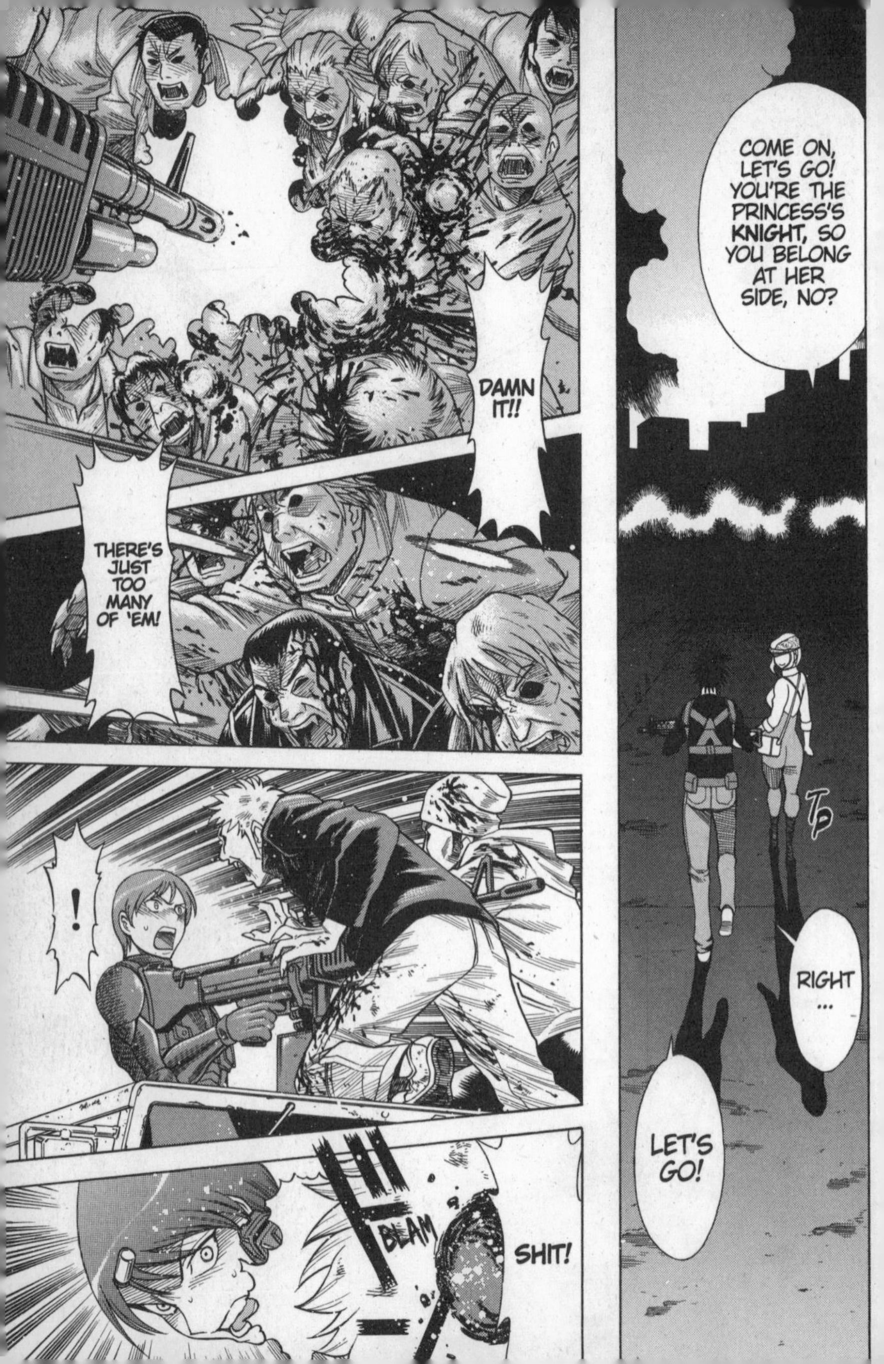
COME ON, LET'S GO! YOU'RE THE PRINCESS'S KNIGHT, SO YOU BELONG AT HER SIDE, NO?
RIGHT ...
LET'S GO!
DAMN IT!!
THERE'S JUST TOO MANY OF 'EM!
!
BLAM
SHIT!

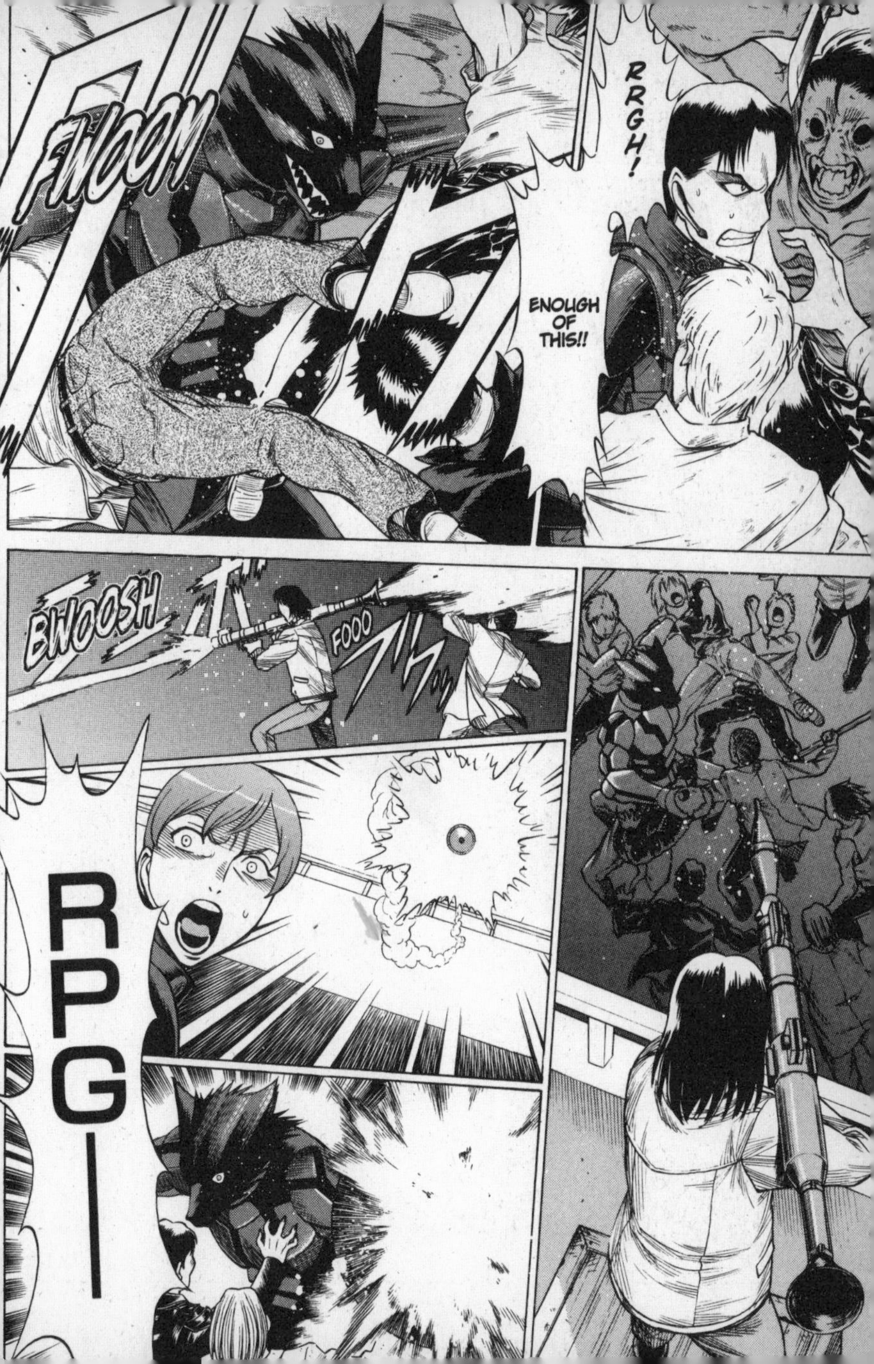
RRGH!
ENOUGH OF THIS!!
FWOOM
BWOOSH
FOOO
RPG—

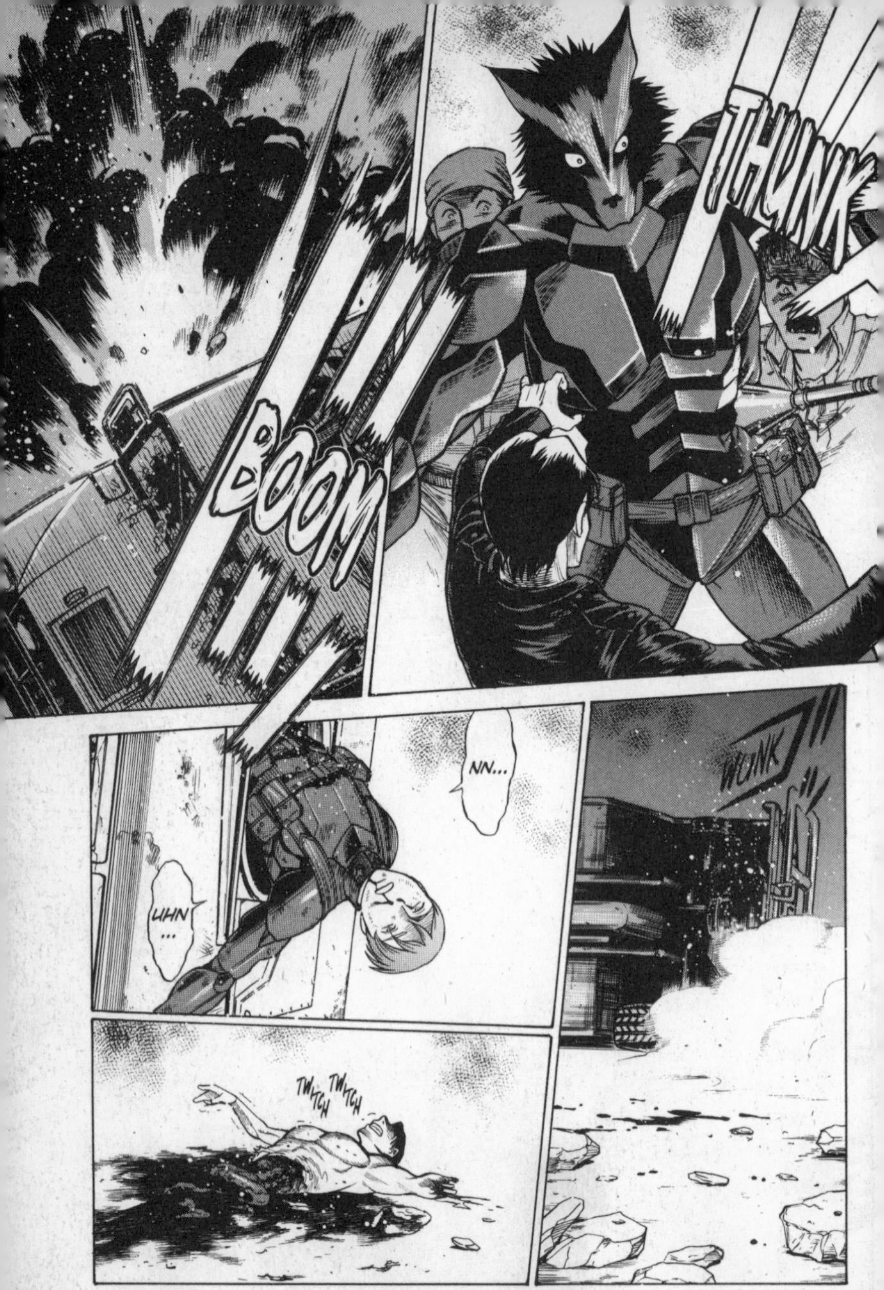
THUNK
BOOM
WUNK
NN...
UHN ...
TWITCH TWITCH

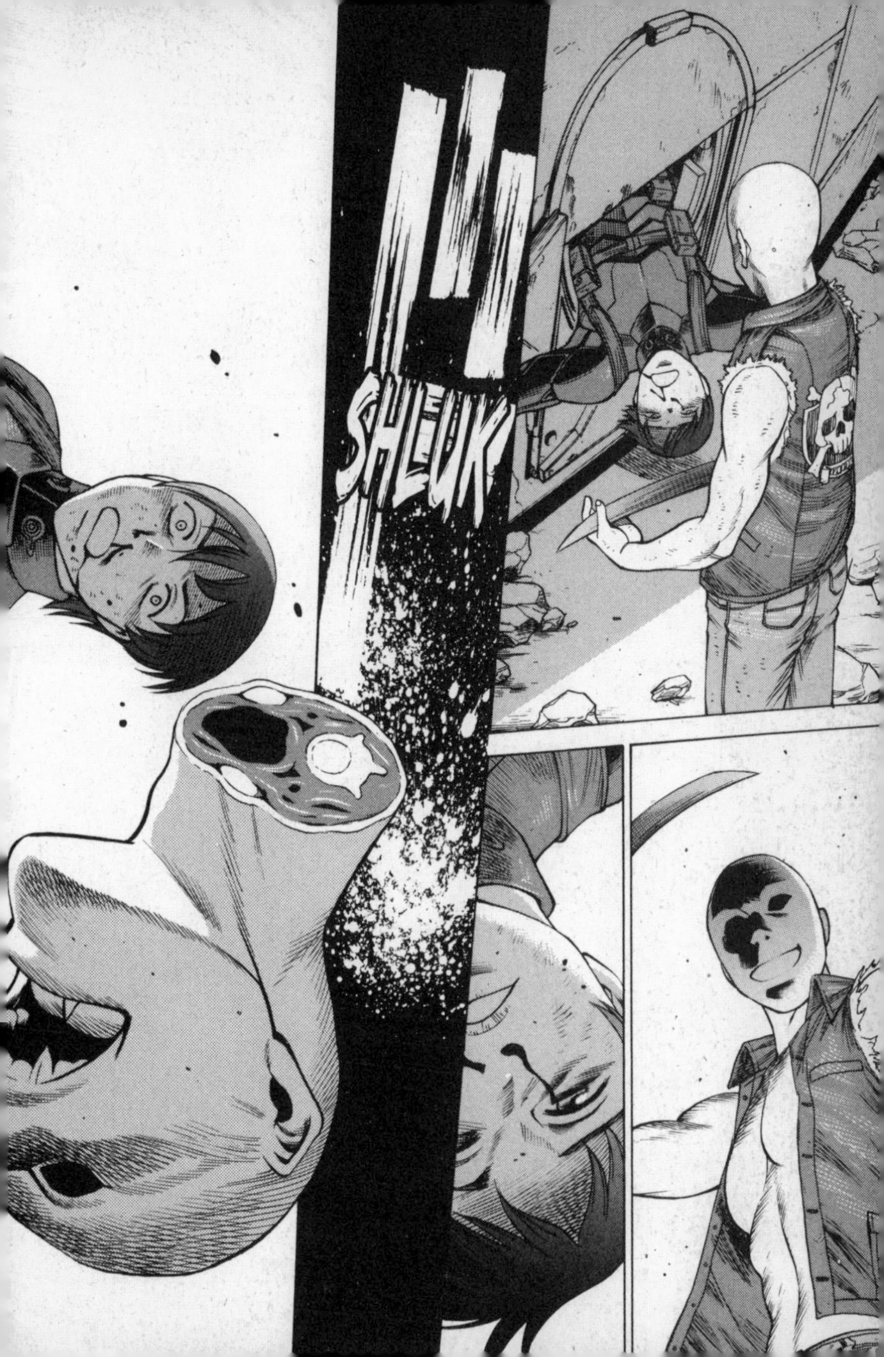
SHLUK!

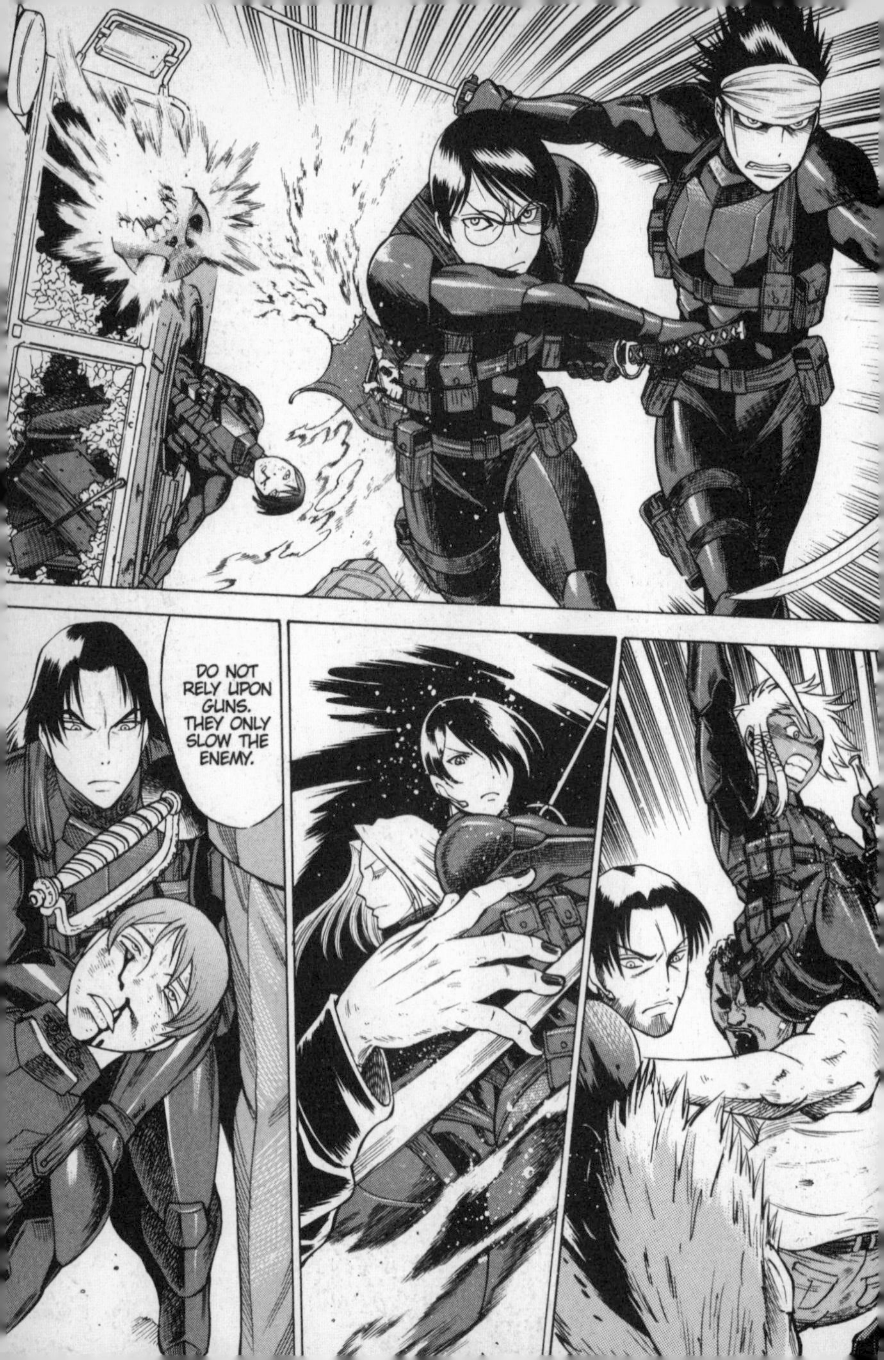
DO NOT RELY UPON GUNS. THEY ONLY SLOW THE ENEMY.

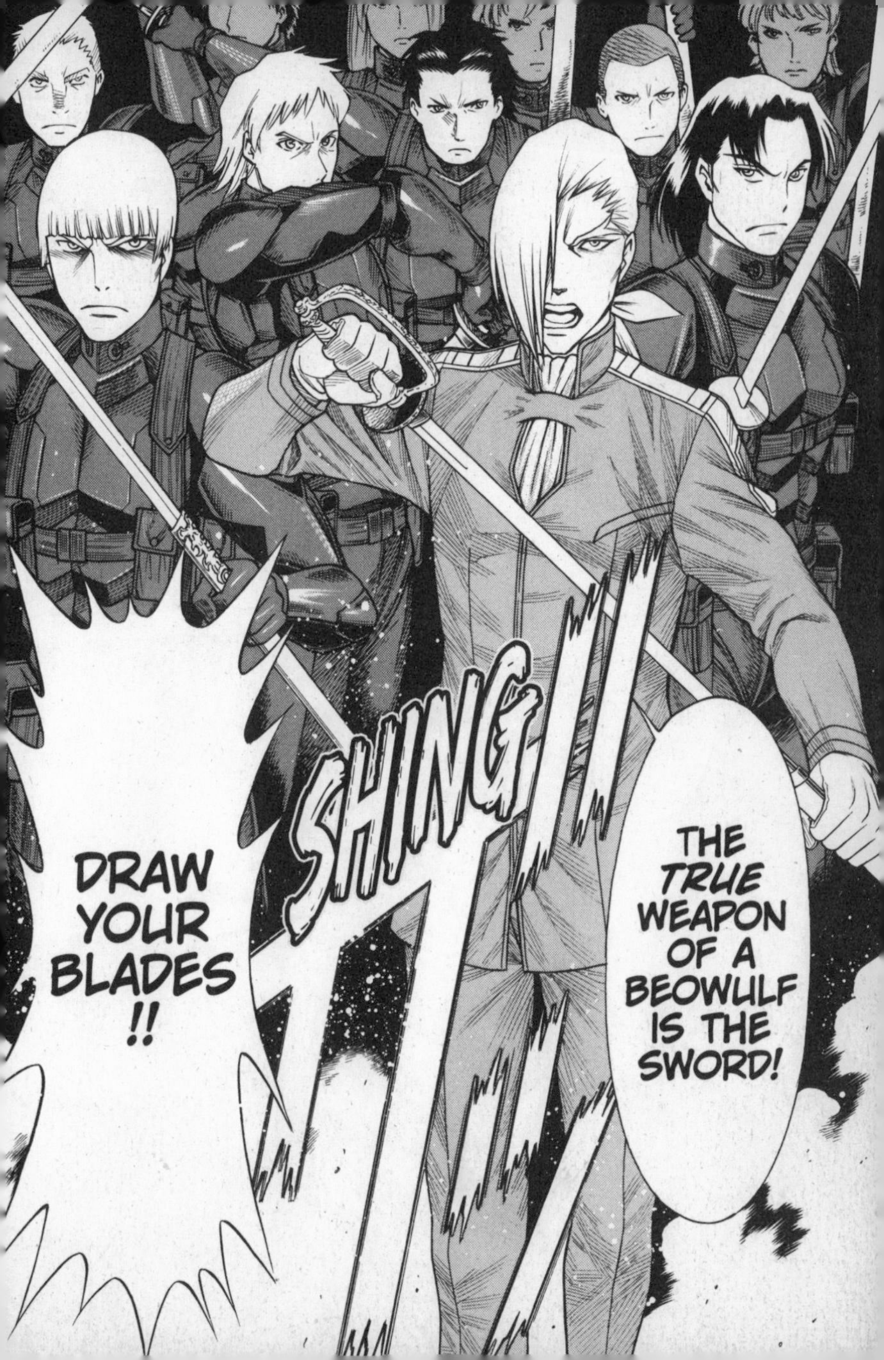
THE *TRUE* WEAPON OF A BEOWULF IS THE SWORD!
SHING
DRAW YOUR BLADES !!

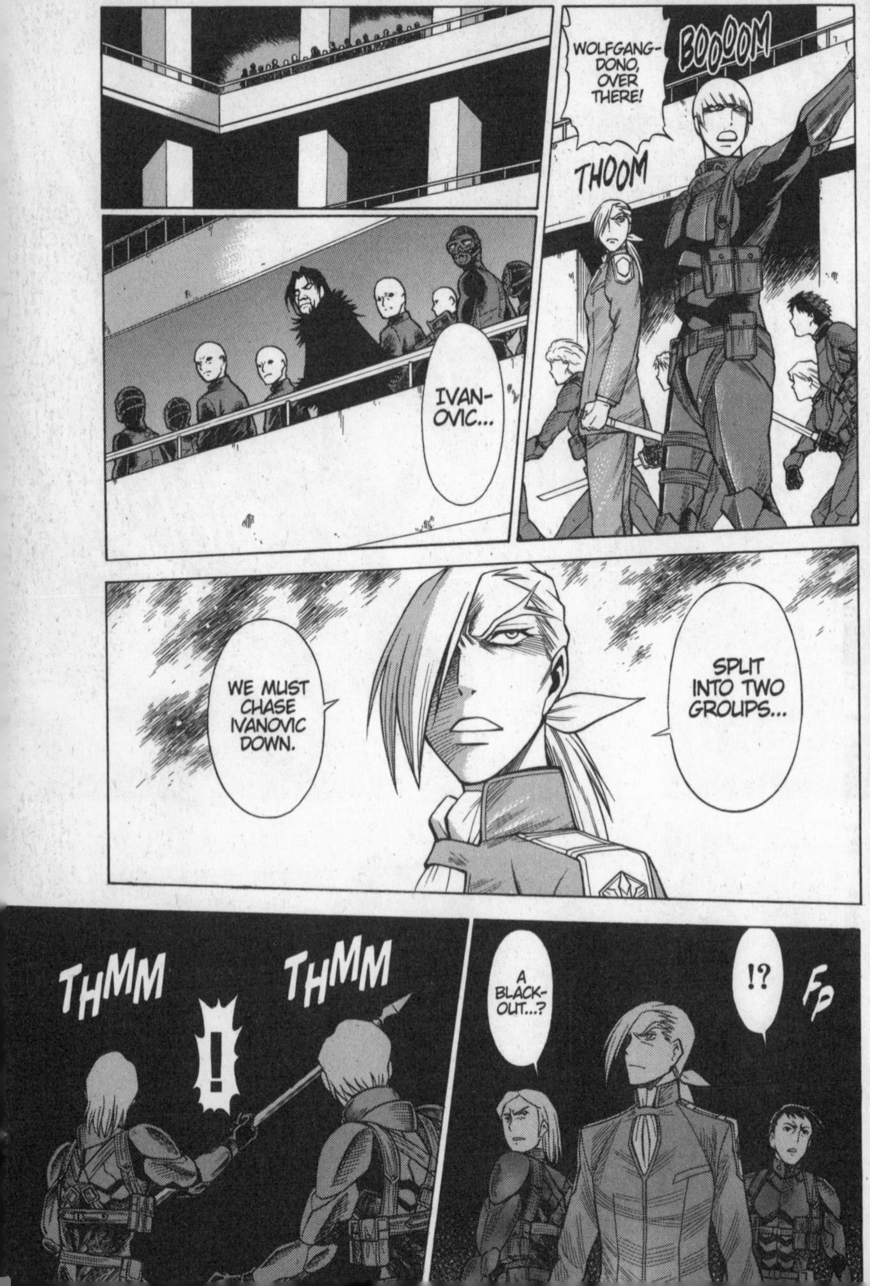
BOOOOM
WOLFGANG-DONO, OVER THERE!
THOOM
IVAN-OVIC...
SPLIT INTO TWO GROUPS...
WE MUST CHASE IVANOVIC DOWN.
Fp
!?
A BLACK-OUT...?
THMM
!
THMM

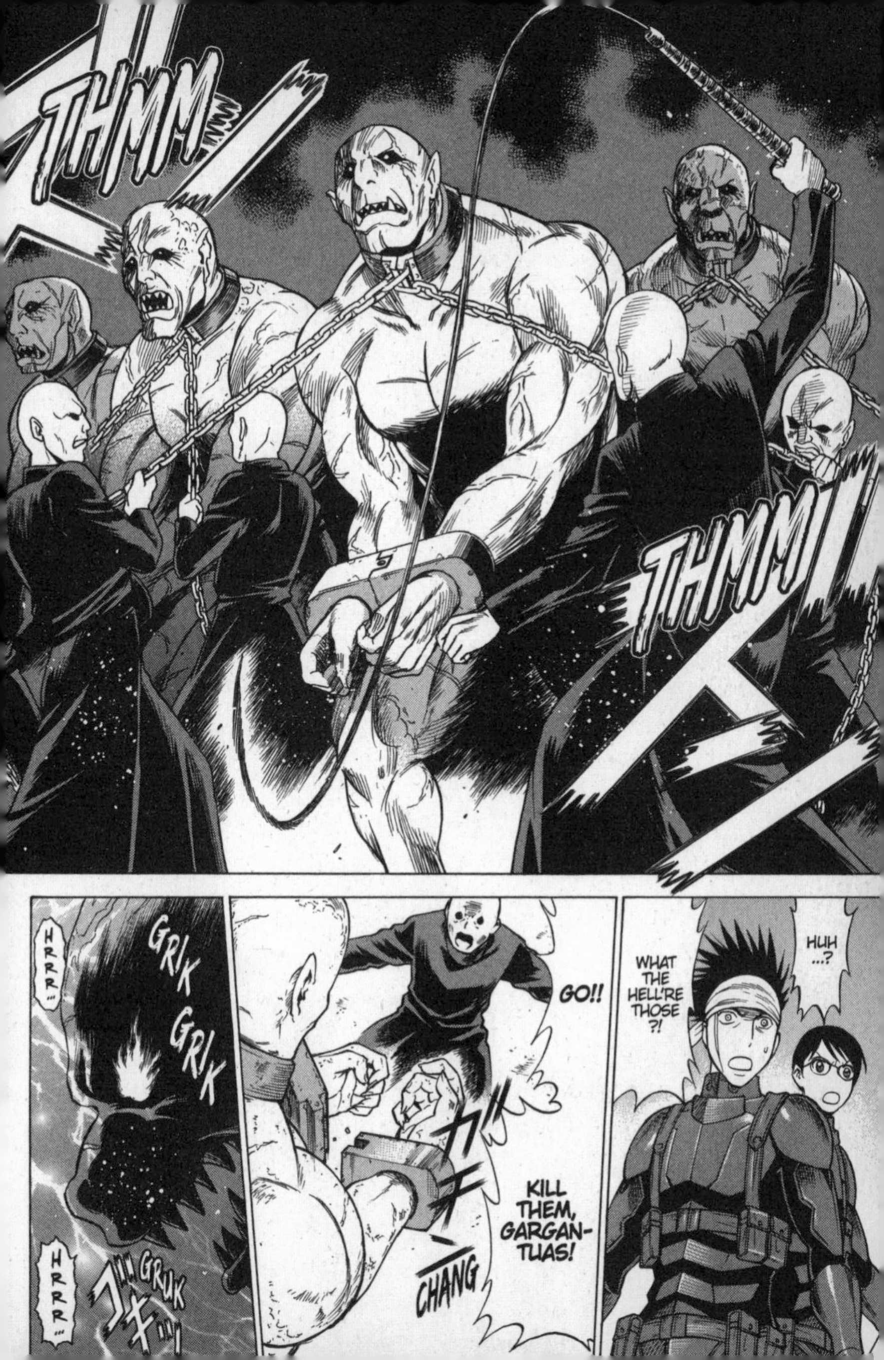
THMM
THMM
HUH ...?
WHAT THE HELL'RE THOSE ?!
GO!!
KILL THEM, GARGANTUAS!
CHANG
HRRR...
GRIK GRIK
HRRR...
GRUK

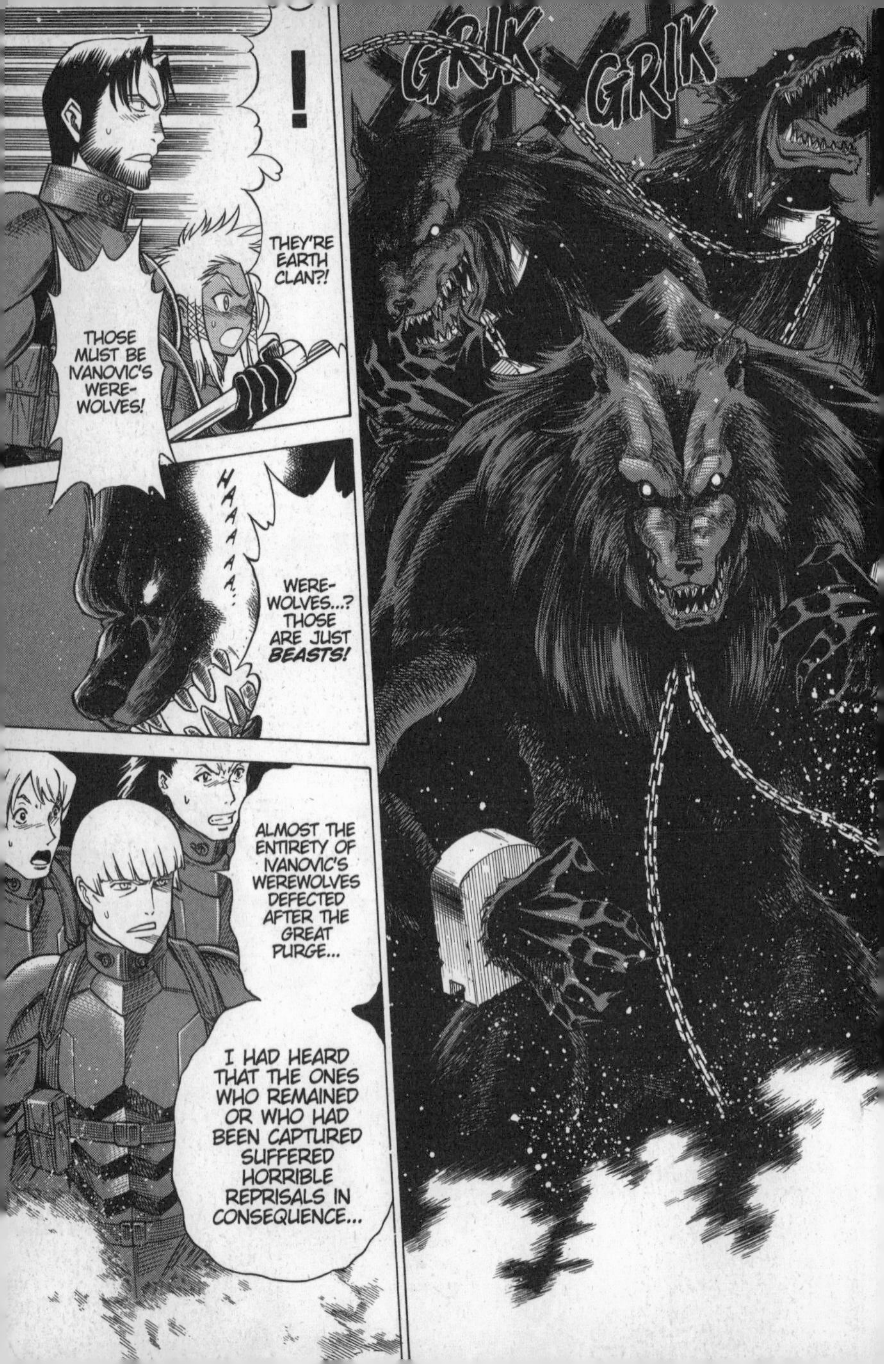
GRIK GRIK
!
THEY'RE EARTH CLAN?!
THOSE MUST BE IVANOVIC'S WERE-WOLVES!
HAAAAA...
WERE-WOLVES...? THOSE ARE JUST *BEASTS!*
ALMOST THE ENTIRETY OF IVANOVIC'S WEREWOLVES DEFECTED AFTER THE GREAT PURGE...
I HAD HEARD THAT THE ONES WHO REMAINED OR WHO HAD BEEN CAPTURED SUFFERED HORRIBLE REPRISALS IN CONSEQUENCE...

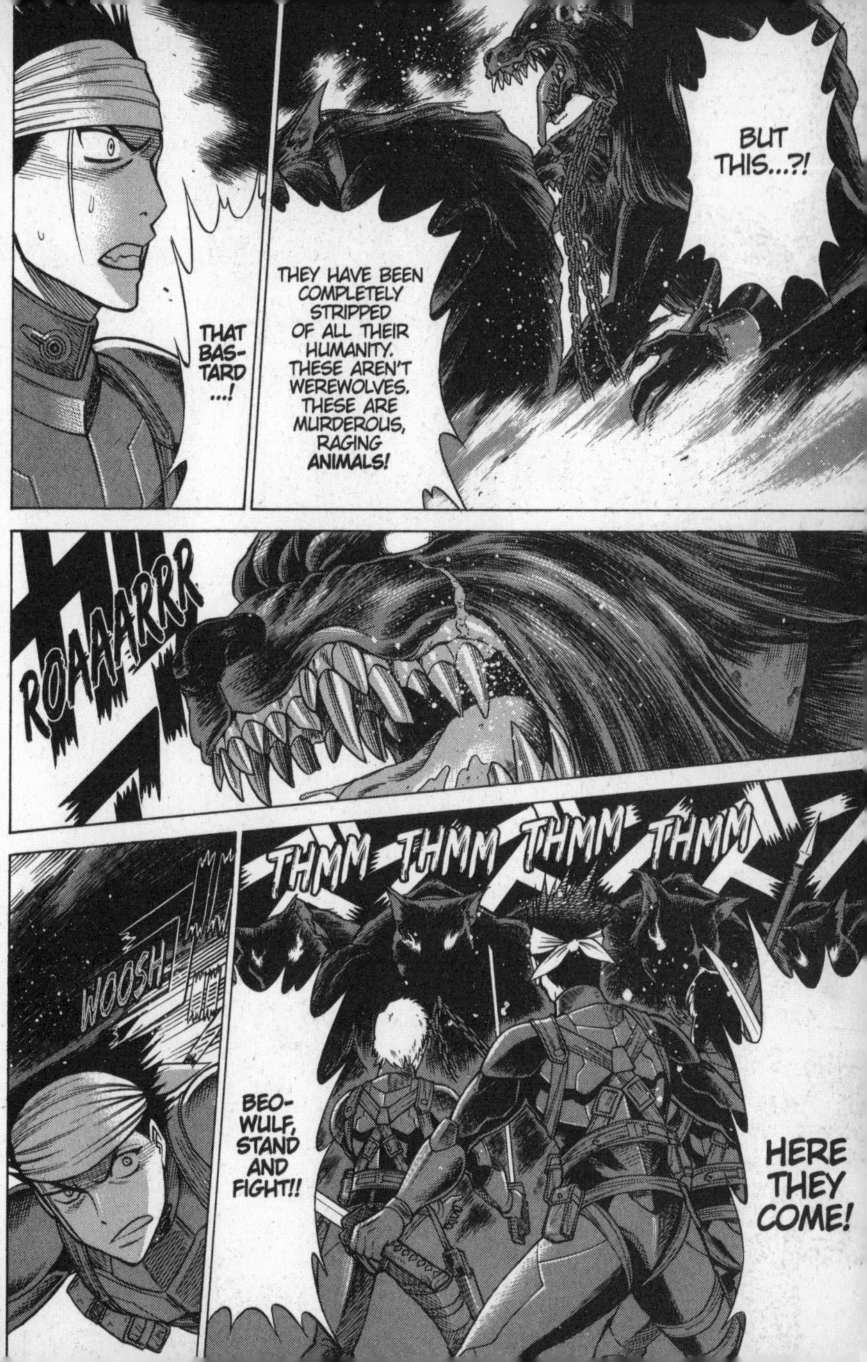
BUT THIS...?!
THEY HAVE BEEN COMPLETELY STRIPPED OF ALL THEIR HUMANITY. THESE AREN'T WEREWOLVES. THESE ARE MURDEROUS, RAGING ANIMALS!
THAT BAS-TARD ...!
ROAAARRR
THMM THMM THMM THMM
HERE THEY COME!
BEO-WULF, STAND AND FIGHT!!
WOOSH

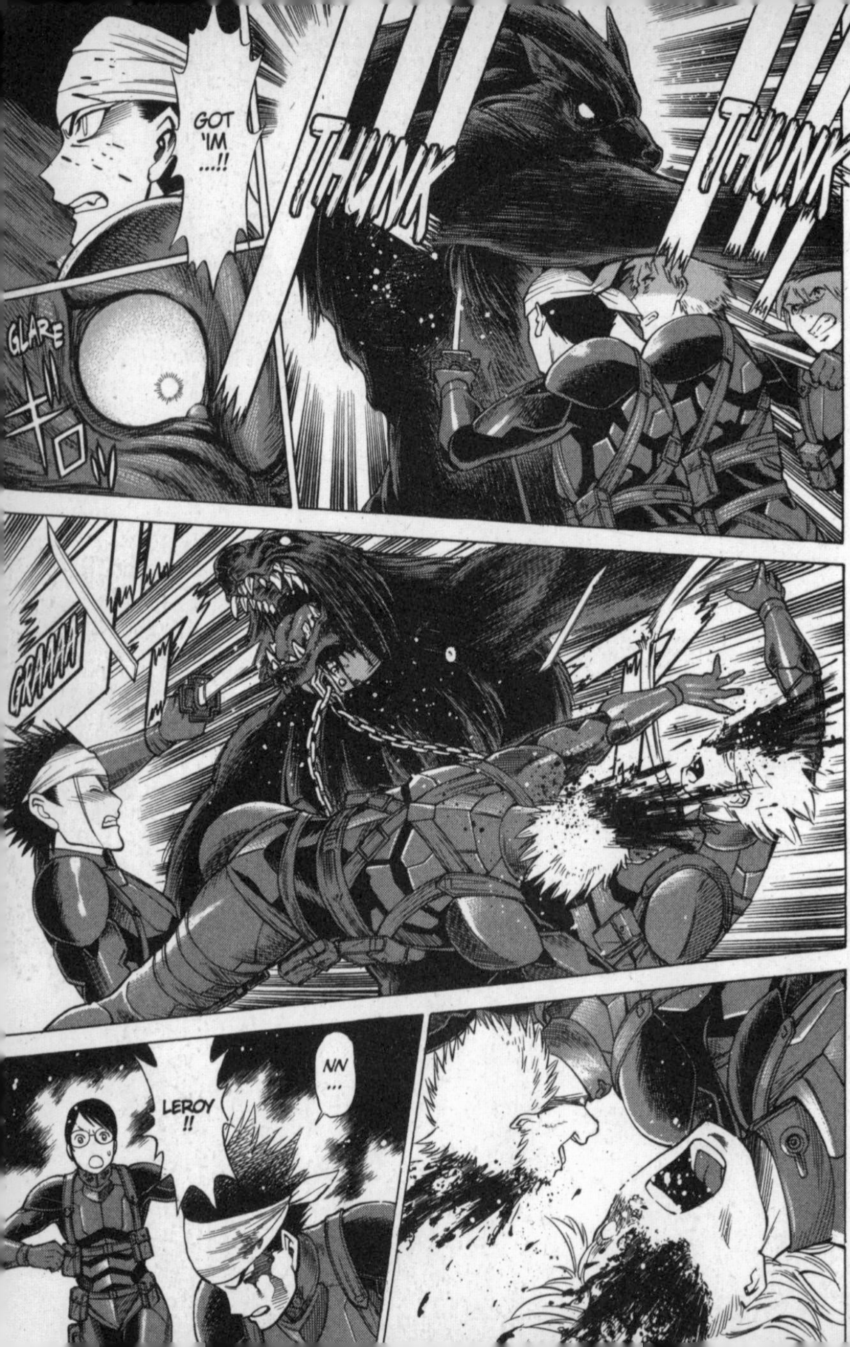
THUNK
THUNK
GOT 'IM ...!!
GLARE
GRAAAH
NN ...
LEROY !!

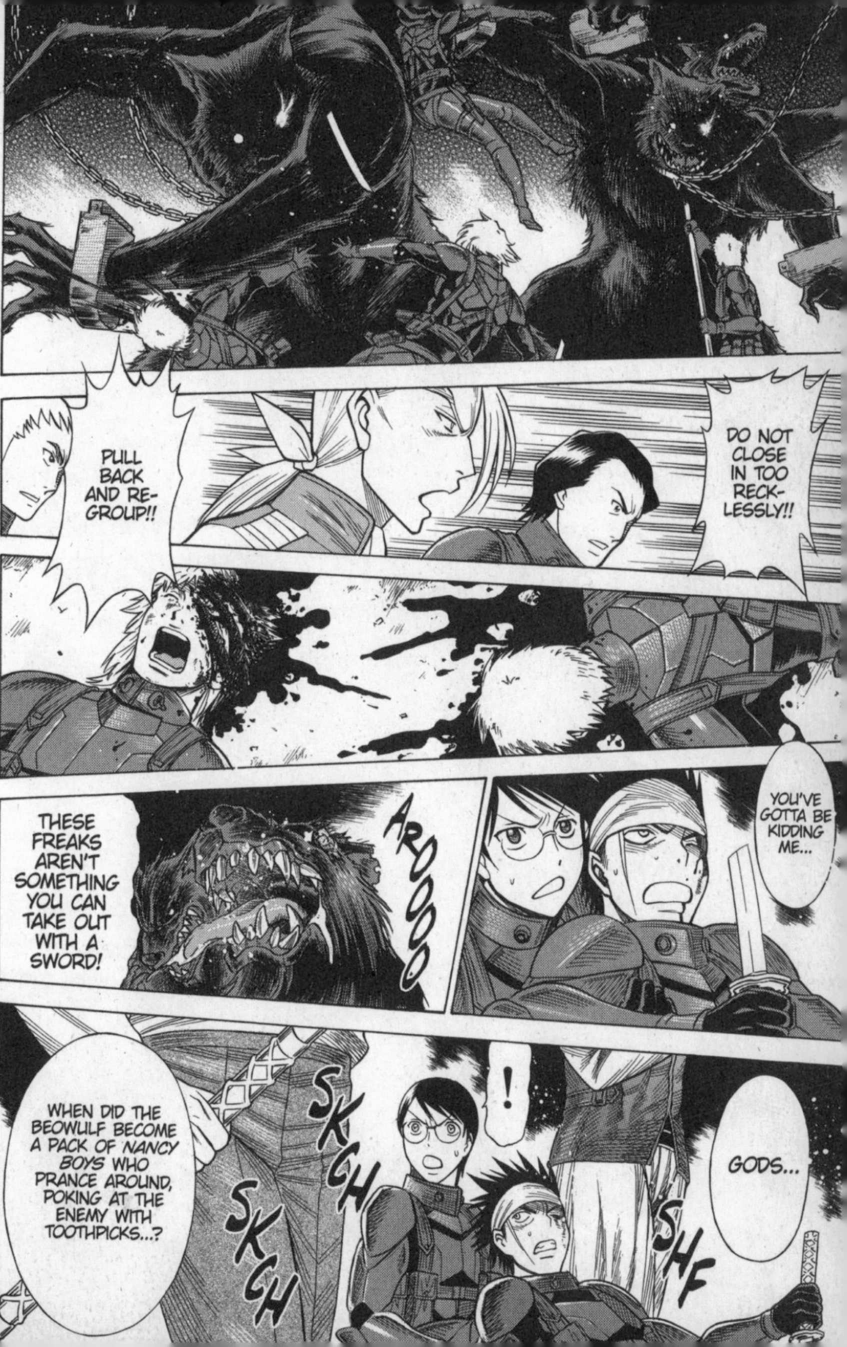
DO NOT CLOSE IN TOO RECK-LESSLY!!
PULL BACK AND RE-GROUP!!
YOU'VE GOTTA BE KIDDING ME...
AROOOOO
THESE FREAKS AREN'T SOMETHING YOU CAN TAKE OUT WITH A SWORD!
GODS...
!
SKCH
WHEN DID THE BEOWULF BECOME A PACK OF *NANCY BOYS* WHO PRANCE AROUND, POKING AT THE ENEMY WITH TOOTHPICKS...?
SHF
SKCH

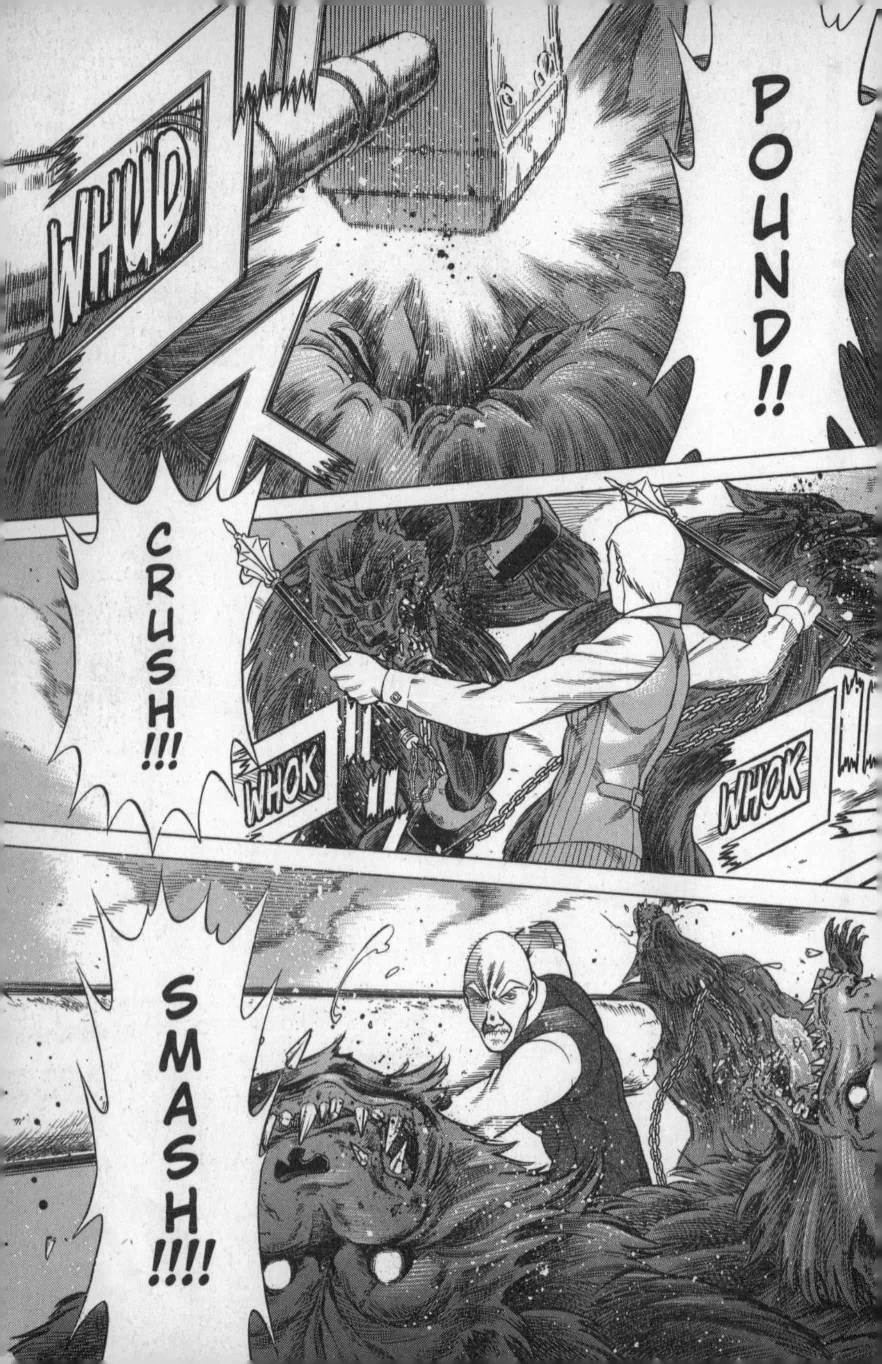
POUND!!
WHUD
WHOK
CRUSH!!!
WHOK
SMASH!!!!

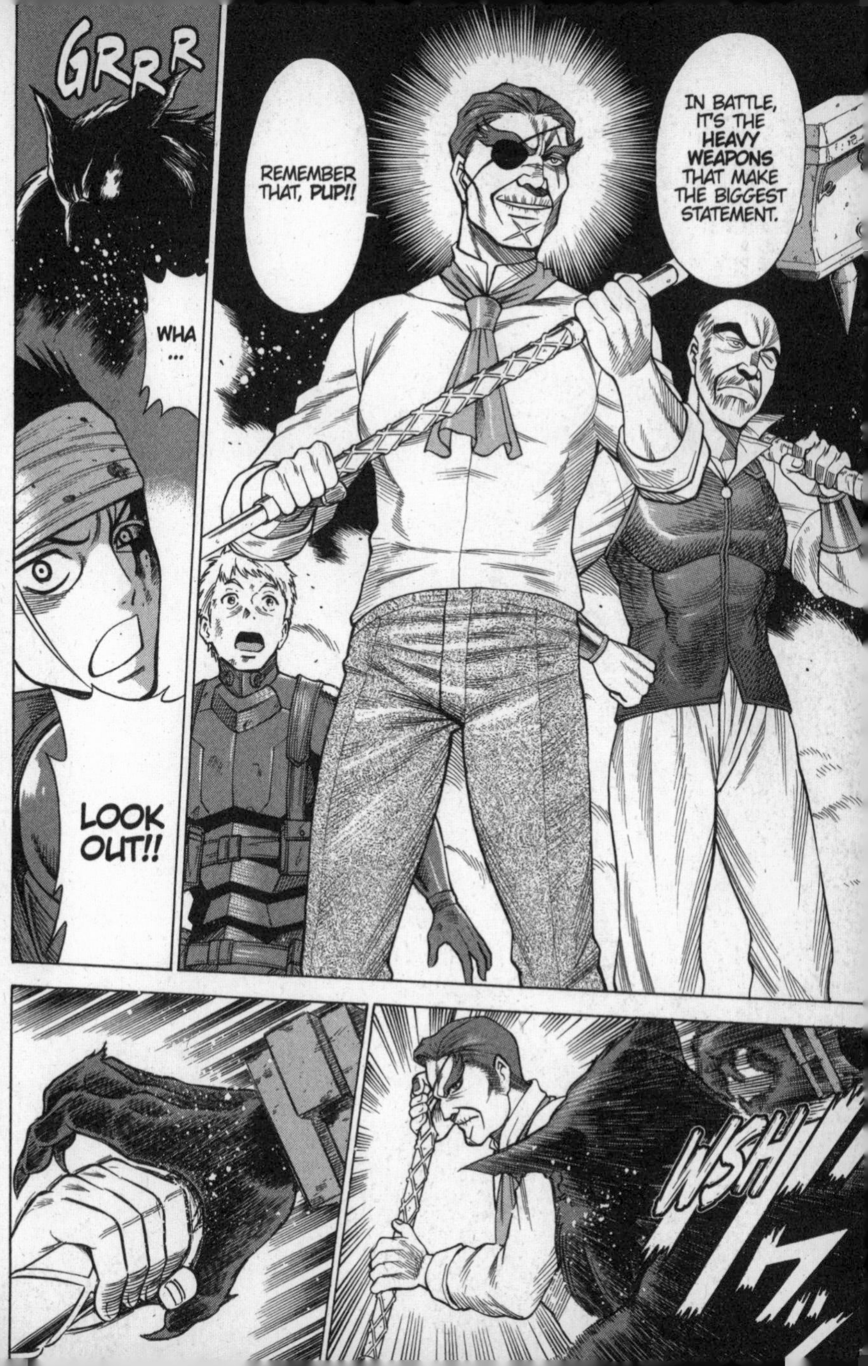
IN BATTLE, IT'S THE HEAVY WEAPONS THAT MAKE THE BIGGEST STATEMENT.
REMEMBER THAT, PUP!!
GRRR
WHA ...
LOOK OUT!!
WSH

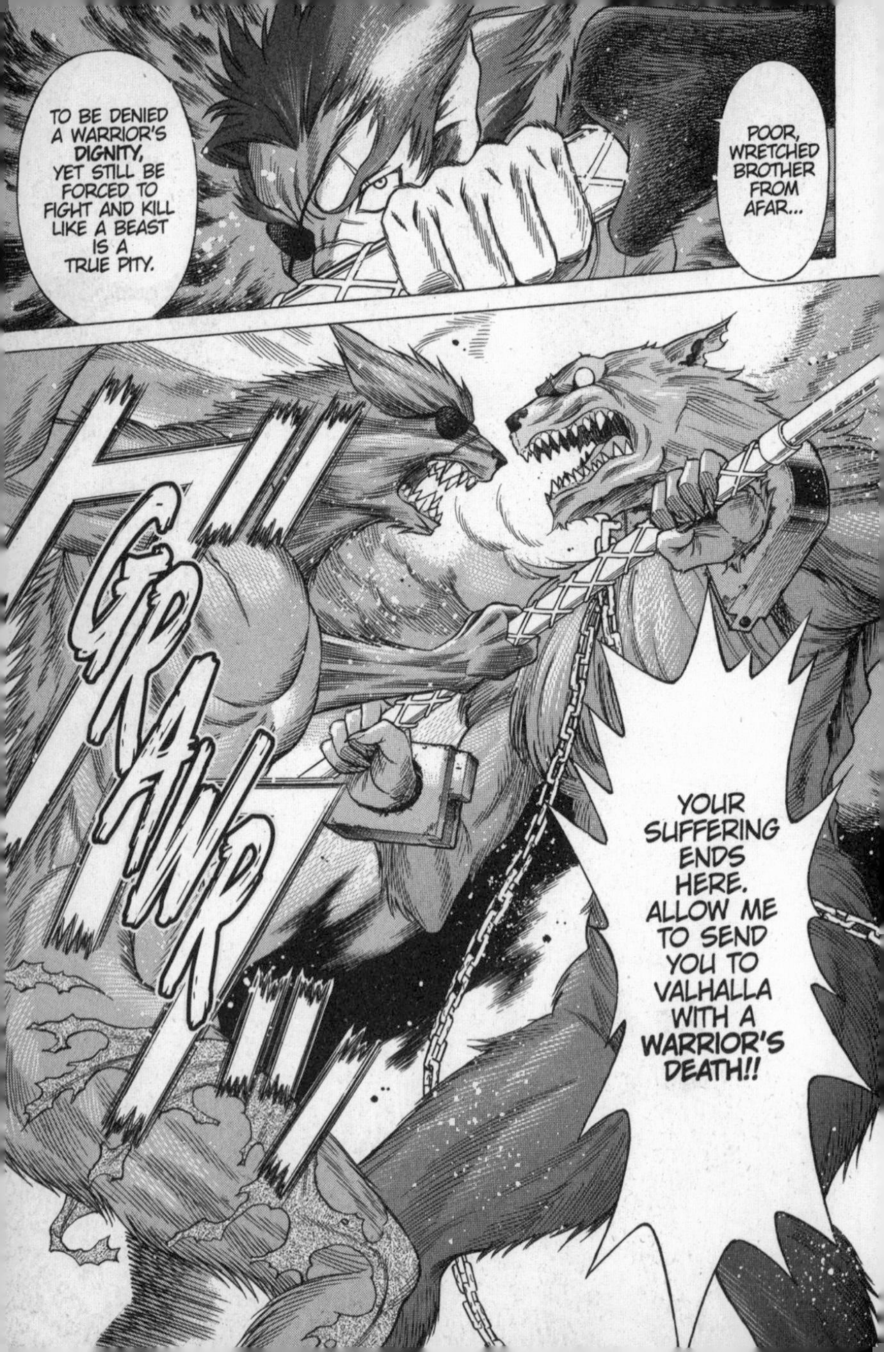
POOR, WRETCHED BROTHER FROM AFAR...
TO BE DENIED A WARRIOR'S DIGNITY, YET STILL BE FORCED TO FIGHT AND KILL LIKE A BEAST IS A TRUE PITY.
YOUR SUFFERING ENDS HERE. ALLOW ME TO SEND YOU TO VALHALLA WITH A WARRIOR'S DEATH!!

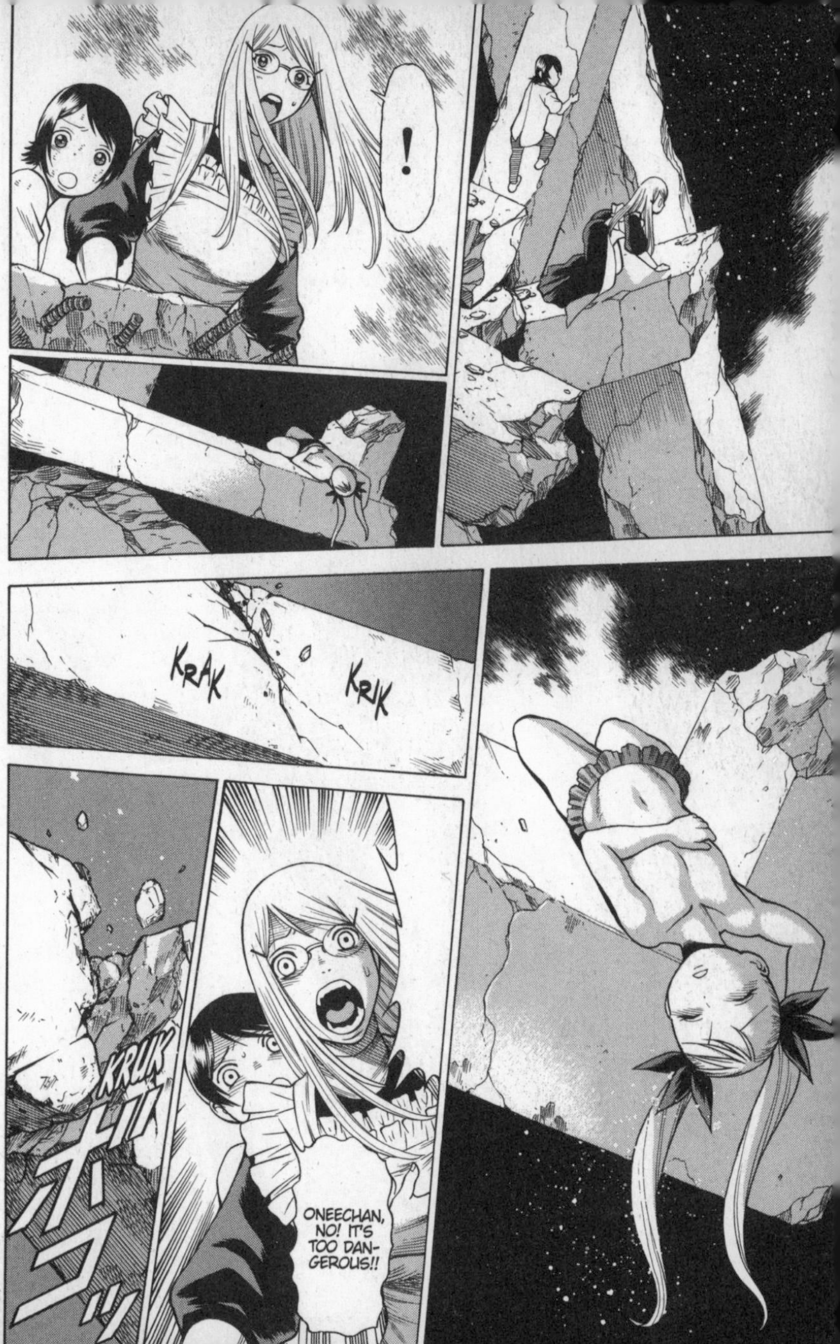
!
KRAK
KRIK
ONEECHAN, NO! IT'S TOO DANGEROUS!!
KRUK

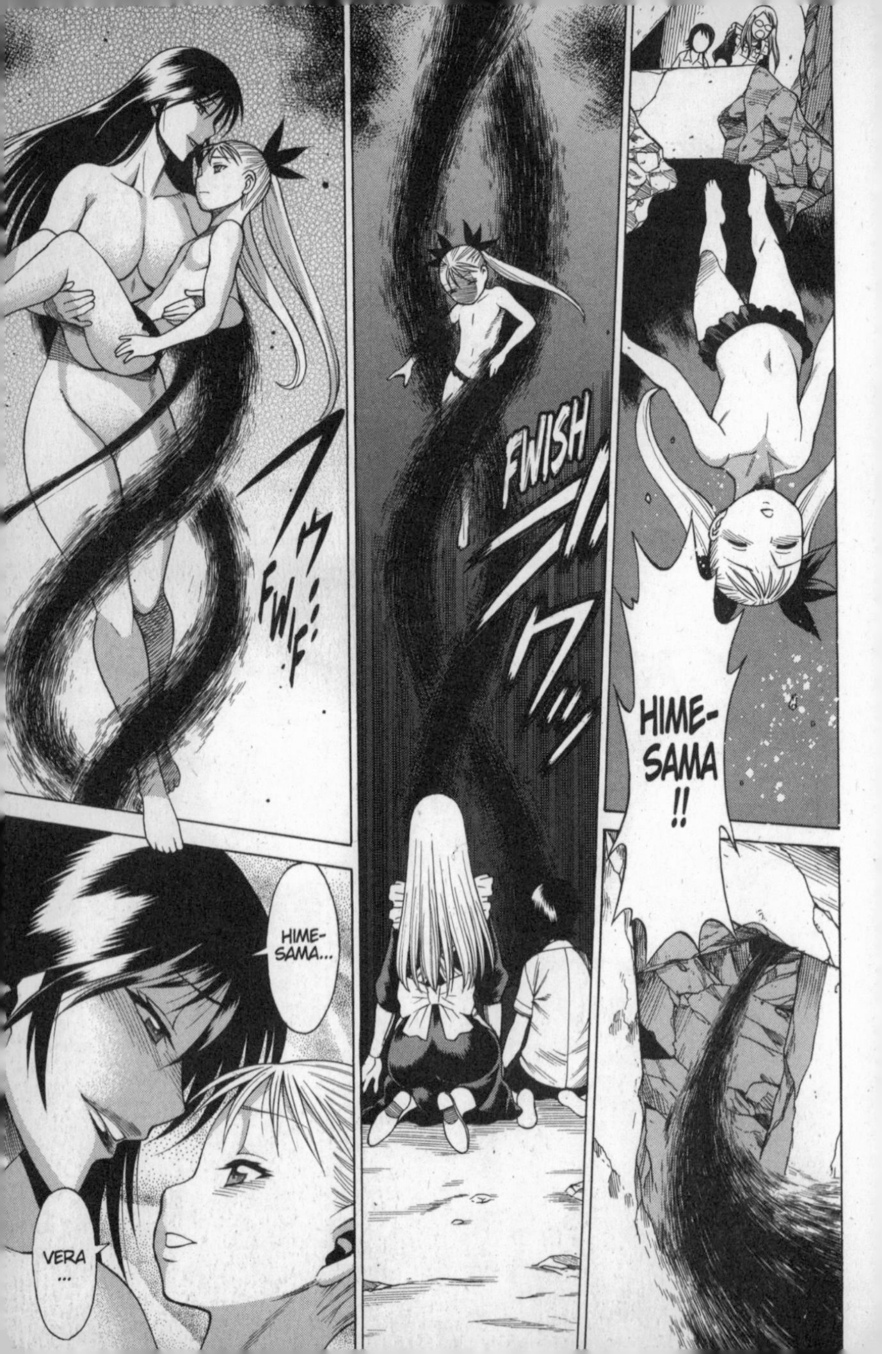
HIME-SAMA!!
FWISH
FWIF
HIME-SAMA...
VERA...

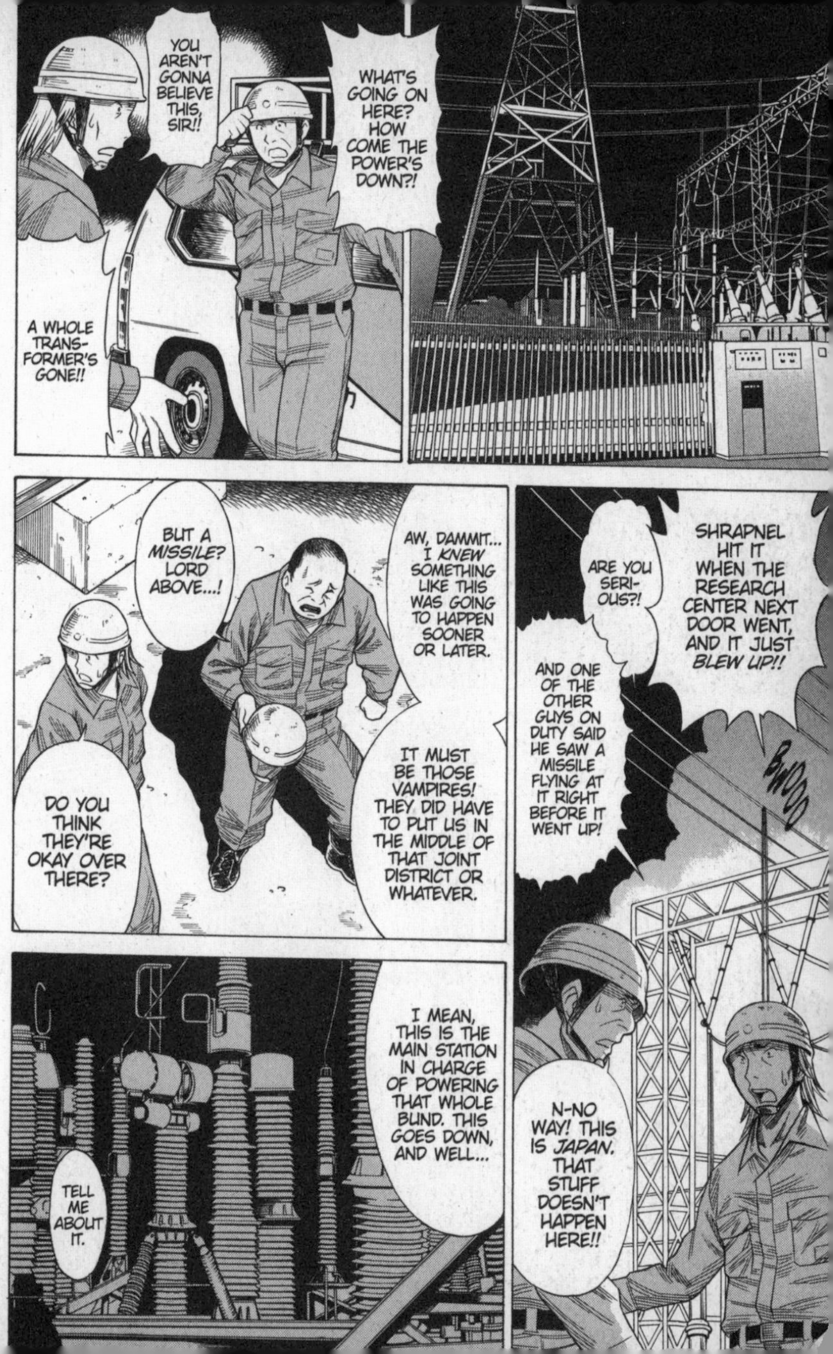
WHAT'S GOING ON HERE? HOW COME THE POWER'S DOWN?!
YOU AREN'T GONNA BELIEVE THIS, SIR!!
A WHOLE TRANSFORMER'S GONE!!
SHRAPNEL HIT IT WHEN THE RESEARCH CENTER NEXT DOOR WENT, AND IT JUST *BLEW UP!!*
ARE YOU SERIOUS?!
AND ONE OF THE OTHER GUYS ON DUTY SAID HE SAW A MISSILE FLYING AT IT RIGHT BEFORE IT WENT UP!
AW, DAMMIT... I *KNEW* SOMETHING LIKE THIS WAS GOING TO HAPPEN SOONER OR LATER.
BUT A *MISSILE*? LORD ABOVE...!
IT MUST BE THOSE VAMPIRES! THEY DID HAVE TO PUT US IN THE MIDDLE OF THAT JOINT DISTRICT OR WHATEVER.
DO YOU THINK THEY'RE OKAY OVER THERE?
N-NO WAY! THIS IS *JAPAN*. THAT STUFF DOESN'T HAPPEN HERE!!
I MEAN, THIS IS THE MAIN STATION IN CHARGE OF POWERING THAT WHOLE BUND. THIS GOES DOWN, AND WELL...
TELL ME ABOUT IT.

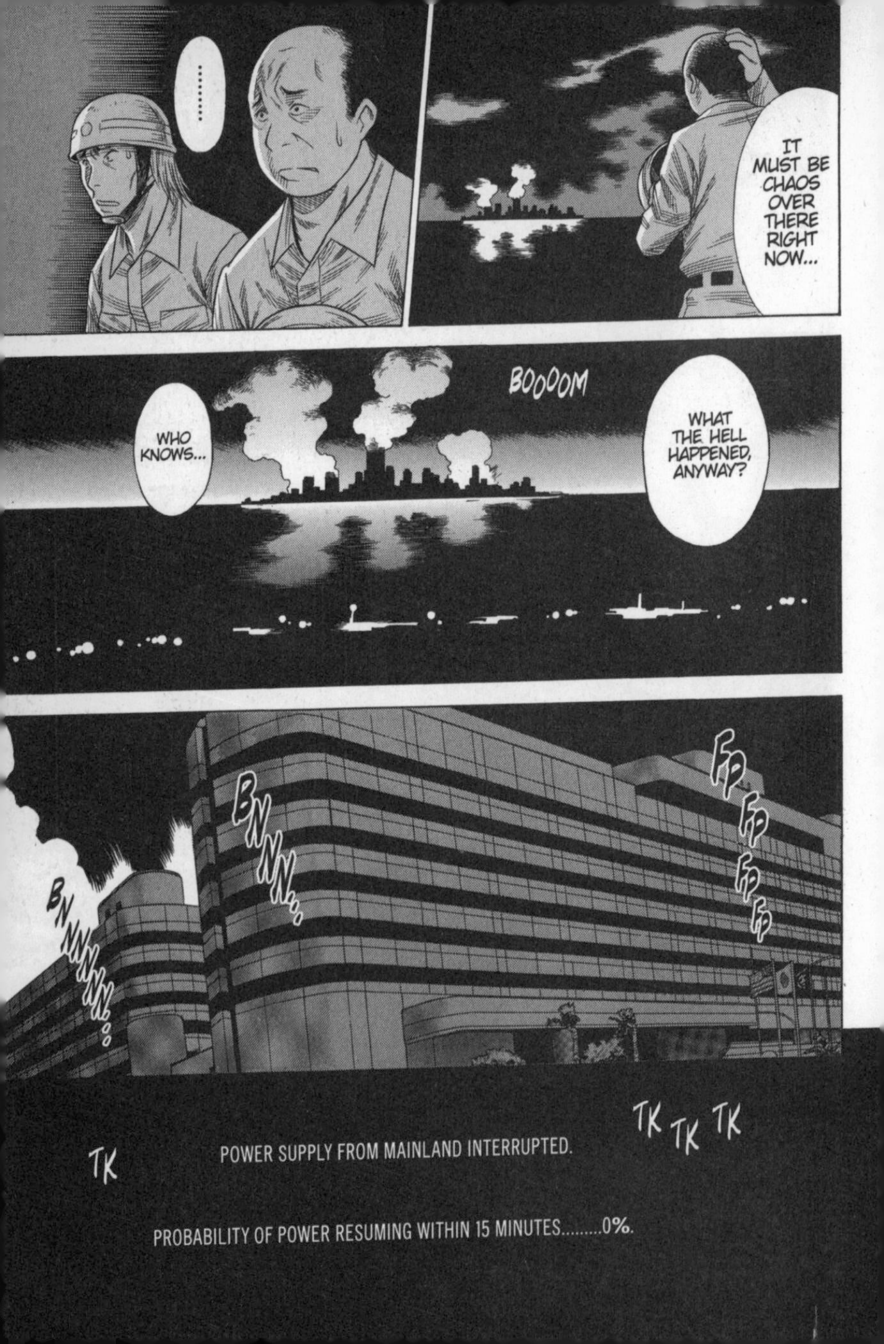
IT MUST BE CHAOS OVER THERE RIGHT NOW...
......
WHAT THE HELL HAPPENED, ANYWAY?
BOOOOM
WHO KNOWS...
FP FP FP FP
BNNN..
BNNNNN..
TK TK TK
TK
POWER SUPPLY FROM MAINLAND INTERRUPTED.
PROBABILITY OF POWER RESUMING WITHIN 15 MINUTES.........0%.

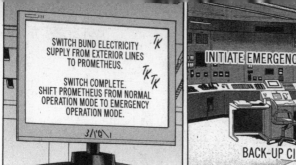

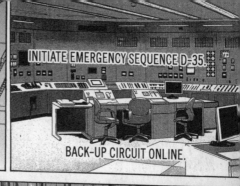

INITIATE EMERGENCY SEQUENCE D-35.
BACK-UP CIRCUIT ONLINE.
SWITCH BUND ELECTRICITY SUPPLY FROM EXTERIOR LINES TO PROMETHEUS.
TK
TKTK
SWITCH COMPLETE.
SHIFT PROMETHEUS FROM NORMAL OPERATION MODE TO EMERGENCY OPERATION MODE.
INCREASE POWER GENERATION RATIO FROM 75% TO 135%.
VWMM
ゴウーン
VWMM
ゴウーン
VWMM
ゴウーン
CRITICAL OPERATIONS WITHIN ACCEPTABLE PARAMETERS.
RESUME POWER SUPPLY TO BUND.
VWMM
ゴウーン
VWMM
ゴウーン
VWMM
ゴウーン

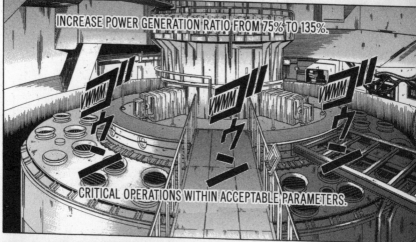

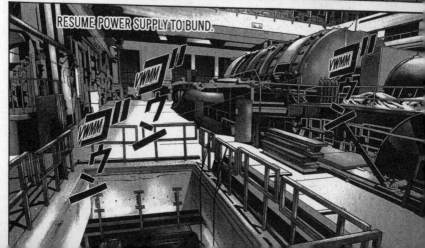

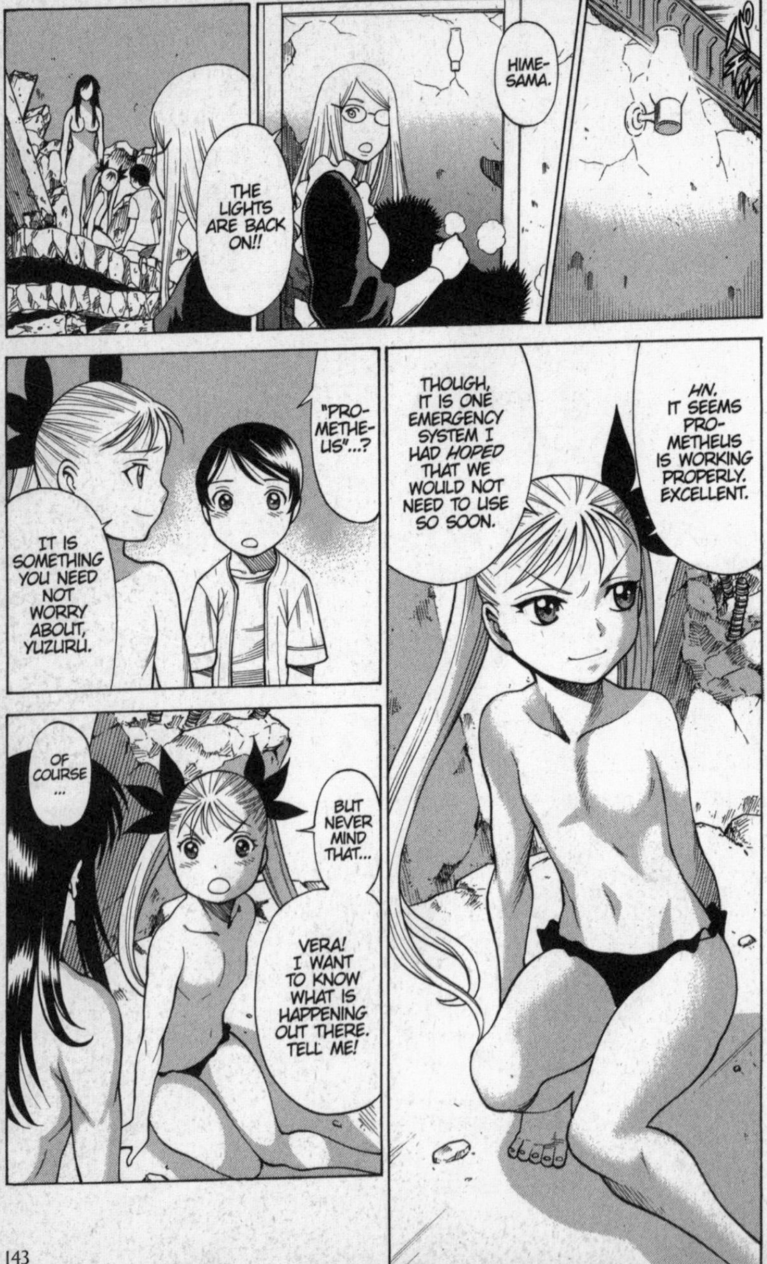
HIME-SAMA.
THE LIGHTS ARE BACK ON!!
HN. IT SEEMS PROMETHEUS IS WORKING PROPERLY. EXCELLENT.
THOUGH, IT IS ONE EMERGENCY SYSTEM I HAD *HOPED* THAT WE WOULD NOT NEED TO USE SO SOON.
"PROMETHEUS"...?
IT IS SOMETHING YOU NEED NOT WORRY ABOUT, YUZURU.
BUT NEVER MIND THAT...
VERA! I WANT TO KNOW WHAT IS HAPPENING OUT THERE. TELL ME!
OF COURSE ...

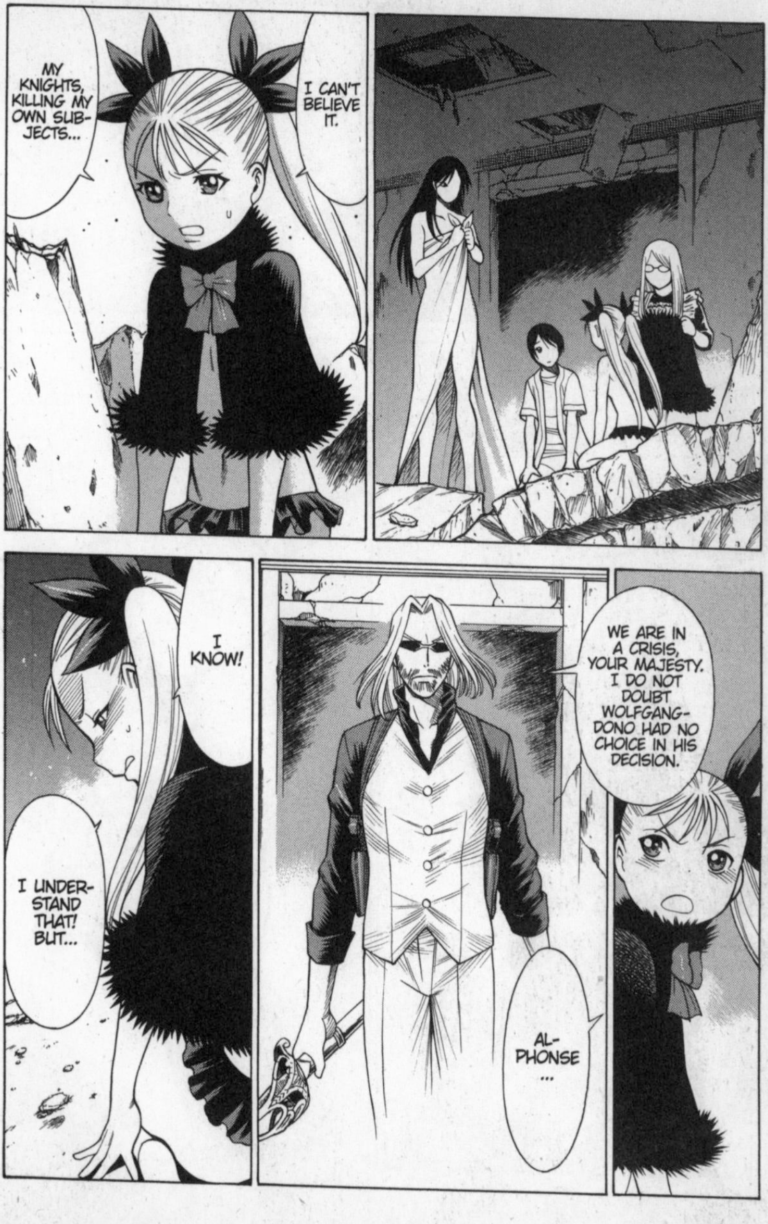
I CAN'T BELIEVE IT.
MY KNIGHTS, KILLING MY OWN SUBJECTS...
WE ARE IN A CRISIS, YOUR MAJESTY. I DO NOT DOUBT WOLFGANG-DONO HAD NO CHOICE IN HIS DECISION.
ALPHONSE...
I KNOW!
I UNDERSTAND THAT! BUT...

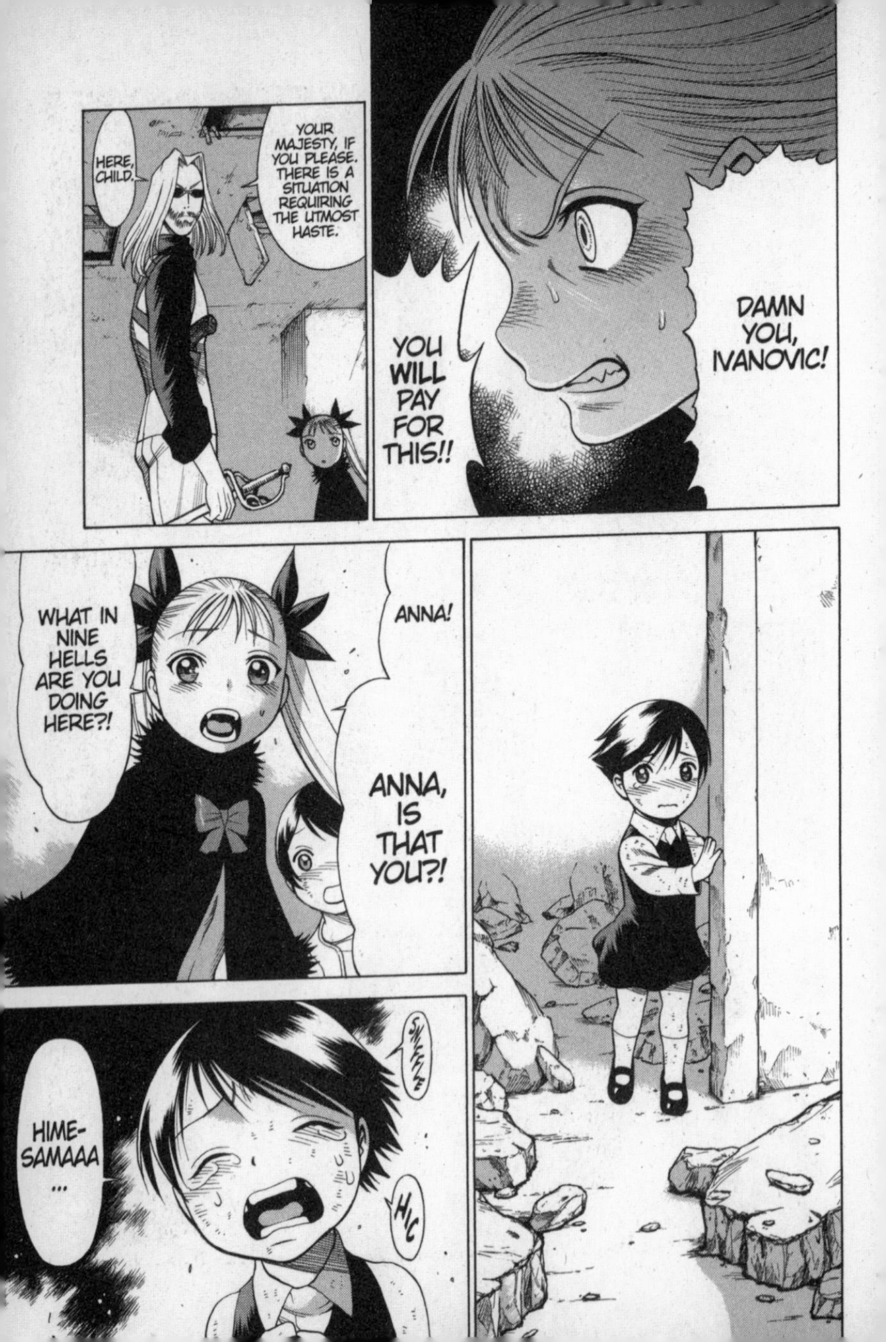

DAMN YOU, IVANOVIC!
YOU WILL PAY FOR THIS!!
YOUR MAJESTY, IF YOU PLEASE. THERE IS A SITUATION REQUIRING THE UTMOST HASTE.
HERE, CHILD.
ANNA!
ANNA, IS THAT YOU?!
WHAT IN NINE HELLS ARE YOU DOING HERE?!
SNIFFLE
HIC
HIME-SAMAAA...

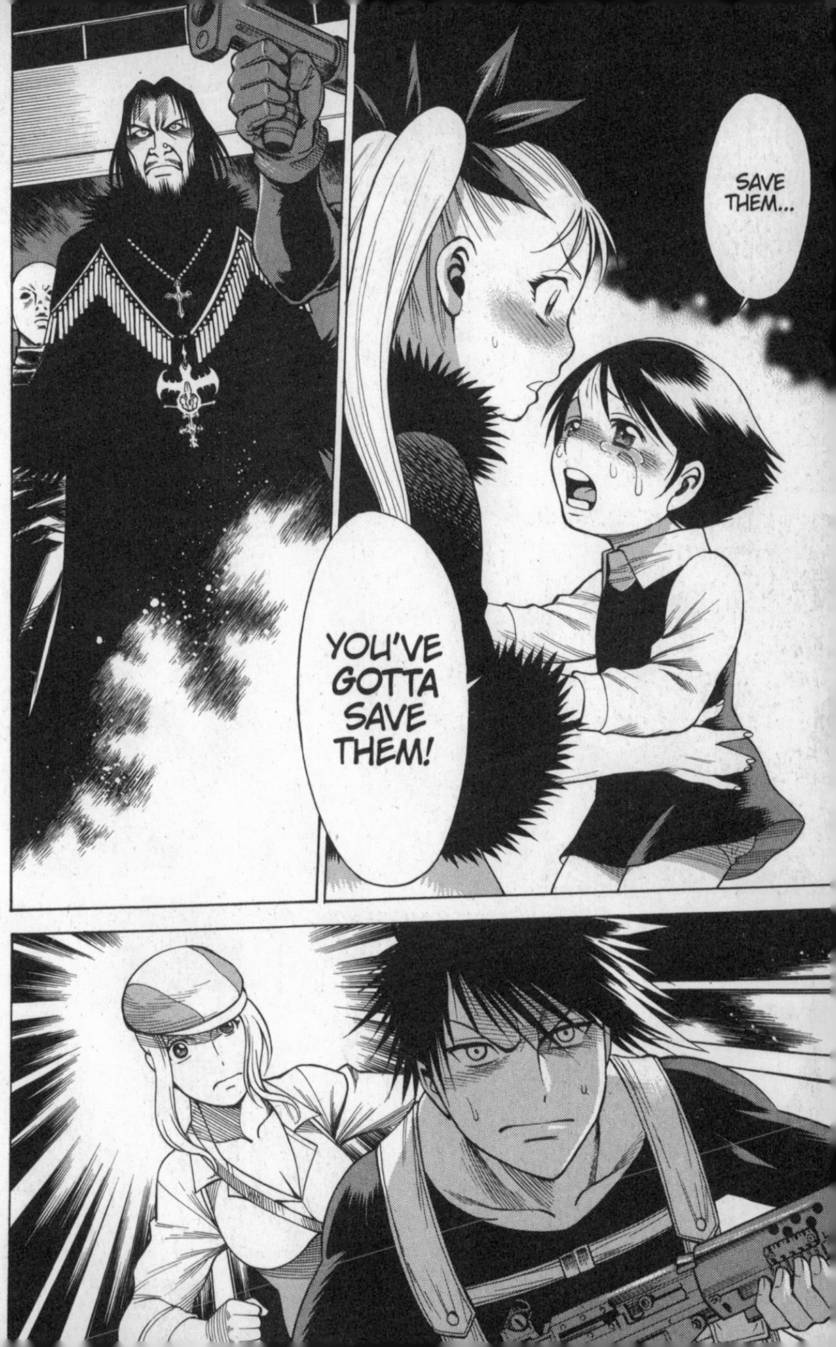
SAVE THEM...
YOU'VE GOTTA SAVE THEM!

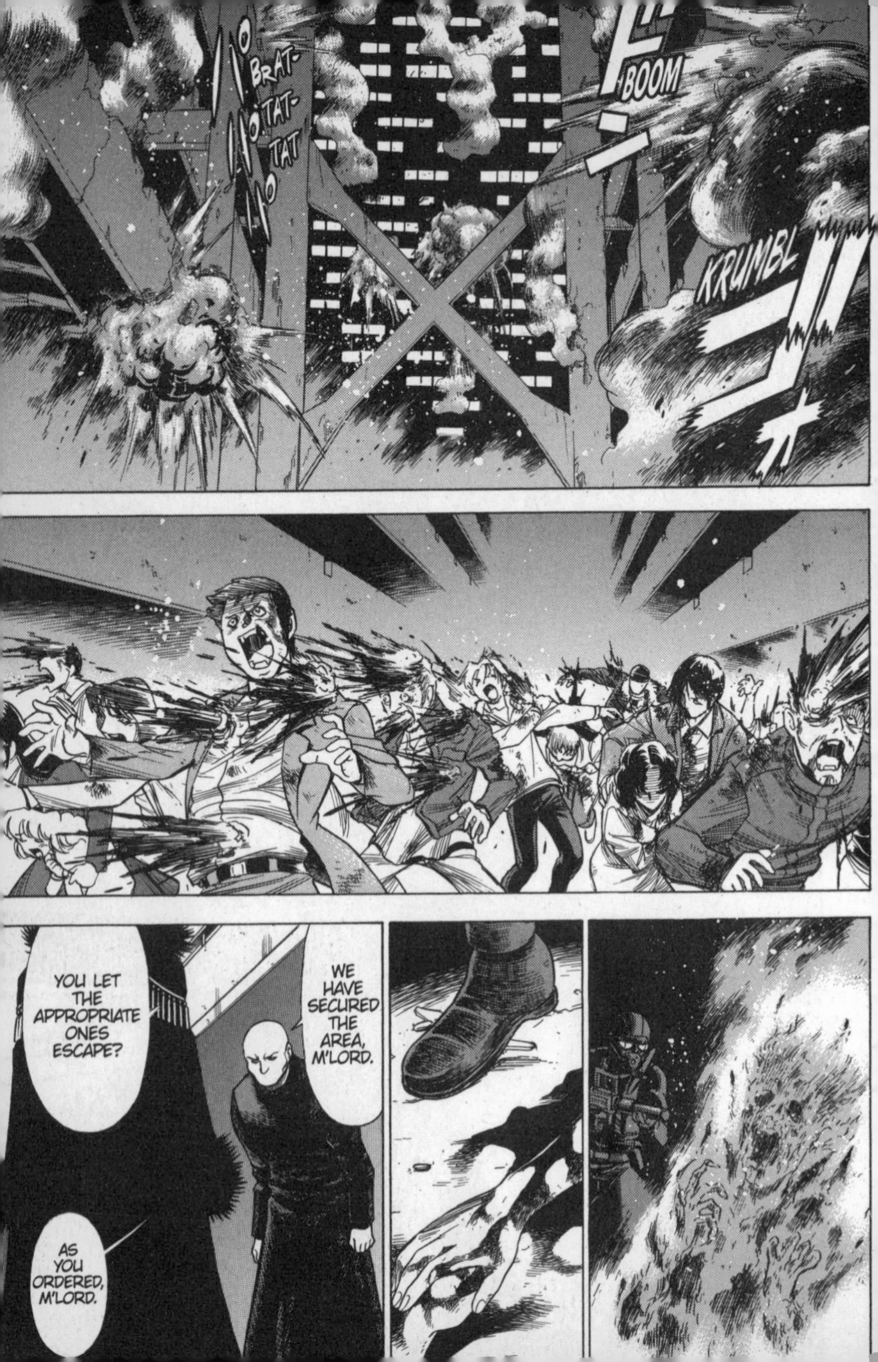
BOOM
KRUMBL
BRAT-TAT-TAT
WE HAVE SECURED THE AREA, M'LORD.
YOU LET THE APPROPRIATE ONES ESCAPE?
AS YOU ORDERED, M'LORD.

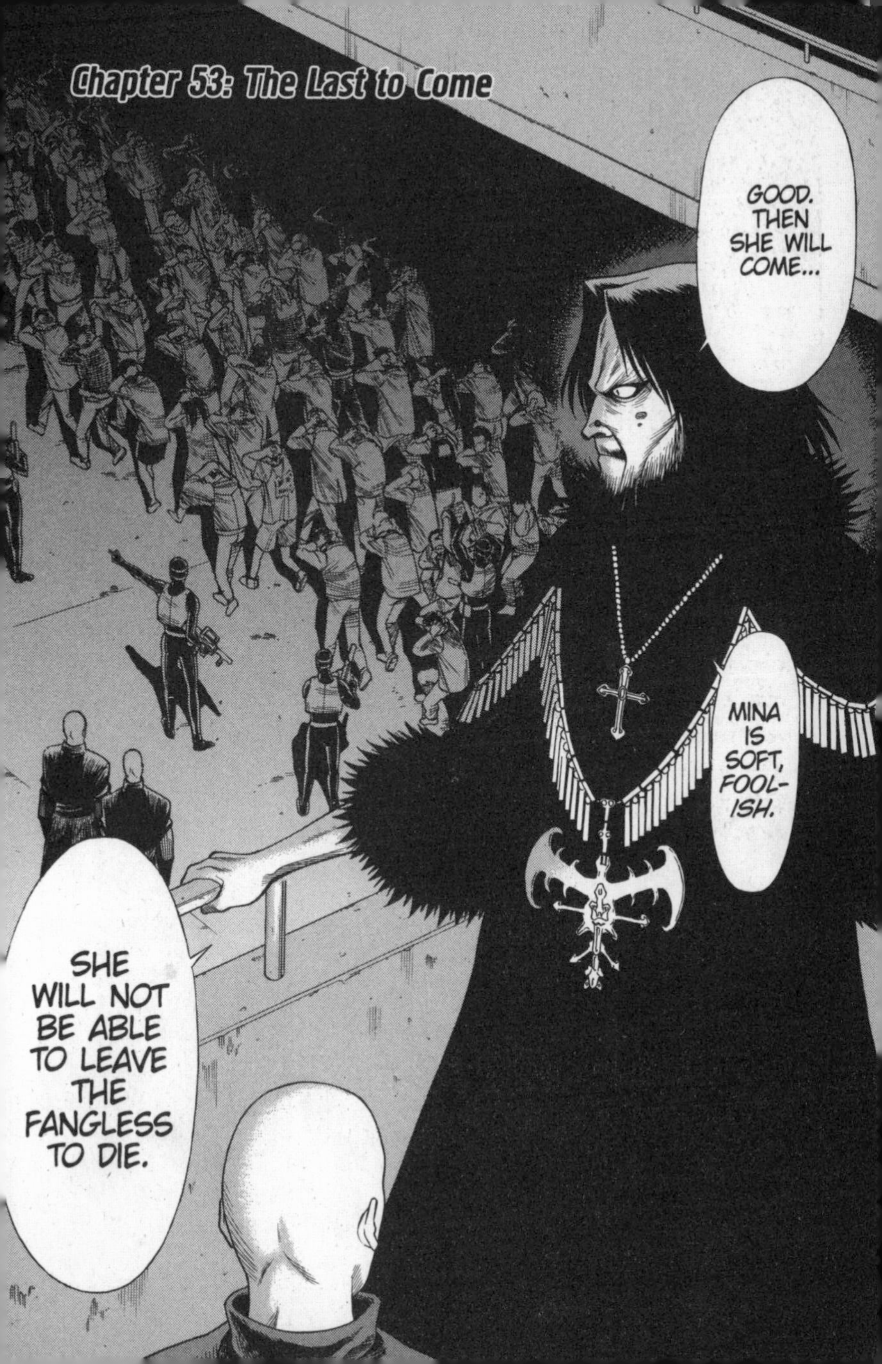
Chapter 53: The Last to Come
GOOD. THEN SHE WILL COME...
MINA IS SOFT, FOOL-ISH.
SHE WILL NOT BE ABLE TO LEAVE THE FANGLESS TO DIE.

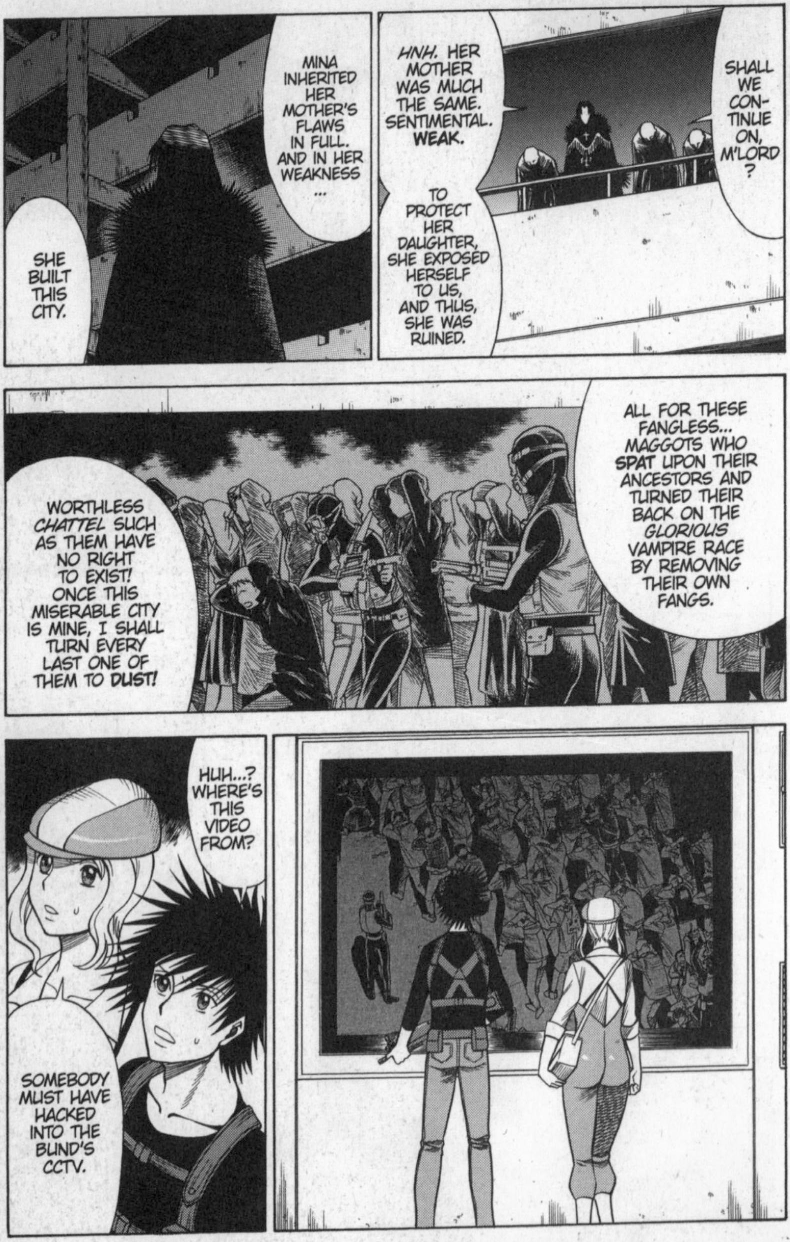

SHALL WE CON-TINUE ON, M'LORD?
HNH. HER MOTHER WAS MUCH THE SAME. SENTIMENTAL. WEAK.
TO PROTECT HER DAUGHTER, SHE EXPOSED HERSELF TO US, AND THUS, SHE WAS RUINED.
MINA INHERITED HER MOTHER'S FLAWS IN FULL. AND IN HER WEAKNESS ...
SHE BUILT THIS CITY.
ALL FOR THESE FANGLESS... MAGGOTS WHO SPAT UPON THEIR ANCESTORS AND TURNED THEIR BACK ON THE GLORIOUS VAMPIRE RACE BY REMOVING THEIR OWN FANGS.
WORTHLESS CHATTEL SUCH AS THEM HAVE NO RIGHT TO EXIST! ONCE THIS MISERABLE CITY IS MINE, I SHALL TURN EVERY LAST ONE OF THEM TO DUST!
HUH...? WHERE'S THIS VIDEO FROM?
SOMEBODY MUST HAVE HACKED INTO THE BUND'S CCTV.

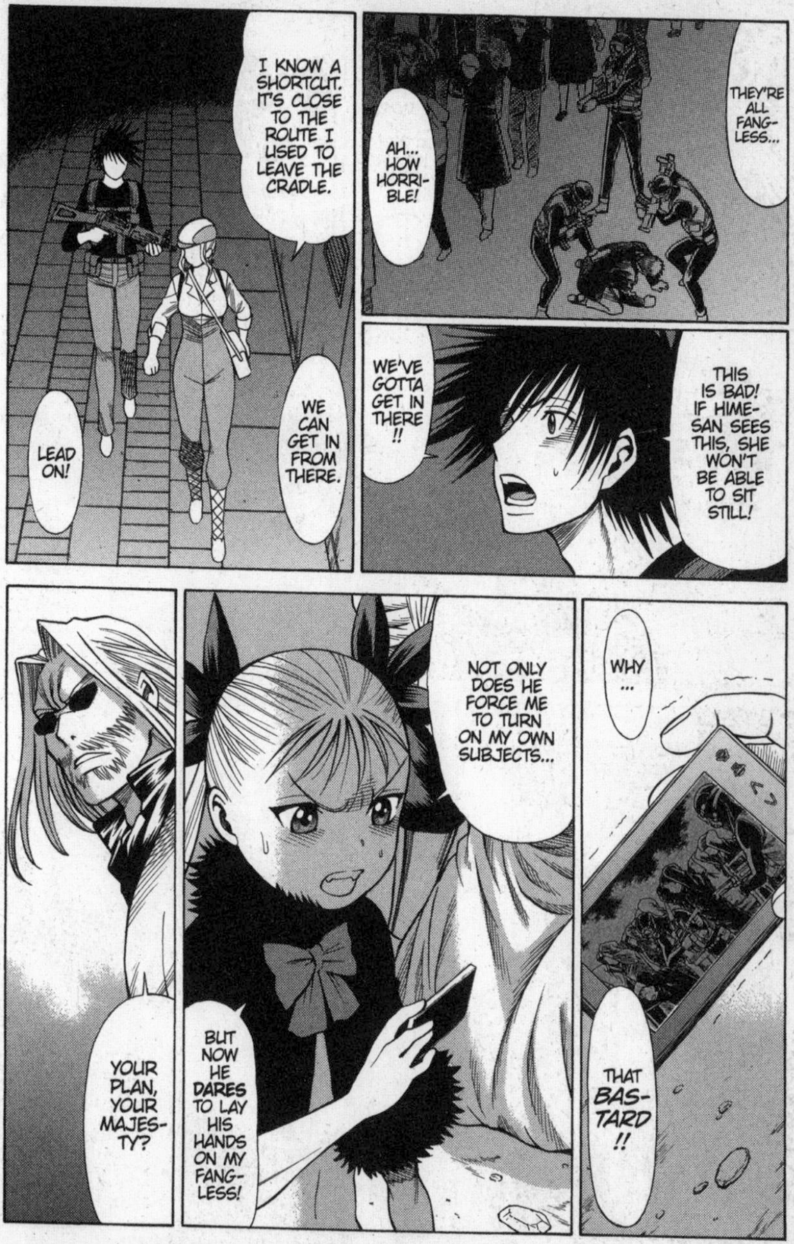
THEY'RE ALL FANG-LESS...
AH... HOW HORRI-BLE!
THIS IS BAD! IF HIME-SAN SEES THIS, SHE WON'T BE ABLE TO SIT STILL!
WE'VE GOTTA GET IN THERE !!
I KNOW A SHORTCUT. IT'S CLOSE TO THE ROUTE I USED TO LEAVE THE CRADLE.
WE CAN GET IN FROM THERE.
LEAD ON!
WHY ...
THAT BAS-TARD !!
NOT ONLY DOES HE FORCE ME TO TURN ON MY OWN SUBJECTS...
BUT NOW HE DARES TO LAY HIS HANDS ON MY FANG-LESS!
YOUR PLAN, YOUR MAJES-TY?

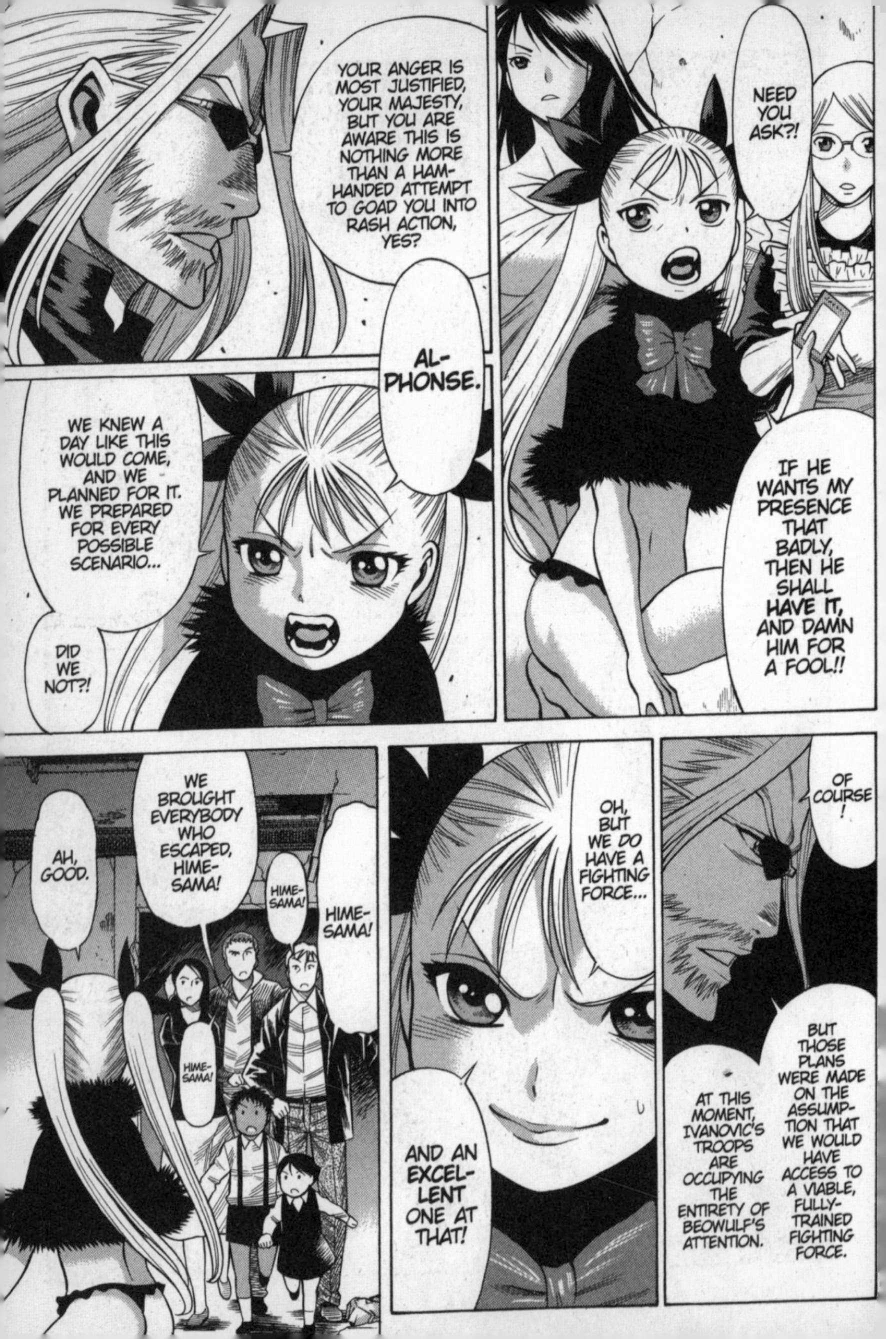
NEED YOU ASK?!
IF HE WANTS MY PRESENCE THAT BADLY, THEN HE SHALL HAVE IT, AND DAMN HIM FOR A FOOL!!
YOUR ANGER IS MOST JUSTIFIED, YOUR MAJESTY, BUT YOU ARE AWARE THIS IS NOTHING MORE THAN A HAM-HANDED ATTEMPT TO GOAD YOU INTO RASH ACTION, YES?
AL-PHONSE.
WE KNEW A DAY LIKE THIS WOULD COME, AND WE PLANNED FOR IT. WE PREPARED FOR EVERY POSSIBLE SCENARIO...
DID WE NOT?!
OF COURSE!
BUT THOSE PLANS WERE MADE ON THE ASSUMP-TION THAT WE WOULD HAVE ACCESS TO A VIABLE, FULLY-TRAINED FIGHTING FORCE.
AT THIS MOMENT, IVANOVIC'S TROOPS ARE OCCUPYING THE ENTIRETY OF BEOWULF'S ATTENTION.
OH, BUT WE DO HAVE A FIGHTING FORCE...
AND AN EXCEL-LENT ONE AT THAT!
WE BROUGHT EVERYBODY WHO ESCAPED, HIME-SAMA!
HIME-SAMA!
HIME-SAMA!
AH, GOOD.
HIME-SAMA!

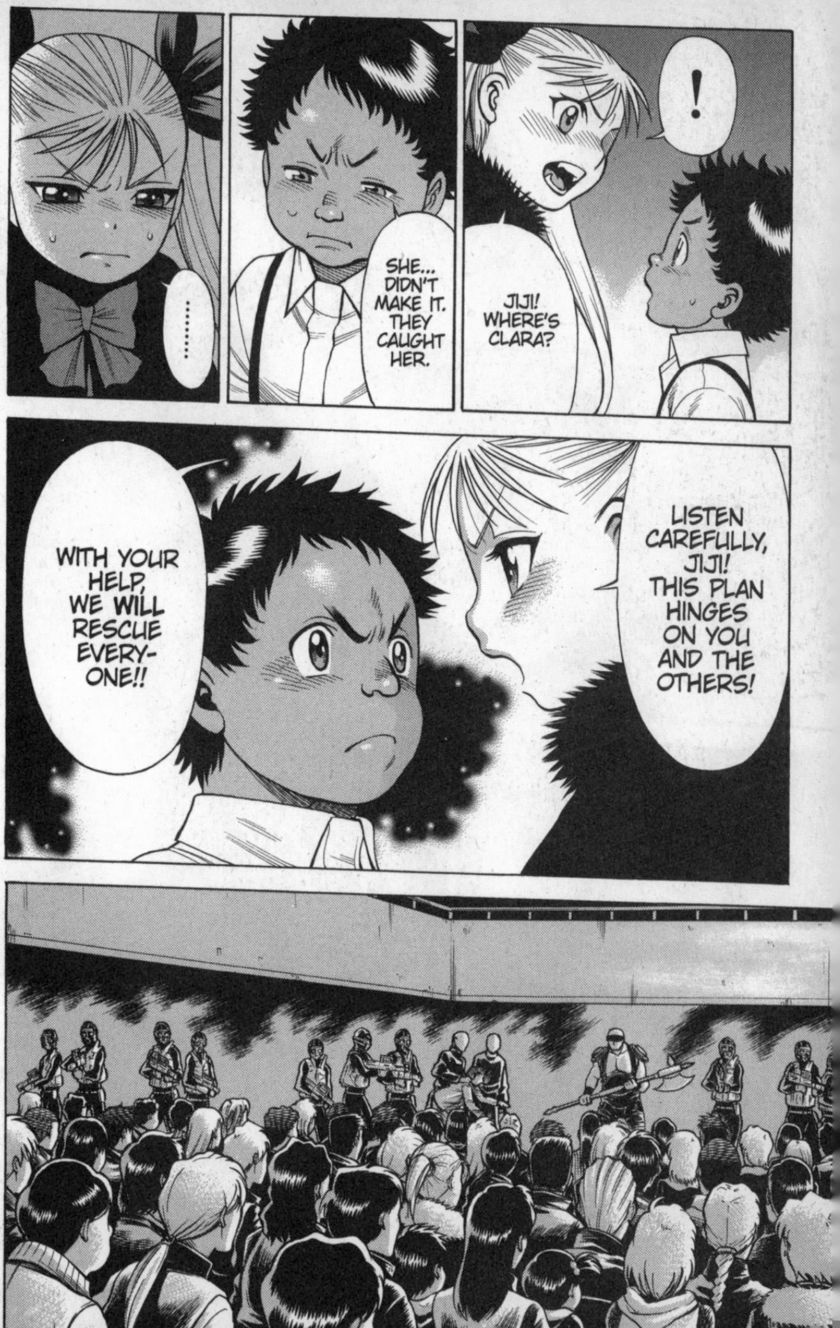
!
JIJI! WHERE'S CLARA?
SHE... DIDN'T MAKE IT. THEY CAUGHT HER.
......
LISTEN CAREFULLY, JIJI! THIS PLAN HINGES ON YOU AND THE OTHERS!
WITH YOUR HELP, WE WILL RESCUE EVERY-ONE!!

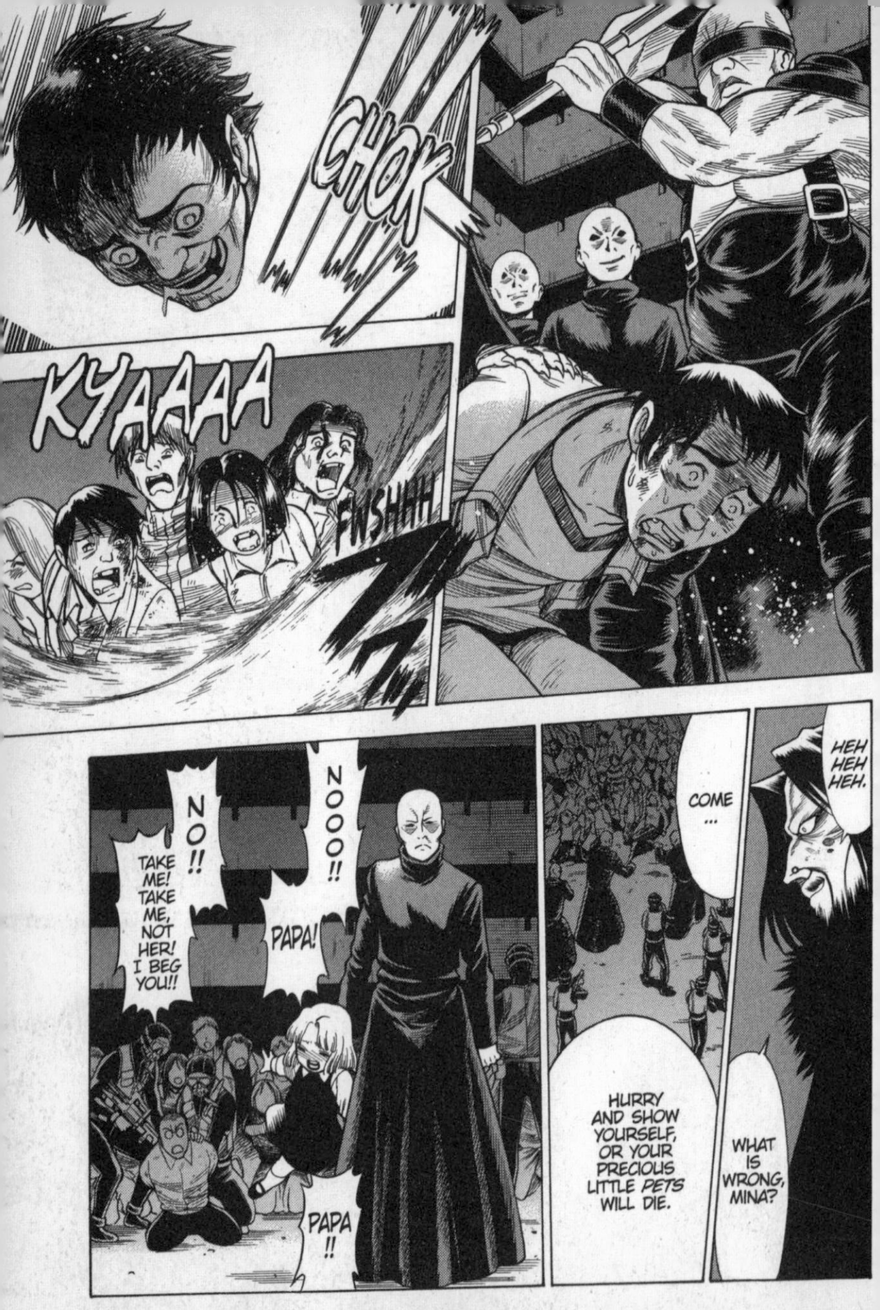
CHOK
KYAAAA
FWSHHH
HEH HEH HEH.
WHAT IS WRONG, MINA?
COME ...
HURRY AND SHOW YOURSELF, OR YOUR PRECIOUS LITTLE PETS WILL DIE.
NOOOO!!
PAPA!
NO!!
TAKE ME! TAKE ME, NOT HER! I BEG YOU!!
PAPA!!

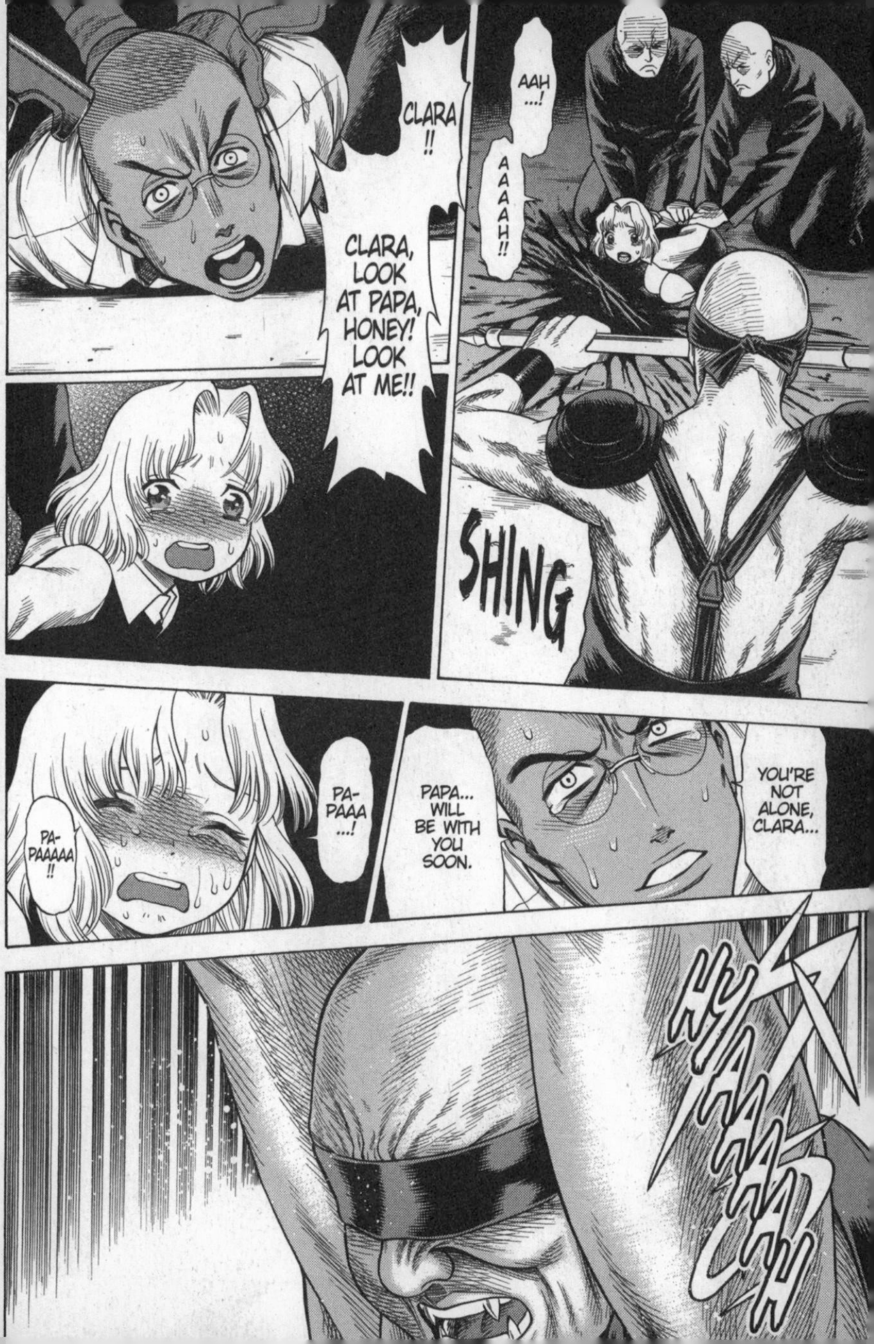
AAH ...!
AAAAAH!!
SHING
CLARA !!
CLARA, LOOK AT PAPA, HONEY! LOOK AT ME!!
YOU'RE NOT ALONE, CLARA...
PAPA... WILL BE WITH YOU SOON.
PA-PAAAA ...!
PA-PAAAAA !!

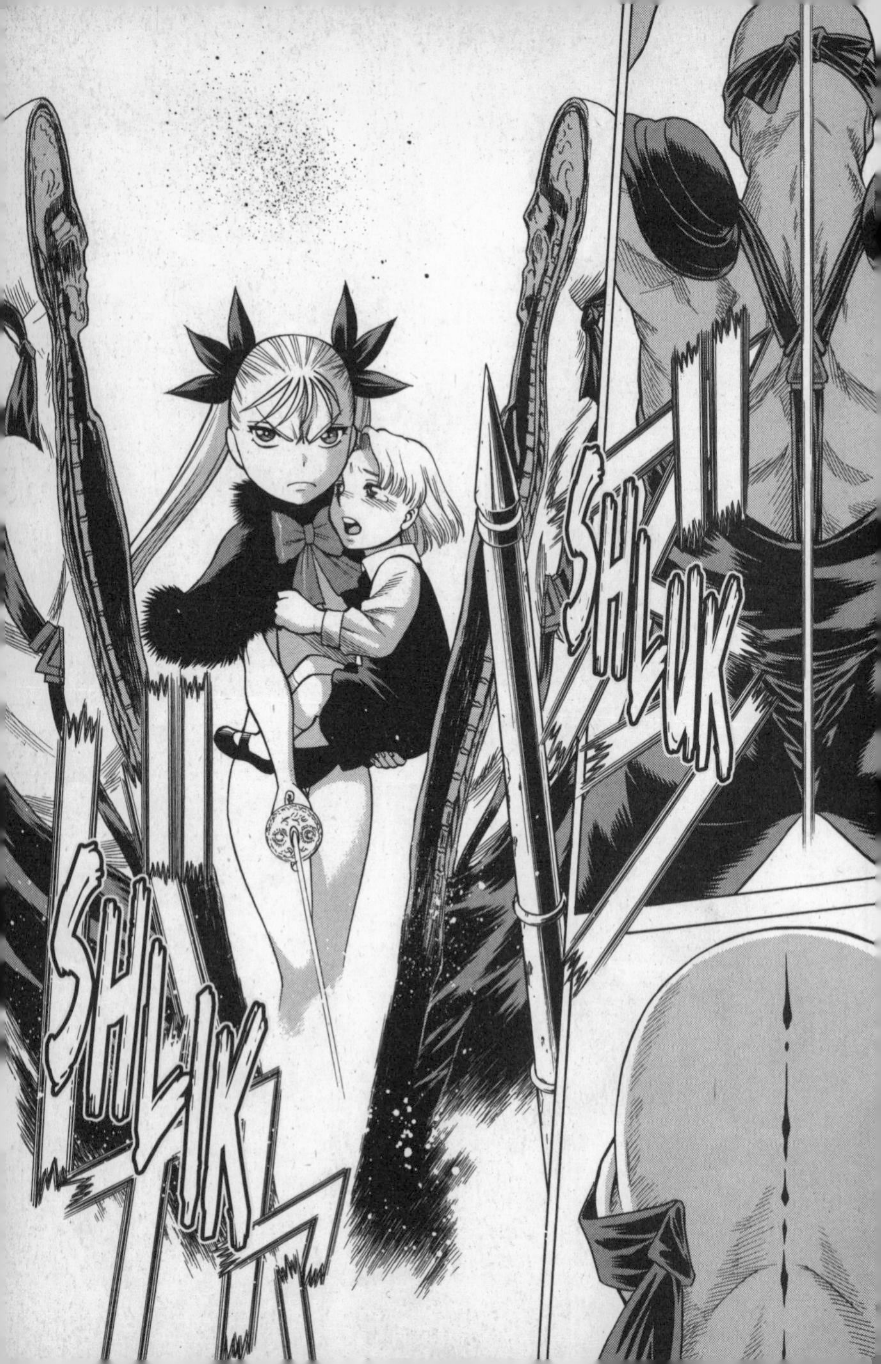
SHLIK
SHLIK

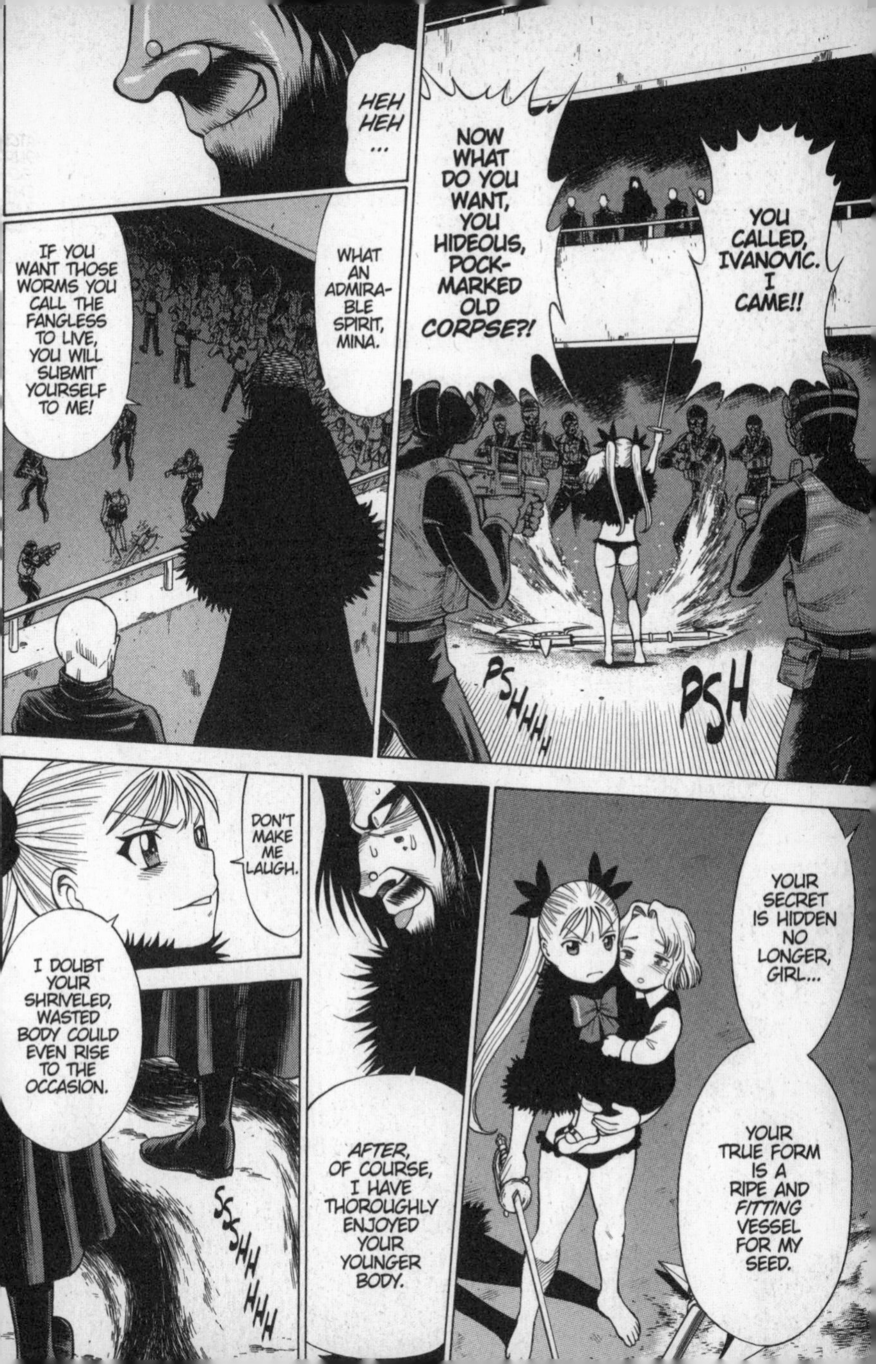

YOU CALLED, IVANOVIC. I CAME!!
NOW WHAT DO YOU WANT, YOU HIDEOUS, POCK-MARKED OLD CORPSE?!
PSH
PSHHHH
HEH HEH ...
WHAT AN ADMIRA-BLE SPIRIT, MINA.
IF YOU WANT THOSE WORMS YOU CALL THE FANGLESS TO LIVE, YOU WILL SUBMIT YOURSELF TO ME!
YOUR SECRET IS HIDDEN NO LONGER, GIRL...
YOUR TRUE FORM IS A RIPE AND FITTING VESSEL FOR MY SEED.
AFTER, OF COURSE, I HAVE THOROUGHLY ENJOYED YOUR YOUNGER BODY.
DON'T MAKE ME LAUGH.
I DOUBT YOUR SHRIVELED, WASTED BODY COULD EVEN RISE TO THE OCCASION.
SSSHHHHHH

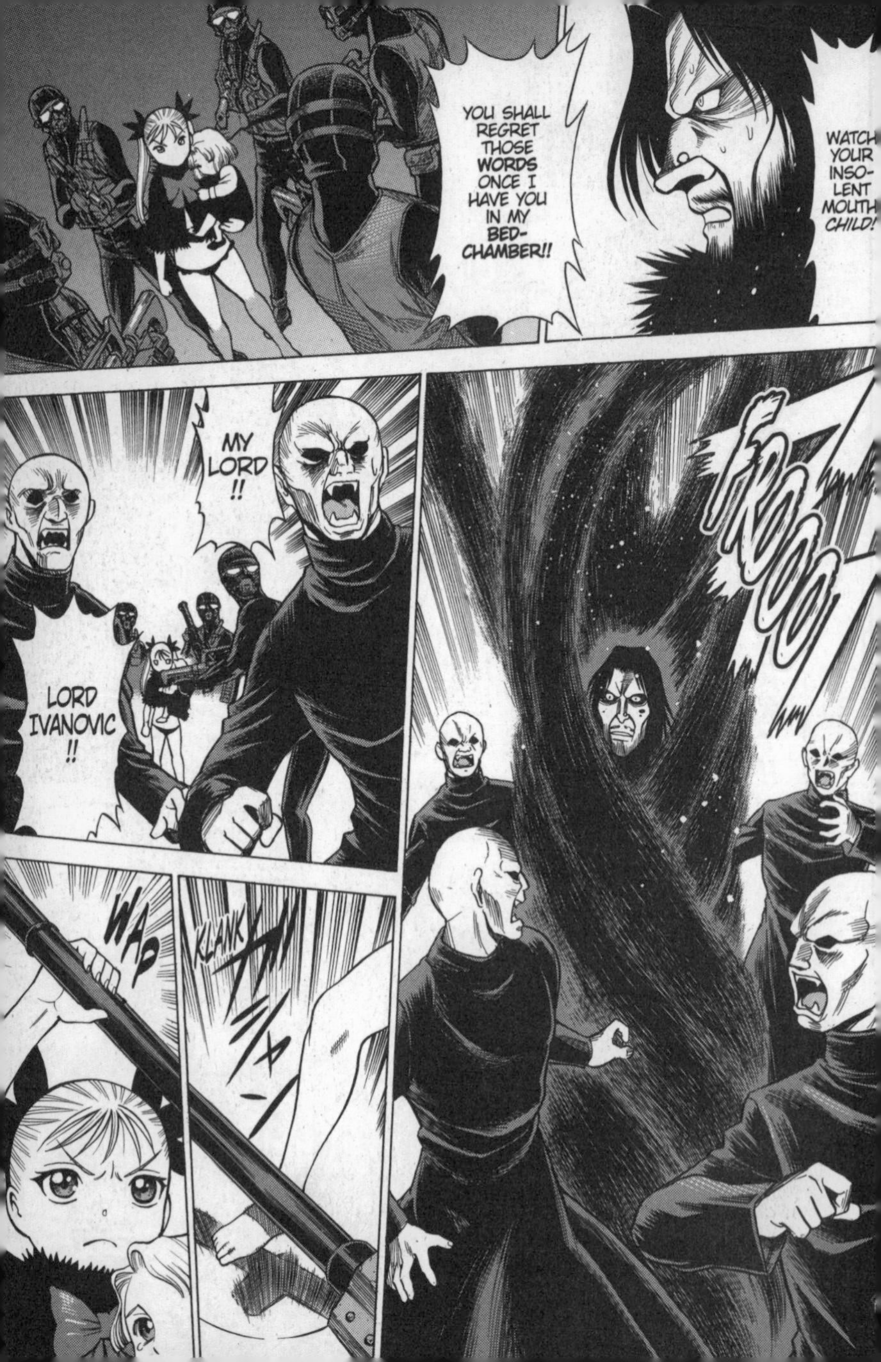
WATCH YOUR INSO-LENT MOUTH CHILD!
YOU SHALL REGRET THOSE WORDS ONCE I HAVE YOU IN MY BED-CHAMBER!!
FROOOO
MY LORD!!
LORD IVANOVIC!!
KLANK
WAP

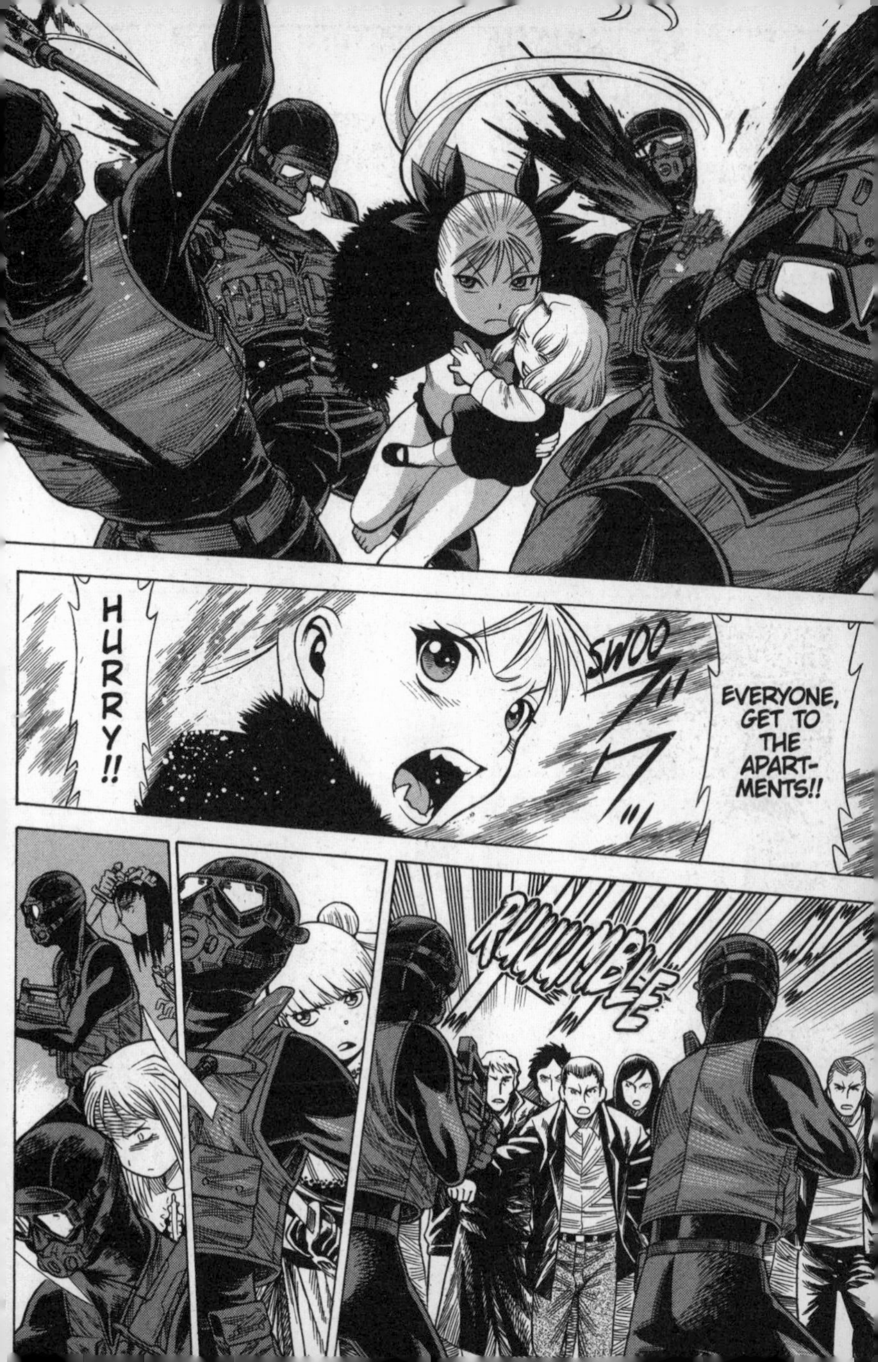
EVERYONE, GET TO THE APARTMENTS!!
SWOO
HURRY!!
RUUUMBLE

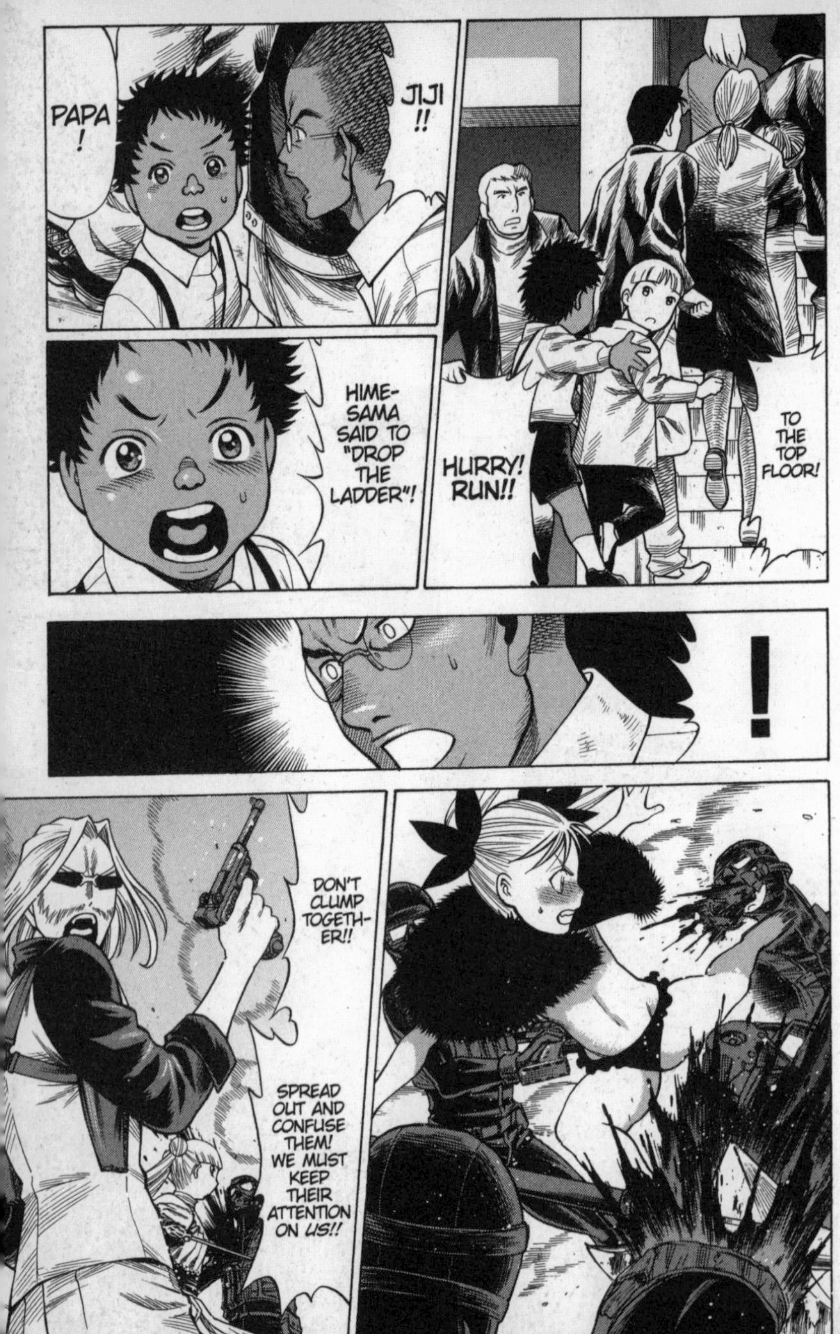
TO THE TOP FLOOR!
HURRY! RUN!!
JIJI!!
PAPA!
HIME-SAMA SAID TO "DROP THE LADDER"!
!
DON'T CLUMP TOGETHER!!
SPREAD OUT AND CONFUSE THEM! WE MUST KEEP THEIR ATTENTION ON US!!

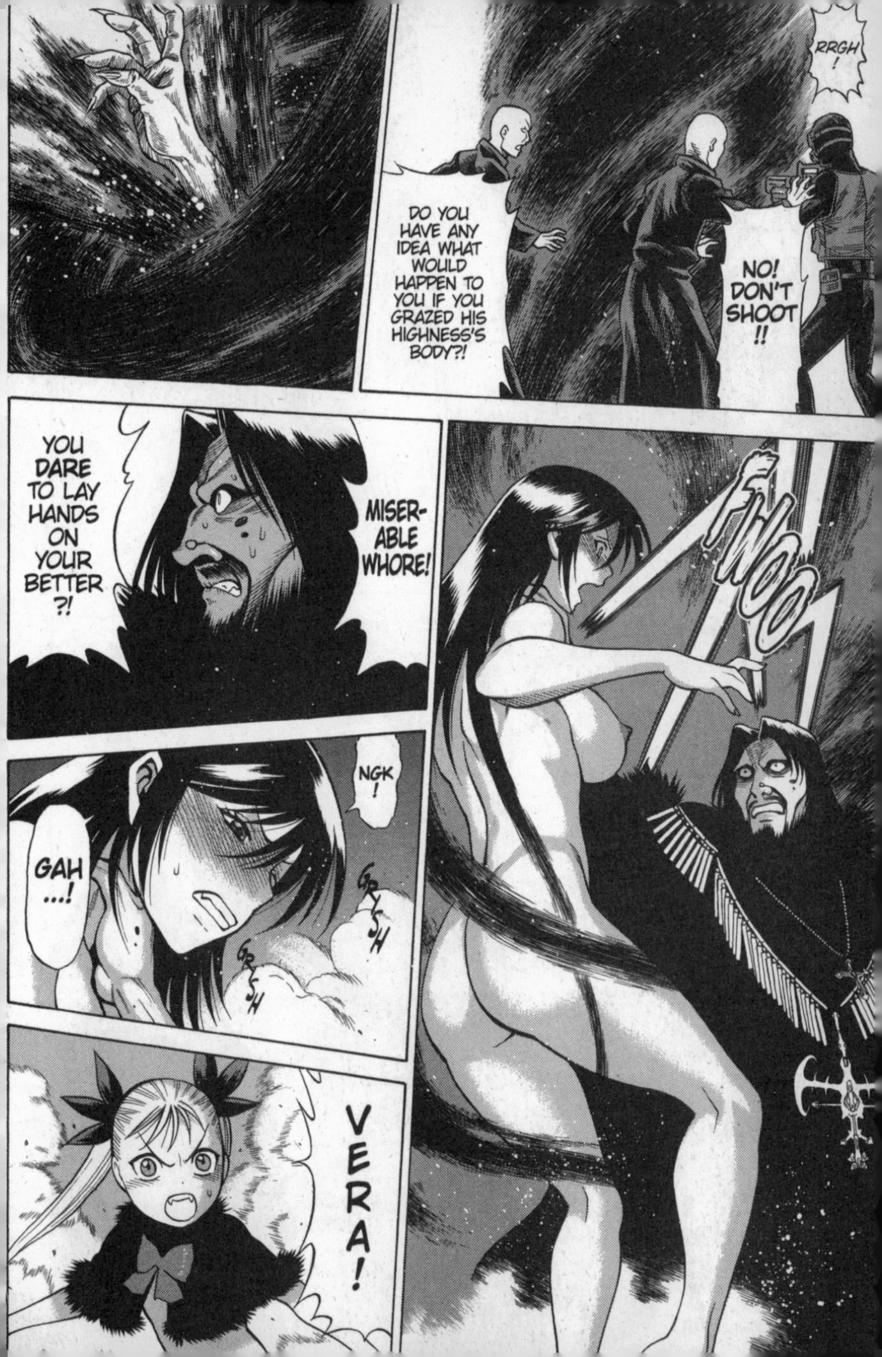
RRGH!
NO! DON'T SHOOT!!
DO YOU HAVE ANY IDEA WHAT WOULD HAPPEN TO YOU IF YOU GRAZED HIS HIGHNESS'S BODY?!
FWOOM
MISER-ABLE WHORE!
YOU DARE TO LAY HANDS ON YOUR BETTER?!
NGK!
GAH...!
GRISH
GRISH
VERA!

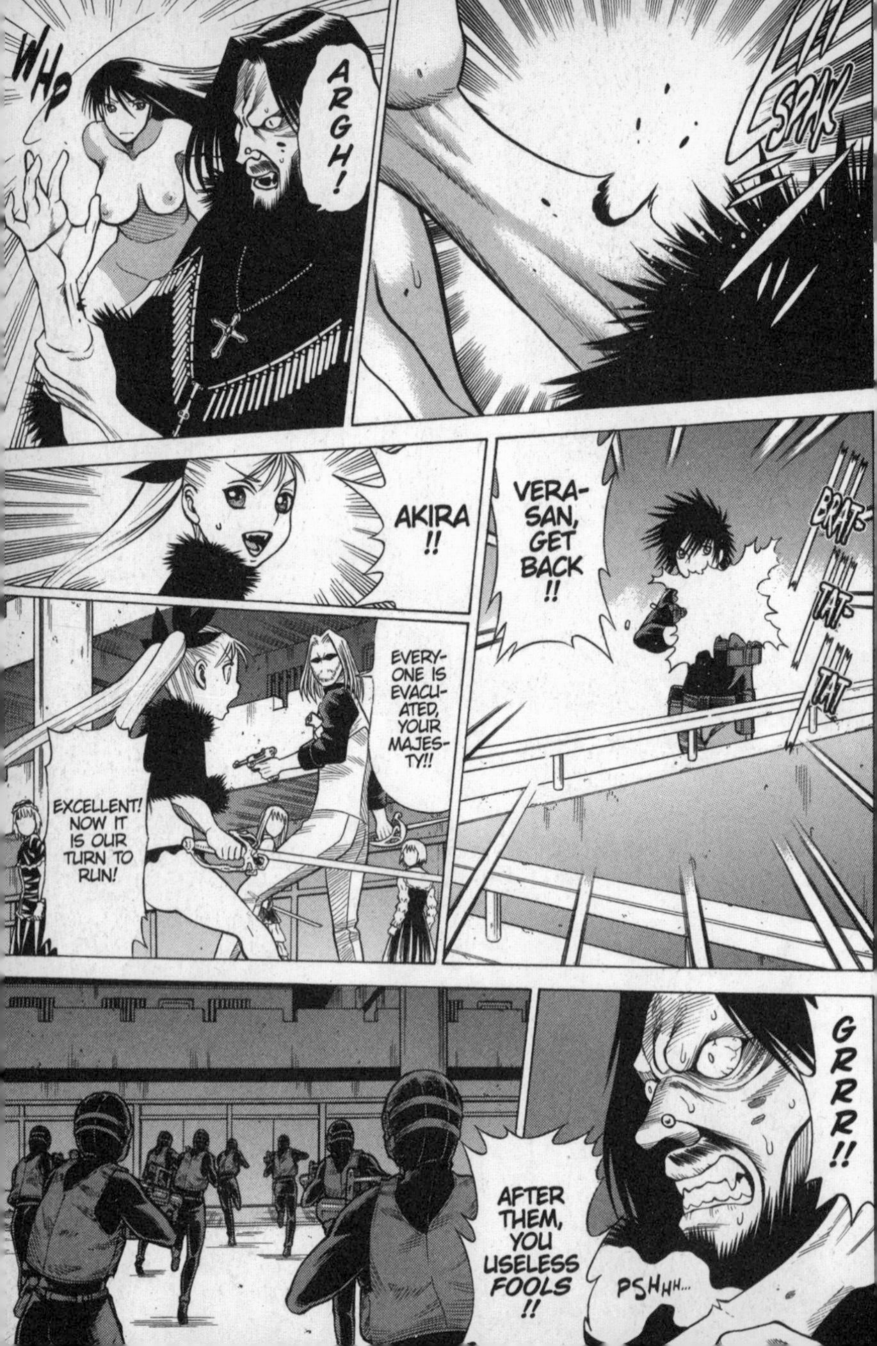
SPAK
ARGH!
WHP
VERA-SAN, GET BACK!!
BRAT-TAT-TAT
AKIRA!!
EVERY-ONE IS EVACU-ATED, YOUR MAJES-TY!!
EXCELLENT! NOW IT IS OUR TURN TO RUN!
GRRR!!
AFTER THEM, YOU USELESS FOOLS!!
PSHHH...

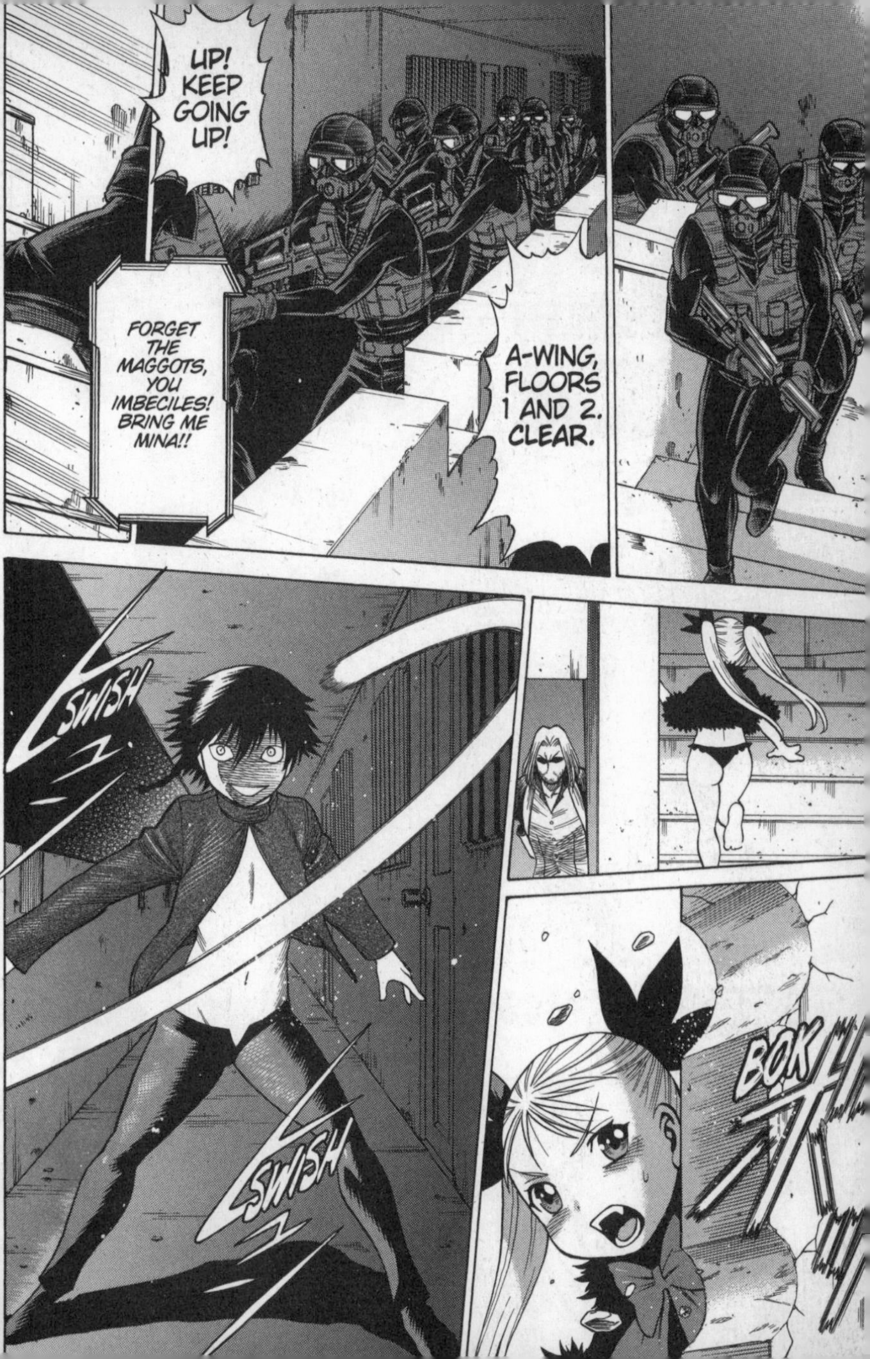
A-WING, FLOORS 1 AND 2. CLEAR.
UP! KEEP GOING UP!
FORGET THE MAGGOTS, YOU IMBECILES! BRING ME MINA!!
BOK
SWISH
SWISH

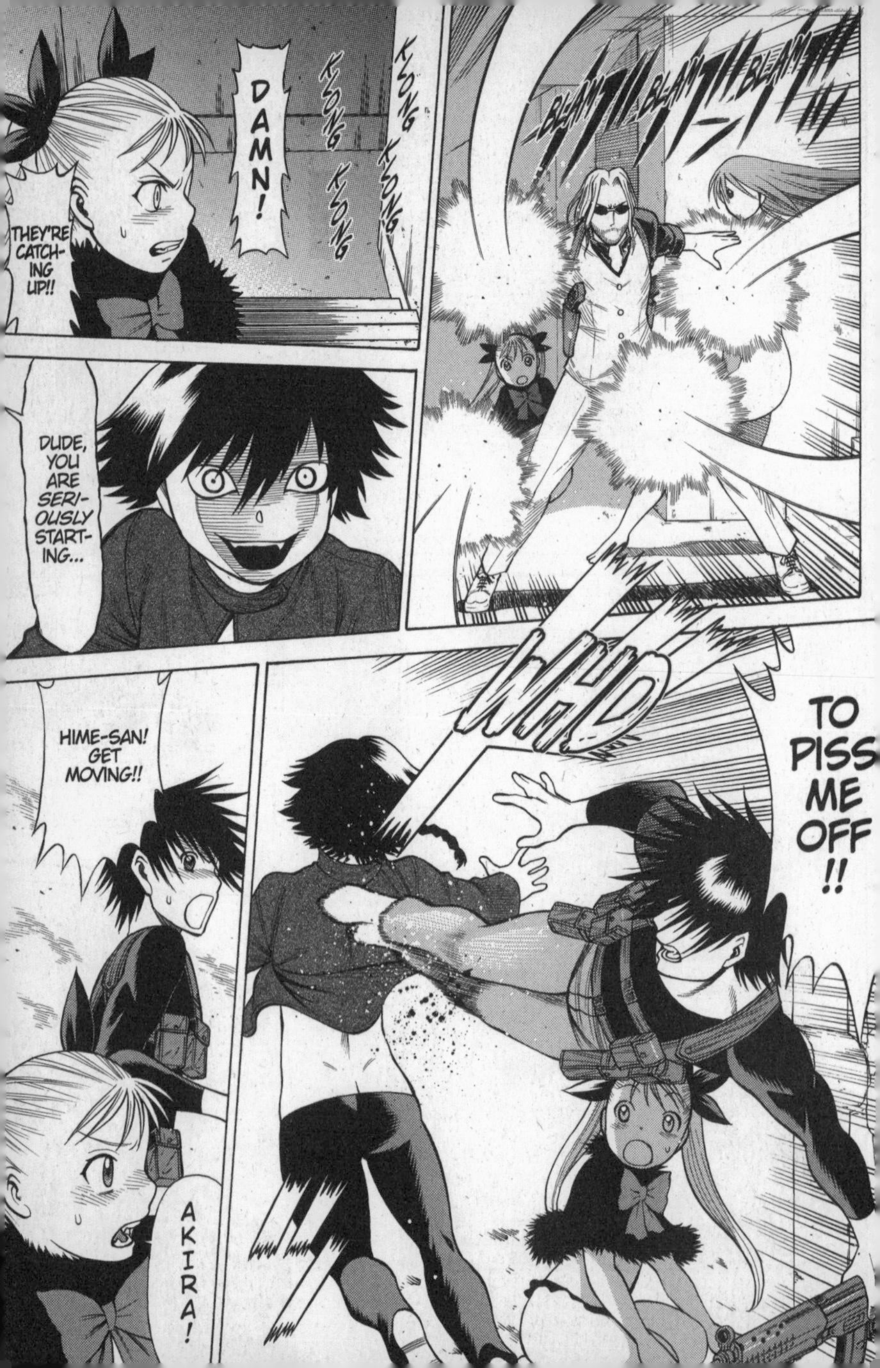
BLAM!! BLAM!! BLAM!!
KLONG KLONG KLONG
KLONG KLONG KLONG
DAMN!
THEY'RE CATCHING UP!!
DUDE, YOU ARE SERIOUSLY STARTING...
WHO
TO PISS ME OFF!!
HIME-SAN! GET MOVING!!
AKIRA!

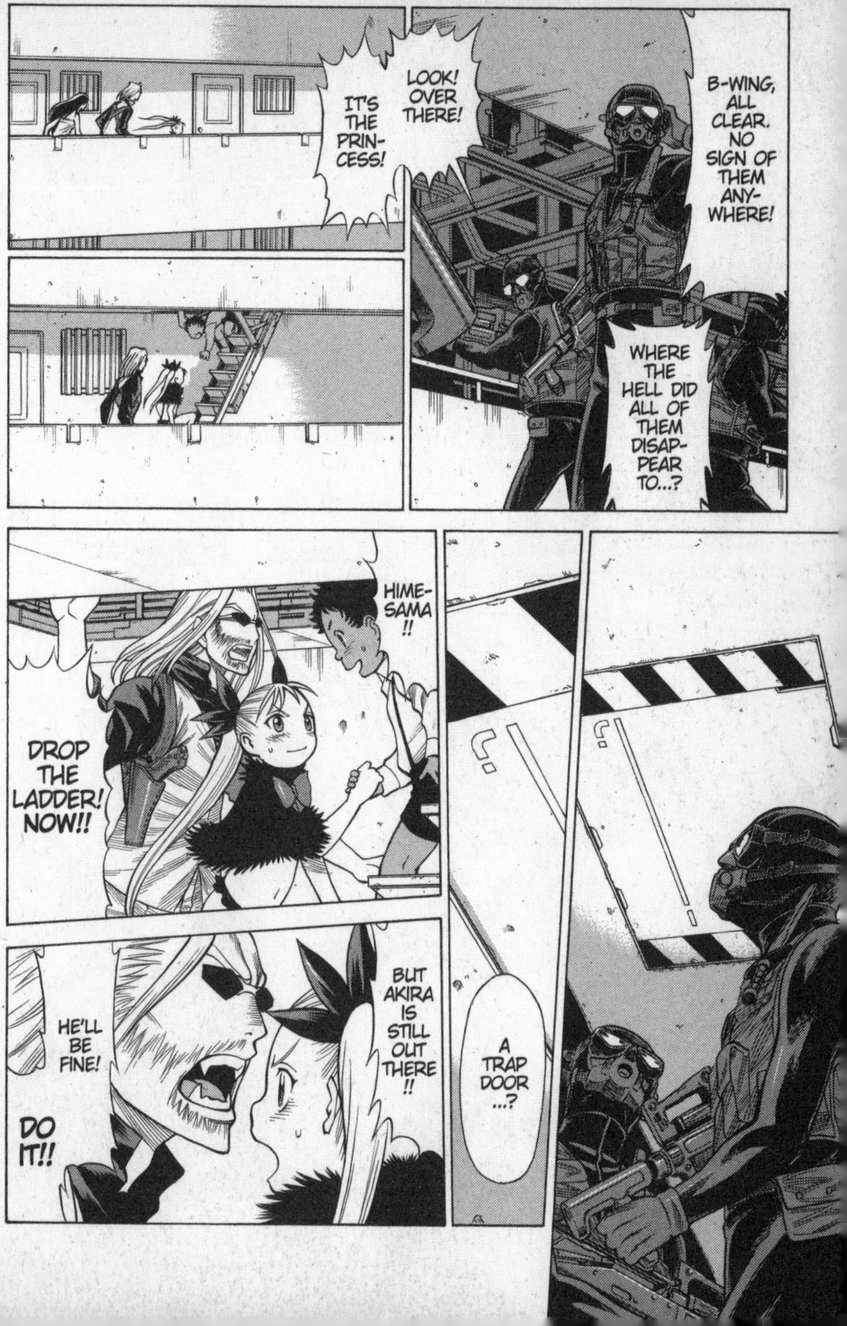
B-WING, ALL CLEAR. NO SIGN OF THEM ANYWHERE!
WHERE THE HELL DID ALL OF THEM DISAPPEAR TO...?
LOOK! OVER THERE!
IT'S THE PRINCESS!
A TRAP DOOR ...?
HIME-SAMA!!
DROP THE LADDER! NOW!!
BUT AKIRA IS STILL OUT THERE!!
HE'LL BE FINE!
DO IT!!

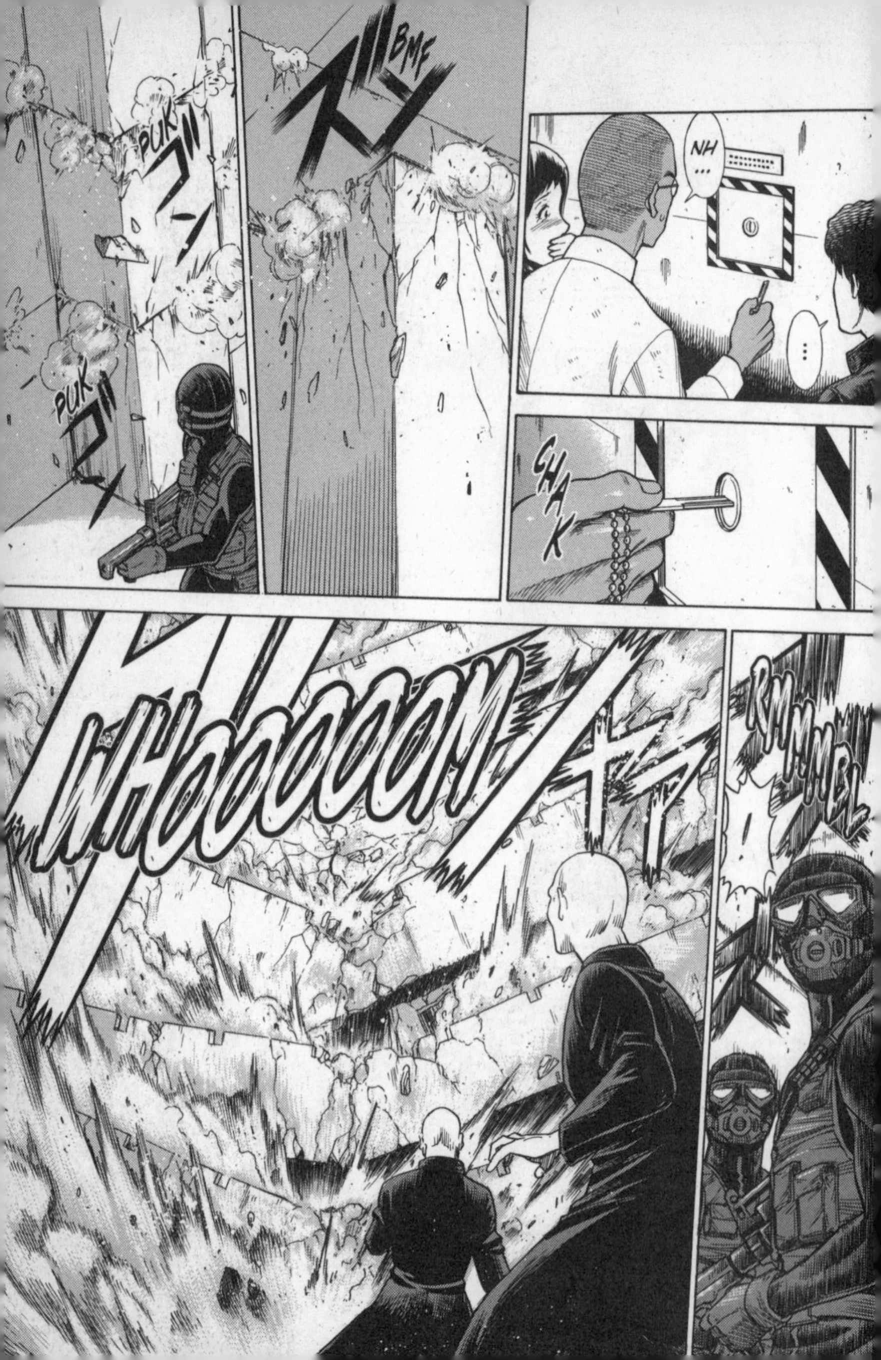
NH ...
...
CHAK
BMF
PUK
PUK
RMMMBL
WHOOOOM

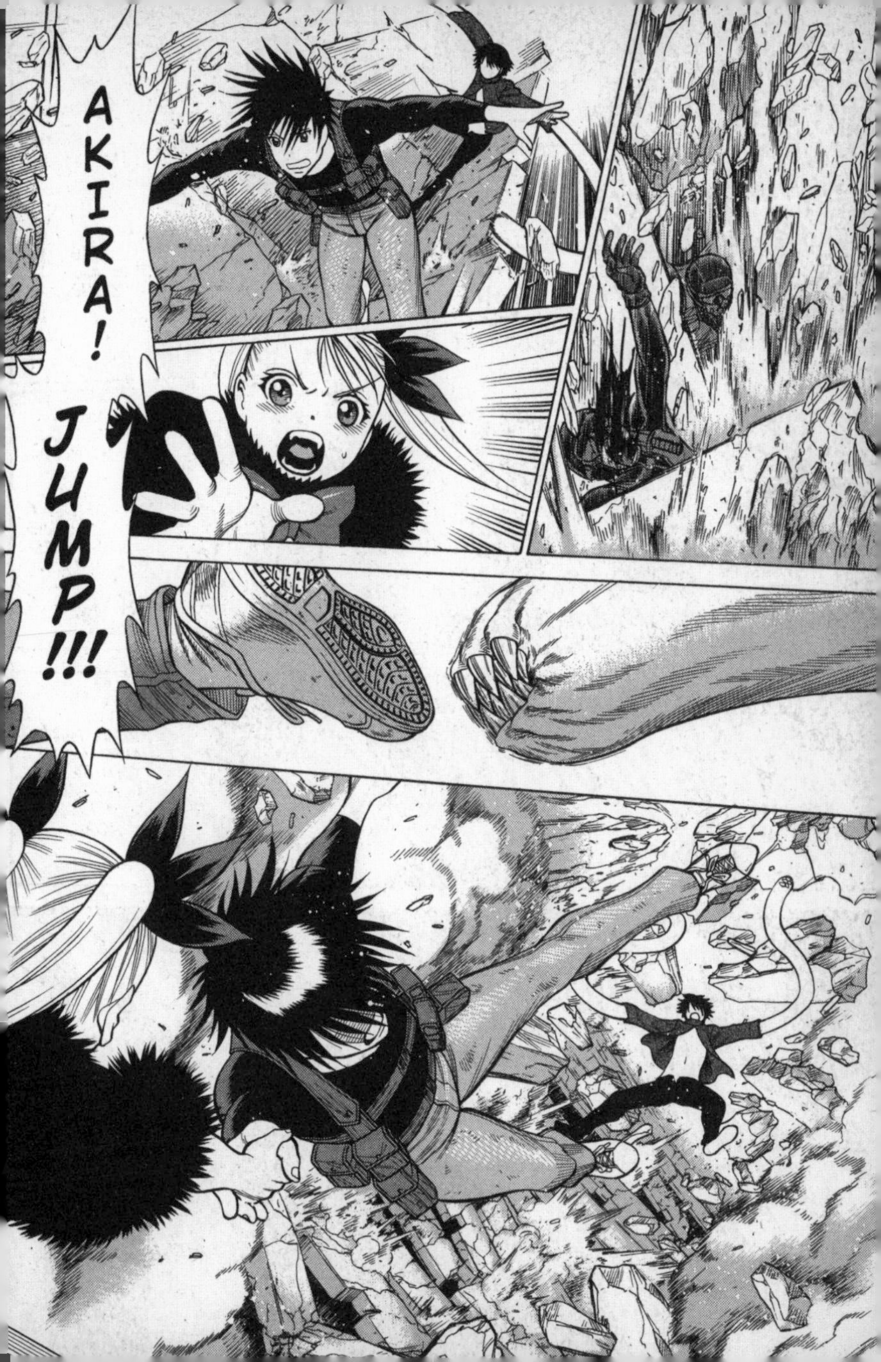
AKIRA! JUMP!!!

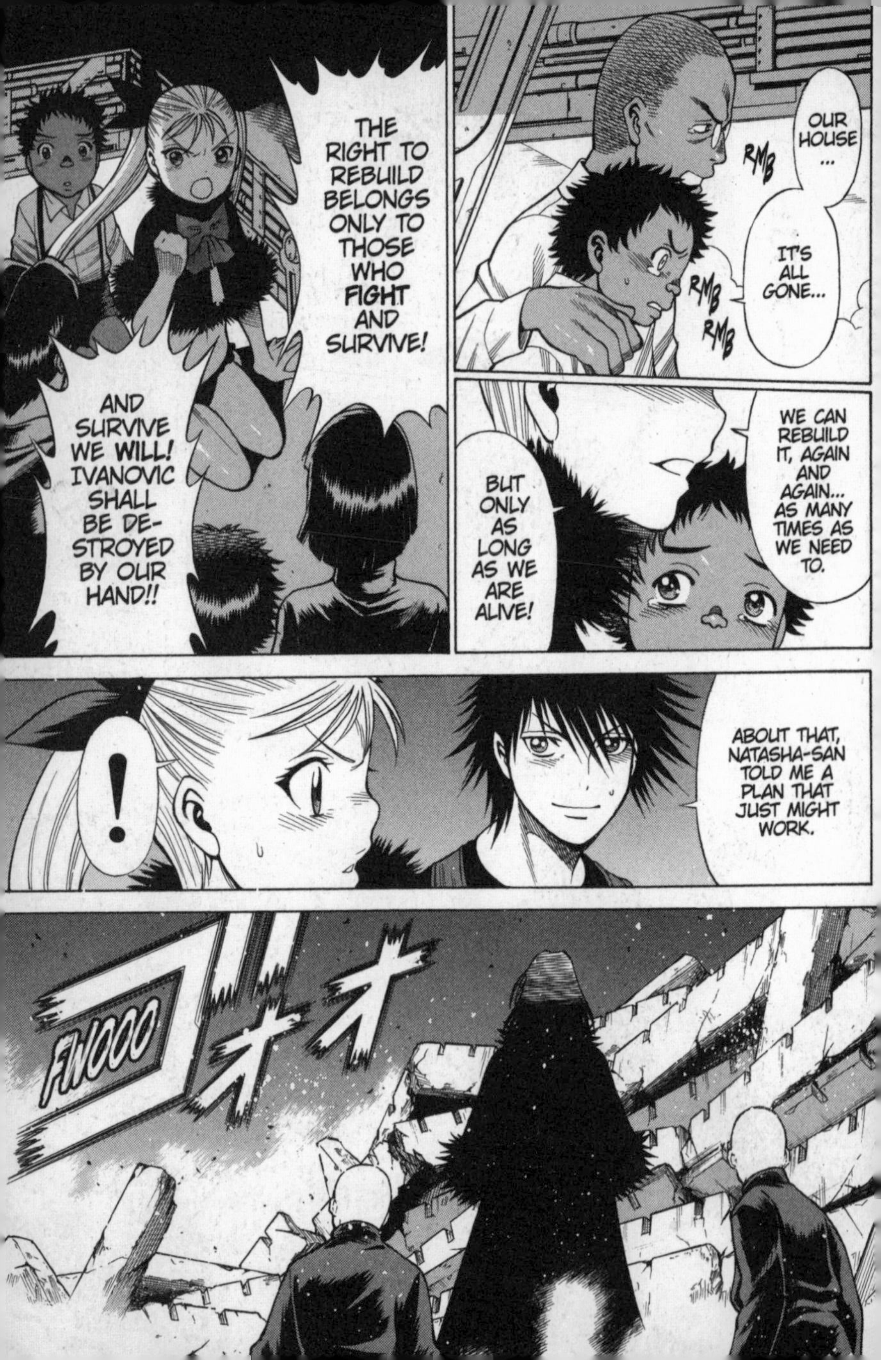
OUR HOUSE ...
RMB
IT'S ALL GONE...
RMB RMB
WE CAN REBUILD IT, AGAIN AND AGAIN... AS MANY TIMES AS WE NEED TO.
BUT ONLY AS LONG AS WE ARE ALIVE!
THE RIGHT TO REBUILD BELONGS ONLY TO THOSE WHO FIGHT AND SURVIVE!
AND SURVIVE WE WILL! IVANOVIC SHALL BE DE-STROYED BY OUR HAND!!
ABOUT THAT, NATASHA-SAN TOLD ME A PLAN THAT JUST MIGHT WORK.
!
FWOOO

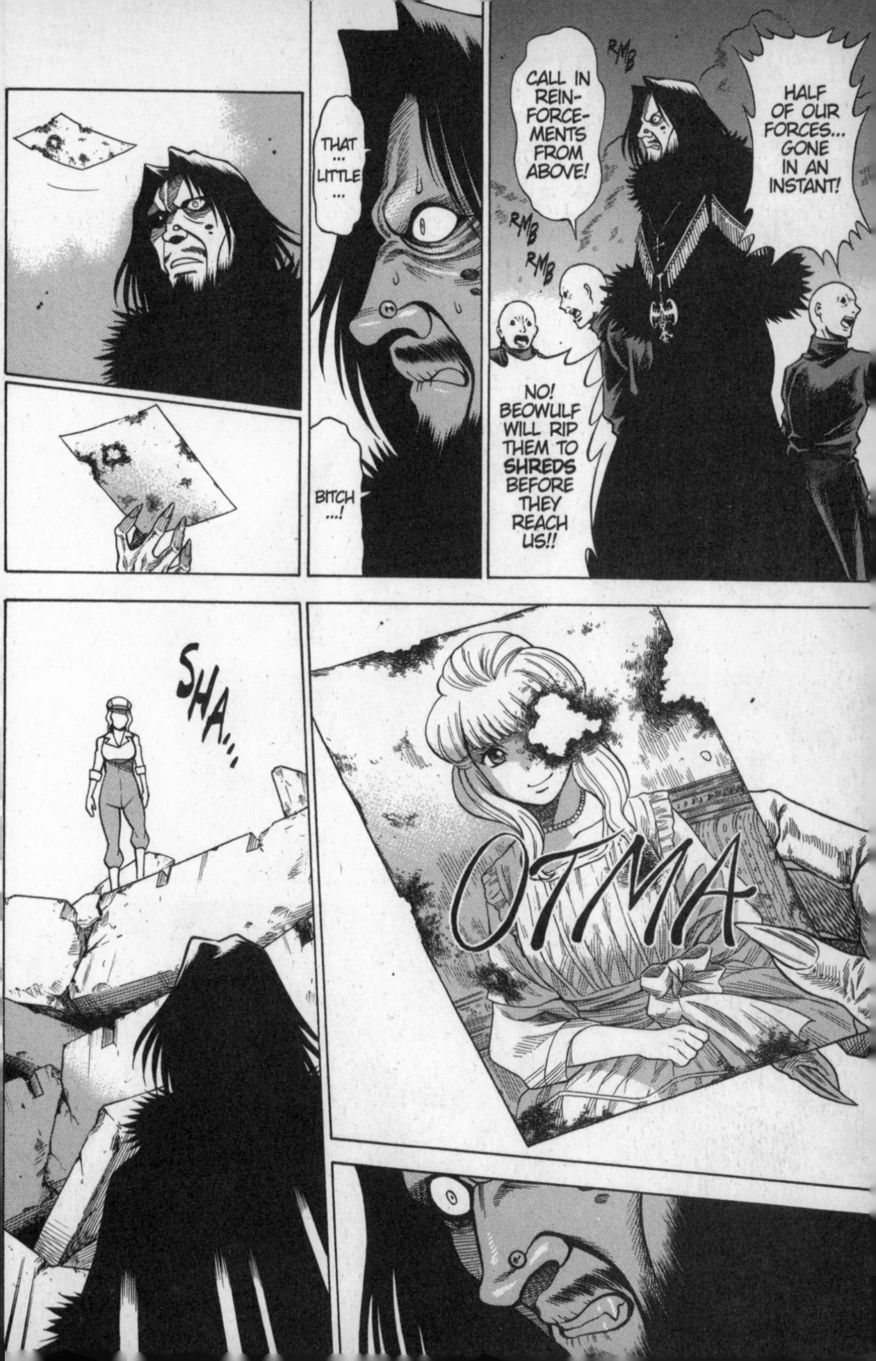
HALF OF OUR FORCES... GONE IN AN INSTANT!
RMB
CALL IN REIN-FORCE-MENTS FROM ABOVE!
RMB
RMB
NO! BEOWULF WILL RIP THEM TO **SHREDS** BEFORE THEY REACH US!!
THAT ... LITTLE ...
BITCH ...!
OTMA
SHA...

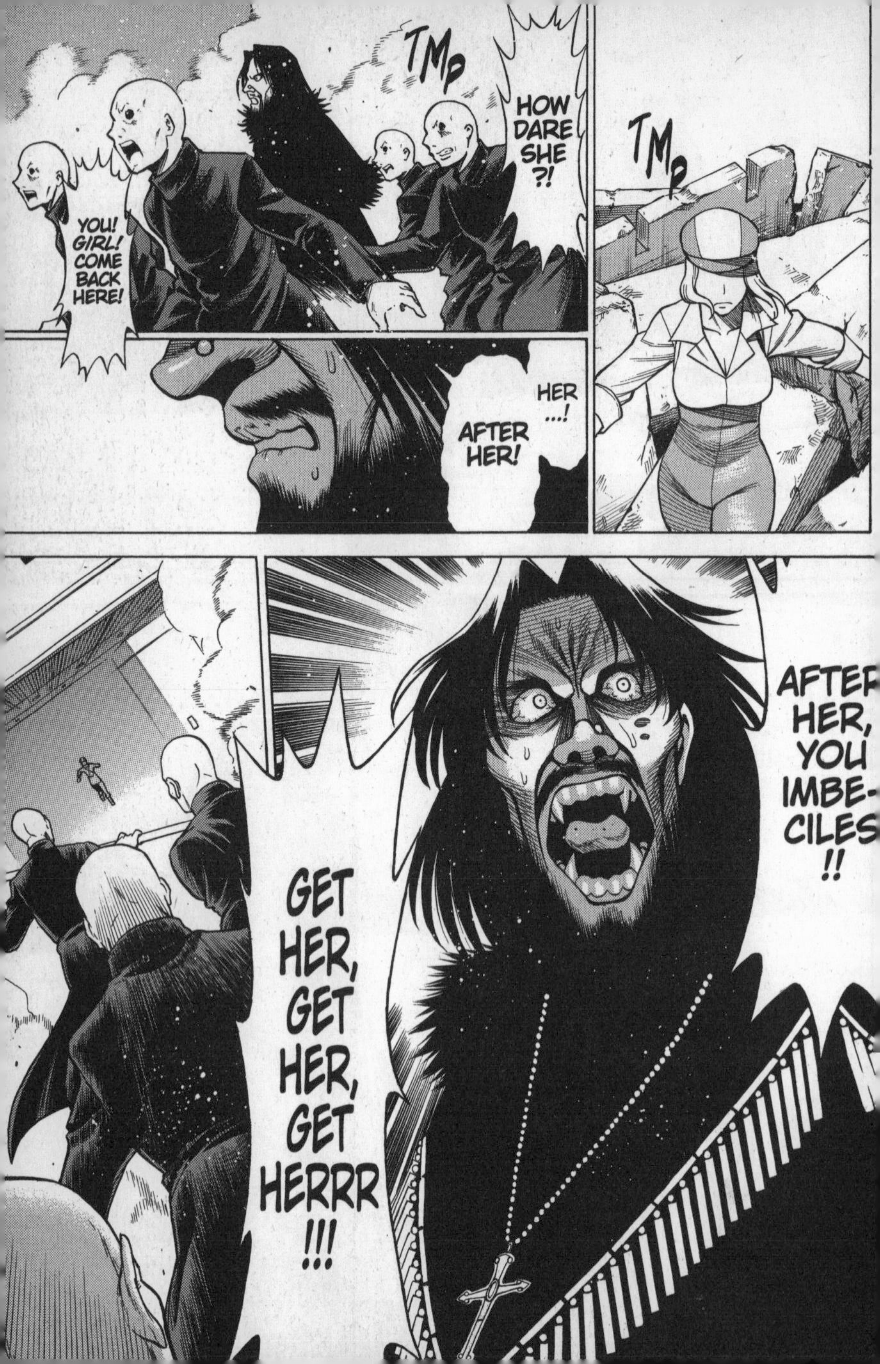
TMP
TMP
HOW DARE SHE?!
YOU! GIRL! COME BACK HERE!
HER ...!
AFTER HER!
AFTER HER, YOU IMBECILES!!
GET HER, GET HER, GET HERRR!!!

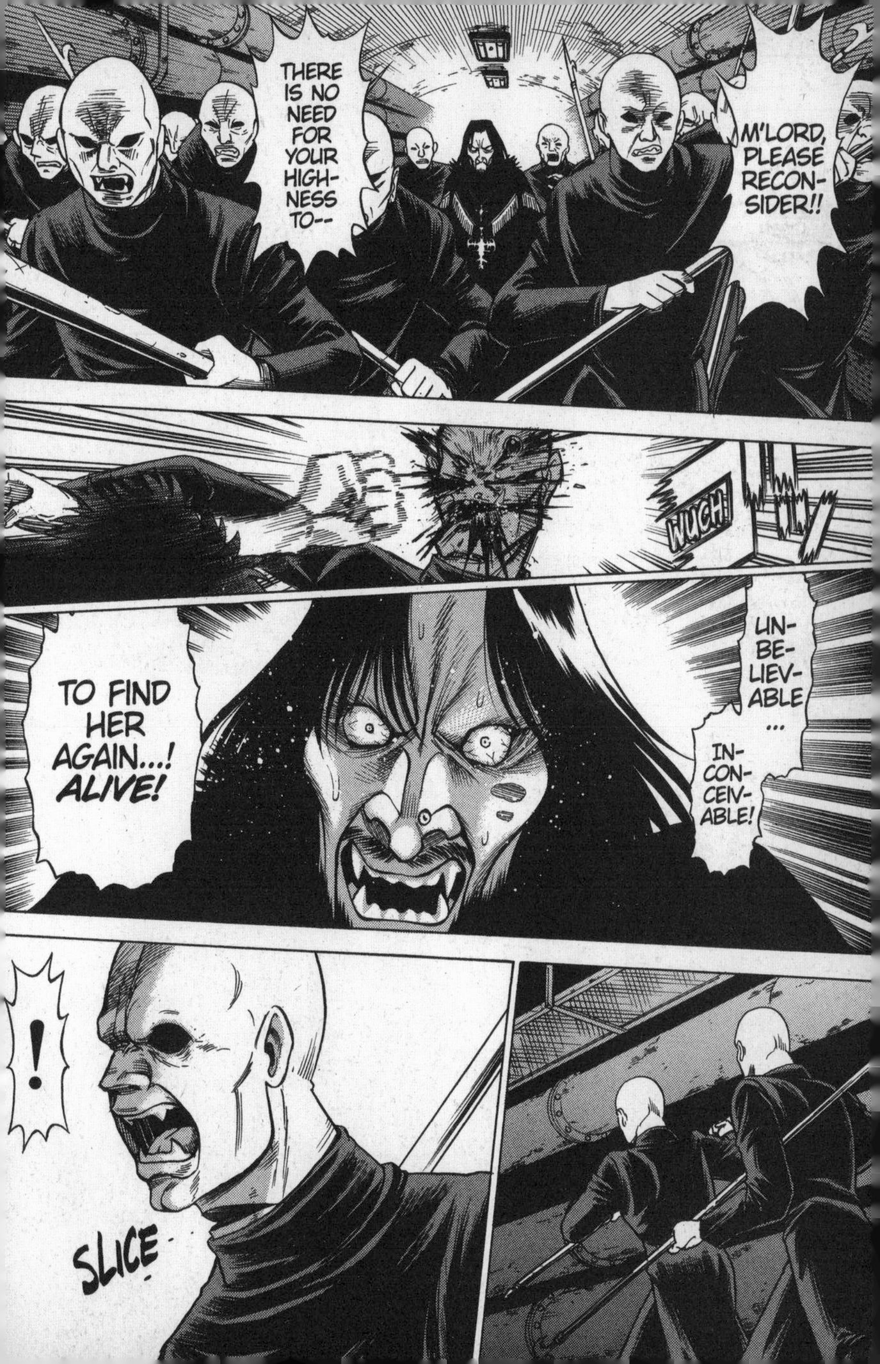
M'LORD, PLEASE RECONSIDER!!
THERE IS NO NEED FOR YOUR HIGHNESS TO--
WUCH
UNBELIEVABLE...
INCONCEIVABLE!
TO FIND HER AGAIN...! ALIVE!
!
SLICE

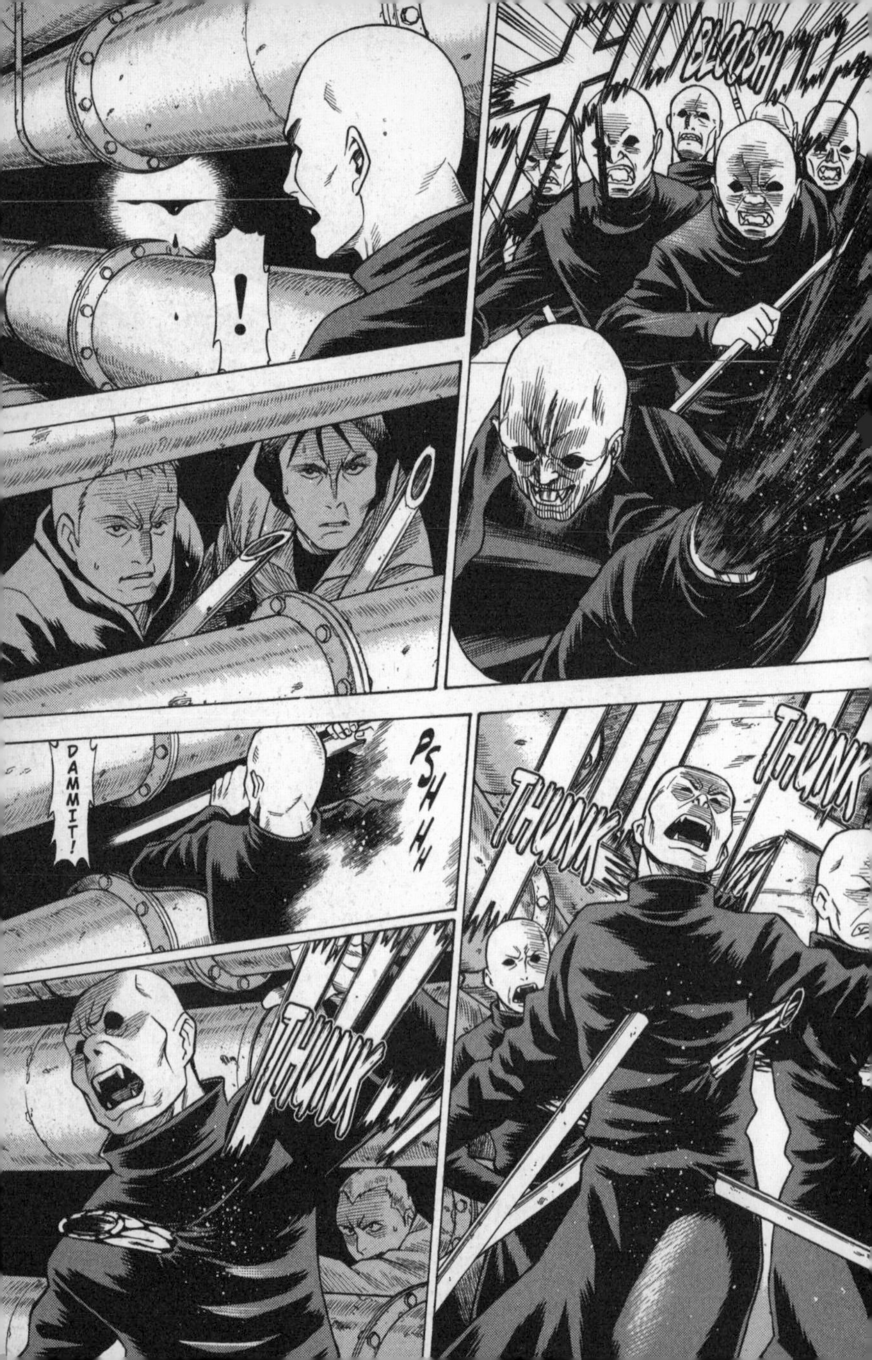
BLOOSH
!
THUNK
THUNK
DAMMIT!
PSHHH
THUNK

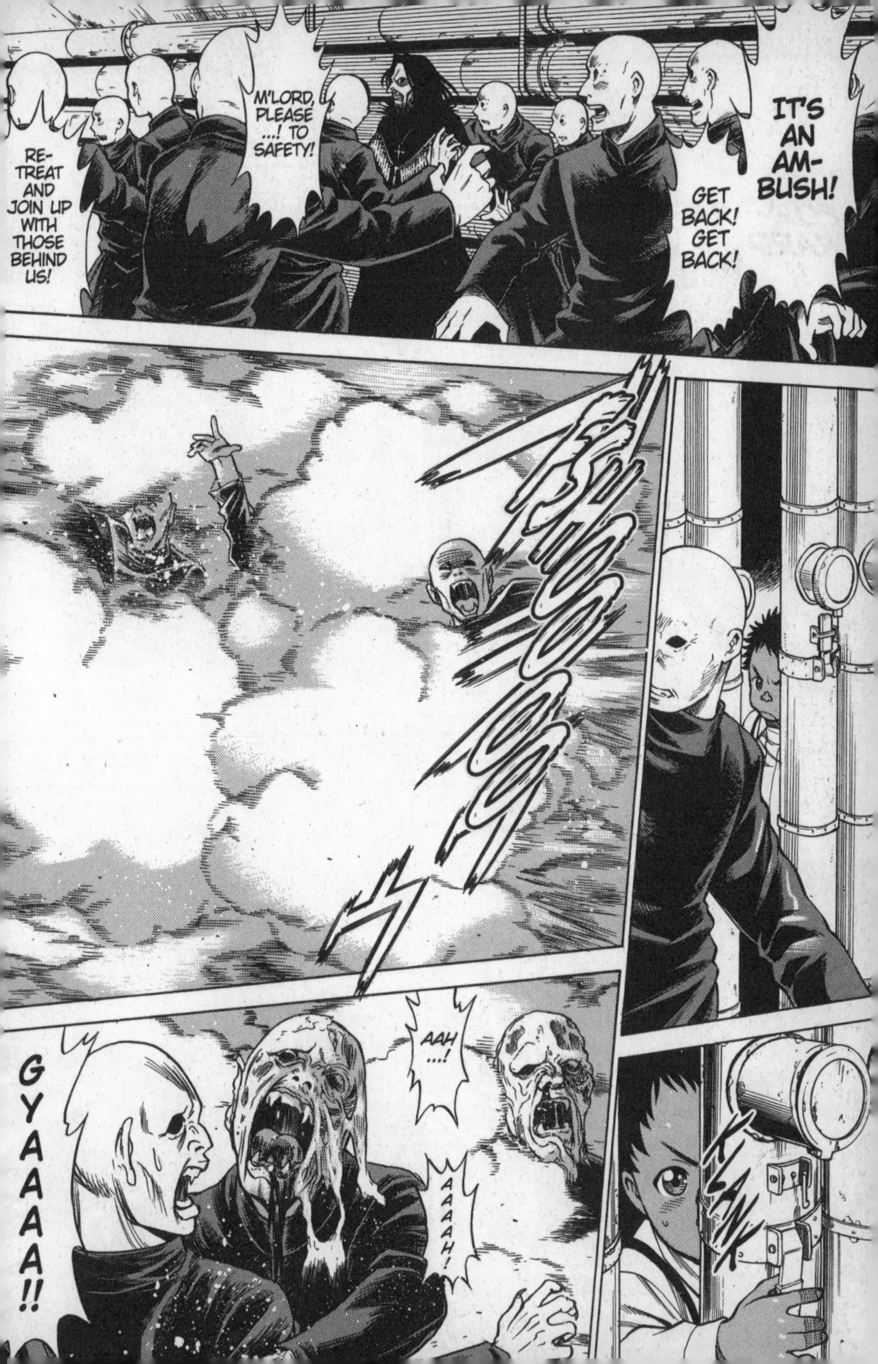
IT'S AN AM-BUSH!
GET BACK! GET BACK!
M'LORD, PLEASE ...! TO SAFETY!
RE-TREAT AND JOIN UP WITH THOSE BEHIND US!
KLANK
AAH ...!
AAAAAH!
GYAAAAAA!!

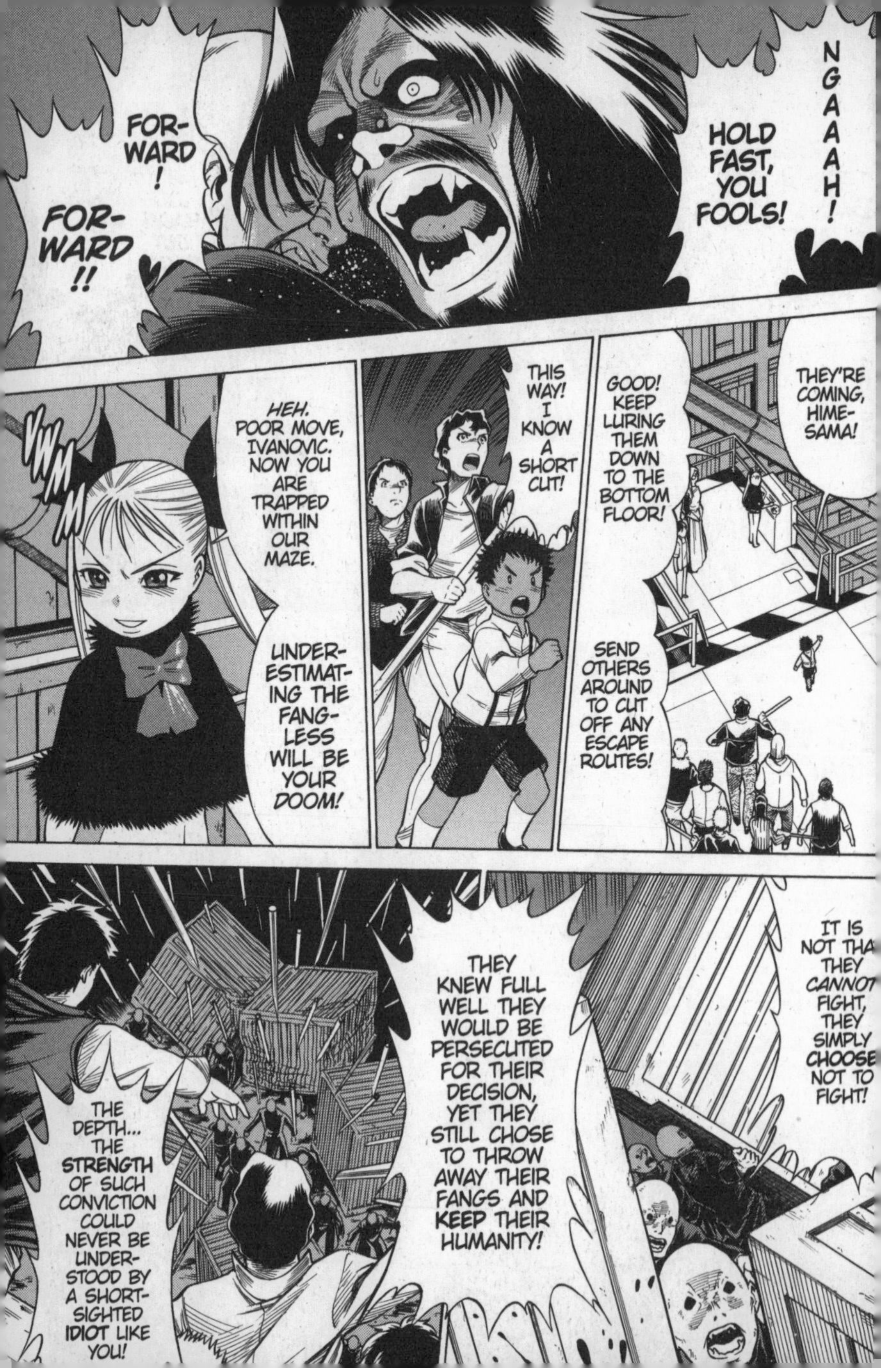
NGAAAAH!
HOLD FAST, YOU FOOLS!
FOR-WARD!
FOR-WARD!!
THEY'RE COMING, HIME-SAMA!
GOOD! KEEP LURING THEM DOWN TO THE BOTTOM FLOOR!
SEND OTHERS AROUND TO CUT OFF ANY ESCAPE ROUTES!
THIS WAY! I KNOW A SHORT CUT!
HEH. POOR MOVE, IVANOVIC. NOW YOU ARE TRAPPED WITHIN OUR MAZE.
UNDER-ESTIMATING THE FANG-LESS WILL BE YOUR DOOM!
IT IS NOT THA THEY CANNO FIGHT, THEY SIMPLY CHOOSE NOT TO FIGHT!
THEY KNEW FULL WELL THEY WOULD BE PERSECUTED FOR THEIR DECISION, YET THEY STILL CHOSE TO THROW AWAY THEIR FANGS AND KEEP THEIR HUMANITY!
THE DEPTH... THE STRENGTH OF SUCH CONVICTION COULD NEVER BE UNDER-STOOD BY A SHORT-SIGHTED IDIOT LIKE YOU!

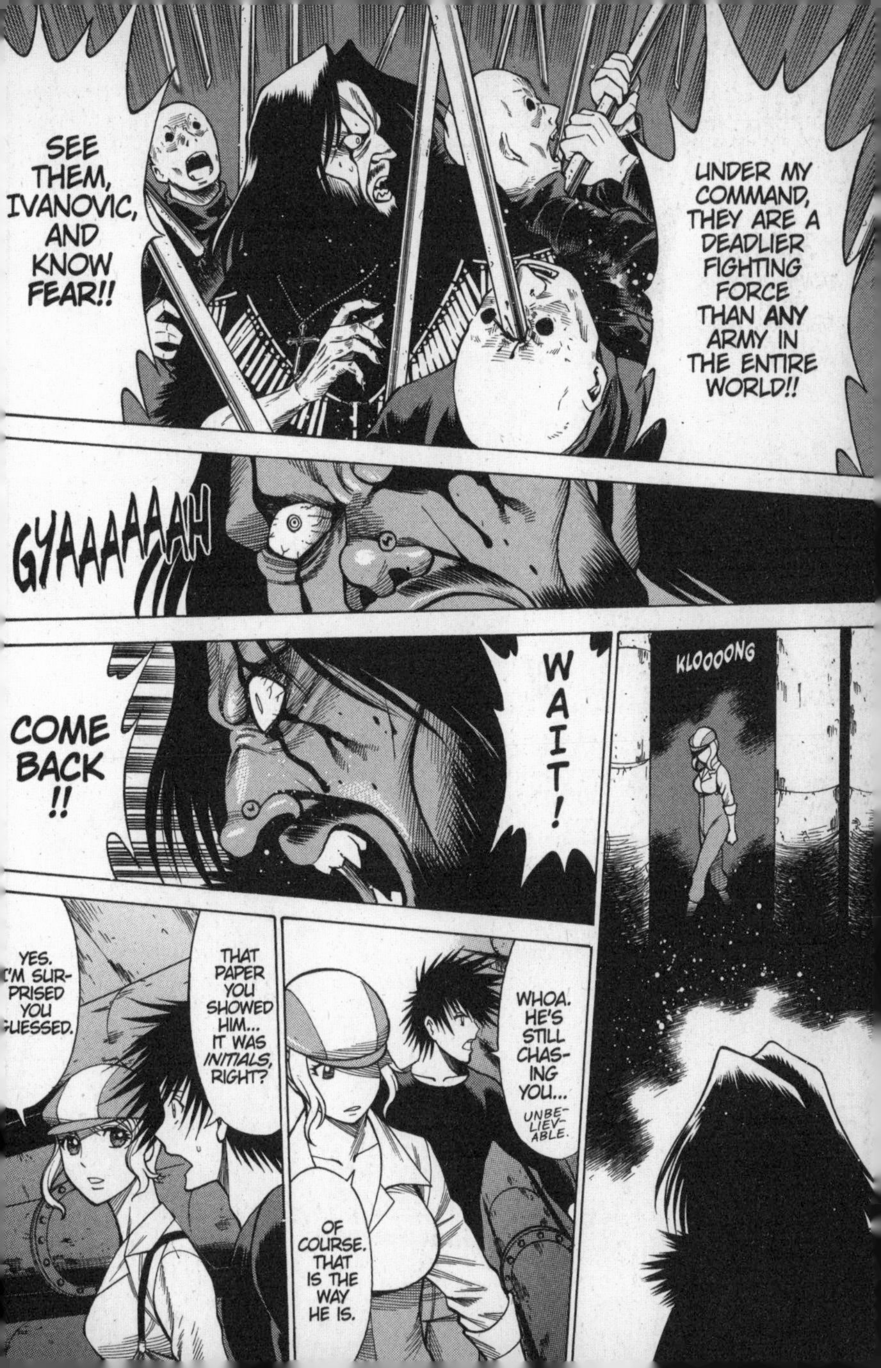
UNDER MY COMMAND, THEY ARE A DEADLIER FIGHTING FORCE THAN ANY ARMY IN THE ENTIRE WORLD!!
SEE THEM, IVANOVIC, AND KNOW FEAR!!
GYAAAAAAH
KLOOOONG
WAIT!
COME BACK!!
WHOA. HE'S STILL CHAS-ING YOU...
UNBE-LIEV-ABLE.
OF COURSE. THAT IS THE WAY HE IS.
THAT PAPER YOU SHOWED HIM... IT WAS INITIALS, RIGHT?
YES. I'M SUR-PRISED YOU GUESSED.

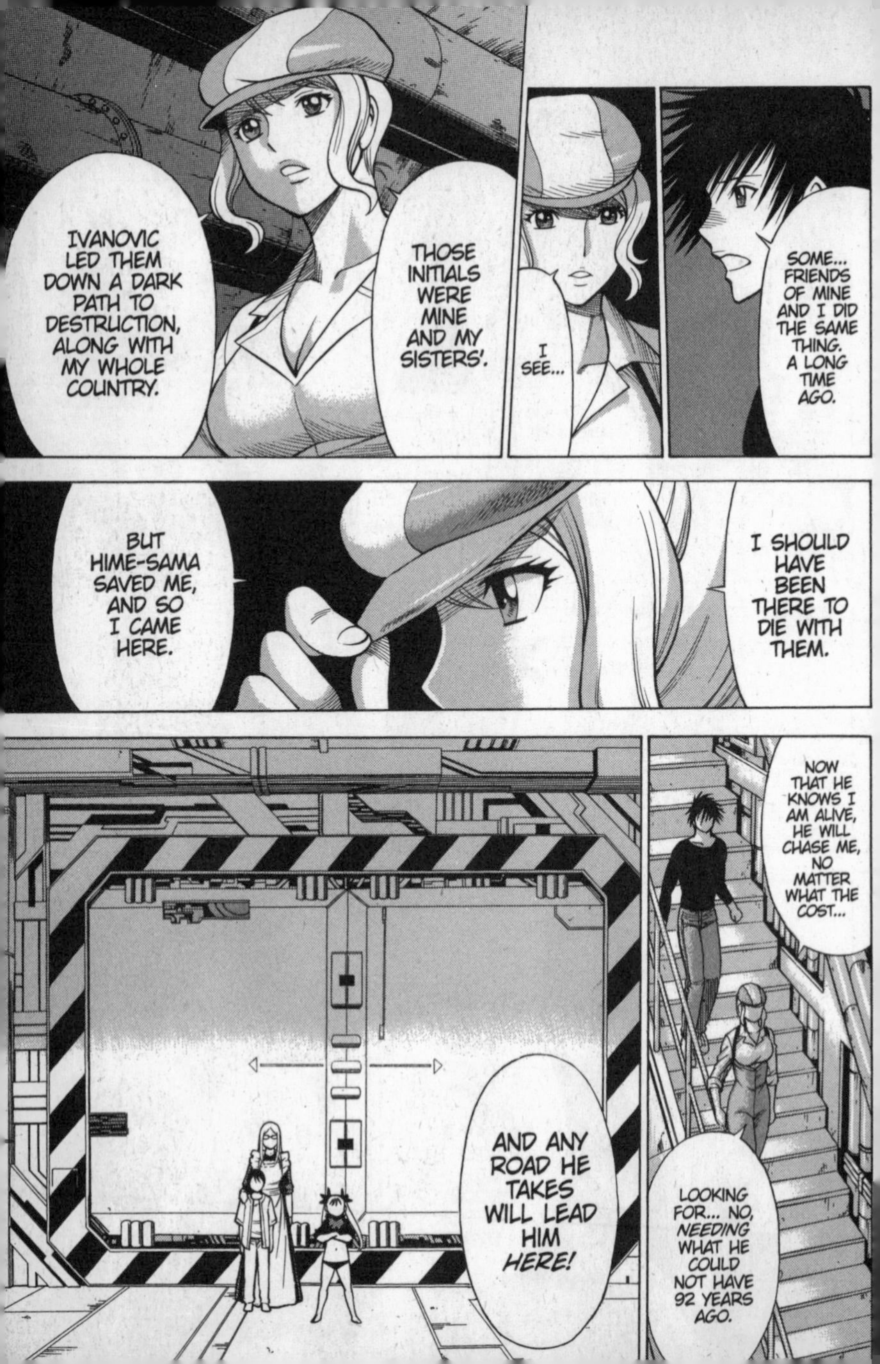
SOME... FRIENDS OF MINE AND I DID THE SAME THING. A LONG TIME AGO.
I SEE...
THOSE INITIALS WERE MINE AND MY SISTERS'.
IVANOVIC LED THEM DOWN A DARK PATH TO DESTRUCTION, ALONG WITH MY WHOLE COUNTRY.
I SHOULD HAVE BEEN THERE TO DIE WITH THEM.
BUT HIME-SAMA SAVED ME, AND SO I CAME HERE.
NOW THAT HE KNOWS I AM ALIVE, HE WILL CHASE ME, NO MATTER WHAT THE COST...
LOOKING FOR... NO, *NEEDING* WHAT HE COULD NOT HAVE 92 YEARS AGO.
AND ANY ROAD HE TAKES WILL LEAD HIM *HERE!*

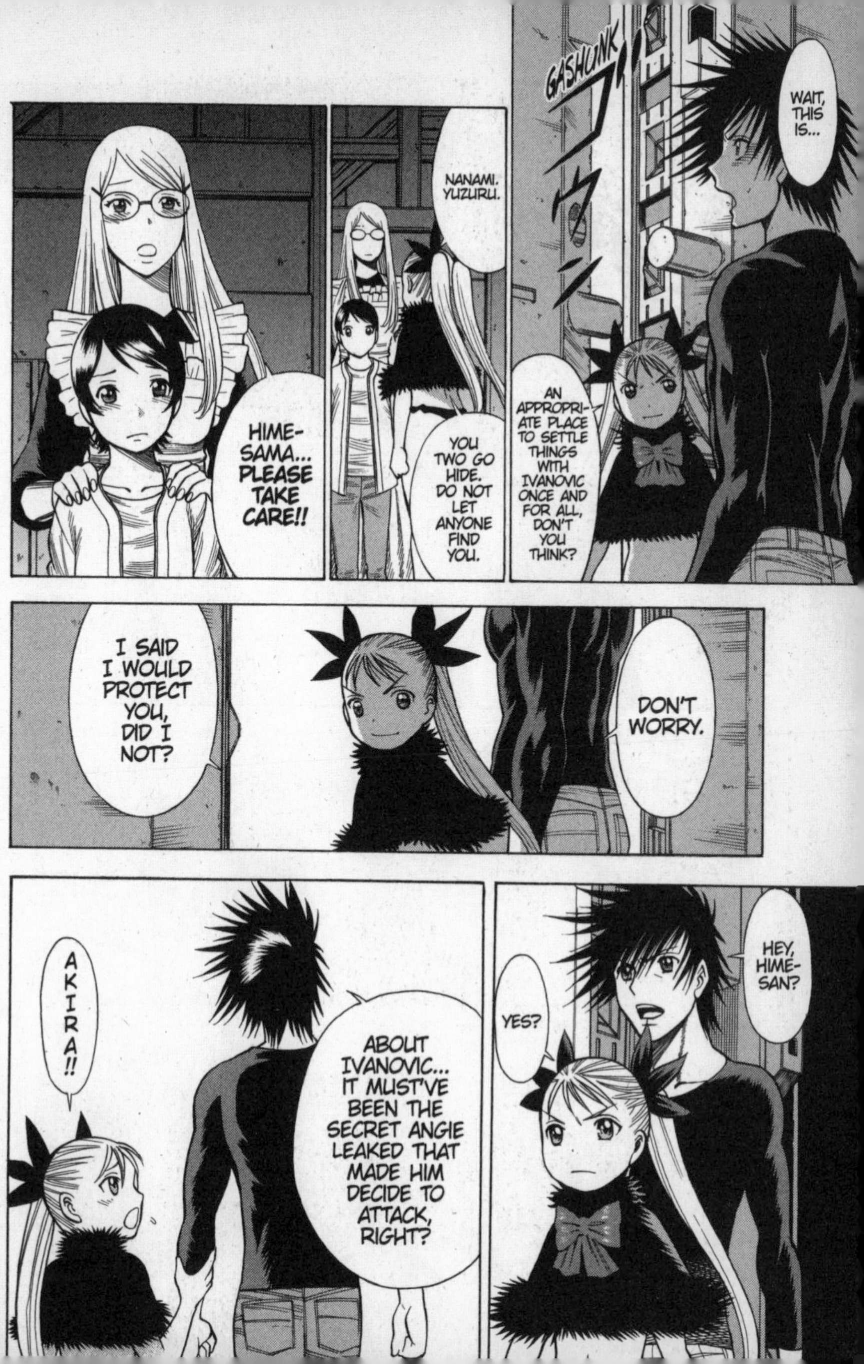
GASHUNK
WAIT, THIS IS...
AN APPROPRIATE PLACE TO SETTLE THINGS WITH IVANOVIC ONCE AND FOR ALL, DON'T YOU THINK?
NANAMI. YUZURU.
YOU TWO GO HIDE. DO NOT LET ANYONE FIND YOU.
HIME-SAMA... PLEASE TAKE CARE!!
DON'T WORRY.
I SAID I WOULD PROTECT YOU, DID I NOT?
HEY, HIME-SAN?
YES?
ABOUT IVANOVIC... IT MUST'VE BEEN THE SECRET ANGIE LEAKED THAT MADE HIM DECIDE TO ATTACK, RIGHT?
AKIRA!!

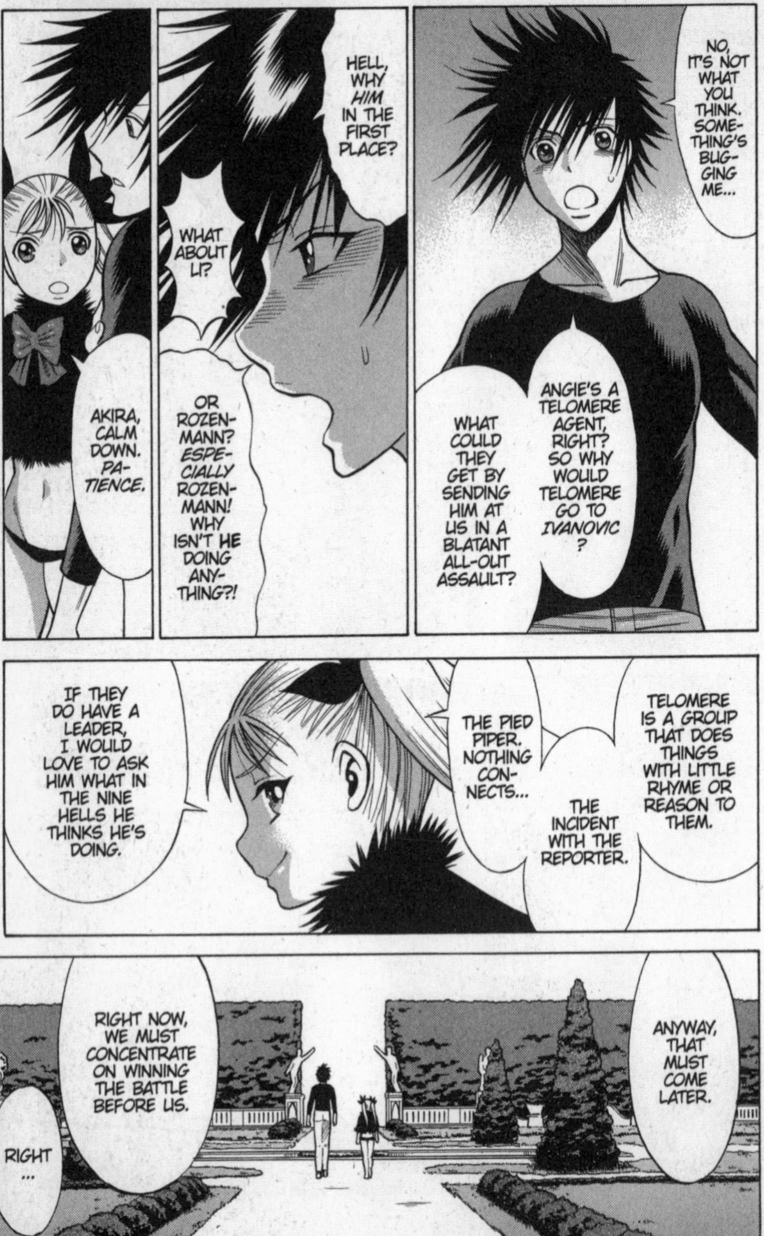
NO, IT'S NOT WHAT YOU THINK. SOMETHING'S BUGGING ME...
ANGIE'S A TELOMERE AGENT, RIGHT? SO WHY WOULD TELOMERE GO TO *IVANOVIC*?
WHAT COULD THEY GET BY SENDING HIM AT US IN A BLATANT ALL-OUT ASSAULT?
HELL, WHY *HIM* IN THE FIRST PLACE?
WHAT ABOUT LI?
OR ROZENMANN? *ESPECIALLY* ROZENMANN! WHY ISN'T HE DOING ANYTHING?!
AKIRA, CALM DOWN. *PATIENCE.*
TELOMERE IS A GROUP THAT DOES THINGS WITH LITTLE RHYME OR REASON TO THEM.
THE INCIDENT WITH THE REPORTER.
THE PIED PIPER. NOTHING CONNECTS...
IF THEY DO HAVE A LEADER, I WOULD LOVE TO ASK HIM WHAT IN THE NINE HELLS HE THINKS HE'S DOING.
ANYWAY, THAT MUST COME LATER.
RIGHT NOW, WE MUST CONCENTRATE ON WINNING THE BATTLE BEFORE US.
RIGHT ...

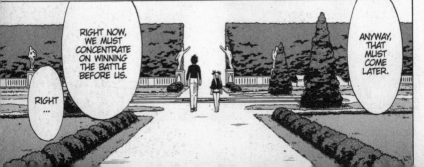

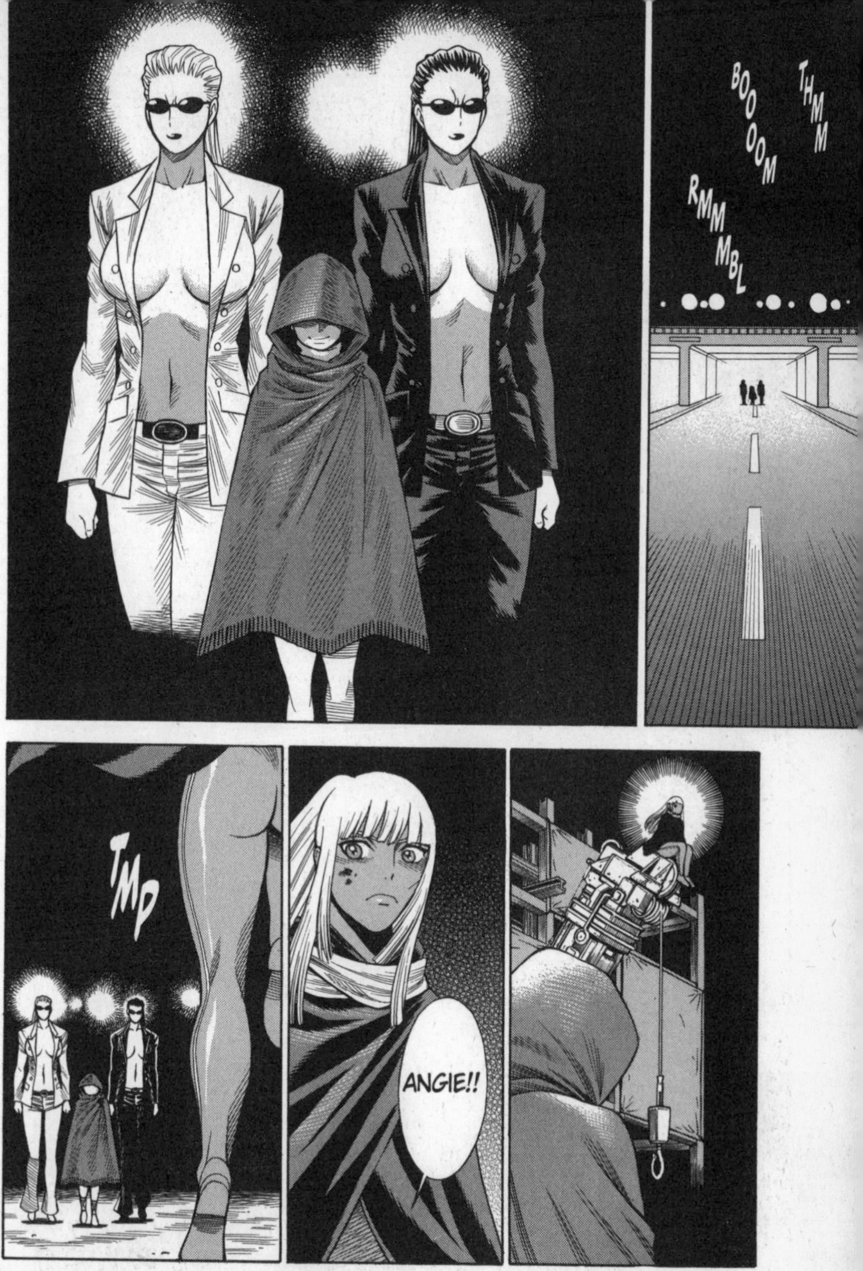
THMM
BOOOOM
RMMMBL
ANGIE!!
TMP

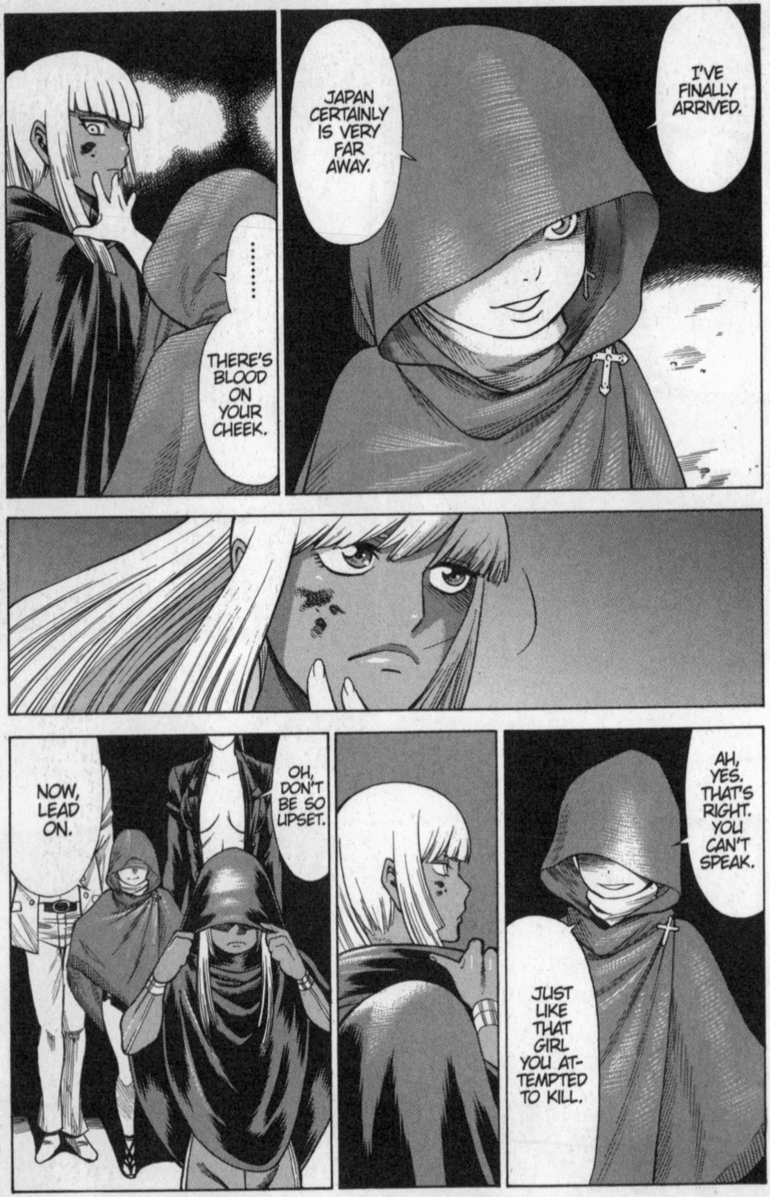
I'VE FINALLY ARRIVED.
JAPAN CERTAINLY IS VERY FAR AWAY.
......
THERE'S BLOOD ON YOUR CHEEK.
AH, YES. THAT'S RIGHT. YOU CAN'T SPEAK.
JUST LIKE THAT GIRL YOU AT-TEMPTED TO KILL.
OH, DON'T BE SO UPSET.
NOW, LEAD ON.

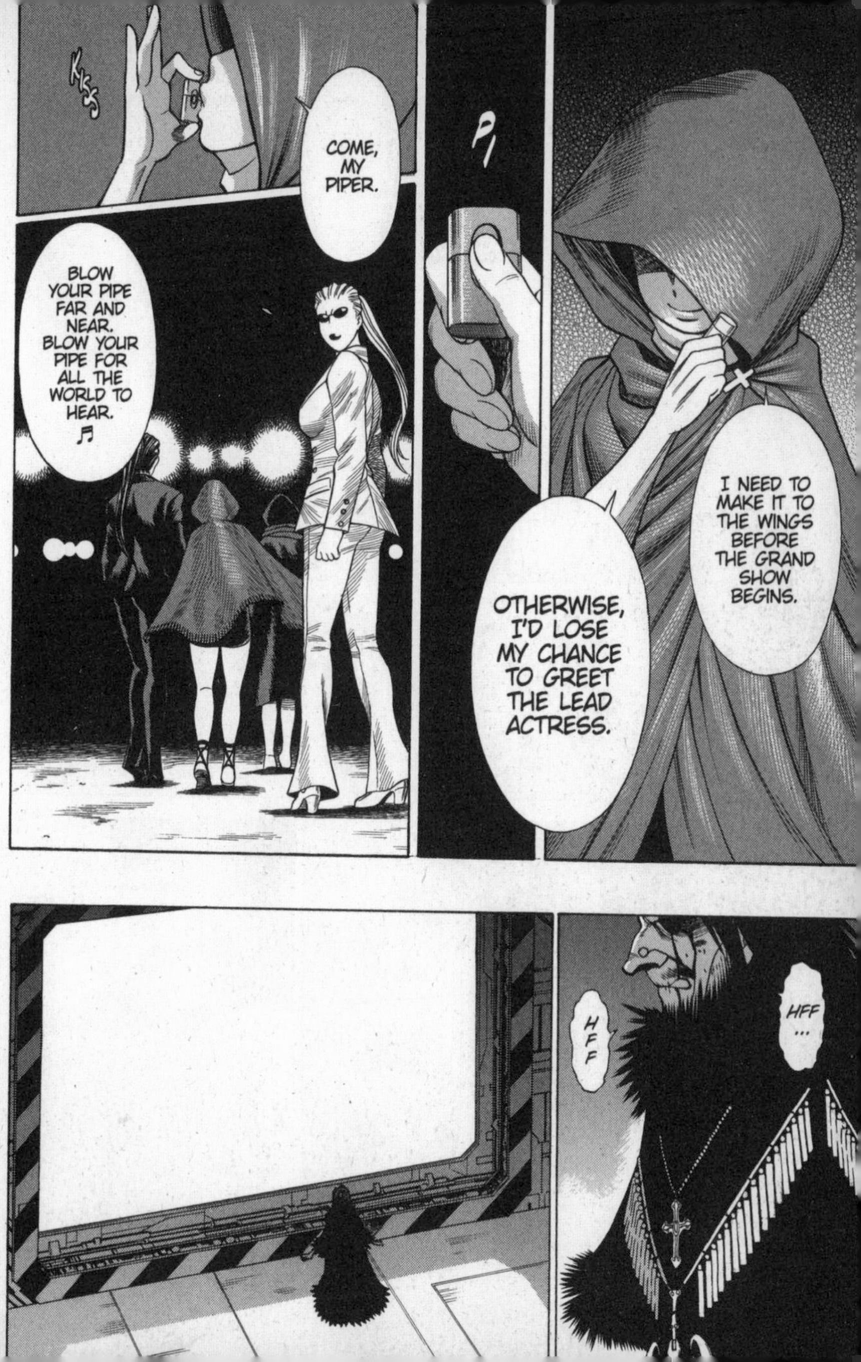
I NEED TO MAKE IT TO THE WINGS BEFORE THE GRAND SHOW BEGINS.
OTHERWISE, I'D LOSE MY CHANCE TO GREET THE LEAD ACTRESS.
PI
KISS
COME, MY PIPER.
BLOW YOUR PIPE FAR AND NEAR. BLOW YOUR PIPE FOR ALL THE WORLD TO HEAR. ♬
HFF...
HFF

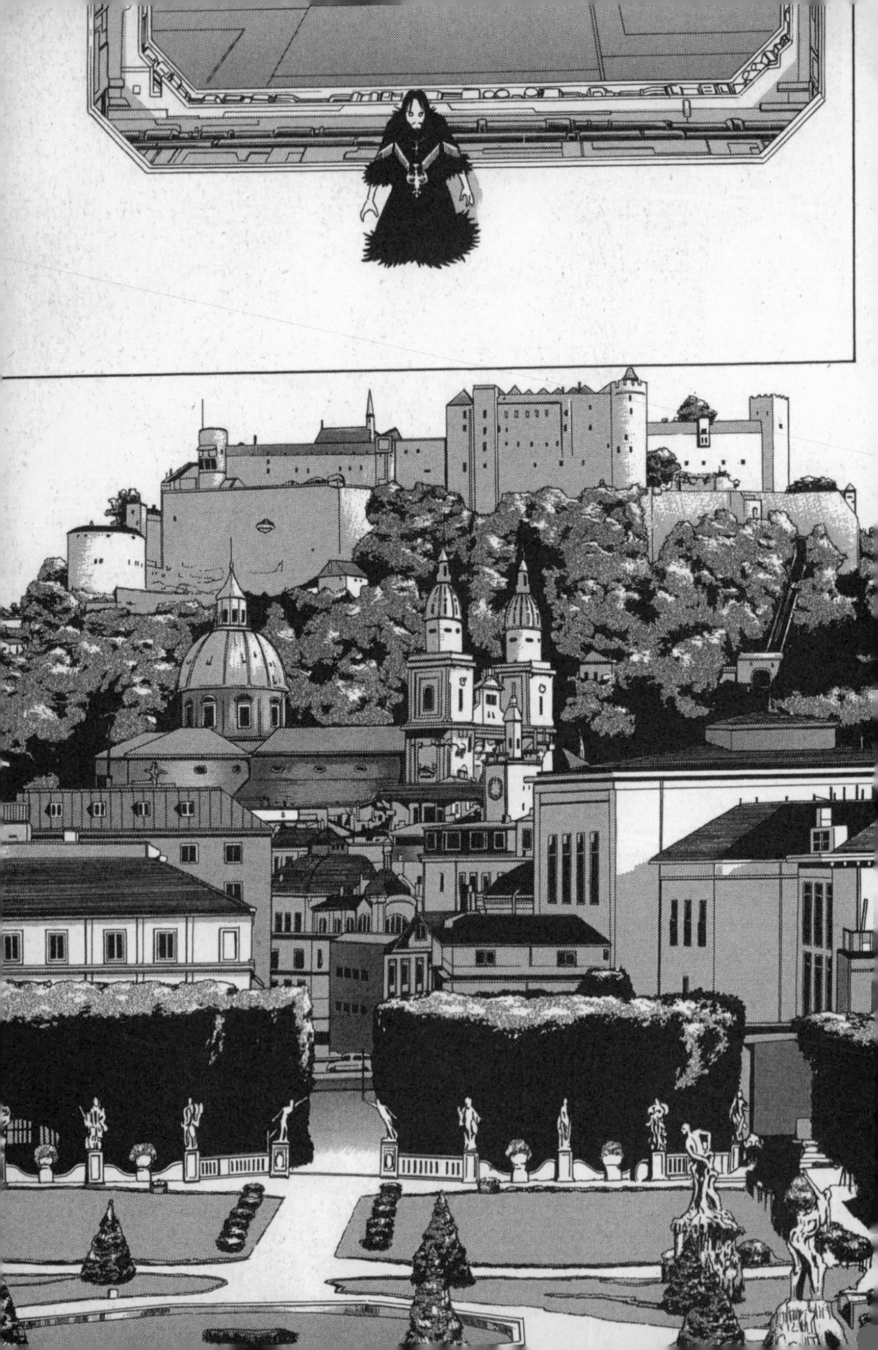

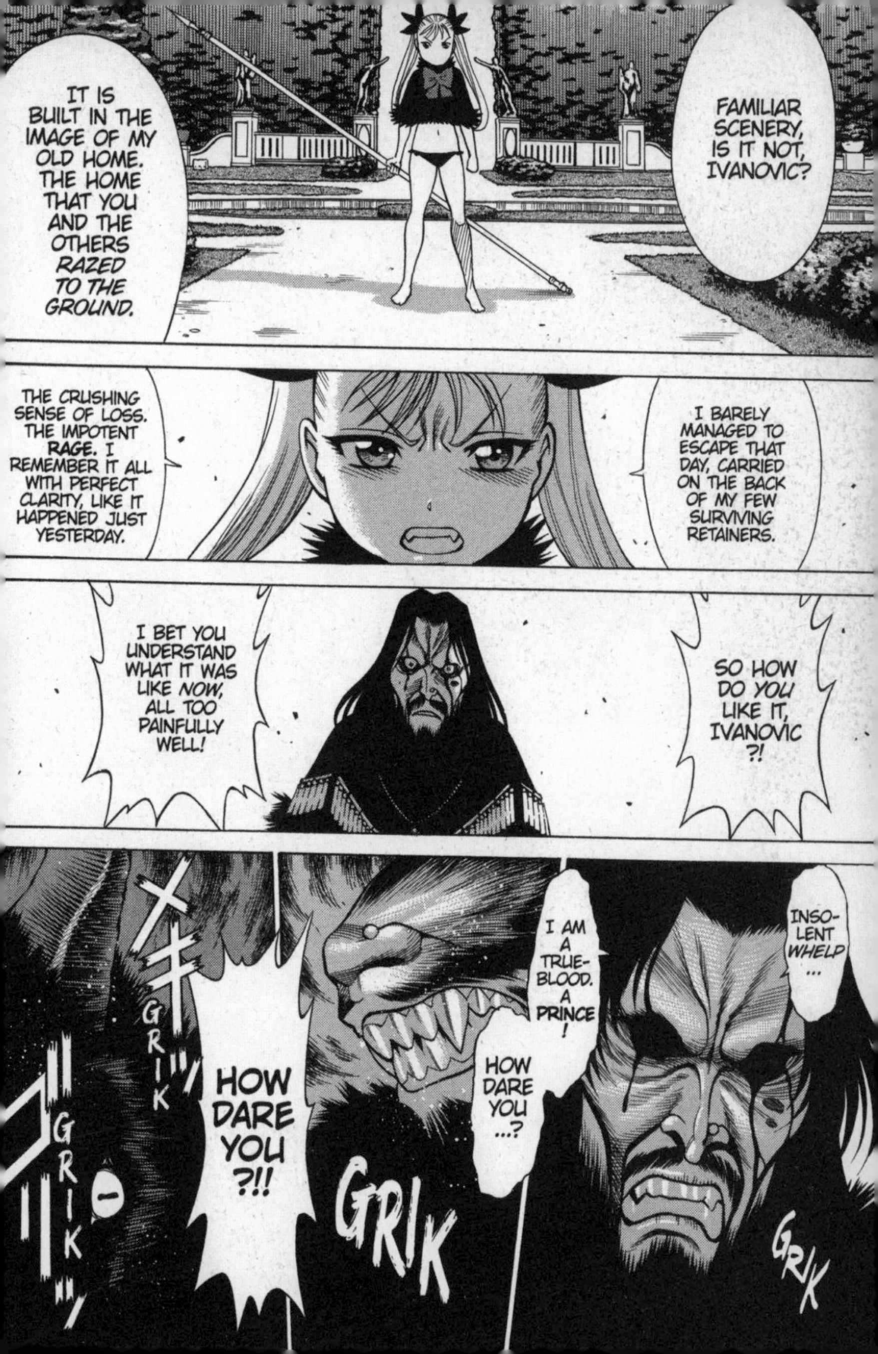
FAMILIAR SCENERY, IS IT NOT, IVANOVIC?
IT IS BUILT IN THE IMAGE OF MY OLD HOME. THE HOME THAT YOU AND THE OTHERS *RAZED* TO THE GROUND.
I BARELY MANAGED TO ESCAPE THAT DAY, CARRIED ON THE BACK OF MY FEW SURVIVING RETAINERS.
THE CRUSHING SENSE OF LOSS. THE IMPOTENT RAGE. I REMEMBER IT ALL WITH PERFECT CLARITY, LIKE IT HAPPENED JUST YESTERDAY.
SO HOW DO *YOU* LIKE IT, IVANOVIC ?!
I BET YOU UNDERSTAND WHAT IT WAS LIKE *NOW*, ALL TOO PAINFULLY WELL!
INSOLENT *WHELP* ...
I AM A TRUEBLOOD. A PRINCE!
HOW DARE YOU ...?
GRIK
GRIK
HOW DARE YOU ?!!
GRIK
GRIK

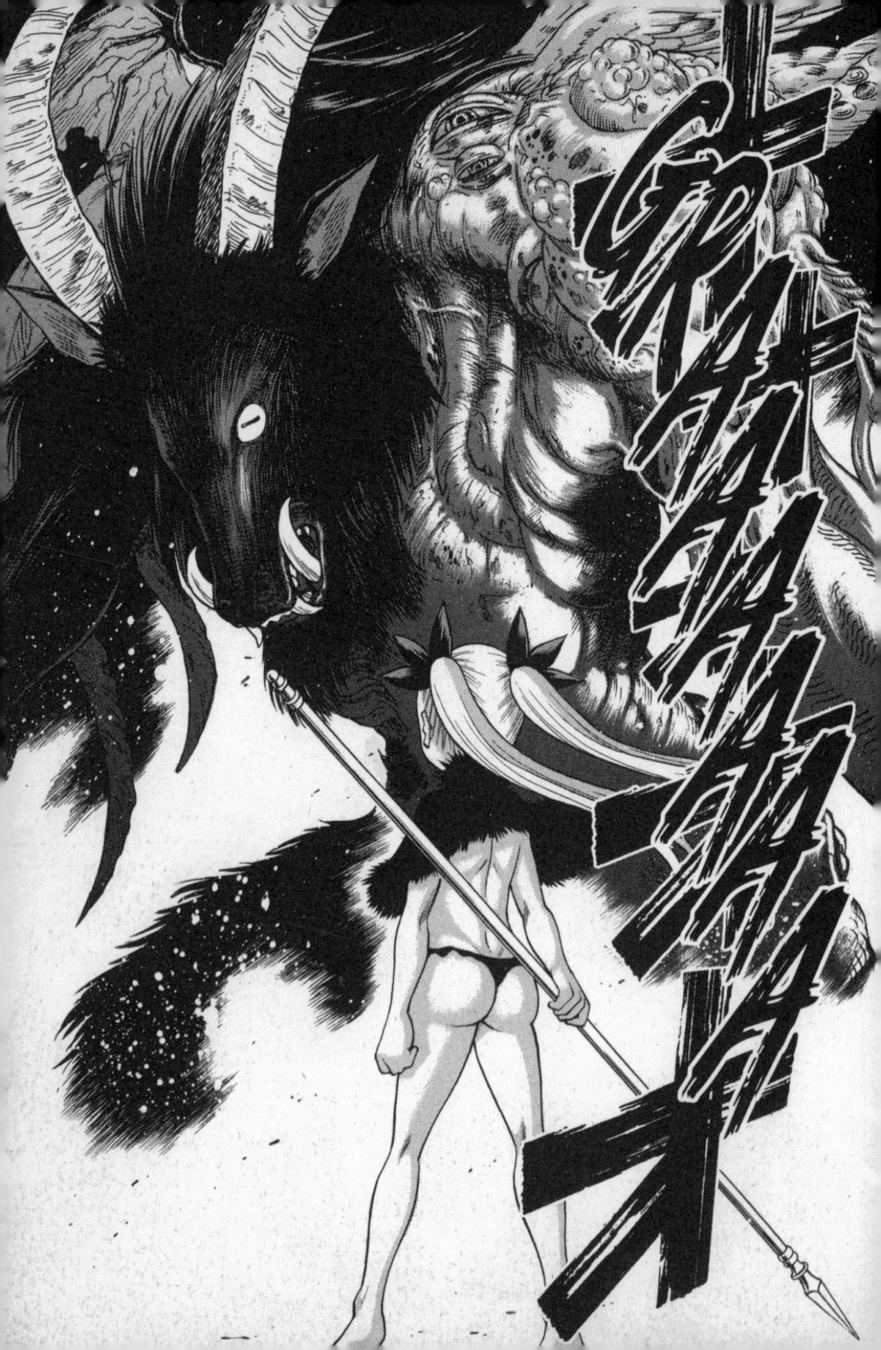

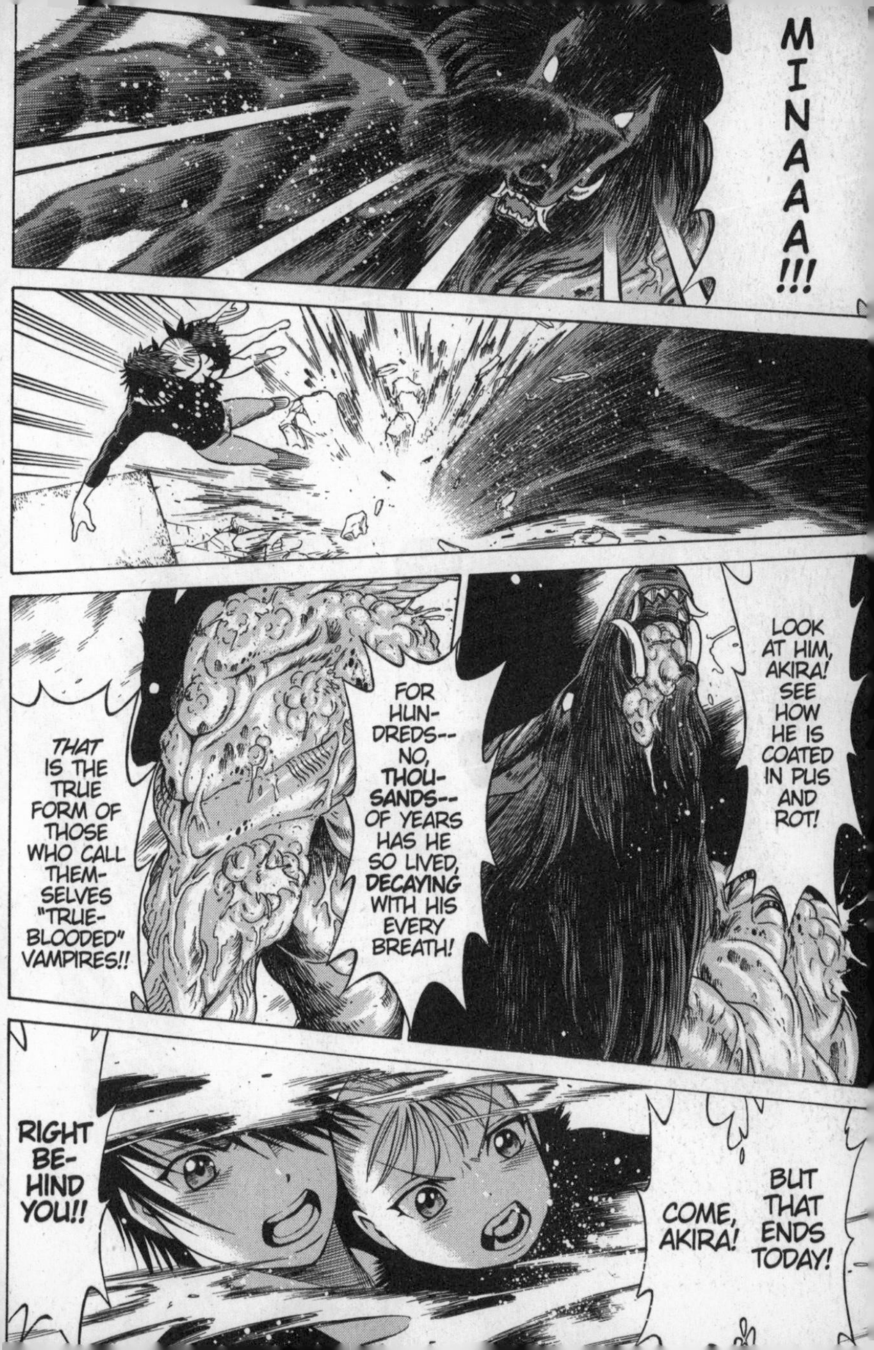
MINAAAA!!!
LOOK AT HIM, AKIRA! SEE HOW HE IS COATED IN PUS AND ROT!
FOR HUNDREDS--NO, THOUSANDS--OF YEARS HAS HE SO LIVED, DECAYING WITH HIS EVERY BREATH!
THAT IS THE TRUE FORM OF THOSE WHO CALL THEMSELVES "TRUE-BLOODED" VAMPIRES!!
BUT THAT ENDS TODAY!
COME, AKIRA!
RIGHT BEHIND YOU!!

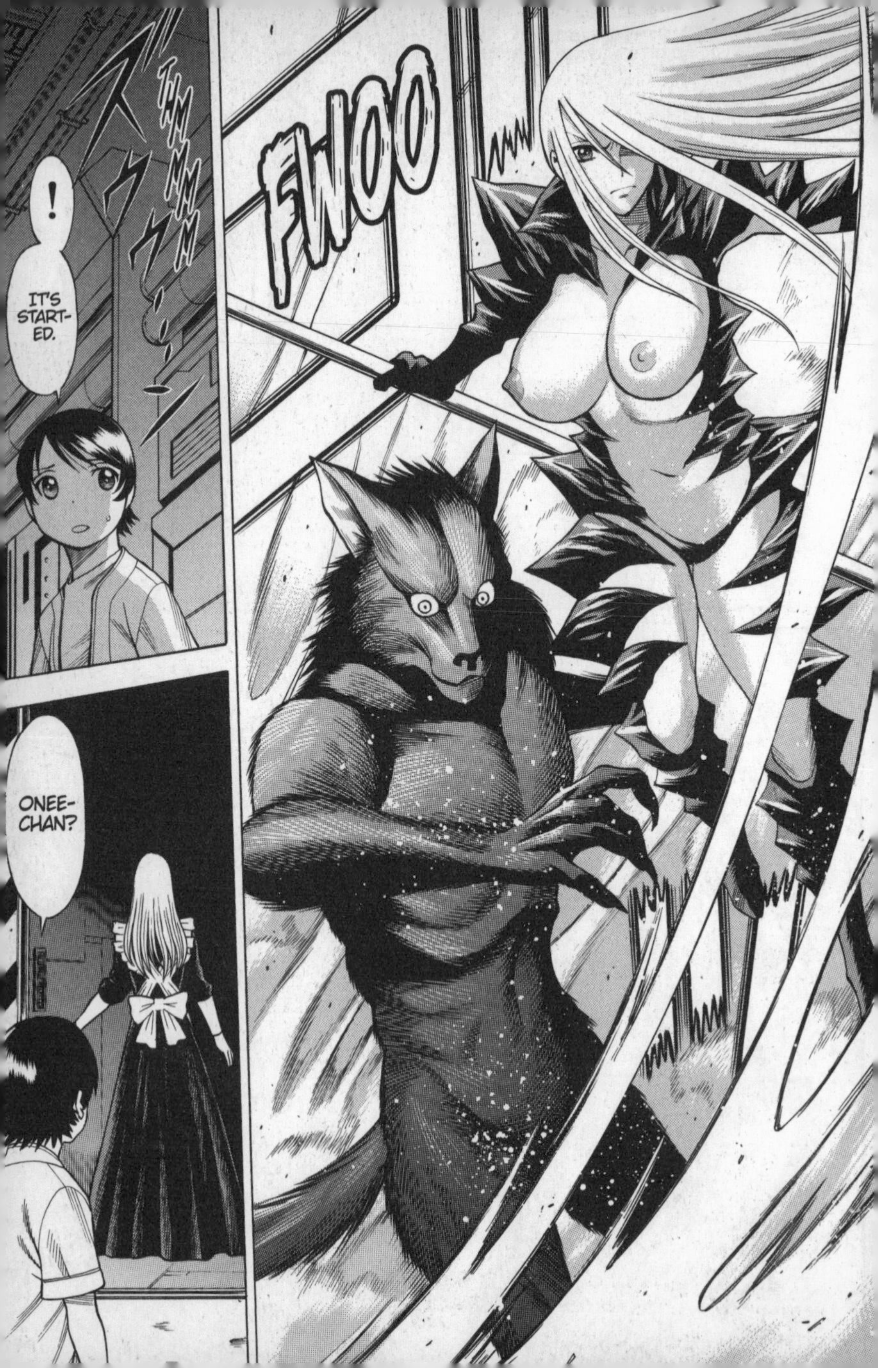
FWOO
THMMMMM
!
IT'S STARTED.
ONEE-CHAN?

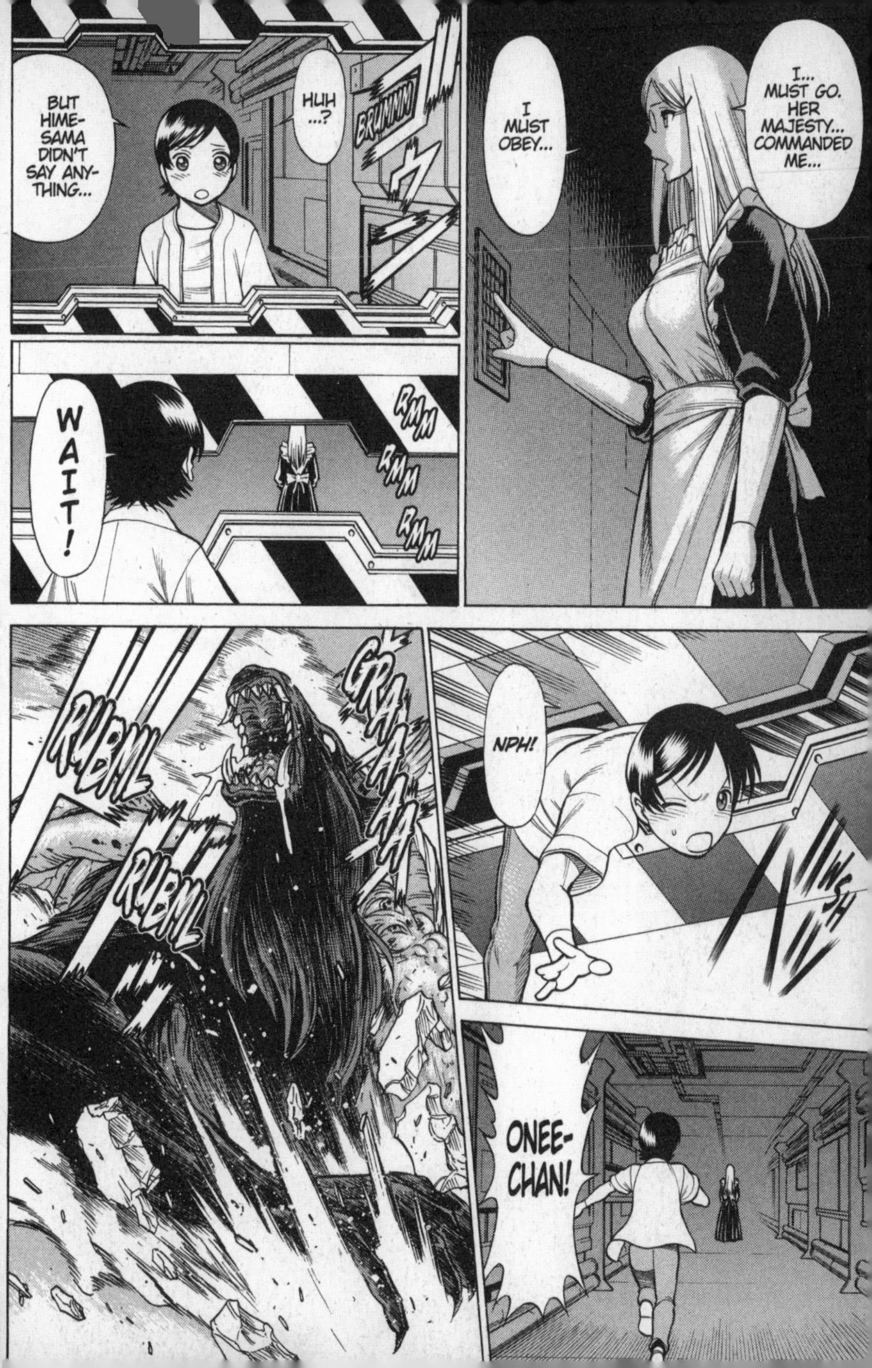
I... MUST GO. HER MAJESTY... COMMANDED ME...
I MUST OBEY...
BRUNNN
HUH ...?
BUT HIME-SAMA DIDN'T SAY ANY-THING...
RMM RMM RMM
WAIT!
NPH!
WSH
ONEE-CHAN!
GRAAAA
RUBML
RUBML

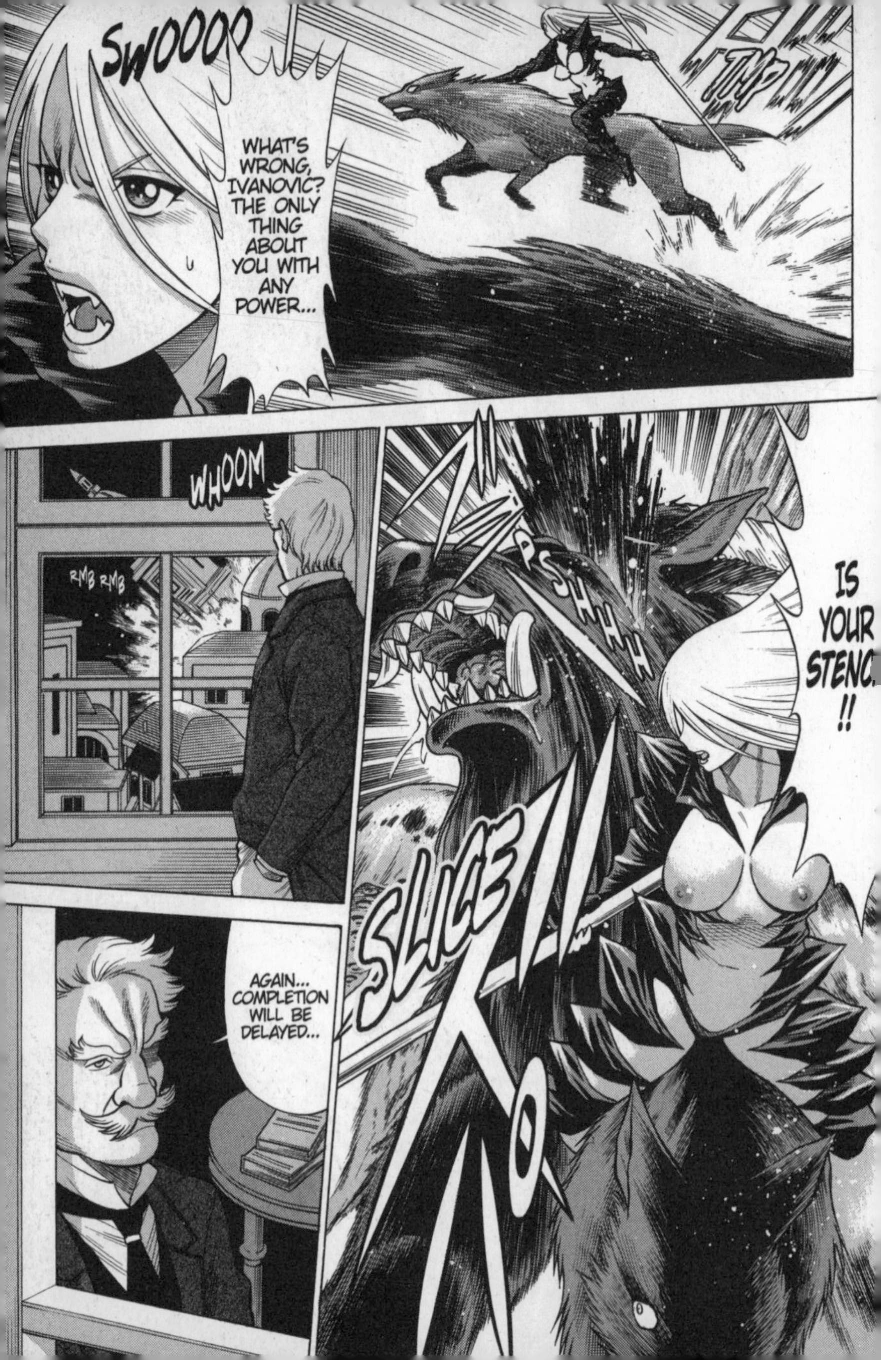
SWOOOP
WHAT'S WRONG, IVANOVIC? THE ONLY THING ABOUT YOU WITH ANY POWER...
IS YOUR STENC
!!
PSHHHH
SLICE
WHOOM
RMB RMB
AGAIN... COMPLETION WILL BE DELAYED...

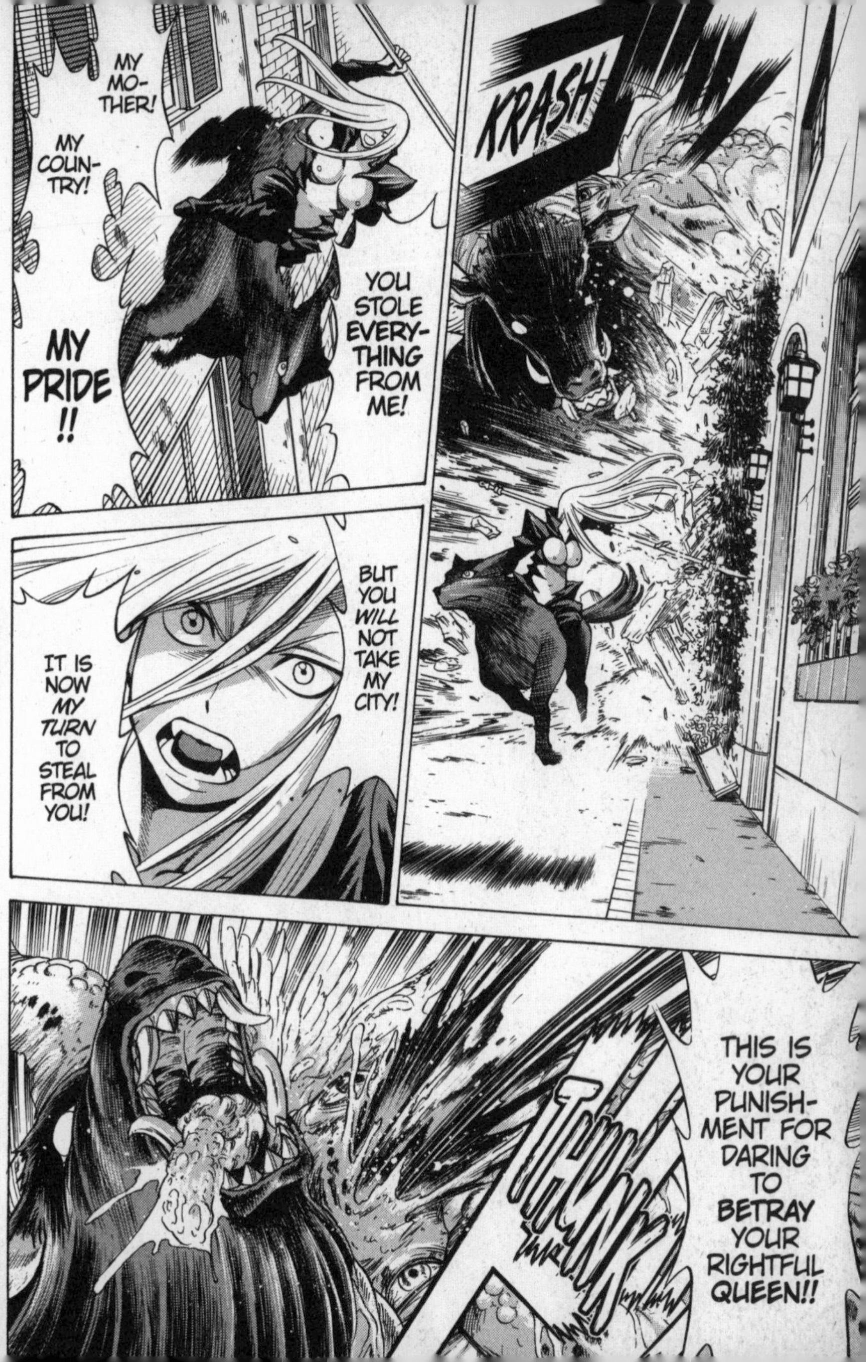
KRASH
MY MO-THER!
MY COUN-TRY!
MY PRIDE!!
YOU STOLE EVERY-THING FROM ME!
BUT YOU WILL NOT TAKE MY CITY!
IT IS NOW MY TURN TO STEAL FROM YOU!
THIS IS YOUR PUNISH-MENT FOR DARING TO BETRAY YOUR RIGHTFUL QUEEN!!

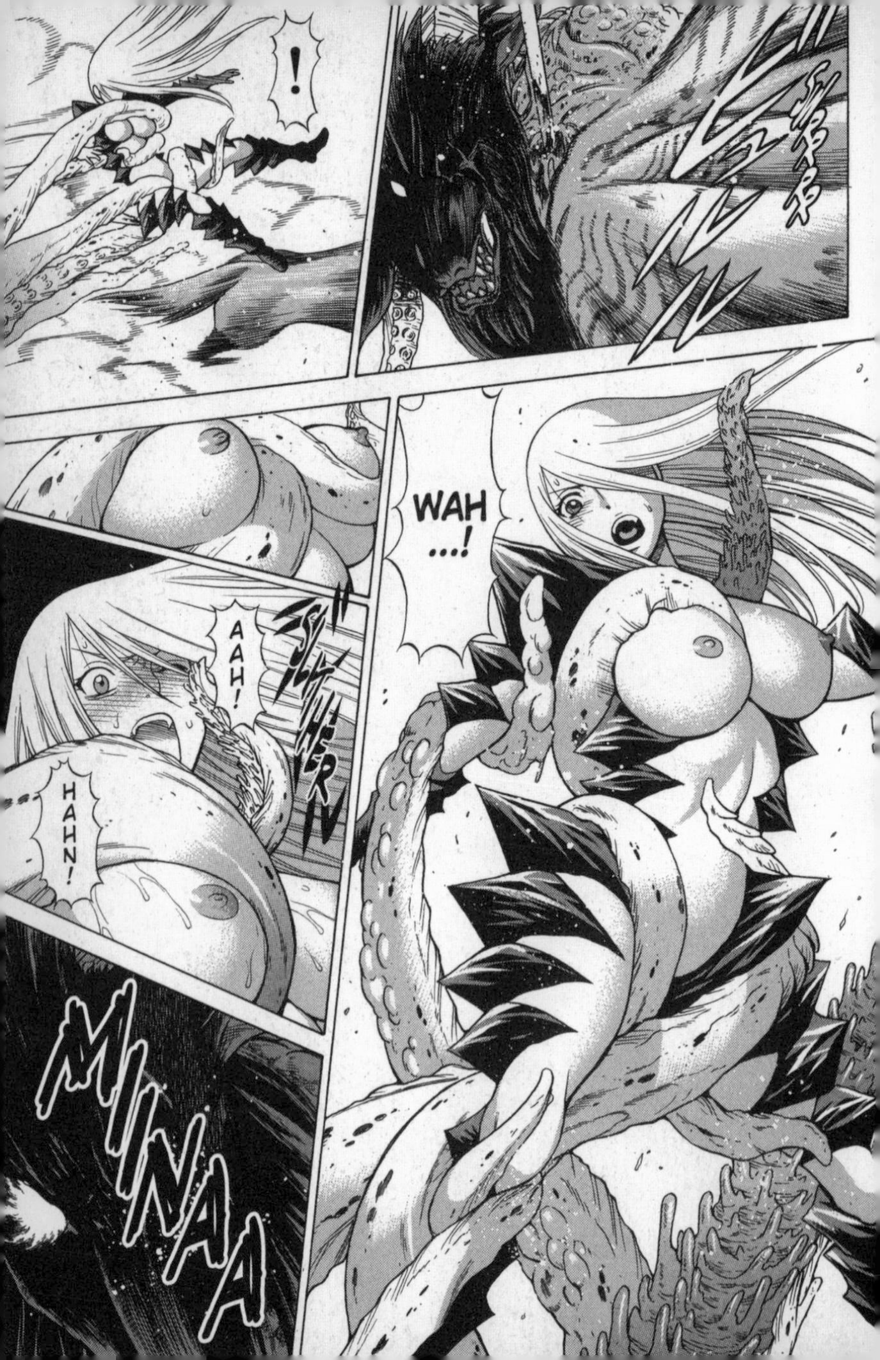
SHRRRR
!
WAH ...!
AAH!
SLITHER
HAHN!
MINAA

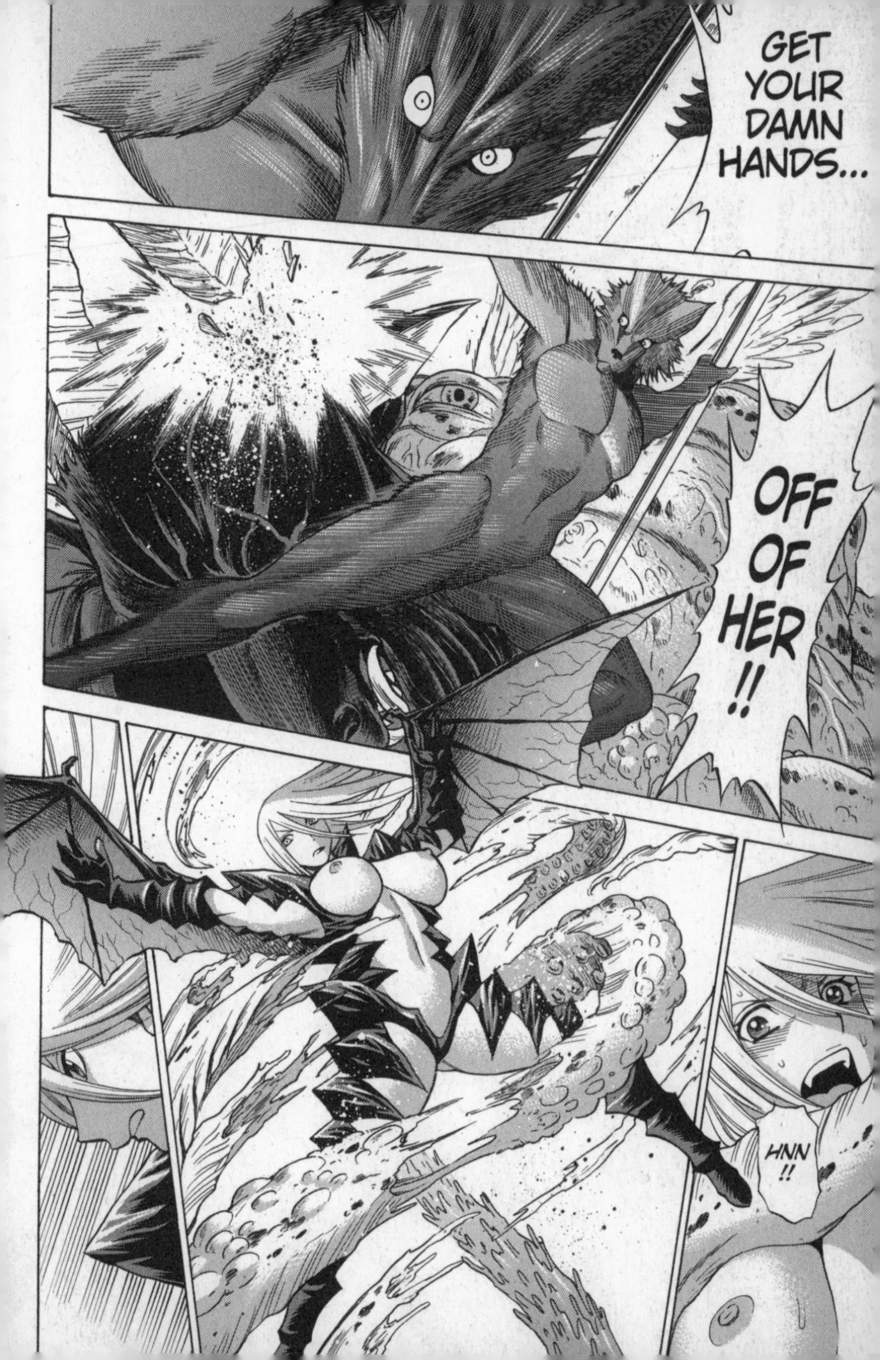
GET YOUR DAMN HANDS...
OFF OF HER !!
HNN !!

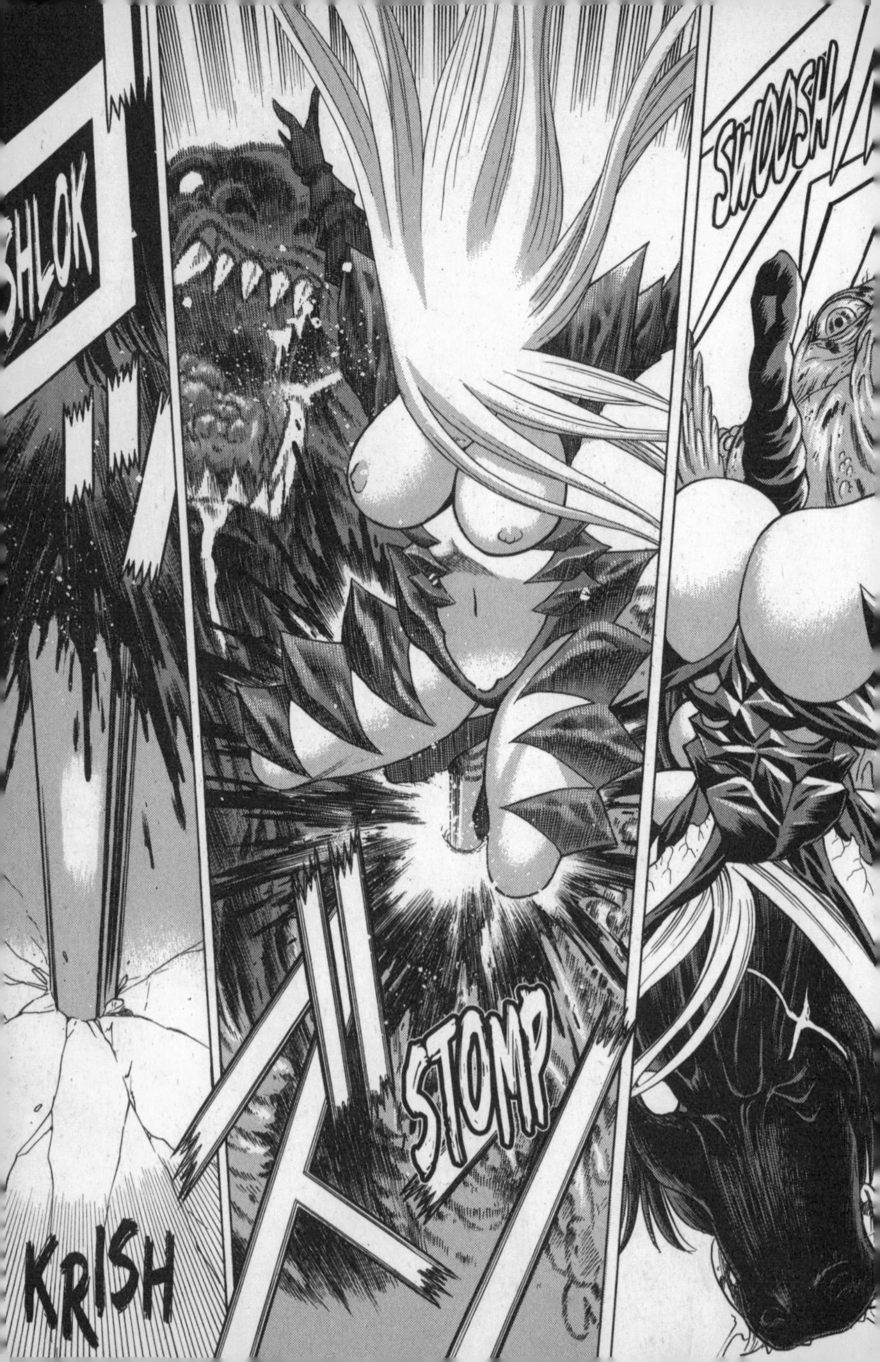
SHLOOSH
STOMP
SHLOK
KRISH

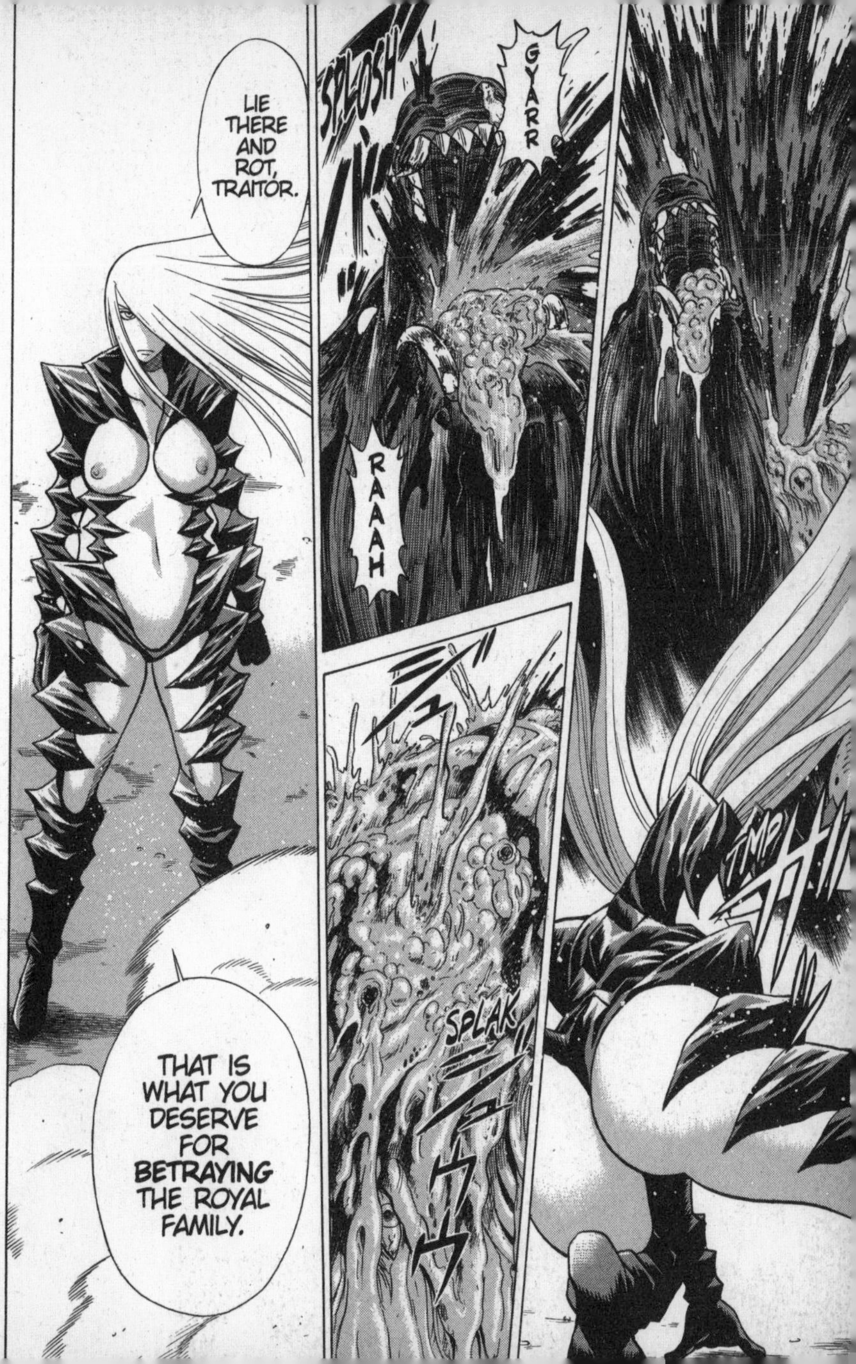
TMP
SPLOSH
GYARR
RAAAH
SPLAK
LIE THERE AND ROT, TRAITOR.
THAT IS WHAT YOU DESERVE FOR BETRAYING THE ROYAL FAMILY.

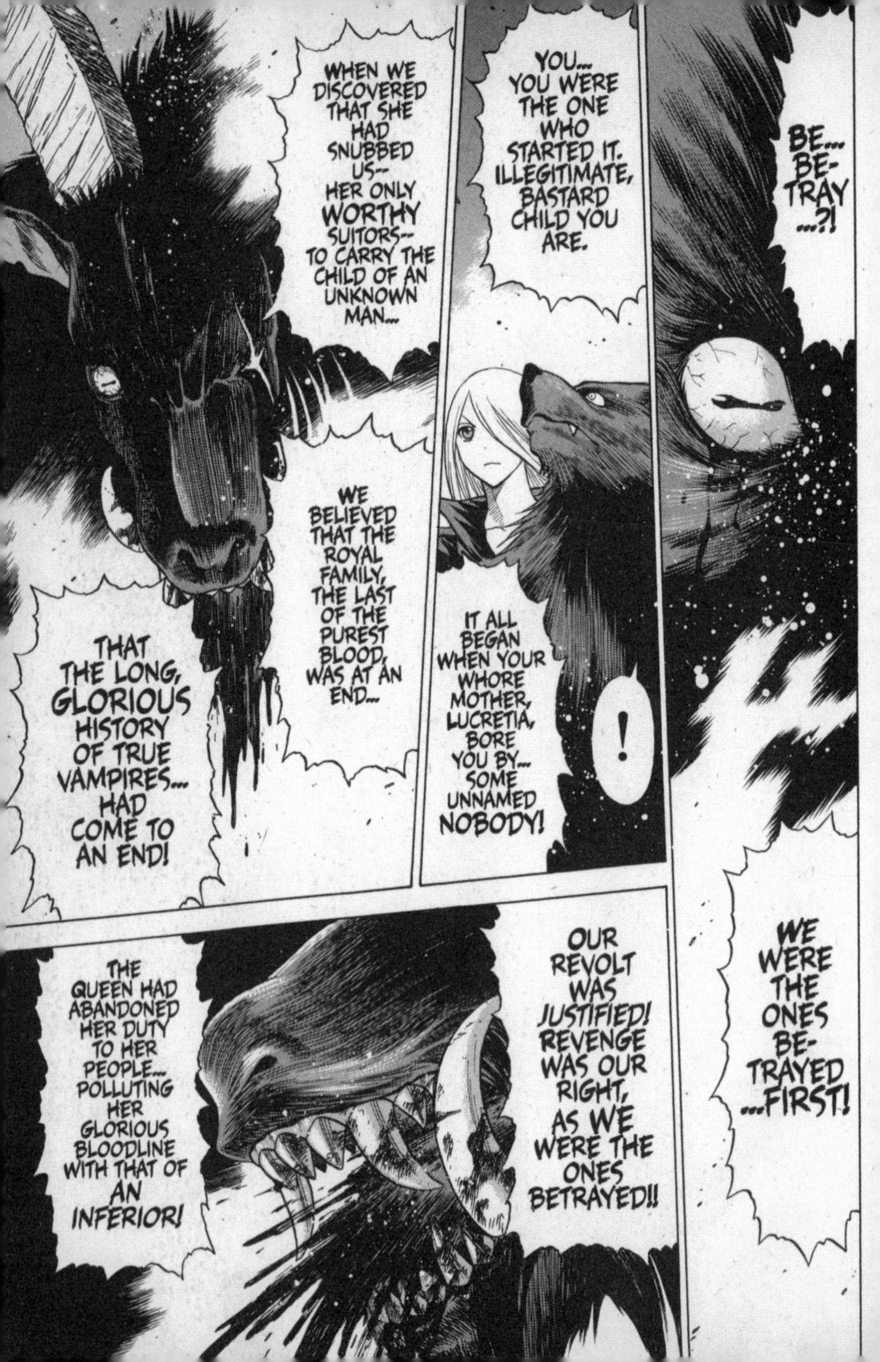

BE... BE-TRAY...?!
WE WERE THE ONES BE-TRAYED ...FIRST!
YOU... YOU WERE THE ONE WHO STARTED IT. ILLEGITIMATE, BASTARD CHILD YOU ARE.
IT ALL BEGAN WHEN YOUR WHORE MOTHER, LUCRETIA, BORE YOU BY... SOME UNNAMED NOBODY!
!
WHEN WE DISCOVERED THAT SHE HAD SNUBBED US-- HER ONLY WORTHY SUITORS-- TO CARRY THE CHILD OF AN UNKNOWN MAN...
WE BELIEVED THAT THE ROYAL FAMILY, THE LAST OF THE PUREST BLOOD, WAS AT AN END...
THAT THE LONG, GLORIOUS HISTORY OF TRUE VAMPIRES... HAD COME TO AN END!
OUR REVOLT WAS JUSTIFIED! REVENGE WAS OUR RIGHT, AS WE WERE THE ONES BETRAYED!!
THE QUEEN HAD ABANDONED HER DUTY TO HER PEOPLE... POLLUTING HER GLORIOUS BLOODLINE WITH THAT OF AN INFERIOR!

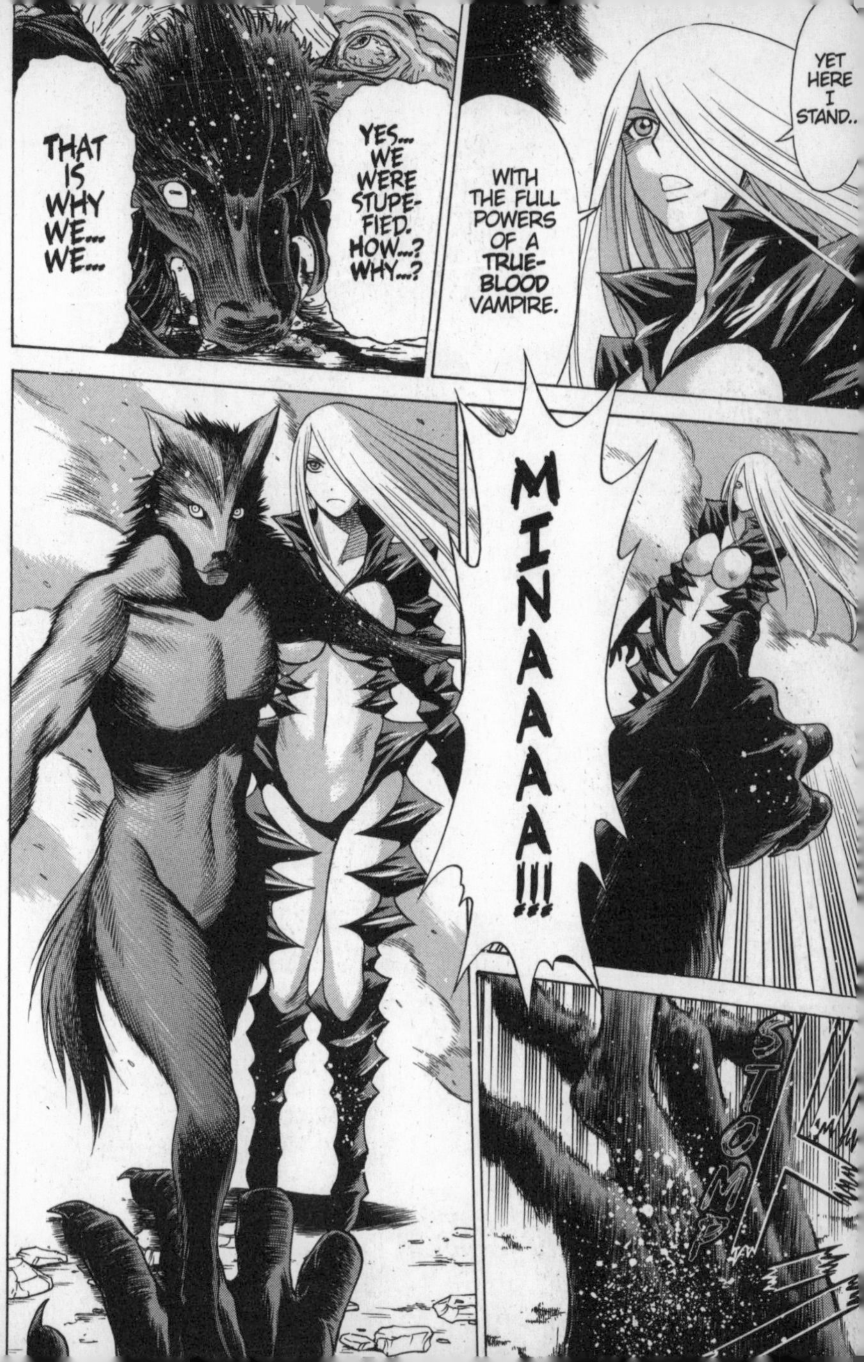
YET HERE I STAND..
WITH THE FULL POWERS OF A TRUE-BLOOD VAMPIRE.
YES... WE WERE STUPE-FIED. HOW...? WHY...?
THAT IS WHY WE... WE...
MINAAAA!!!
STOMP

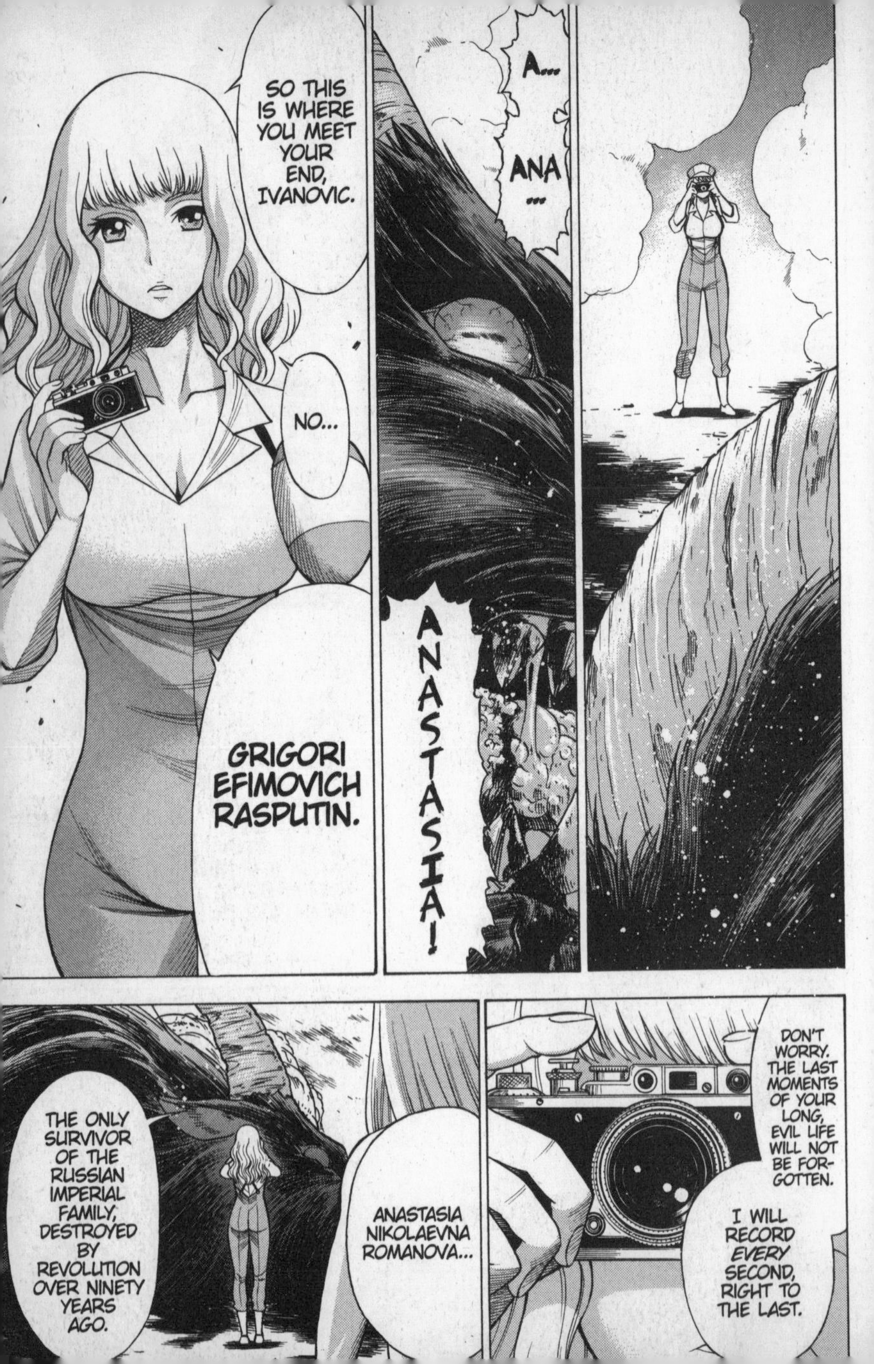
A... ANA ...
ANASTASIA!
SO THIS IS WHERE YOU MEET YOUR END, IVANOVIC.
NO...
GRIGORI EFIMOVICH RASPUTIN.
DON'T WORRY. THE LAST MOMENTS OF YOUR LONG, EVIL LIFE WILL NOT BE FOR-GOTTEN.
I WILL RECORD *EVERY* SECOND, RIGHT TO THE LAST.
ANASTASIA NIKOLAEVNA ROMANOVA...
THE ONLY SURVIVOR OF THE RUSSIAN IMPERIAL FAMILY, DESTROYED BY REVOLUTION OVER NINETY YEARS AGO.

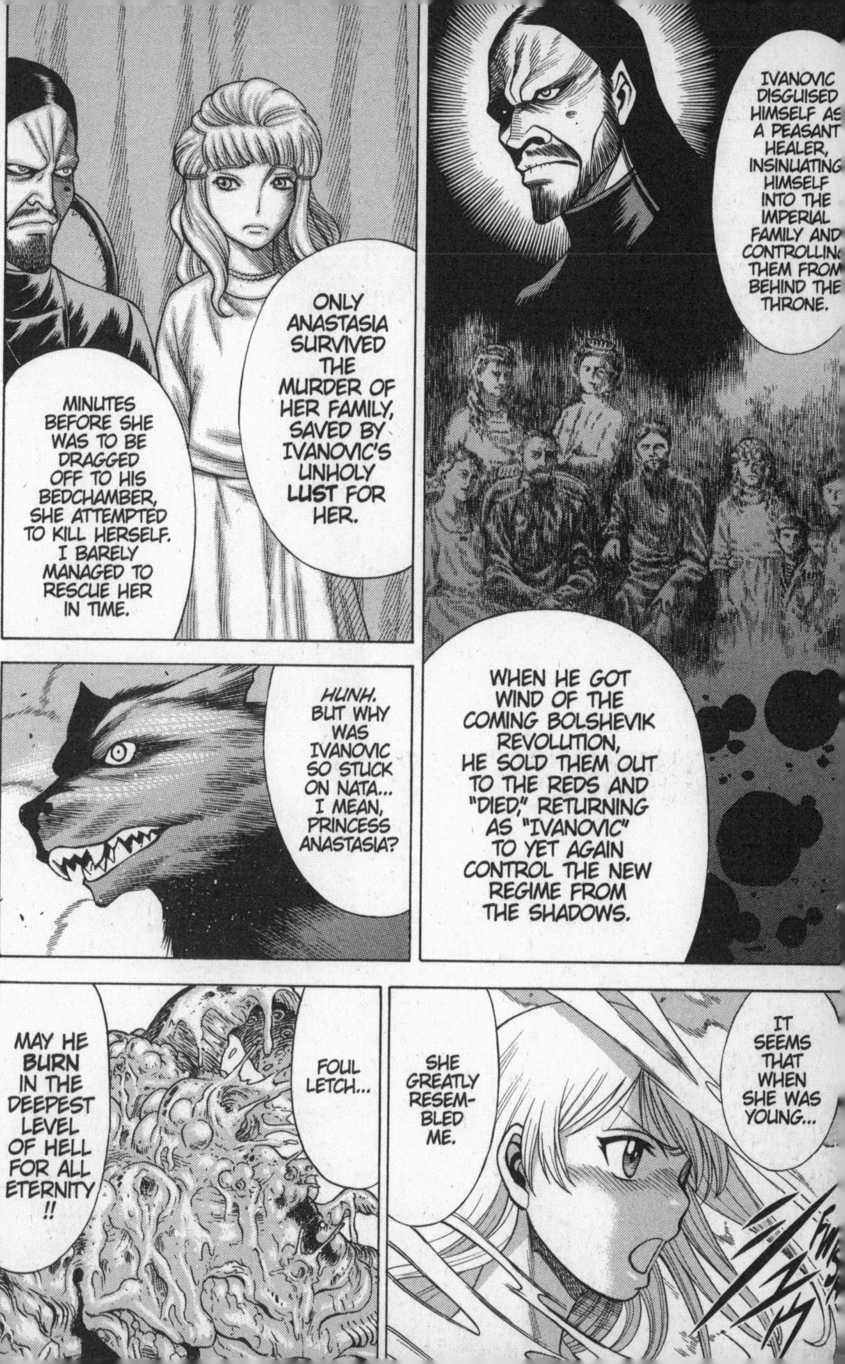
IVANOVIC DISGUISED HIMSELF AS A PEASANT HEALER, INSINUATING HIMSELF INTO THE IMPERIAL FAMILY AND CONTROLLING THEM FROM BEHIND THE THRONE.
WHEN HE GOT WIND OF THE COMING BOLSHEVIK REVOLUTION, HE SOLD THEM OUT TO THE REDS AND "DIED," RETURNING AS "IVANOVIC" TO YET AGAIN CONTROL THE NEW REGIME FROM THE SHADOWS.
ONLY ANASTASIA SURVIVED THE MURDER OF HER FAMILY, SAVED BY IVANOVIC'S UNHOLY **LUST** FOR HER.
MINUTES BEFORE SHE WAS TO BE DRAGGED OFF TO HIS BEDCHAMBER, SHE ATTEMPTED TO KILL HERSELF. I BARELY MANAGED TO RESCUE HER IN TIME.
HUNH. BUT WHY WAS IVANOVIC SO STUCK ON NATA... I MEAN, PRINCESS ANASTASIA?
IT SEEMS THAT WHEN SHE WAS YOUNG...
SHE GREATLY RESEMBLED ME.
FOUL LETCH...
MAY HE **BURN** IN THE DEEPEST LEVEL OF HELL FOR ALL ETERNITY!!

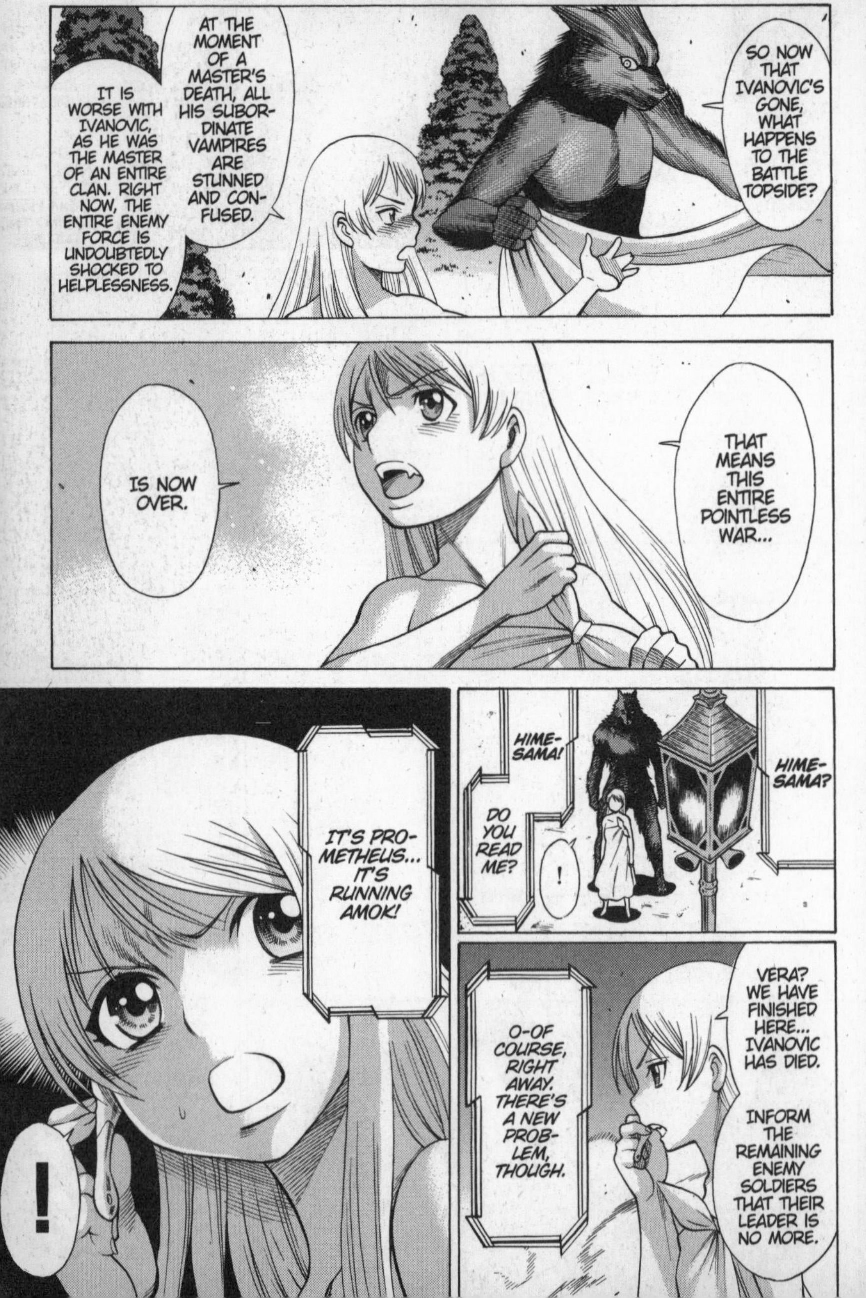
SO NOW THAT IVANOVIC'S GONE, WHAT HAPPENS TO THE BATTLE TOPSIDE?
AT THE MOMENT OF A MASTER'S DEATH, ALL HIS SUBOR-DINATE VAMPIRES ARE STUNNED AND CON-FUSED.
IT IS WORSE WITH IVANOVIC, AS HE WAS THE MASTER OF AN ENTIRE CLAN. RIGHT NOW, THE ENTIRE ENEMY FORCE IS UNDOUBTEDLY SHOCKED TO HELPLESSNESS.
THAT MEANS THIS ENTIRE POINTLESS WAR...
IS NOW OVER.
HIME-SAMA?
HIME-SAMA!
DO YOU READ ME?
!
VERA? WE HAVE FINISHED HERE... IVANOVIC HAS DIED.
INFORM THE REMAINING ENEMY SOLDIERS THAT THEIR LEADER IS NO MORE.
O-OF COURSE, RIGHT AWAY. THERE'S A NEW PROB-LEM, THOUGH.
IT'S PRO-METHEUS... IT'S RUNNING AMOK!
!

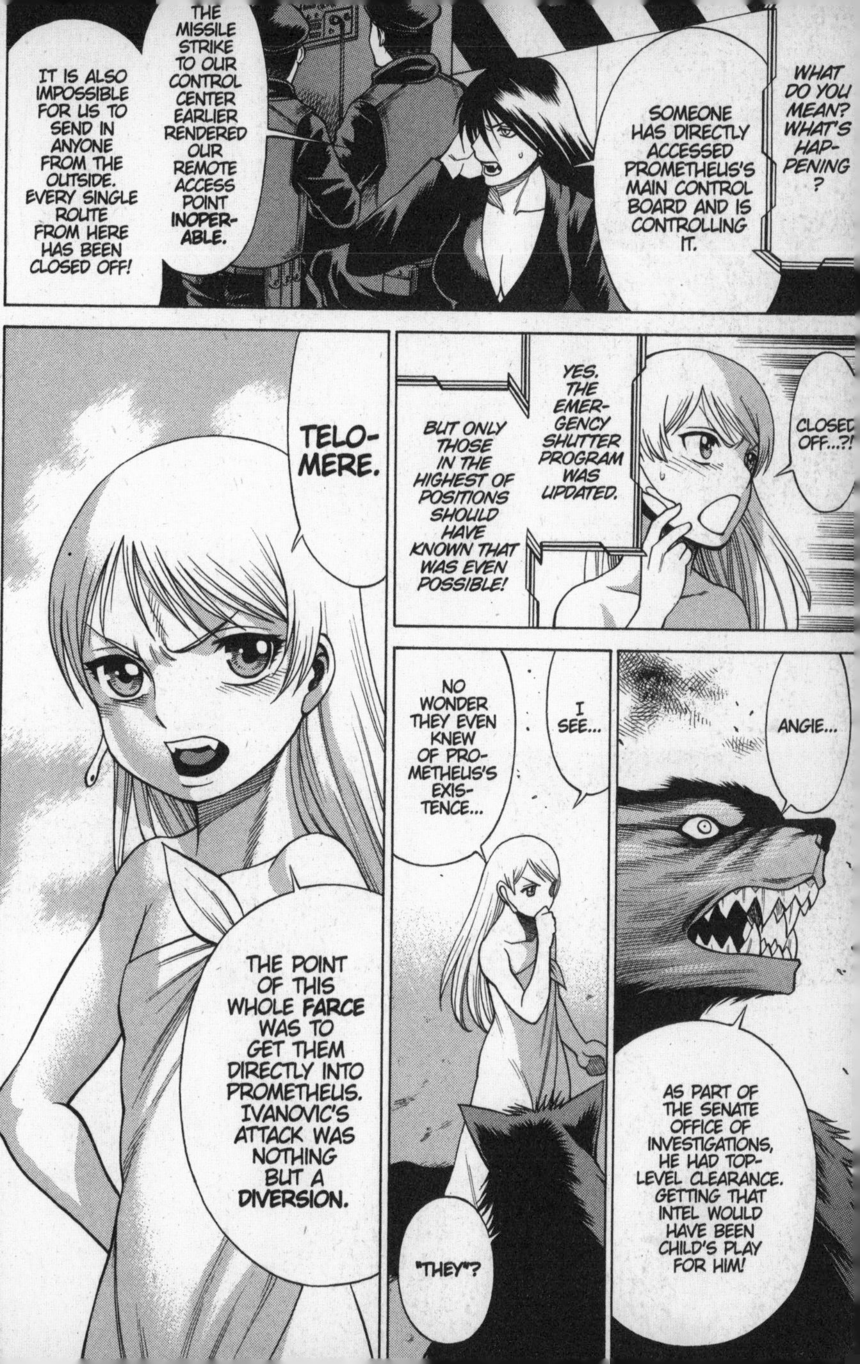
WHAT DO YOU MEAN? WHAT'S HAP-PENING?
SOMEONE HAS DIRECTLY ACCESSED PROMETHEUS'S MAIN CONTROL BOARD AND IS CONTROLLING IT.
THE MISSILE STRIKE TO OUR CONTROL CENTER EARLIER RENDERED OUR REMOTE ACCESS POINT INOPER-ABLE.
IT IS ALSO IMPOSSIBLE FOR US TO SEND IN ANYONE FROM THE OUTSIDE. EVERY SINGLE ROUTE FROM HERE HAS BEEN CLOSED OFF!
CLOSED OFF...?!
YES. THE EMER-GENCY SHUTTER PROGRAM WAS UPDATED.
BUT ONLY THOSE IN THE HIGHEST OF POSITIONS SHOULD HAVE KNOWN THAT WAS EVEN POSSIBLE!
ANGIE...
AS PART OF THE SENATE OFFICE OF INVESTIGATIONS, HE HAD TOP-LEVEL CLEARANCE. GETTING THAT INTEL WOULD HAVE BEEN CHILD'S PLAY FOR HIM!
I SEE...
NO WONDER THEY EVEN KNEW OF PRO-METHEUS'S EXIS-TENCE...
"THEY"?
TELO-MERE.
THE POINT OF THIS WHOLE FARCE WAS TO GET THEM DIRECTLY INTO PROMETHEUS. IVANOVIC'S ATTACK WAS NOTHING BUT A DIVERSION.

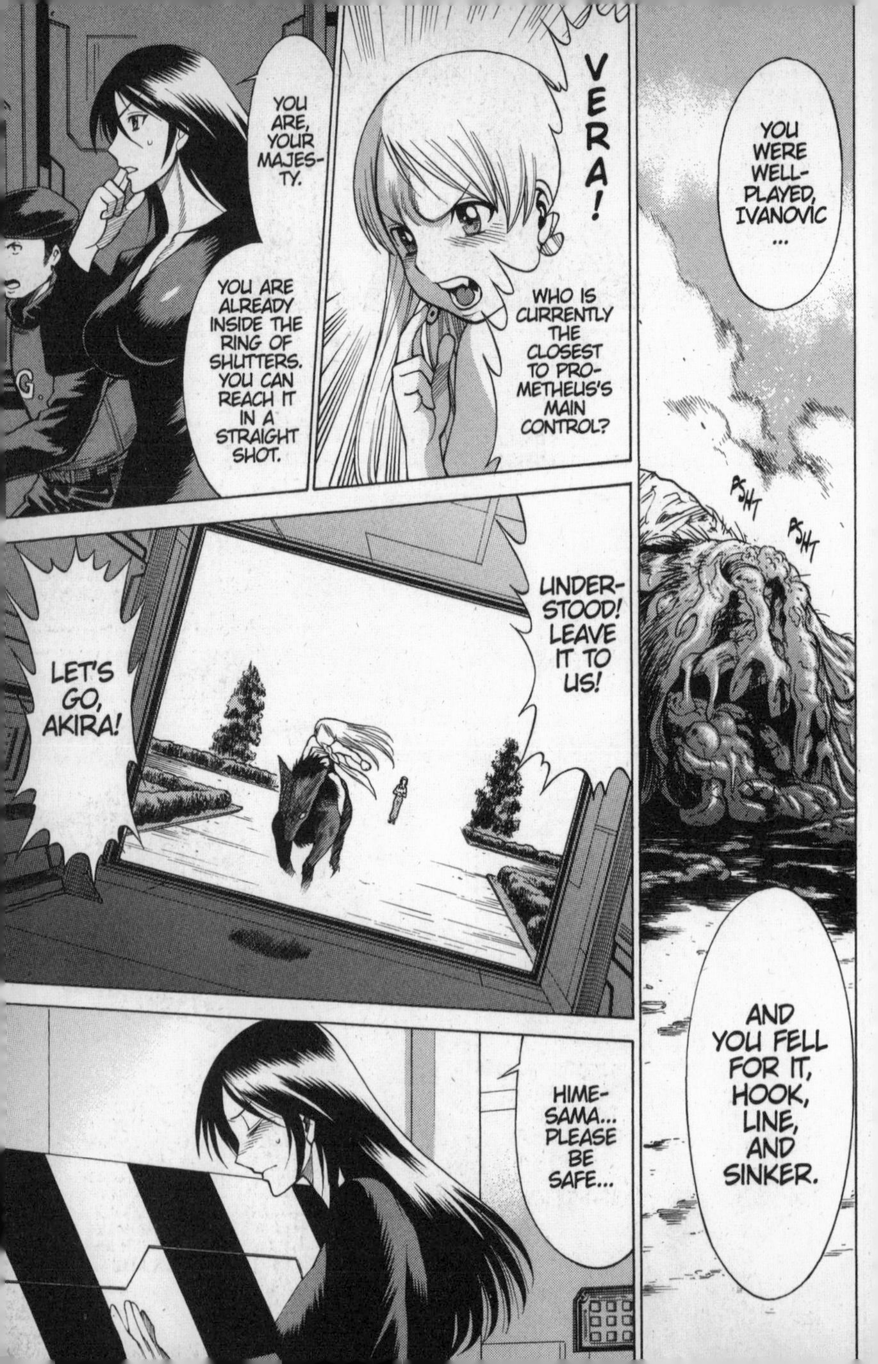
YOU WERE WELL-PLAYED, IVANOVIC ...
PSHT
PSHT
AND YOU FELL FOR IT, HOOK, LINE, AND SINKER.
VERA!
WHO IS CURRENTLY THE CLOSEST TO PRO-METHEUS'S MAIN CONTROL?
YOU ARE, YOUR MAJES-TY.
YOU ARE ALREADY INSIDE THE RING OF SHUTTERS. YOU CAN REACH IT IN A STRAIGHT SHOT.
UNDER-STOOD! LEAVE IT TO US!
LET'S GO, AKIRA!
HIME-SAMA... PLEASE BE SAFE...

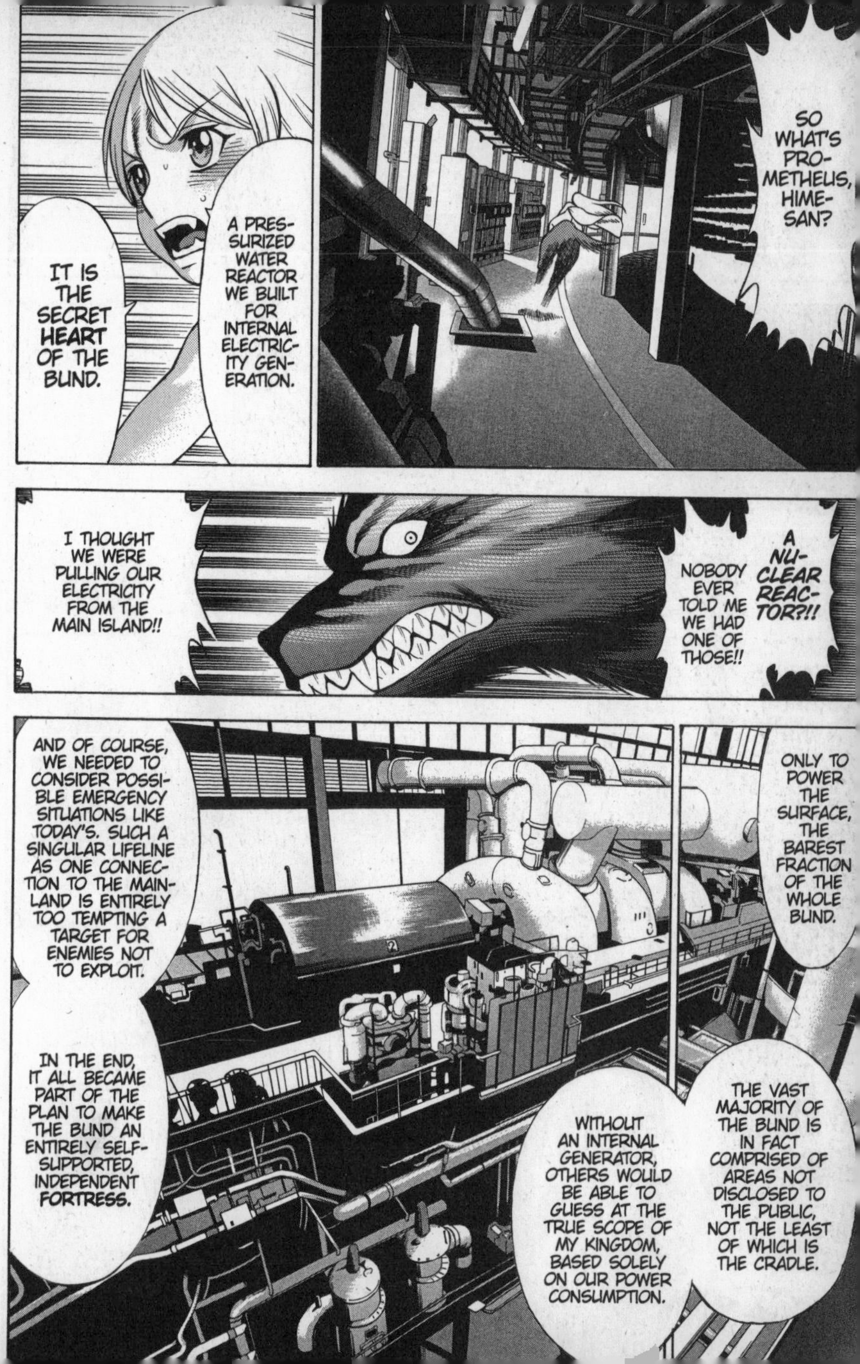
SO WHAT'S PROMETHEUS, HIME-SAN?
A PRESSURIZED WATER REACTOR WE BUILT FOR INTERNAL ELECTRICITY GENERATION.
IT IS THE SECRET HEART OF THE BUND.
A NUCLEAR REACTOR?!!
NOBODY EVER TOLD ME WE HAD ONE OF THOSE!!
I THOUGHT WE WERE PULLING OUR ELECTRICITY FROM THE MAIN ISLAND!!
ONLY TO POWER THE SURFACE, THE BAREST FRACTION OF THE WHOLE BUND.
THE VAST MAJORITY OF THE BUND IS IN FACT COMPRISED OF AREAS NOT DISCLOSED TO THE PUBLIC, NOT THE LEAST OF WHICH IS THE CRADLE.
WITHOUT AN INTERNAL GENERATOR, OTHERS WOULD BE ABLE TO GUESS AT THE TRUE SCOPE OF MY KINGDOM, BASED SOLELY ON OUR POWER CONSUMPTION.
AND OF COURSE, WE NEEDED TO CONSIDER POSSIBLE EMERGENCY SITUATIONS LIKE TODAY'S. SUCH A SINGULAR LIFELINE AS ONE CONNECTION TO THE MAINLAND IS ENTIRELY TOO TEMPTING A TARGET FOR ENEMIES NOT TO EXPLOIT.
IN THE END, IT ALL BECAME PART OF THE PLAN TO MAKE THE BUND AN ENTIRELY SELF-SUPPORTED, INDEPENDENT FORTRESS.

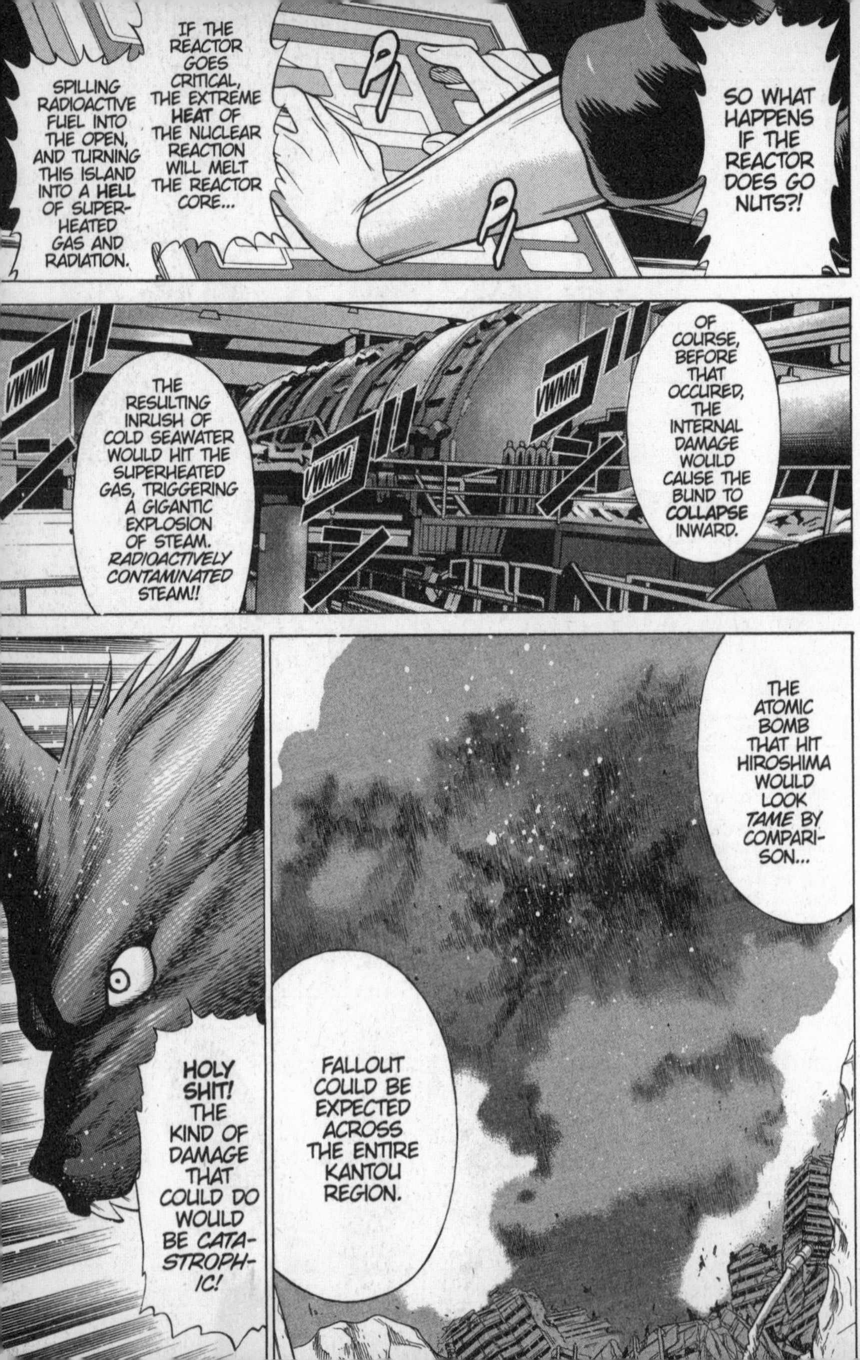
SO WHAT HAPPENS IF THE REACTOR DOES GO NUTS?!
IF THE REACTOR GOES CRITICAL, THE EXTREME HEAT OF THE NUCLEAR REACTION WILL MELT THE REACTOR CORE...
SPILLING RADIOACTIVE FUEL INTO THE OPEN, AND TURNING THIS ISLAND INTO A HELL OF SUPER-HEATED GAS AND RADIATION.
VWMM
OF COURSE, BEFORE THAT OCCURED, THE INTERNAL DAMAGE WOULD CAUSE THE BUND TO COLLAPSE INWARD.
VWMM
VWMM
THE RESULTING INRUSH OF COLD SEAWATER WOULD HIT THE SUPERHEATED GAS, TRIGGERING A GIGANTIC EXPLOSION OF STEAM. *RADIOACTIVELY CONTAMINATED* STEAM!!
THE ATOMIC BOMB THAT HIT HIROSHIMA WOULD LOOK *TAME* BY COMPARI-SON...
FALLOUT COULD BE EXPECTED ACROSS THE ENTIRE KANTOU REGION.
HOLY SHIT! THE KIND OF DAMAGE THAT COULD DO WOULD BE *CATA-STROPH-IC!*

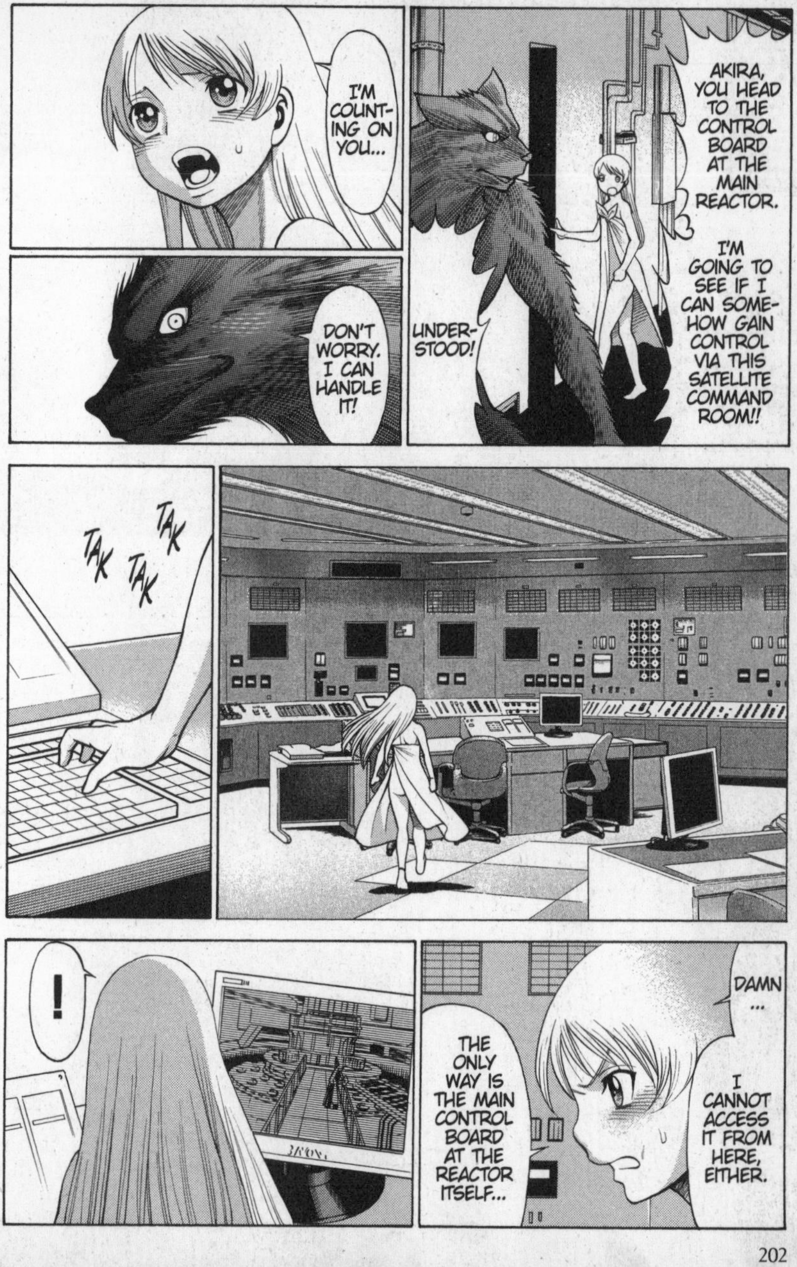
AKIRA, YOU HEAD TO THE CONTROL BOARD AT THE MAIN REACTOR.
I'M GOING TO SEE IF I CAN SOME-HOW GAIN CONTROL VIA THIS SATELLITE COMMAND ROOM!!
UNDER-STOOD!
I'M COUNT-ING ON YOU...
DON'T WORRY. I CAN HANDLE IT!
TAK TAK TAK
DAMN...
I CANNOT ACCESS IT FROM HERE, EITHER.
THE ONLY WAY IS THE MAIN CONTROL BOARD AT THE REACTOR ITSELF...
!

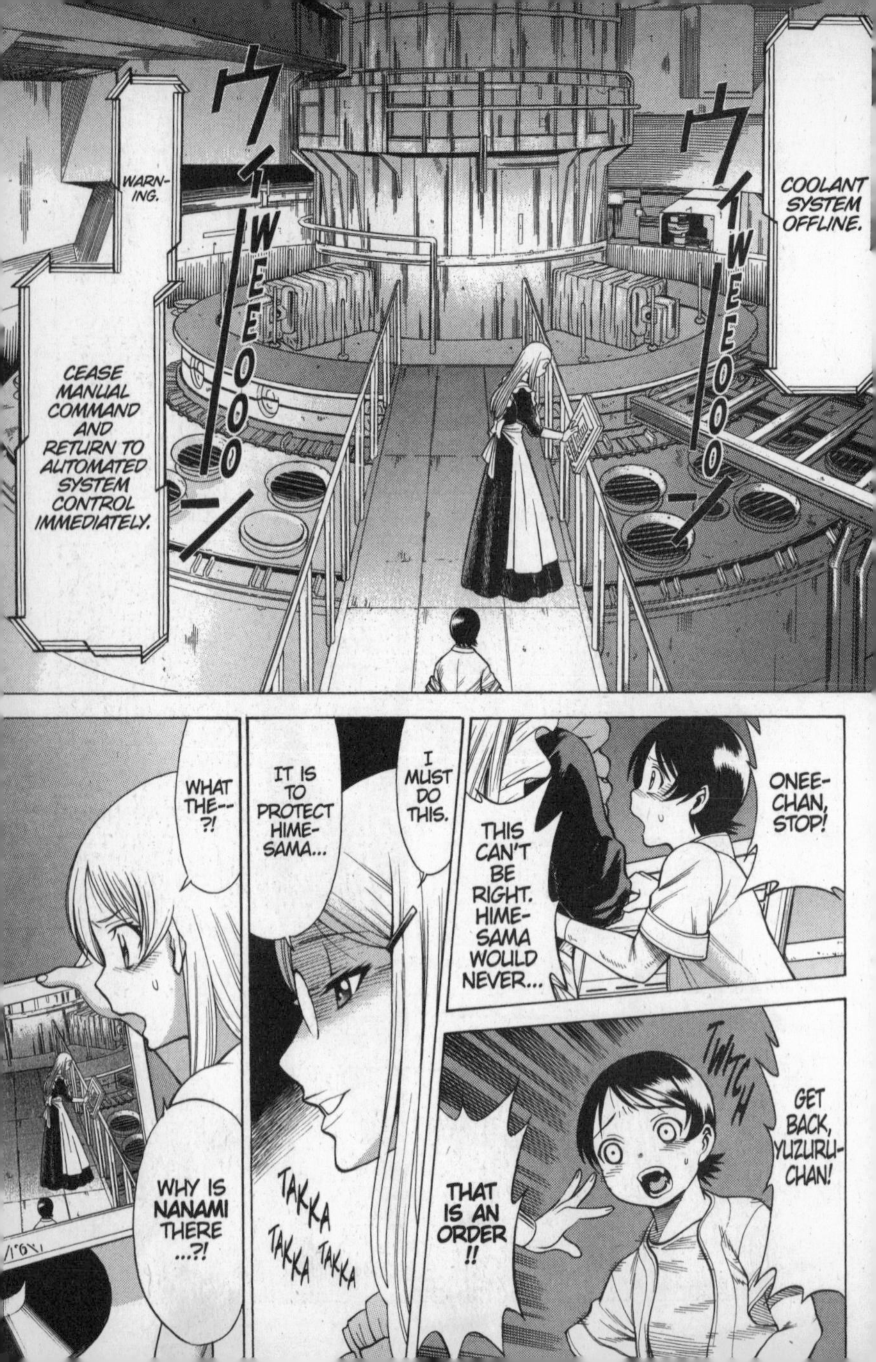
COOLANT SYSTEM OFFLINE.
ウイ
WEEOOO
WARN-ING.
ウイ
WEEOOO
CEASE MANUAL COMMAND AND RETURN TO AUTOMATED SYSTEM CONTROL IMMEDIATELY.
ONEE-CHAN, STOP!
THIS CAN'T BE RIGHT. HIME-SAMA WOULD NEVER...
TWITCH
GET BACK, YUZURU-CHAN!
THAT IS AN ORDER!!
I MUST DO THIS.
IT IS TO PROTECT HIME-SAMA...
TAKKA TAKKA TAKKA TAKKA
WHAT THE--?!
WHY IS NANAMI THERE...?!

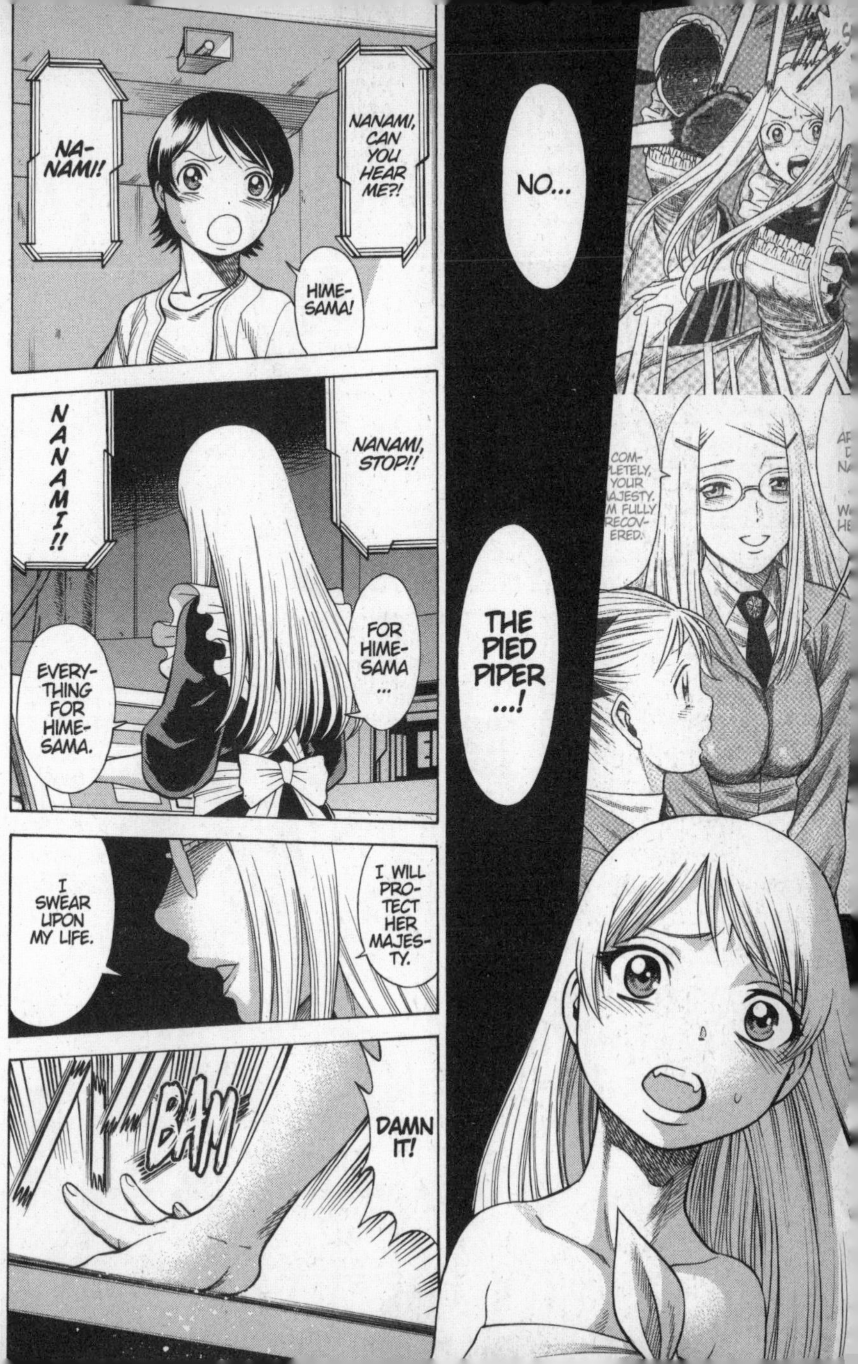
COMPLETELY, YOUR AJESTY. M FULLY RECOVERED.
NO...
THE PIED PIPER...!
NANAMI, CAN YOU HEAR ME?!
HIME-SAMA!
NANAMI!
NANAMI, STOP!!
FOR HIME-SAMA...
NANAMI!!
EVERYTHING FOR HIME-SAMA.
I WILL PROTECT HER MAJESTY.
I SWEAR UPON MY LIFE.
DAMN IT!
BAM

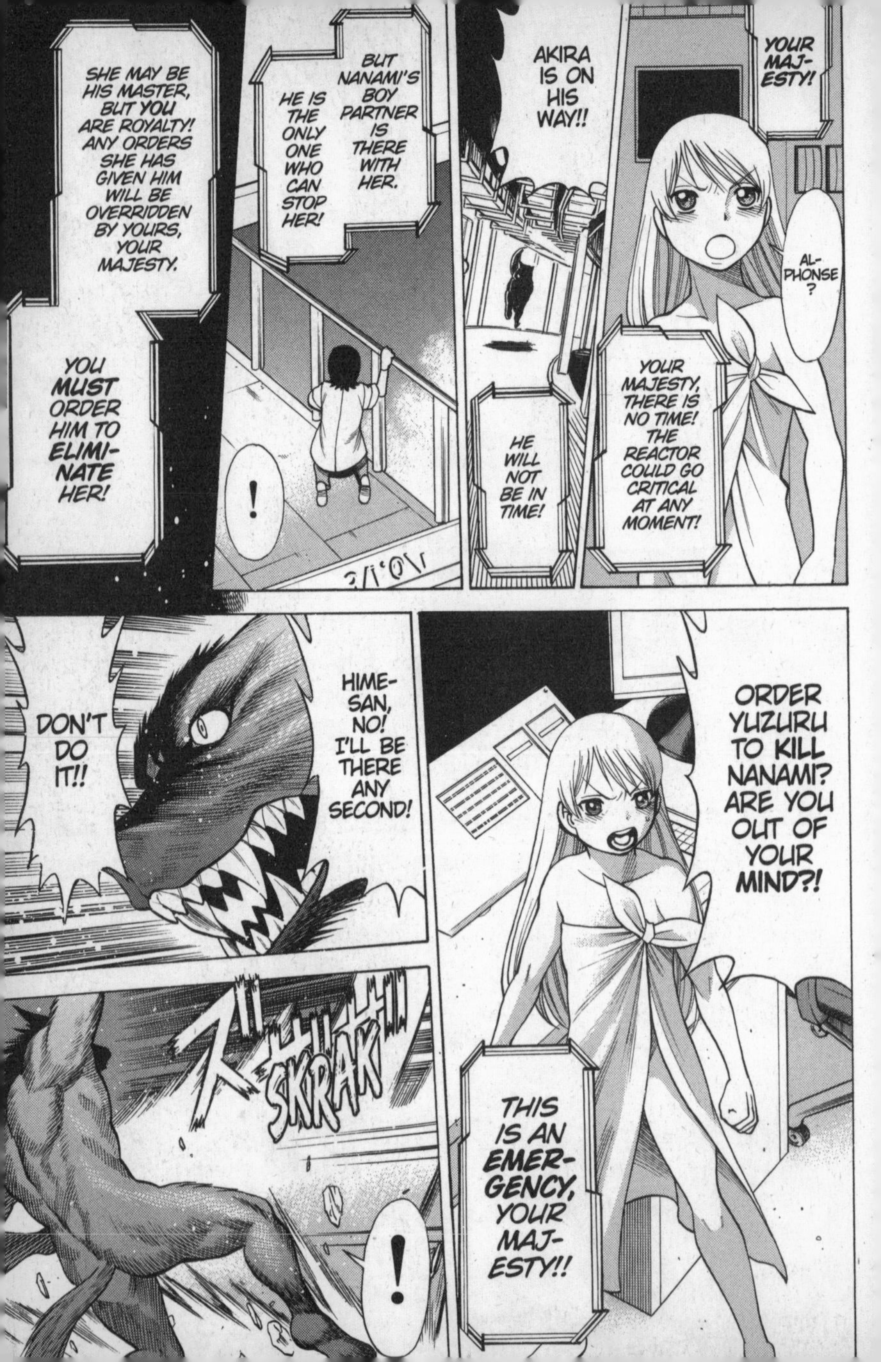
YOUR MAJESTY!
ALPHONSE?
YOUR MAJESTY, THERE IS NO TIME! THE REACTOR COULD GO CRITICAL AT ANY MOMENT!
AKIRA IS ON HIS WAY!!
HE WILL NOT BE IN TIME!
BUT NANAMI'S BOY PARTNER IS THERE WITH HER.
HE IS THE ONLY ONE WHO CAN STOP HER!
!
SHE MAY BE HIS MASTER, BUT YOU ARE ROYALTY! ANY ORDERS SHE HAS GIVEN HIM WILL BE OVERRIDDEN BY YOURS, YOUR MAJESTY.
YOU MUST ORDER HIM TO ELIMINATE HER!
ORDER YUZURU TO KILL NANAMI? ARE YOU OUT OF YOUR MIND?!
THIS IS AN EMERGENCY, YOUR MAJESTY!!
HIME-SAN, NO! I'LL BE THERE ANY SECOND!
DON'T DO IT!!
SKRAK
!

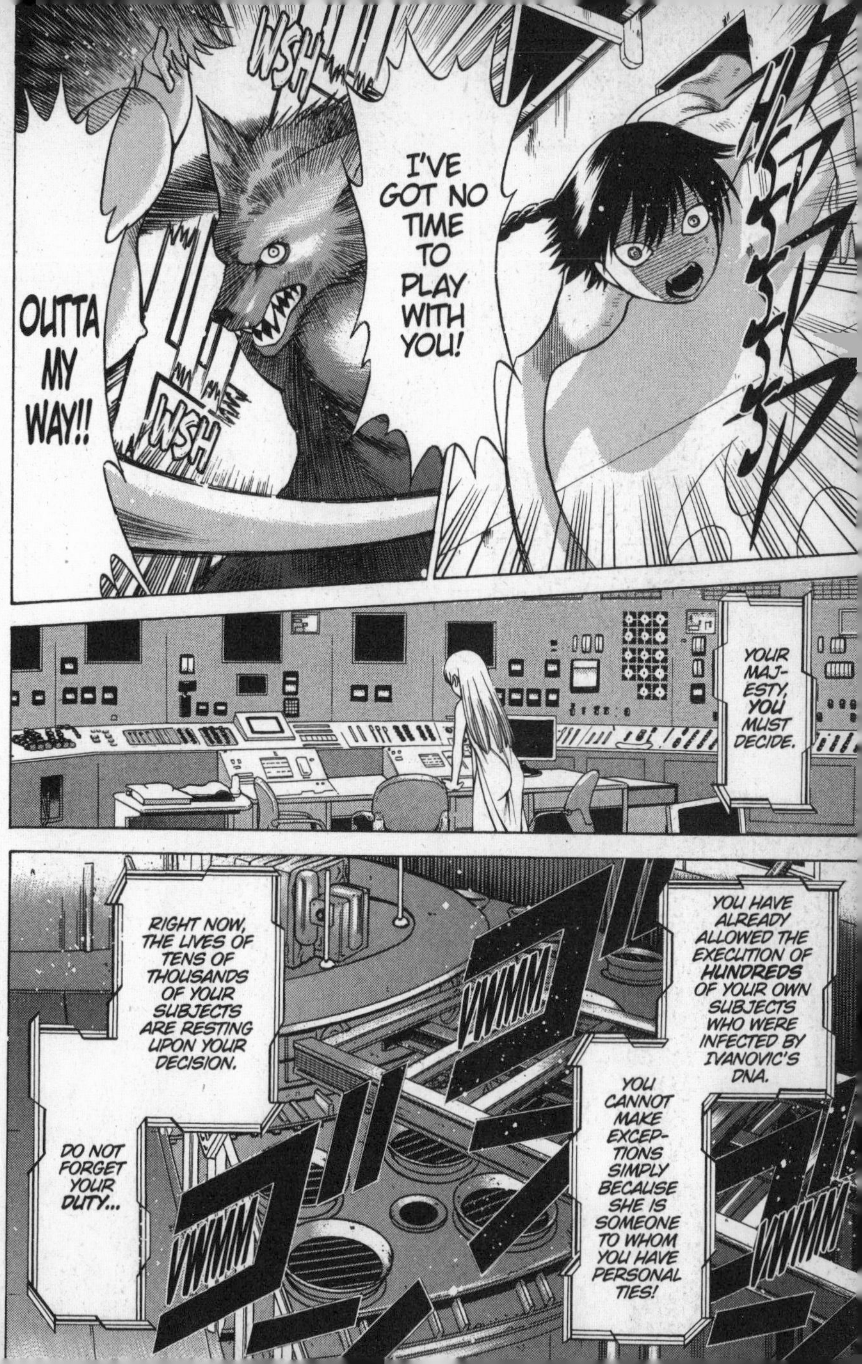
WSH
I'VE GOT NO TIME TO PLAY WITH YOU!
OUTTA MY WAY!!
WSH
YOUR MAJESTY, YOU MUST DECIDE.
YOU HAVE ALREADY ALLOWED THE EXECUTION OF HUNDREDS OF YOUR OWN SUBJECTS WHO WERE INFECTED BY IVANOVIC'S DNA.
RIGHT NOW, THE LIVES OF TENS OF THOUSANDS OF YOUR SUBJECTS ARE RESTING UPON YOUR DECISION.
VWMM
YOU CANNOT MAKE EXCEPTIONS SIMPLY BECAUSE SHE IS SOMEONE TO WHOM YOU HAVE PERSONAL TIES!
VWMM
DO NOT FORGET YOUR DUTY...
VWMM

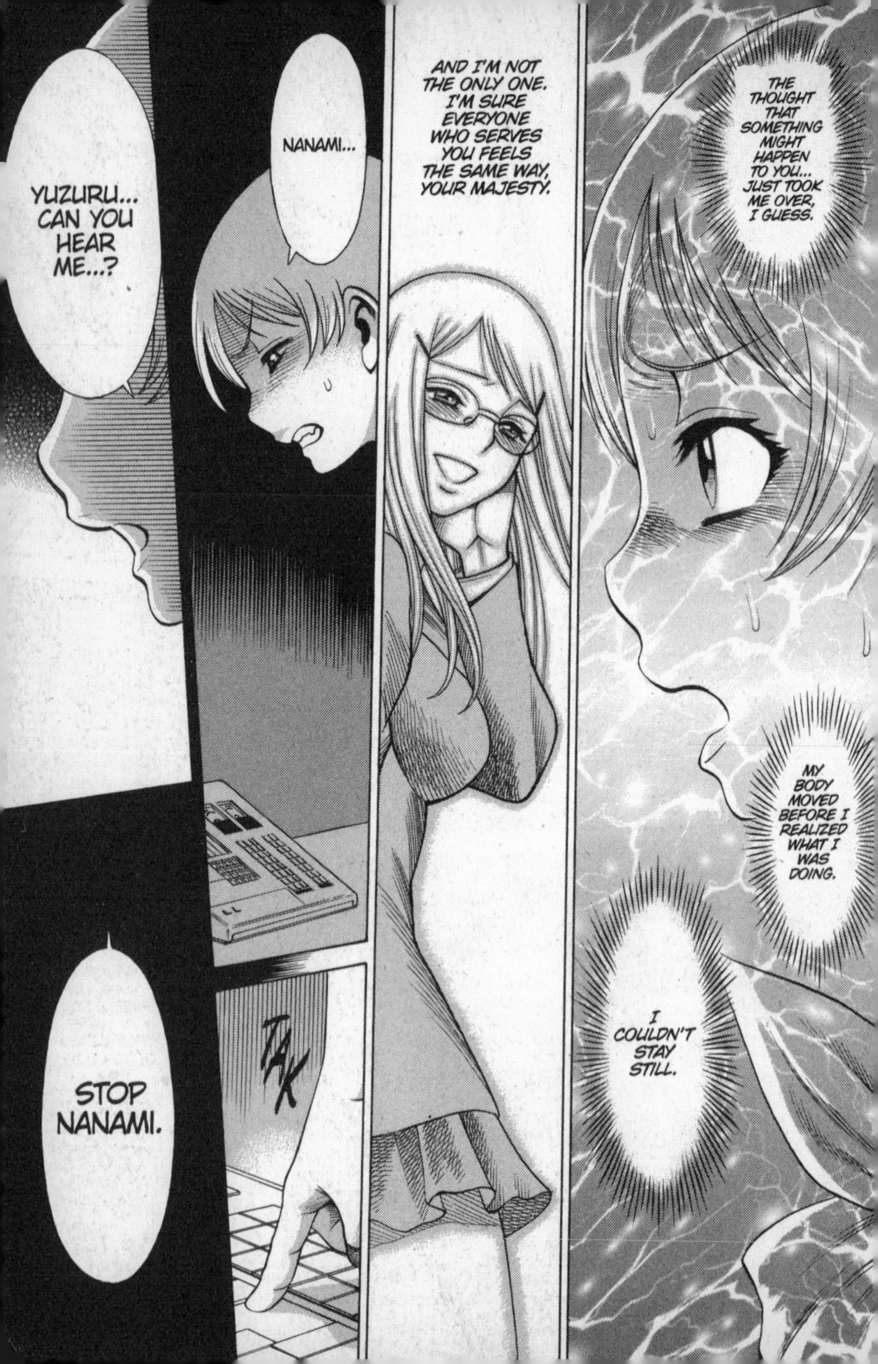
THE THOUGHT THAT SOMETHING MIGHT HAPPEN TO YOU... JUST TOOK ME OVER, I GUESS.
MY BODY MOVED BEFORE I REALIZED WHAT I WAS DOING.
I COULDN'T STAY STILL.
AND I'M NOT THE ONLY ONE. I'M SURE EVERYONE WHO SERVES YOU FEELS THE SAME WAY, YOUR MAJESTY.
NANAMI...
YUZURU... CAN YOU HEAR ME...?
TAK
STOP NANAMI.

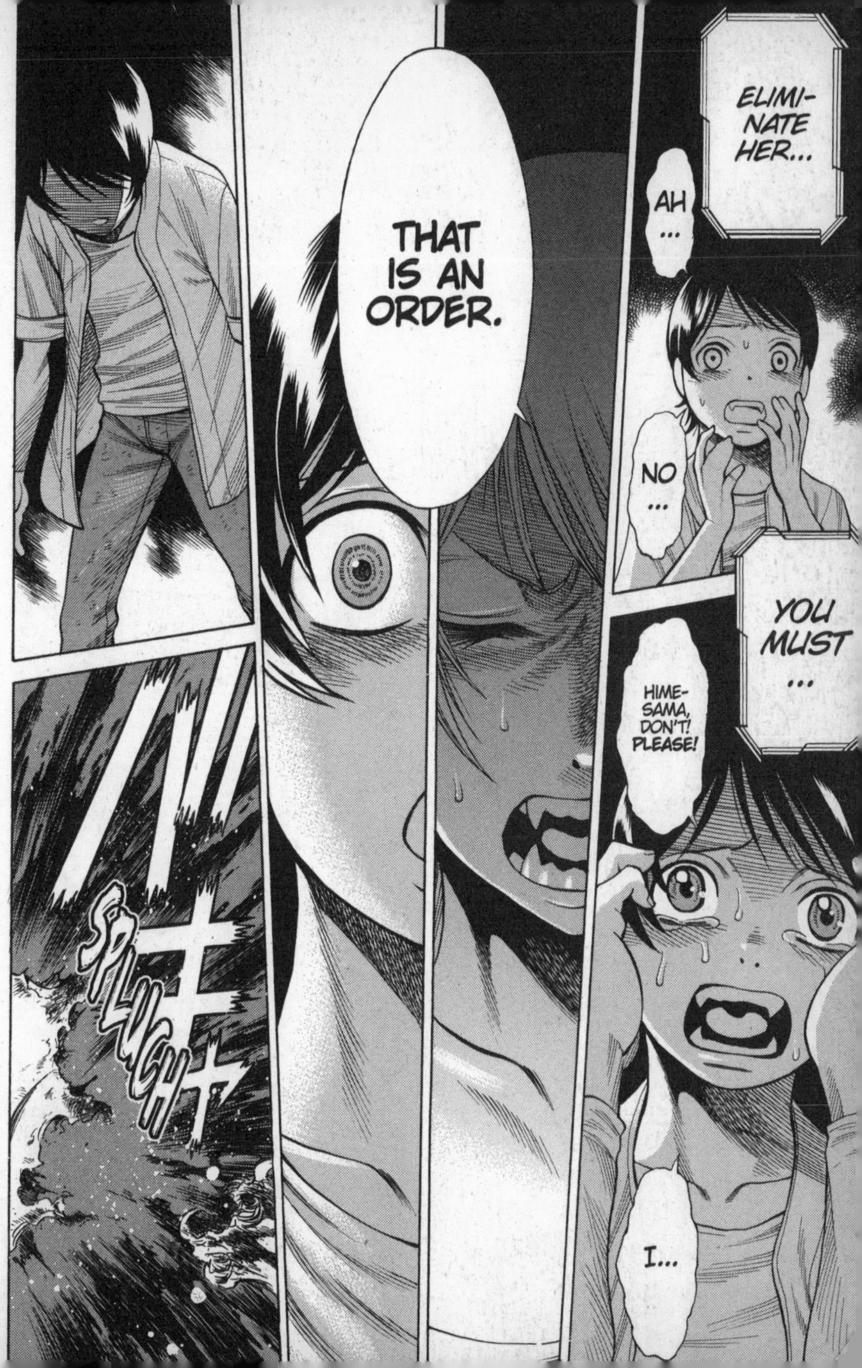

ELIMINATE HER...
AH ...
NO ...
YOU MUST ...
HIME-SAMA, DON'T! PLEASE!
I...
THAT IS AN ORDER.
SPLUGH

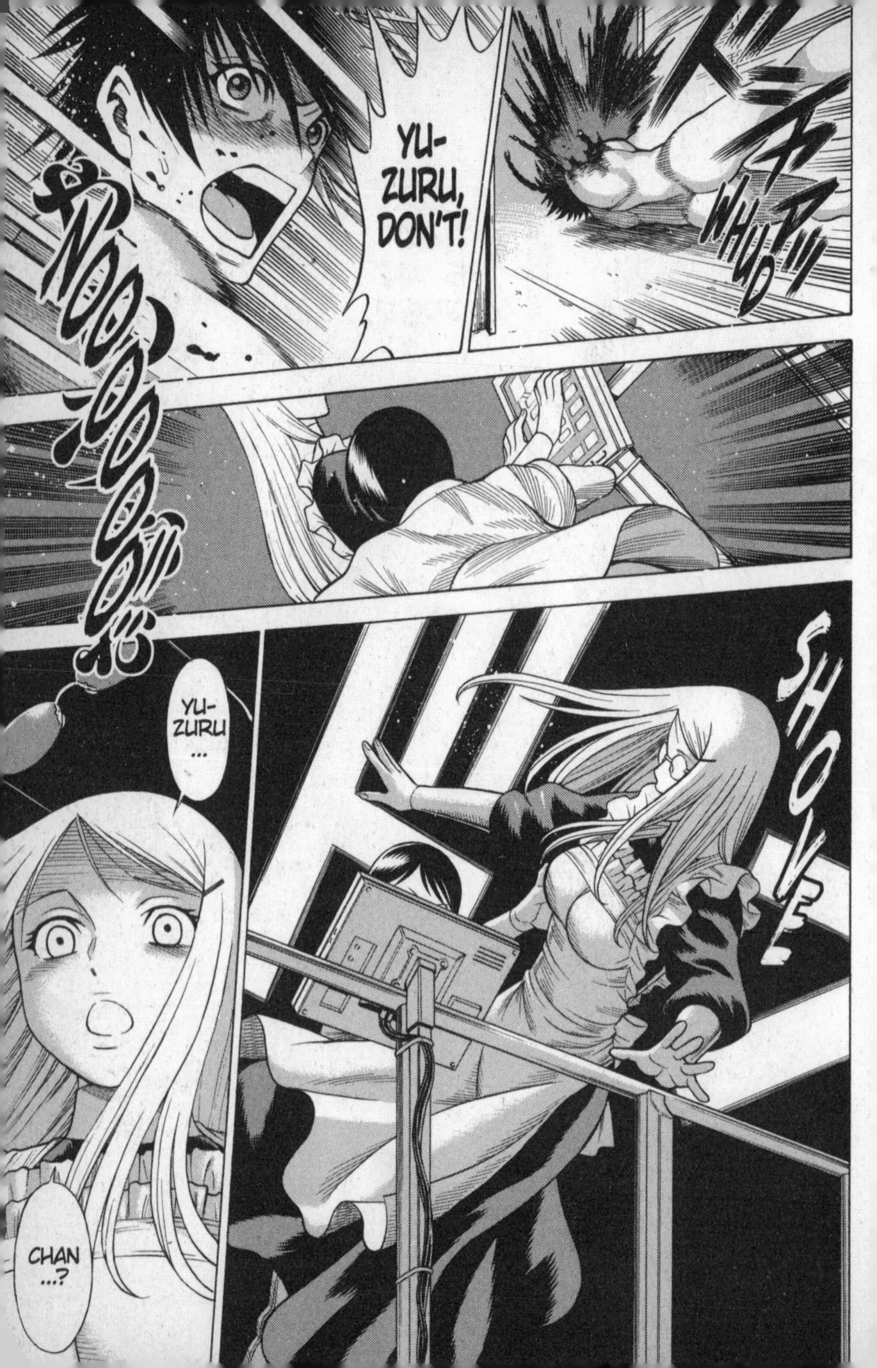

WHUD
YU-
ZURU,
DON'T!
NOOOOOOOO!!
SHOVE!
YU-
ZURU
...
CHAN
...?

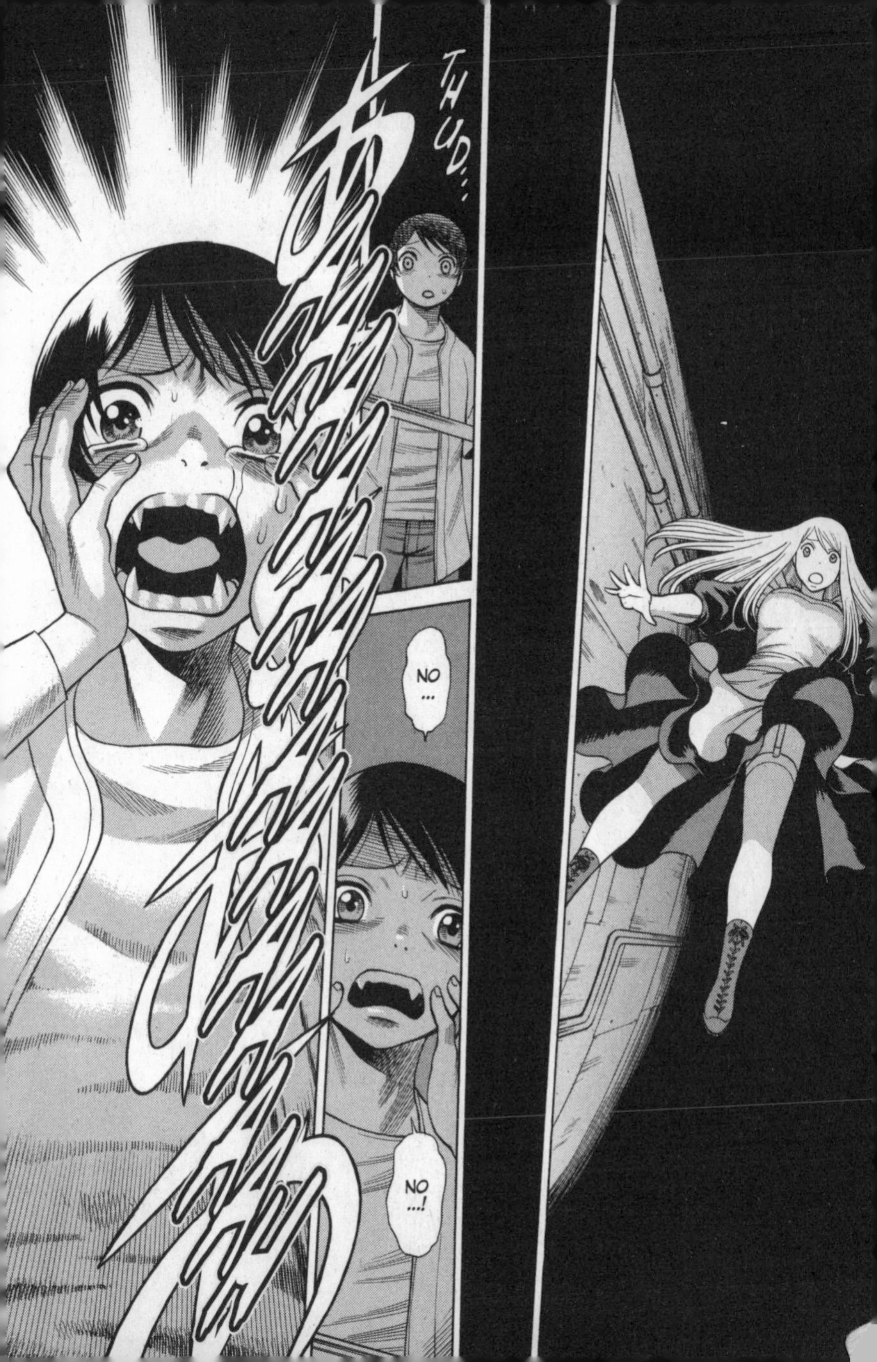
THUD...
NO...
NO...!

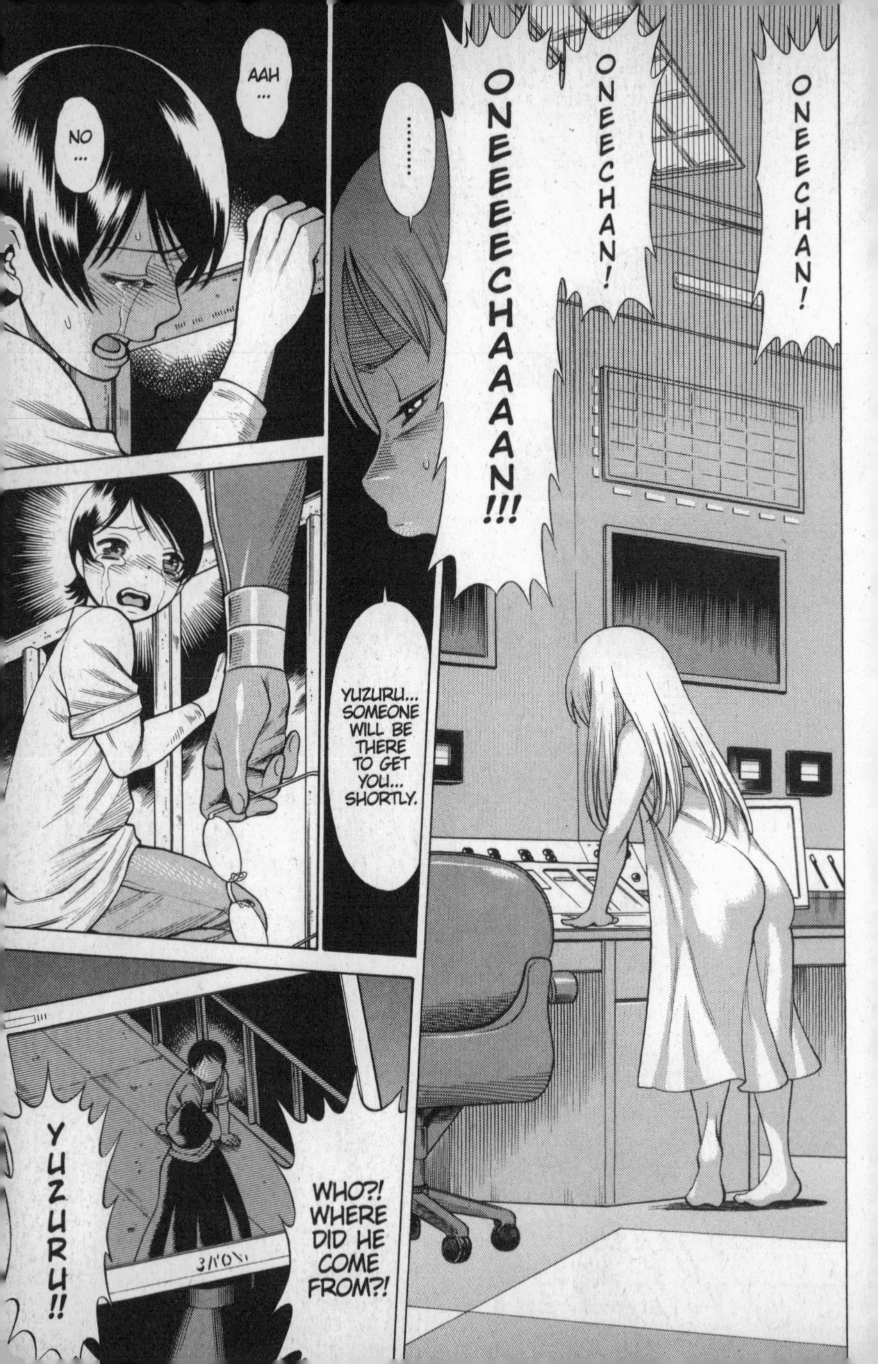
ONEECHAN!
ONEECHAN!
ONEEEECHAAAAAN!!!
......
YUZURU... SOMEONE WILL BE THERE TO GET YOU... SHORTLY.
AAH...
NO...
WHO?! WHERE DID HE COME FROM?!
YUZURU!!

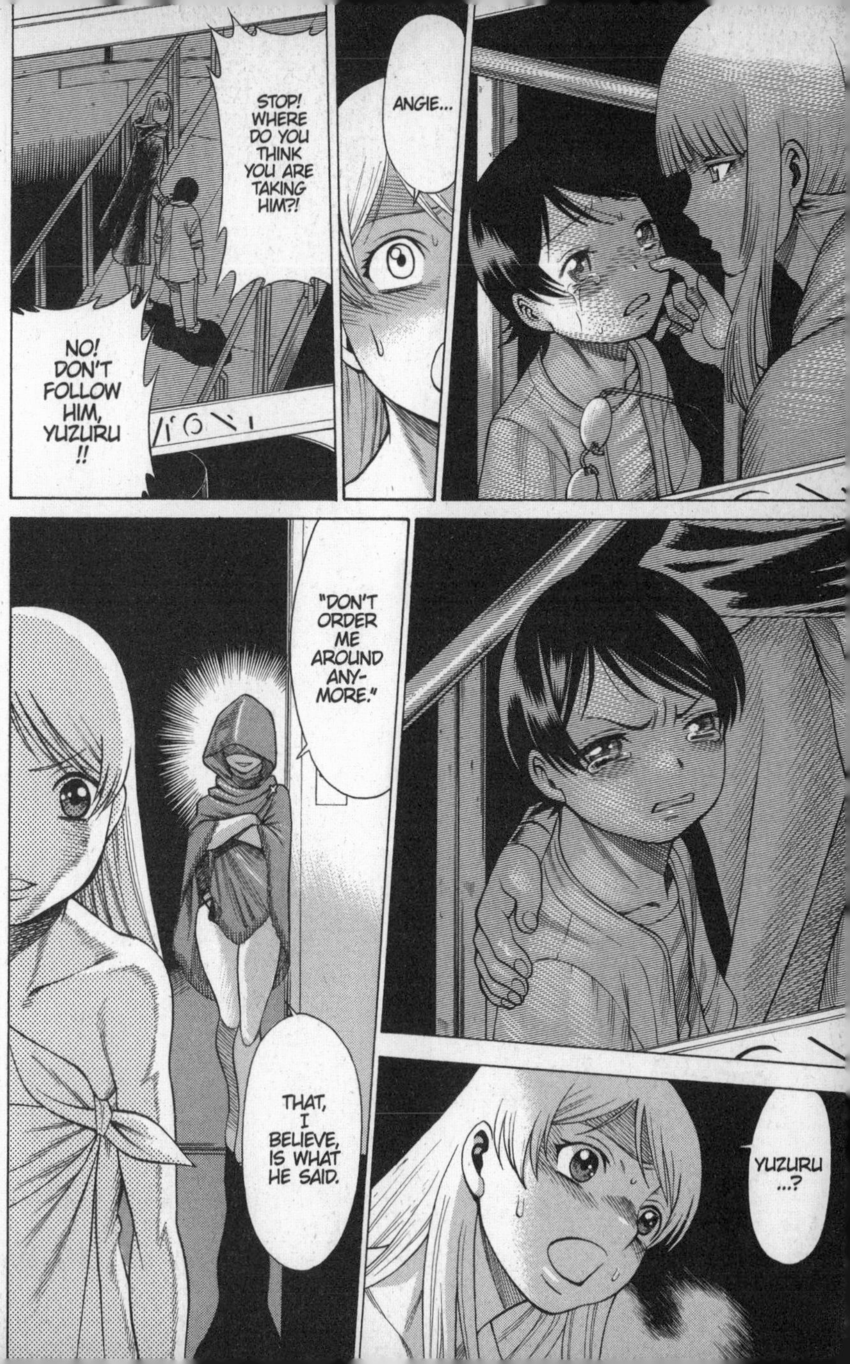
ANGIE...
STOP! WHERE DO YOU THINK YOU ARE TAKING HIM?!
NO! DON'T FOLLOW HIM, YUZURU!!
YUZURU...?
"DON'T ORDER ME AROUND ANYMORE."
THAT, I BELIEVE, IS WHAT HE SAID.

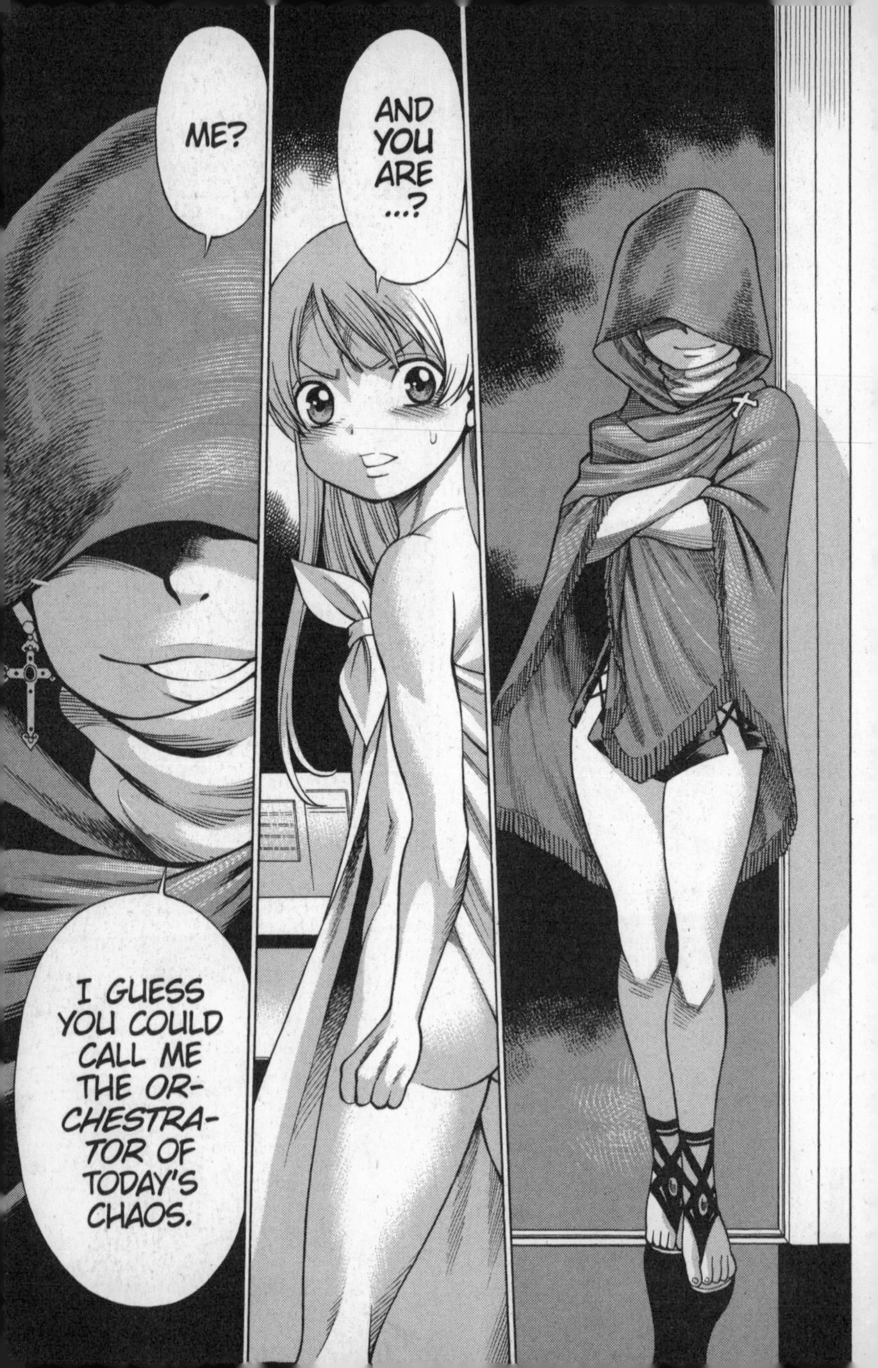
AND YOU ARE ...?
ME?
I GUESS YOU COULD CALL ME THE OR-CHESTRA-TOR OF TODAY'S CHAOS.

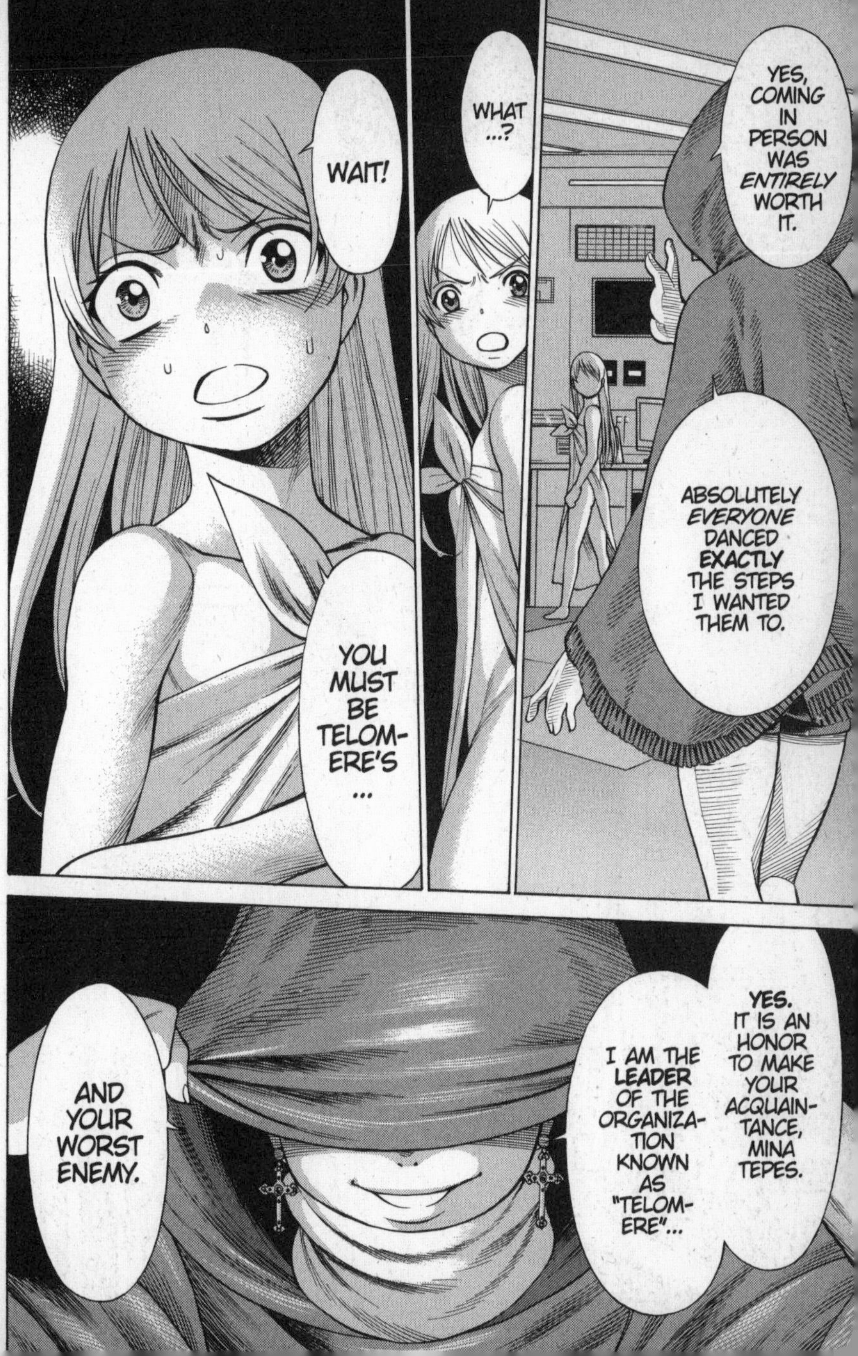
YES, COMING IN PERSON WAS *ENTIRELY* WORTH IT.
ABSOLUTELY *EVERYONE* DANCED **EXACTLY** THE STEPS I WANTED THEM TO.
WHAT ...?
WAIT!
YOU MUST BE TELOM-ERE'S ...
YES. IT IS AN HONOR TO MAKE YOUR ACQUAIN-TANCE, MINA TEPES.
I AM THE **LEADER** OF THE ORGANIZA-TION KNOWN AS "TELOM-ERE"...
AND YOUR WORST ENEMY.

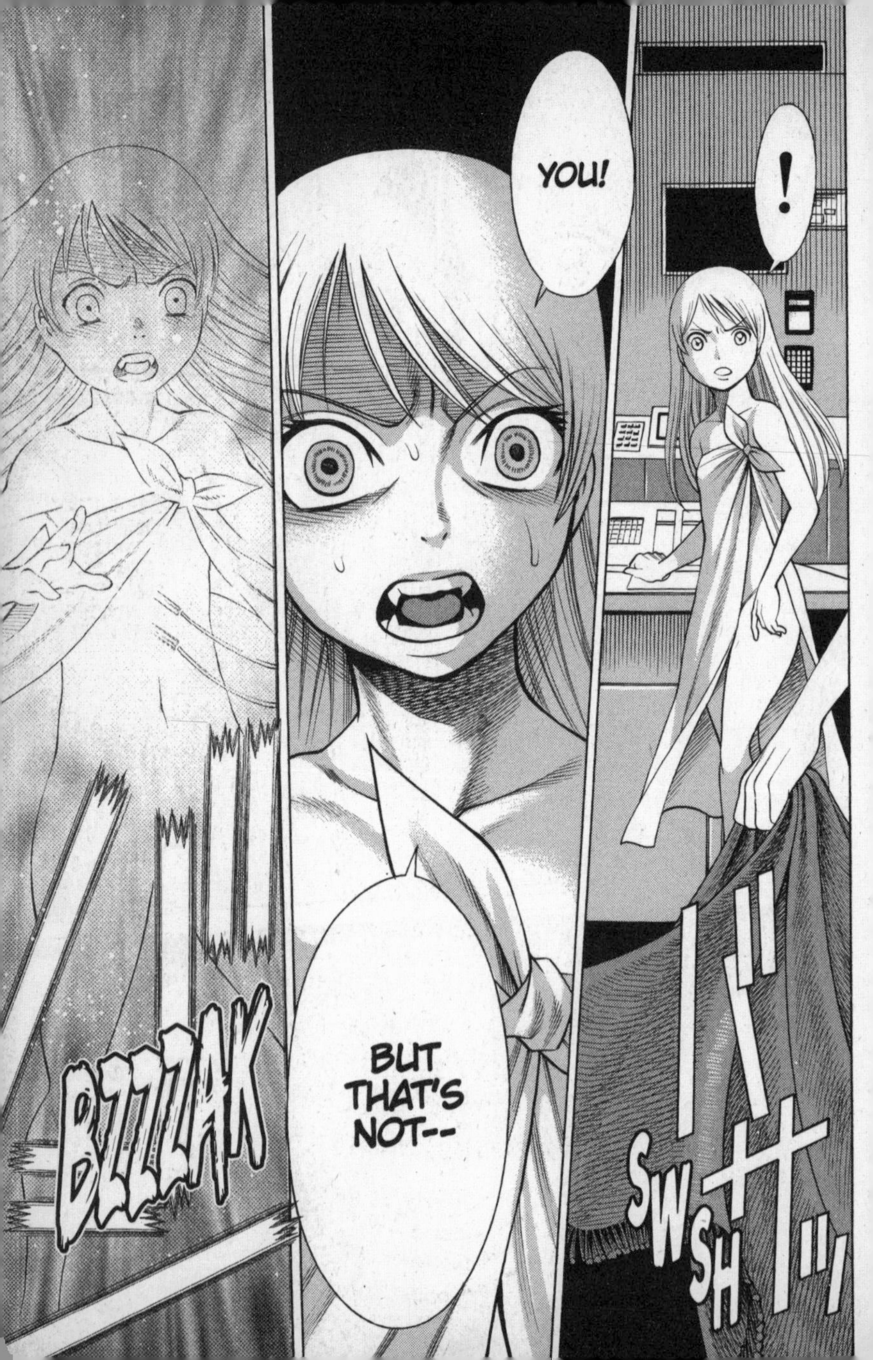
!
SWSH
YOU!
BUT THAT'S NOT--
BZZZAK

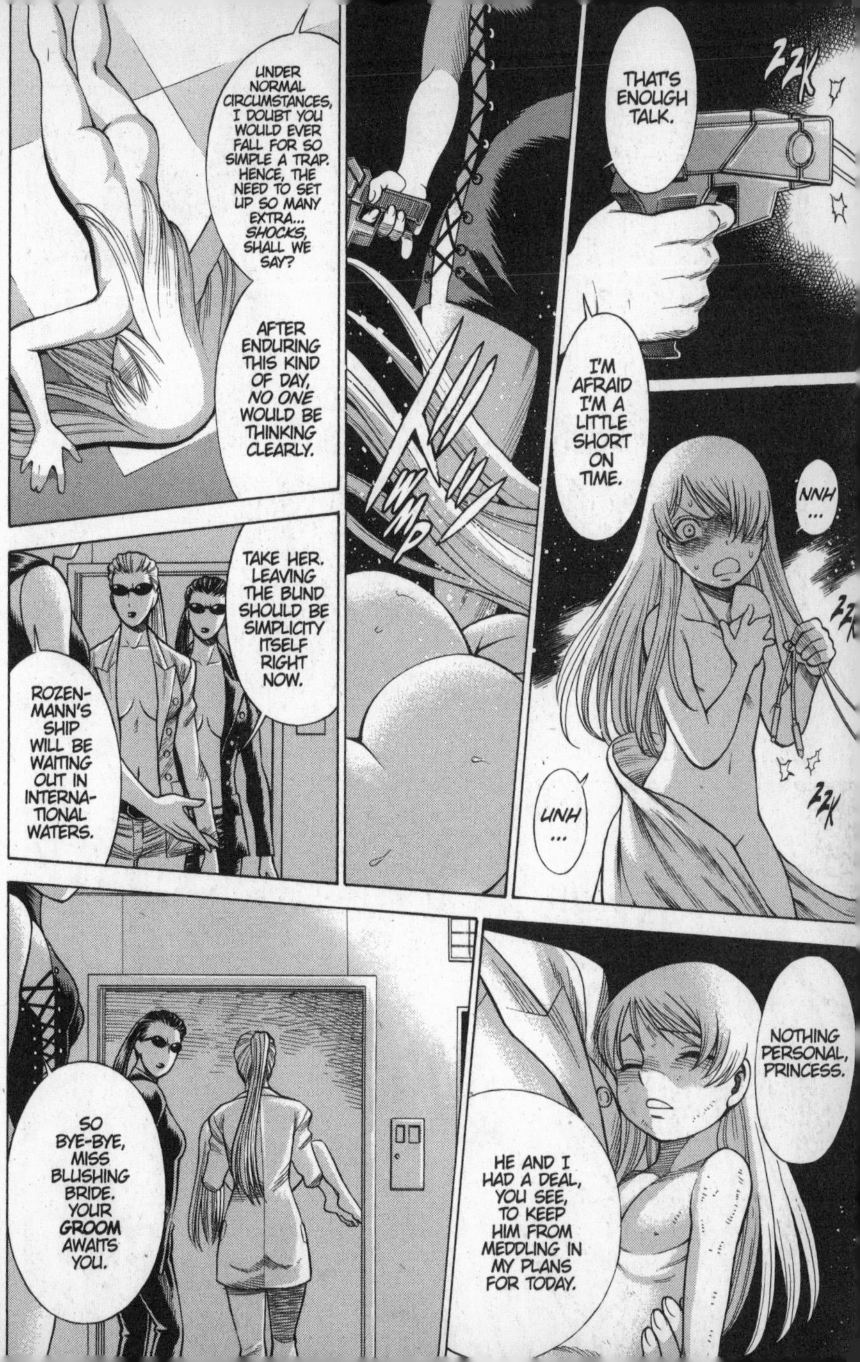
ZZK
THAT'S ENOUGH TALK.
I'M AFRAID I'M A LITTLE SHORT ON TIME.
NNH ...
ZZK
ZZK
UNH ...
WHMP
UNDER NORMAL CIRCUMSTANCES, I DOUBT YOU WOULD EVER FALL FOR SO SIMPLE A TRAP. HENCE, THE NEED TO SET UP SO MANY EXTRA... *SHOCKS*, SHALL WE SAY?
AFTER ENDURING THIS KIND OF DAY, *NO ONE* WOULD BE THINKING CLEARLY.
TAKE HER. LEAVING THE BUND SHOULD BE SIMPLICITY ITSELF RIGHT NOW.
ROZEN-MANN'S SHIP WILL BE WAITING OUT IN INTERNA-TIONAL WATERS.
NOTHING PERSONAL, PRINCESS.
HE AND I HAD A DEAL, YOU SEE, TO KEEP HIM FROM MEDDLING IN MY PLANS FOR TODAY.
SO BYE-BYE, MISS BLUSHING BRIDE. YOUR GROOM AWAITS YOU.

IT IS TIME TO RAISE THE CURTAIN ON MY GRAND PLAY.

NOW THEN...

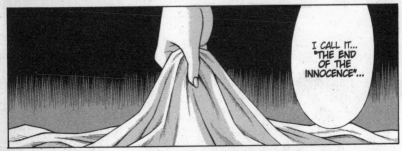

I CALL IT... "THE END OF THE INNOCENCE"...

HM...?

OH. YES.

HIME-SAN! ARE YOU OKAY?!

WHAM

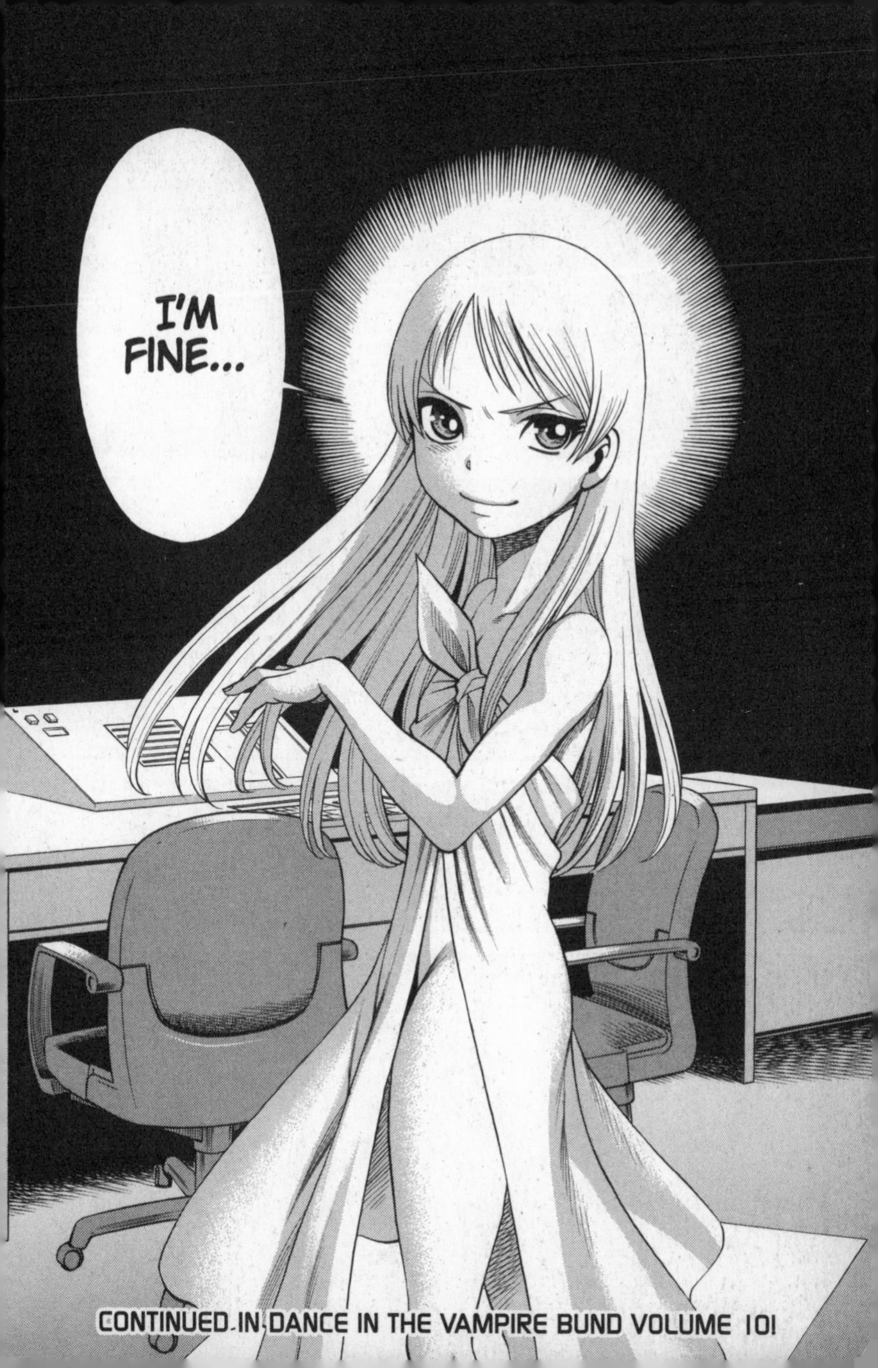
I'M FINE...
CONTINUED IN DANCE IN THE VAMPIRE BUND VOLUME 10!

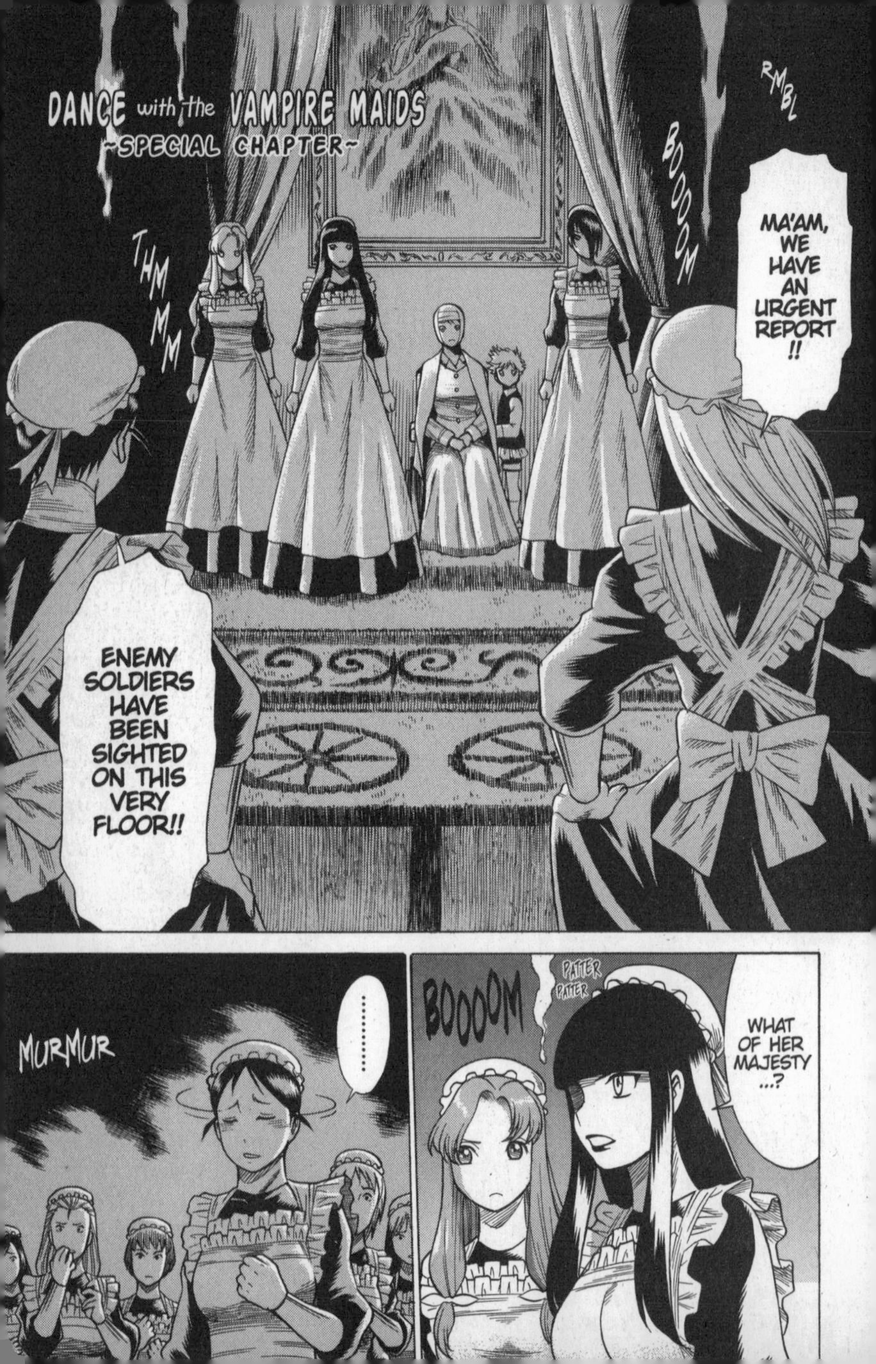
DANCE with the VAMPIRE MAIDS
~SPECIAL CHAPTER~
RMBL
BOOOOM
MA'AM, WE HAVE AN URGENT REPORT!!
THMMMM
ENEMY SOLDIERS HAVE BEEN SIGHTED ON THIS VERY FLOOR!!
WHAT OF HER MAJESTY ...?
PATTER PATTER
BOOOOM
......
MURMUR

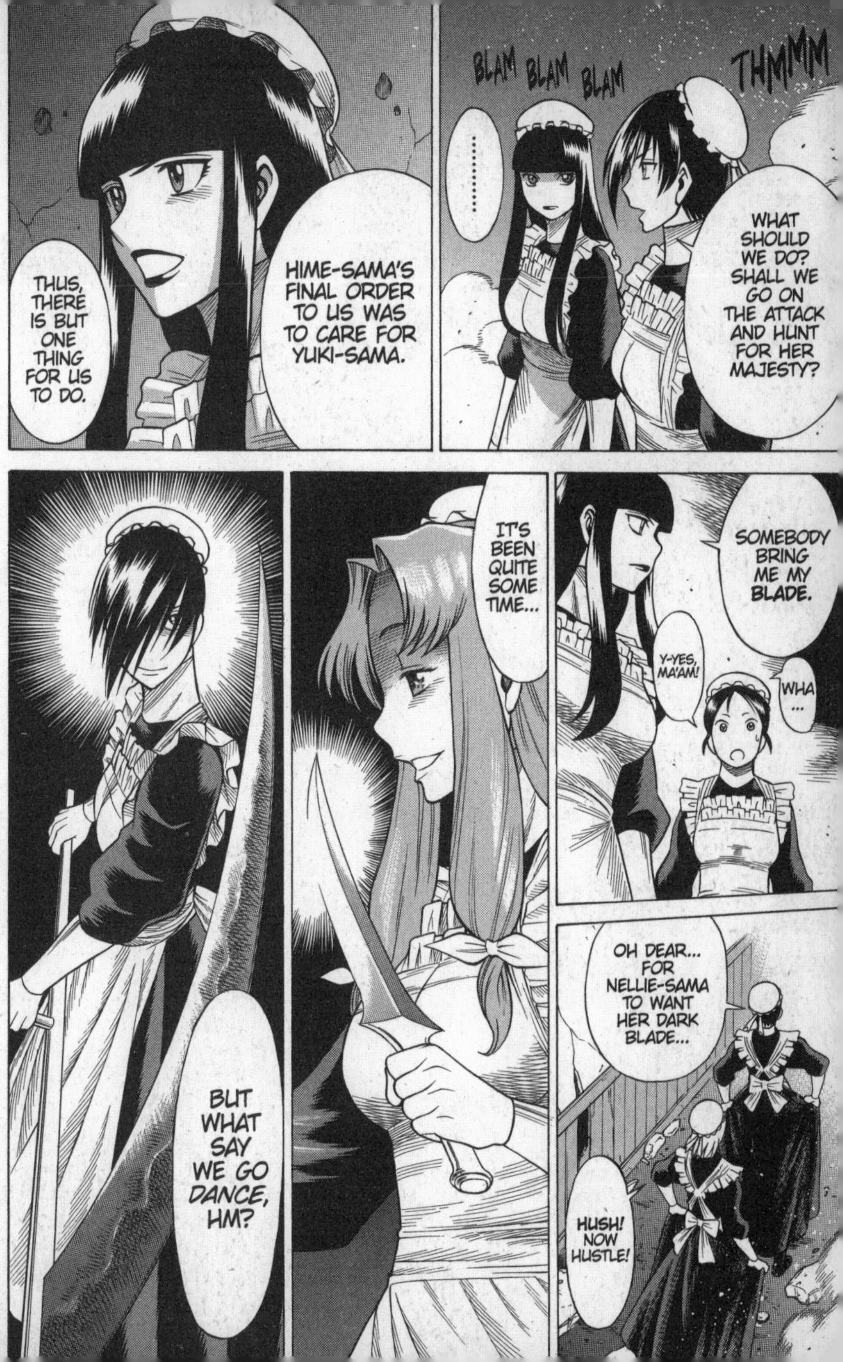
THMMM
BLAM BLAM BLAM
WHAT SHOULD WE DO? SHALL WE GO ON THE ATTACK AND HUNT FOR HER MAJESTY?
......
HIME-SAMA'S FINAL ORDER TO US WAS TO CARE FOR YUKI-SAMA.
THUS, THERE IS BUT ONE THING FOR US TO DO.
SOMEBODY BRING ME MY BLADE.
WHA...
Y-YES, MA'AM!
OH DEAR... FOR NELLIE-SAMA TO WANT HER DARK BLADE...
HUSH! NOW HUSTLE!
IT'S BEEN QUITE SOME TIME...
BUT WHAT SAY WE GO DANCE, HM?

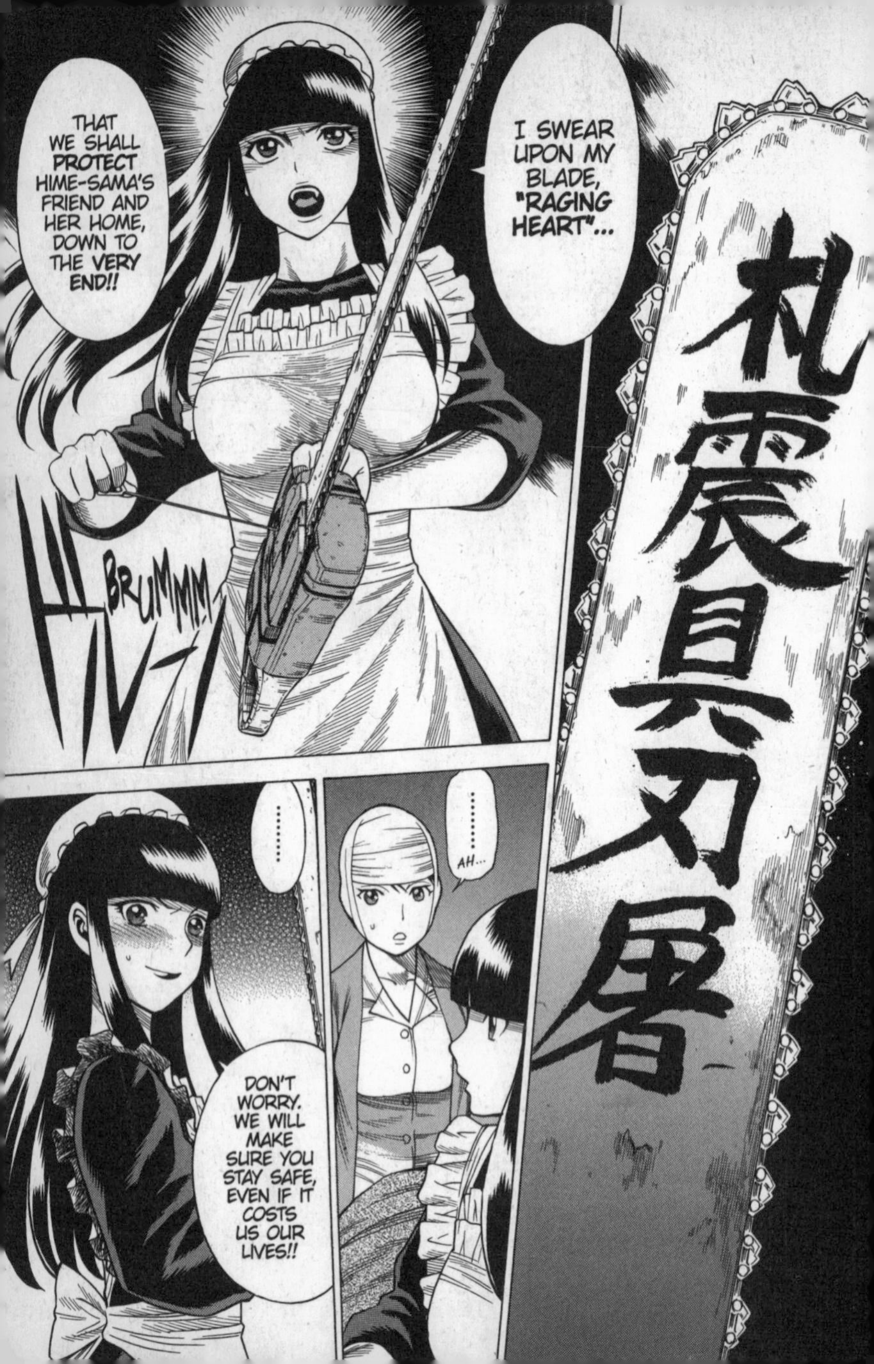
I SWEAR UPON MY BLADE, "RAGING HEART"...
THAT WE SHALL PROTECT HIME-SAMA'S FRIEND AND HER HOME, DOWN TO THE VERY END!!
BRUMMM
......
AH...
......
DON'T WORRY. WE WILL MAKE SURE YOU STAY SAFE, EVEN IF IT COSTS US OUR LIVES!!

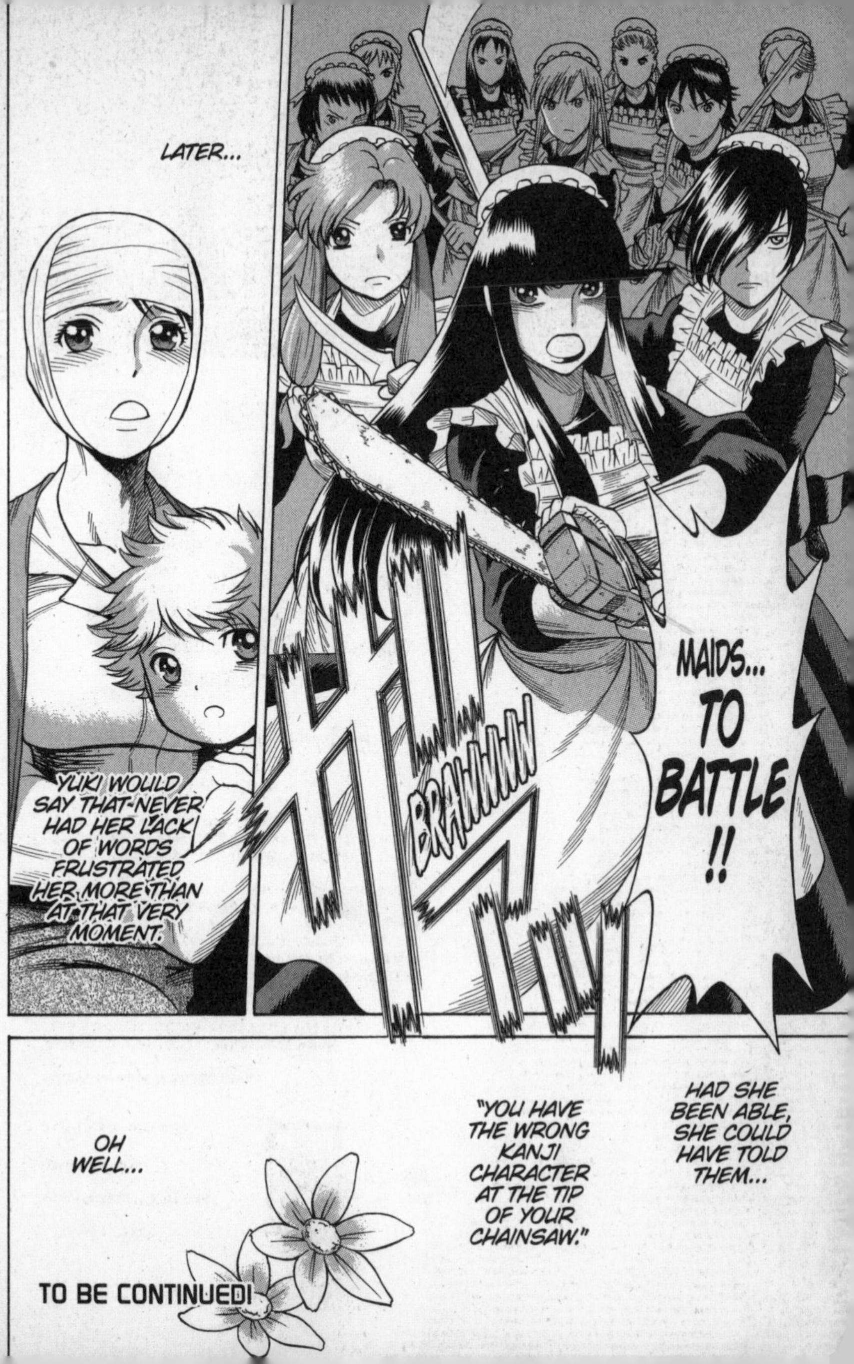
MAIDS... TO BATTLE !!
BRAWWWW
LATER...
YUKI WOULD SAY THAT NEVER HAD HER LACK OF WORDS FRUSTRATED HER MORE THAN AT THAT VERY MOMENT.
HAD SHE BEEN ABLE, SHE COULD HAVE TOLD THEM...
"YOU HAVE THE WRONG KANJI CHARACTER AT THE TIP OF YOUR CHAINSAW."
OH WELL...
TO BE CONTINUED!

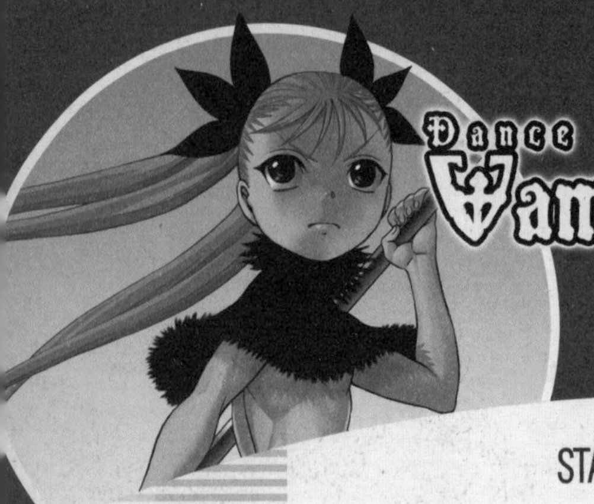

Dance in the Vampire Bund

Volume 9

story & art by Nozomu Tamaki

STAFF CREDITS

translation Adrienne Beck
adaptation Janet Houck
retouch & lettering Roland Amago
cover design Nicky Lim
layout Bambi Eloriaga-Amago
copy editor Shanti Whitesides
editor Adam Arnold

publisher Seven Seas Entertainment

DANCE IN THE VAMPIRE BUND VOL. 9

Visit us online at www.gomanga.com

ISBN: 978-1-934876-87-9

Printed in Canada

First printing: December 2010

10 9 8 7 6 5 4 3 2 1

TRANSLATION NOTE

Chapter 53
Olga, Tatiana, Maria, and Anastasia were the four daughters of Tzar Nicholas II, the last Tzar of Imperial Russia. They actually were known to occasionally sign letters using "OTMA" as a nickname. All four were killed during the Bolshevik Revolution, on July 17, 1918.

THE END

YOU'RE READING THE WRONG WAY

This is the last page of
Dance in the Vampire Bund
Volume 9

This book reads from right to left, Japanese style. To read from the beginning, flip the book over to the other side, start with the top right panel, and take it from there.

If this is your first time reading manga, just follow the diagram. It may seem backwards at first, but you'll get used to it! Have fun!